RED CARPET

RED CARPET

★ ★

HOLLYWOOD, CHINA, AND THE GLOBAL BATTLE FOR CULTURAL SUPREMACY

Erich Schwartzel

PENGUIN PRESS
NEW YORK
2022

PENGUIN PRESS
An imprint of Penguin Random House LLC
penguinrandomhouse.com

Image credits appear on page 367.

LIBRARY OF CONGRESS CATALOGING-IN-PUBLICATION DATA

Names: Schwartzel, Erich, author.
Title: Red carpet : Hollywood, China, and the global battle for cultural supremacy / Erich Schwartzel.
Description: New York : Penguin Press, 2022. | Includes bibliographical references and index. |
Identifiers: LCCN 2021027952 (print) | LCCN 2021027953 (ebook) |
ISBN 9781984878991 (hardcover) | ISBN 9781984879004 (ebook)
Subjects: LCSH: Motion picture industry—United States. |
Motion picture industry—United States—Finance. | Motion picture industry—China. |
Motion picture industry—Government policy—China. |
United States—Relations—China. | China—Relations—United States.
Classification: LCC PN1993.5.U6 S355 2022 (print) | LCC PN1993.5.U6 (ebook) |
DDC 791.430973—dc23/eng/20211027
LC record available at https://lccn.loc.gov/2021027952
LC ebook record available at https://lccn.loc.gov/2021027953

Printed in the United States of America
1   3   5   7   9   10   8   6   4   2

DESIGNED BY MEIGHAN CAVANAUGH

For my parents,
Paul and Romayne Schwartzel

Every film that goes from America abroad, wherever it shall be sent, shall correctly portray to the world the purposes, the ideals, the accomplishments, the opportunities, and the life of America. We are going to sell America to the world with American motion pictures.

—WILL HAYS, PRESIDENT OF THE MOTION PICTURE
PRODUCERS AND DISTRIBUTORS OF AMERICA, 1923

During its 5,000-year history, the Chinese nation has created a brilliant and profound culture. We should disseminate the most fundamental Chinese culture in a popular way.

—XI JINPING, PRESIDENT OF CHINA, 2014

CONTENTS

PART III

INTRODUCTION

n the weeks following the 2008 Summer Olympics in Beijing, a group of Chinese executives traveled to Los Angeles for a crash course in influence. Inside the UCLA classroom of film professor Robert Rosen, a parade of Hollywood executives conducted a series of lectures on America's entertainment industry. The students had been chosen by their country's State Administration of Radio, Film, and Television, and they were in Los Angeles with a mandate: to learn how the American film industry had achieved its status as the leader in global culture—and how China could re-create that achievement back home.

The head of Universal Pictures, the studio behind *Frankenstein, Back to the Future,* and *The Fast and the Furious,* spoke about his film operation, a conglomerate grown out of a collection of nickelodeons founded in 1912. So did the CEO of Metro-Goldwyn-Mayer, a company that was established before the talkie and eventually produced *The Wizard of Oz, West Side Story,* and *The Silence of the Lambs.* An agent at William Morris, the talent agency that counted Matt Damon and Denzel Washington as clients, talked about how he managed America's biggest movie stars. An independent producer explained the art of putting a movie's finances together, and the head of the Motion Picture Association of America detailed his organization's lobbying work on behalf of the nation's entertainers in Washington. It was hard to imagine a more glamorous set of day jobs, positions that turned the men and women who held them into stewards and emissaries of American culture.

That China would send officials to Los Angeles to learn from America's most famous capitalist enterprise would have been unthinkable just decades before, when the Cultural Revolution and the massacre of protesters at Tiananmen Square left little doubt about the government's attitude toward free expression. Yet China in 2008 was ascendant itself, even if that rise occurred out of view of many Americans—including many in Hollywood, where the country's work was just beginning. At the time, the Chinese visitors' unassuming exterior masked incredible power. One young executive worked at a movie channel with eight hundred million viewers, a scale beyond what any of his Hollywood instructors could fathom.

It would take only a decade for the positioning of the two parties in that classroom—the Chinese as students and the Hollywood executives as teachers—to seem both prescient and absurd. In the years that followed, the dynamic would reverse, and it would be Hollywood looking to China for help.

Consider the future of the entities represented in that classroom alone. Within a decade of those classes, Universal would complete a $500 million financing deal with a Chinese firm, cast Chinese actresses in its biggest movies, and construct a Universal theme park outside China's capital city. Metro-Goldwyn-Mayer would shop itself for a Chinese takeover and censor James Bond movies to make sure Chinese citizens never looked weak when matched against England's ageless secret agent.

William Morris would open an office in China to help the country's new class of A-listers win over global audiences. Producers would rewrite scripts, trading New York for Shanghai if it meant getting a movie financed by Chinese billionaires. The MPAA and other officials in Washington would do anything they could to maintain access to the Chinese box office, which grew at a clip as domestic moviegoing flatlined.

Chinese theaters were largely closed off to the world until 1994, when Hollywood studios started exporting ten movies a year to the country. At the time, $3 million was a record-setting gross. By the time those Chinese students arrived at UCLA fourteen years later, the market was growing but still a bundle of optimistic projections. By 2020, China would be the number one box-office market in the world, home to grosses that routinely neared $1 billion—a market that became too big to ignore and too lucrative to anger. Through it all, China would continue to see Hollywood much as those early visitors did: as the ultimate template for building a show business that helped fuel a country's rise, their goal a twenty-first-century sequel to what America's entertainers had done for their country over the course of a hundred years. The Chinese were quick studies.

I JOINED THE LOS ANGELES bureau of *The Wall Street Journal* in the summer of 2013. I had spent the previous four years covering the energy industry for the *Pittsburgh Post-Gazette*, reporting on a fracking boom in Appalachia that had transformed the region's politics, economy, and culture. I was hired to be a fresh set of eyes on the *Journal*'s Hollywood coverage, and I soon started seeing China everywhere I looked.

One announcement followed another: Chinese star Fan Bingbing was appearing in the new *X-Men*. An American theater chain headquartered in Leawood, Kansas, was trading on Wall Street thanks to financing from China's richest man. Paramount Pictures was rushing to edit *World*

War Z to remove a scene that implied a zombie outbreak had originated in China, a plot detail that executives feared would lead to censors denying the movie a Chinese release. Seemingly every producer in town was shopping a script based on the Flying Tigers, the World War II pilots who helped defend China against Japan. Moviegoers in the eastern Chinese city of Qingdao were flocking to see the latest *Transformers*, sending millions of dollars in unexpected grosses back to its studio on Melrose Avenue.

To many observers, it was another round of "dumb money" flowing into Hollywood, long an industry capable of wooing investors with stardust. When I learned there was actually a government agenda out of Beijing backing the efforts—an agenda visible for anyone to see—I realized this would not be a case of fleeting interest. It was immediately clear that Chinese leaders had a plan larger than just box-office grosses. China's economic leverage had quickly translated into political sway, most often in the censorship practiced by Beijing bureaucrats who amassed unprecedented power in executive suites. Unbeknownst to most moviegoers, studios were removing scenes and dialogue from scripts and finished movies to appease Chinese censors—scrubbing any production of plot points that brushed up against sensitive Chinese history or made the country look anything less than a modern, sophisticated world power. Even more disturbing than the movies changing were the ones not getting made at all, for fear of angering Chinese officials. Hollywood became a commercial arm for China's new ambition, and piece by piece, China's interest in the American film industry revealed itself to be a complement to its political ascendance, one that is rewriting the global order of the new century.

The story of this unexpected relationship can be told in three acts. It begins with the founding of Hollywood itself, an industry of workaday seamstresses and actors that in a century transformed into a powerhouse that pulled the world toward the U.S. Hollywood became America's number one export, shipping the swagger of John Wayne, the resistance heroes of *Star Wars*, and the romantic sweep of *Titanic* around the world. For politicians, the movies became a vehicle of influence—especially so in China. Although it had been largely shut off from American culture while it conscripted its own artists and filmmakers into Mao Zedong's revolution, China began to permit Hollywood movies into its theaters in the 1990s as part of a broader modernizing effort. Economics bested Communist Party instincts to hide dangerous thoughts from their people, generating box-office grosses that would prove indispensable to American studio executives.

The second act is the collision that followed, a decade during which Hollywood vulnerabilities met Chinese ambition. Out of nowhere appeared a market with 1.4 billion potential customers—a population of spenders that one Hollywood executive described to me as "a great national resource." Accessing that resource would require bowing to censorship demands and navigating political land mines to build a theme park or secure Chinese financing. Throughout this decade, Chinese producers and politicians maintained the student-teacher relationship evident in that UCLA classroom, turning to Hollywood experts for help building a commercial film industry of their own, one that transformed the theatrical propaganda of previous generations into popcorn entertainment.

The third act focuses the spotlight on China, where President Xi Jinping presides over a movie industry that has become an essential arm of a recast Middle Kingdom, a business modeled after America's but molded to account for the Communist Party's expectation that art will serve the state. The filmography of China in recent years has given its audiences what Americans have taken for granted: stories about people who look like them, who work and play in a country claiming a moment in history. Now China is trying to complete the hardest piece of the puzzle: shipping those movies overseas—and with them the values and vision that they embody and the alternative mode of governance to Western liberal democracy that they promote. As China redraws the geopolitical alignments of the world, it wants to use its movies to redraw the cultural borders atop them.

THE ARC OF CHINA'S INFLUENCE is evident in a single Hollywood franchise, *Top Gun*, in which the geopolitical tensions of the next century came to be reflected in a two-inch patch sewn onto a movie star's costume. The original 1986 film is a hallmark of Ronald Reagan's America—Tom Cruise as the aviator-wearing daredevil Maverick, Berlin's "Take My Breath Away," the hero declaring, "I feel the *need* . . ." In a sign of how deeply the film saw itself as a celebration of the U.S. Navy, producers asked the military to cooperate on the film and acceded to its wishes to make the movie a robust demonstration of American military might. They scrapped a scene involving a crash and turned Maverick's love interest, originally a fellow navy member, into a contractor so audiences didn't see the hero breaking rules about relationships among personnel. Moviegoers didn't mind the jingoism; they wanted to watch their country's naval aviators pull off awesome stunts and save the day. *Top Gun* grossed $177 million in North America. It also did what years of state-produced recruitment videos could not and boosted interest among young men and women in joining the armed forces. Recruiters waited in theater lobbies to catch moviegoers on their way out of the film. (Ray-Ban sales shot up, too.)

In 2017, Paramount Pictures announced it would reboot *Top Gun* with its original star, turning the thirty-one-year-old movie into another example of Hollywood's effective strategy of bathing audiences in nostalgia. But much about the global film market had changed in the intervening years. A $150 million production like *Top Gun: Maverick*, as the sequel would be called, was so expensive that studio chiefs approved the film's production with accounting projections that assumed its global gross would likely include Chinese ticket sales. What's more, some of that $150 million budget came courtesy of Skydance Media, a Los Angeles film and TV company partially financed by Tencent, the Shenzhen-based Chinese tech firm behind the country's most popular messaging app. Chinese money was backing the new *Top Gun* in two ways: in financing behind the scenes and in expected box-office grosses once it hit theaters there.

This all explains what happened to Tom Cruise's bomber jacket.

In the original film, Maverick's bomber featured a patch that highlighted the USS *Galveston* tour of Japan, Taiwan, and other countries in the Pacific, with flags from those countries below his collar—along with his aviators, as iconic a look as the American movie has created. Chinese investors on the movie pointed out to Skydance executives that those 1986 patches now posed a problem. After moving aggressively into Hong Kong, Xi had taken steps to reinforce the view he and many within China held that Taiwan was a part of China as well, and not its own country. Having a global movie star flaunt Taiwan's flag on his back undermined Chinese sovereignty. And given China's decades-long animosity toward Japan, the studio executives reasoned that they should play it safe and erase that patch, too. When Paramount unveiled the poster for *Top Gun: Maverick* in the summer of 2019, it showed Cruise from the back, his signature brown leather jacket in focus and the flags of Taiwan and Japan—U.S. allies in real life—removed. Chinese officials did not even have to weigh in. By 2019, Hollywood had so fully absorbed Beijing's political preferences that such decisions were made by teams in Los Angeles without Chinese input. If it could help Paramount executives make their case to Chinese censors that *Top Gun* should show in Chinese theaters, Maverick's bomber would adhere to the One China policy.

This book is the story of what happened between the two *Top Gun*s. It is a story with implications that stretch far beyond the entertainment industry. Hollywood's experience has served as a precursor for numerous American industries trying to balance doing business in China with placating Chinese officials, from Apple to the National Basketball Association. In the months following the COVID-19 outbreak, China's economic recovery proved a financial salvation for struggling companies across numerous sectors, further boosting the country's political leverage through its 1.4 billion consumers.

China's omnipresence on-screen reflects the country's increasing ubiquity in business and in other parts of the world. That ubiquity has also exported a worldwide fear of crossing China. In the course of researching this book, I learned quickly the set of tools—encrypted messaging apps, coded conversations—that executives insisted upon, knowing their communications were monitored by officials in Beijing.

These concerns only grew as tensions between the U.S. and China escalated during Donald Trump's administration and Xi's aggressive crackdown on dissent. As China loomed large in the collective imagination, the lives and experiences of individual Chinese citizens were often lost in sweeping geopolitical analyses. Those deeply involved in Hollywood's economic relationship with China grew quiet too, worried not only about losing their business but also about graver consequences: being called in for questioning, getting thrown out of the country, disappearing.

In early 2020, I had lunch at a vegan restaurant blocks from Warner Bros. with an executive who worked in China. Before we could begin talking, she turned off her cell phone and put it in her purse underneath the table. When that didn't assuage her fears, she took her purse to the other side of the restaurant, asking the staff to keep it behind the counter. She then wondered if she should go put it in her car, since she'd heard that the Chinese government could even surveil a conversation from across the room. Chinese paranoia had infiltrated Burbank, and it was entirely justified.

THIS BOOK SHOULD SERVE AS a pair of X-ray goggles on the most powerful American art form of the last hundred years. The Chinese actress in the scene suddenly makes sense, the detour to Shanghai revealed not as a creative decision but as a commercial one. If a third-act savior emerges to save the hero, chances are he comes from the East.

China's pressure on Hollywood and its own entertainment industry have the potential to challenge the American film industry as the chief narrator of the twenty-first century. Hollywood, by maintaining warm relations with the regime, has bolstered China's campaign for global influence with American movies that either turn every portrayal of the country into a state-sanctioned commercial or avoid anything that challenges how Xi's party sees the world. Movies made by China's own producers have become a proxy for the Cold War the two countries have devolved into, one waged between China and the norms and values of the West. China's mixture of authoritarianism and capitalism has proved for other world leaders an alluring alternative to the free and democratic model that Americans for decades have believed in exporting to other nations— a model powerfully reflected in and endorsed by the movies the United States has sent abroad. In considering the fight for the next generation of moviegoers, look beyond auditoriums in the U.S. and China to the parts of the world where it remains unclear which country will take on the role of superpower benefactor.

In some cases, the rise of China's entertainment industry has deepened our understanding of a country and culture that remain misunderstood, even demonized. In more insidious cases, it has braided a censorious agenda into moviemaking, corrupting America's most effective tool for selling democracy and free expression to the world. Over this next century, China wants to use the movies to brand itself to the world, and it learned how to do so from the best. All of this has happened before our very eyes.

PART I

ONE

Banning Brad Pitt

The dead would be moved for Disneyland. Generations of villagers lay buried under the acreage outside Shanghai that officials had allocated for China's first Disney theme park, but the ancestors would not get in their way. Homes could be razed, remains excavated, and families relocated. Even in the early 1990s, when Peter Murphy, the head of strategic planning for the Walt Disney Company, traveled to Shanghai, it was clear the country held larger ambitions for the miles of rice fields and shanties that the city's construction cranes hadn't reached. To Murphy, the acres of low-ceilinged homes and bicycle riders hardly looked like the setting for a polished, perfect Magic Kingdom where Snow White and Goofy might stroll. But when his host, Shanghai mayor Zhu Rongji, took in the expanse, he saw something different.

"This," Zhu said, "is where Disneyland will be."

When executives suggested it wasn't the right time to open a park, Zhu didn't understand what the holdup was. Chinese construction crews could clear the land the next day, he told Murphy. They could pour foundation on a Saturday and start building that Monday. The Shanghai government had already allocated the land for the future park in 1990, shortly after Zhu visited Disneyland in Southern California. In the minds of Chinese officials some twenty years after the Cultural Revolution, there could be no greater validation for their nation's economic miracle than the erection of their own Disney park in Shanghai.

Murphy suspected that Zhu was right. There would be a Disney theme park in China—someday. But there was a reason that the company operated only four Disney parks around the world at that point. A company built on precision and customers' expectations of perfection didn't simply start building a park when someone suggested it. There was a playbook Disney deployed when introducing its brand to a new country. First, it would broadcast on local airwaves the Disney Channel, a twenty-four-hour network that introduced shows like *Darkwing Duck* and characters like Pluto in short order. Once families grew attached to the characters, Disney would open toy stores where they could express that love by buying stuffed animals and action figures. Only then would the company consider spending billions of dollars to build a theme park, which families wouldn't visit if they hadn't been seeded with affection for the characters in the years-long campaign. China would get its park, but on Disney's time line.

Like China's ruling party, Disney operated in five-year plans, and in the mid-1990s, a crucial part of that plan was generating more business overseas. Fortune 500 companies like Coca-Cola and Ford were selling soda and cars to the Chinese, while Disney remained heavily weighted in the domestic sphere—about 80 percent of its revenue came from American consumers during this time. The Chinese, though, "had a lot of money under their mattress," as Lawrence Murphy, then Disney's chief strategic officer, told his colleagues. The one-child policy, enacted in 1980, had spawned a generation of only children in Chinese homes; for the first time in recent history, Chinese parents had money to spend on their children. Just a few decades earlier, Western entertainment had been banned in China, and only top officials had TV sets. The 1990s would be a decade in which China, in the eyes of American business, turned from a country into a market.

All of that promise and ambition were suddenly endangered in 1996, when Murphy received a phone call to his Los Angeles office. It was the Chinese embassy in Washington. An official there had called Disney's general line and been directed to Murphy.

"You started, in the last forty-eight hours, shooting a film in Morocco about the Dalai Lama called *Kundun*," the embassy official said.

Murphy was dumbstruck. He had never heard of a movie called *Kundun*. He barely paid attention to most movies Disney made. A thirty-four-year-old Wharton MBA and strategic planner known as "the Enforcer" within Disney's notoriously political C-suite, Murphy kept the longest hours among executives and made sure the divisions making movies stayed within their financial parameters. He had little interest in the creative side of moviemaking. Disney's business was one of imagination, filling children with inspiration and aspiration on its best days and cementing gender roles and black-and-white morality on its worst. Murphy might as well have worked as an executive at a car company, taking carburetors instead of fantasy abroad. He called himself a "suit," proudly.

He had to ask around about *Kundun*. His colleagues told him that it was, as the embassy official had said, a drama being directed by Martin Scorsese about the Dalai Lama. It had taken only two days after cameras started rolling for word of the production to travel from its set in Morocco to Beijing, where officials were not happy. After learning about the film and the story it told, Murphy realized that the making of this movie endangered Disney's entire future in China. He didn't know it at the time, but that phone call to his Burbank office was the start of a cautionary tale for all of Hollywood—in fact, it was a sign that the capital offered in China was inextricably tied to politics. On the afternoon of the call from the Chinese embassy, a future in which China would exercise remarkable power in Hollywood—the ability to green-light projects and change scripts like an invisible studio chief—began to take shape.

In the meantime, though, Murphy needed to put out this fire. He called the person who was already on retainer to help Disney navigate the Chinese power structure. Henry Kissinger listened to Murphy as he laid out the *Kundun* issue. Murphy's mind was racing with the implications it might spell for Disney's plans in China, but the former secretary of state remained unfazed by the whole thing. Granted, Kissinger had negotiated Nixon's meeting with Mao Zedong in 1972, a détente that reorganized the world order. Given China's economic growth and the political power it had accrued since Nixon and Mao shook hands in Beijing, it was fitting that, twenty-four years later, he would be called in to save Mickey Mouse.

ACROSS TOWN AT Sony Pictures Entertainment, a government relations executive named Hope Boonshaft received a perplexing phone call of her own only a few months later, in the spring of 1997. Of all things, it also concerned a politically sensitive movie about the Dalai Lama, this one called *Seven Years in Tibet*.

Howard Stringer, Sony Corporation of America's top executive, explained that the film had been shown to some Chinese officials, and it had so offended them that there was now concern that they might expel all Sony business from the country. The film wasn't just putting Sony movies at risk; in the mid-1990s, the Chinese box office could have hardly covered a few executive salaries anyway. It was threatening "big Sony," as employees put it—the manufacturer of computers and televisions that had led Japan's electronics boom since its founding just after the end of World War II. The prospect of losing access to China's factories and customers meant billions of dollars were on the line.

"Howard," Boonshaft said to her boss, "that's a bit above my pay grade." Stringer told her to figure it out.

Work on *Seven Years in Tibet* had begun innocently enough. In the early 1990s, Jean-Jacques Annaud, a French director known for little-seen but well-respected art house movies like *The Bear* and *The Lover*, was drawn to Asia after filming a movie in Vietnam. He had a strong desire to return and explore the continent's spirituality and asked his assistant for books he could adapt into movies on the theme. She brought him Heinrich Harrer's memoir. Harrer was a mountaineer who'd left Nazi Europe to summit Nanga Parbat in British India, only to be taken prisoner and eventually find himself tutoring a teenage Dalai Lama as war broke out between Tibet and China. "Fabulous," thought Annaud as he read the book and assessed its cinematic potential. "Here's a blond Aryan Nazi who becomes the teacher of the Dalai Lama." Brad Pitt, Hollywood's most famous blond, got the part.

The movie was perfectly timed for the Dalai Lama's own star-making moment in Hollywood. He was born in a shed and identified as the fourteenth incarnation of the Dalai Lama at four years old, and now the docile monk lived in Dharamsala, where a government-in-exile of about 113,000 Tibetans sandwiched between China and India is based. As repression of Tibet grew, the Dalai Lama's public persona rose. In 1989 he won the Nobel Peace Prize. In 1992 he guest-edited the December issue of French *Vogue*. The next year, Richard Gere, star of *An Officer and a Gentleman* and *Pretty Woman*, went off script before announcing the winner for Best Art Direction at the Academy Awards to decry the "horrendous, horrendous human rights situation" in Tibet. Sharon Stone called herself a disciple. In a 1997 ceremony in India attended by 1,500 monks and nuns, Steven Seagal, the star of ultraviolent revenge fantasies like *Hard to Kill*, was anointed a *tulku*, a "reincarnated lama and radiant emanation of the Buddha." Disney's ABC put *Dharma & Greg*, about a young American woman embracing Buddhism, on its prime-time lineup. A charming monk who encouraged others to shun all earthly possessions had become the patron saint of Beverly Hills.

His Holiness was so popular, in fact, that soon there were not one but two movies about him under way. Also, among those taken in were *E.T.*

the Extra-Terrestrial screenwriter Melissa Mathison and her husband, Harrison Ford, already a fixture in the Hollywood firmament as the star of *Star Wars* and *Raiders of the Lost Ark*. The couple had traveled to Tibet in 1992 and met a tour guide, Gendun Rinchen, who was accused by China of being a spy and imprisoned for nearly a year. Mathison was there preparing to write *Kundun*, a screenplay about the Dalai Lama's teenage years. Mathison wanted to ground Tibet in the story of the real people caught in a political and spiritual tinderbox. "Part of the tragedy of Tibet is that it's been Shangri-La" in Hollywood movies, she said, presented as a caricature and not as a pressing humanitarian crisis. "Nobody believed it existed in the first place, so its destruction was the destruction of a fantasy." She began telling associates in Hollywood that hers would be the authentic Dalai Lama production of 1997; she and Ford had flown to India and read the *Kundun* script with the man himself. Martin Scorsese came on board to direct. Then the Dalai Lama, ever the diplomat, also endorsed the story that had inspired *Seven Years in Tibet*.

"Harrer is one of the few Westerners who [are] fully acquainted with the Tibetan way of life. His book is beautiful and good," the Dalai Lama said. He added, "Since I was 15 or 16 there has been a tragic situation in my country and most of my life has been spent under difficult circumstances. Buddhist teaching has helped me to retain hope and determination in this time, so perhaps a story about such a person must be a good thing."

The history that both *Kundun* and *Seven Years in Tibet* explored was nearly fifty years old, but it was fresh in the minds of Chinese officials. China invaded Tibet in 1949, its soldiers sweeping through the region and ordering monks to reeducation camps. Soldiers destroyed religious temples and killed villagers. Bronze statues from the region were melted down for copper. A decade later, Chinese soldiers handily defeated a Tibetan insurrection, and the Dalai Lama escaped to India, worried his murder or capture would spell the total end of Tibetan Buddhism. He still lives there today, his power defined more by where he cannot go than by where he can. To Americans, Tibetans can be viewed as spiritual brethren to their country's own colonists, persecuted for their beliefs and forced to find refuge elsewhere. But to many Chinese, the Tibetans' argument for sovereignty, as one scholar put it, is akin to an American hearing about a "rally calling for Hawaii to be returned to the descendants of the last king of those islands." His mere presence—let alone his star power—is a one-man rebuke to what China considers its rightful borders.

There was at least one U.S. executive who knew making a movie about this history was bad for business. Edgar Bronfman Jr., the CEO of Canadian beverage company Seagram, had acquired Universal Studios in 1995. Scorsese had a distribution deal with Universal at the time, but things quickly grew tense between him and the new owner. The director had recently wrapped his three-hour epic *Casino*, and Bronfman wanted him to cut forty-five minutes from the film to make it commercially viable. Scorsese refused, prompting Bronfman to wonder why a studio had employees if they weren't going to listen to the boss. Then Scorsese brought the boss *Kundun*.

"I'm not doing this. I don't need to have my spirits and wine business thrown out of China," Bronfman said. Through his beverage deals, Bronfman was already aware of a principle Hollywood was learning in real time: in China, political mistakes are punished with economic sanctions. Alienating China with a movie wasn't about losing the paltry box-office sales it might yield. It was about allowing that movie to become a contaminant in the larger corporate structure, one that put far larger revenues at risk. For Sony, China was threatening a disruption of an electronics supply chain that would cost billions to rebuild. At Disney, where Scorsese took the project after Bronfman's refusal, it was the TV channel, theme park, and Mickey Mouse plush dolls that might not pass through Chinese borders because of a midbudget drama being made through a production deal signed by a subdivision of a subdivision.

Chinese officials didn't care what the studio executives knew or when they knew it. "We are resolutely opposed to the making of this movie," said Kong Min, an official in China's film bureau, of *Kundun* months before it was scheduled to hit theaters. "It is intended to glorify the Dalai Lama, so it is an interference in China's internal affairs."

When had a movie release ever been received with the language of spy craft? For the first time, a certain kind of message had been sent from China to Hollywood at large, as effective as if couriers had been dispatched to every office with a telegram. There's a saying in Chinese, *shā jī jǐng hóu*, which roughly translates to "kill the chicken to scare the monkeys." The chicken was the person who could be made a public example of; the monkeys were everyone who watched and learned from that person's mistake. The cases of *Seven Years in Tibet* and *Kundun* were the first clash of Hollywood moviemaking with Chinese politics, but as the industry's entanglement with China grew, Sony and Disney would have a lot of company in the coop.

WHEN HE HAD STARTED FILMING, Annaud visited Tibet on a production scouting trip. Though he firmly identified as an atheist, he found himself moved when he watched the monks chant together and blow horns from their mountaintop sanctuaries. China, he began to think, was not unlike his home country, France, or his adopted country, the United States. It had made some mistakes throughout history, and exploring a country's mistakes was what its filmmakers did. Soon he sensed the long reach of an angry China in episodes that presaged what was to come. Officials in the town where production was based, a border region called Ladakh, told him that India, under pressure from China, had threatened to cut off their electricity if filming continued. Then the production was denied permission to open a local bank account. Cutting off the power was one thing. Cutting off the money was another, and Chinese pressure stopped the production for the thirty minutes it took Annaud to secure permission to move *Seven Years in Tibet* to a friendlier country.

The cast and crew decamped to the Andes Mountains along the

border of Chile and Argentina, a range that broached the same altitude as their original location in Ladakh but was safely located halfway around the world. Laborers reconstructed Lhasa. The roughly one hundred monks cast in the movie, some of whom had signed their contracts with purple-inked thumbprints, flew to South America, crying when they saw the movie-set simulacrum of their lost city. They were a lot cast out by the world. The Argentine government had limited the number of monks granted entry, worried they would stay and form a politically problematic settlement. When Argentinian customs agents wouldn't allow Asian yaks in, fearing they carried disease, Annaud's crew sourced new yaks from Montana. These yaks stepped off the cargo plane and into roles for which they'd been miscast; they were not, Annaud realized, working yaks but *"yak de compagnie,"* accustomed to a life of leisure on the Montana prairie and unprepared to haul heavy bags on their backs. Two were eventually trained to the point that Annaud could get the shots he needed. Annaud had effectively re-created Tibet in the Andes, though modern life would sneak in every morning when Argentinian teenagers screamed for Pitt as his motorcade rode into set.

When she sat down to watch the completed film soon after receiving the call from her studio's CEO, Boonshaft had only a cursory understanding of Chinese politics, but it didn't take a sinologist to see why China was going to be offended. The movie opens with a toddler Dalai Lama, still missing a few teeth, receiving gifts from prostrating Tibetans. After Harrer's capture, the Dalai Lama, now a young boy, is drawn to the white man who teaches monks how to ice-skate. Harrer (along with moviegoers) learns what China doesn't want anyone to know: his surrogate son is the spiritual leader of millions. They learn the rarefied world he lives in, where no one is ever to be seated higher than him, speak before he does, or look him in the eye. Harrer becomes his tutor of the outside world, telling him where Paris is, who Jack the Ripper was, what a Molotov cocktail can do. Harrer, in turns, adopts the Tibetan sensibility: he respects all living creatures and learns the omen that an asteroid portends. In this case, the evil omen is Mao, who a radio broadcaster tells us has consolidated power and vows to reclaim Tibet.

China had reason to fear the way the movie presented it. Chinese soldiers mow down statues of Buddha with machine guns, bomb villages, and chase out terrified citizens. The Chinese send officials to reason with the Dalai Lama, offering autonomy and religious freedom if the country accepts China as its political master. The Dalai Lama's teachings of nonviolence and compassion make the Chinese officials look like boorish fools. Harrer leaves Tibet a changed man, of course, one who reconnects with his estranged son and at one point plants a Tibetan flag atop a mountain. The movie's final image: text on the screen reminding the audience of the one million Tibetans dead at the hands of the Chinese occupation.

The lights came up in Boonshaft's screening room on the Sony lot. Years later, Sony would learn how easy it was to cut a single scene or line of dialogue from a movie to get approval from Chinese censors, but this was a 130-minute humanization of a Chinese state enemy and an assault on its most sensitive political issue. Boonshaft hustled to manage damage control, calling Jim Sasser, an old friend from Washington who was then serving as U.S. ambassador to China. He recommended she immediately acquaint herself with local Chinese officials and study Mandarin. It was all a matter of building up *guanxi*, the Chinese mixture of etiquette and politesse that undergirds every relationship in professional Chinese circles. More than simply networking or quid pro quo arrangements, *guanxi* is a level of trust that must be established before any deal is completed or truce reached.

Boonshaft's first step toward building it: traveling across town to introduce herself to the Chinese consul and the Chinese cultural attaché in Los Angeles. Her second step: going to the Tiffany in Beverly Hills to buy offertory presents (she had already learned not to give them clocks, since the Chinese view such gifts as a death omen). Her third step: doing whatever she could to get in their good graces. Even in 1997, Boonshaft could see that China's top priority was to spread its influence abroad. She started screening local Chinese movies on the Sony lot, another suggestion of Sasser's that meant the world to Chinese officials trying to develop the credibility of their own film industry. The screenings were by invitation only, and the consulate managed the guest list. The movies themselves were not high priorities for Sony, but the expense of dessert for the receptions afterward was a small price to pay if it built up goodwill. Those Chinese officials cheered to see Sony executives drop by unannounced and express interest in China's entertainment industry did not know that Boonshaft had invited them for the charm offensive.

She brought herself up to speed on the history of China's relationship with Japan, learning about the Battle of Nanjing, the six-week massacre of some three hundred thousand Chinese civilians at the hands of Japan's Imperial Army. The so-called Rape of Nanjing had occurred sixty years prior, but the Chinese had never forgotten the murders—or Japan's refusal to apologize for them. Sony, Japan's best-known company, did business with China, but Boonshaft always sensed tension. Now the Chinese were unhappy about a movie whose release was still months away.

No matter: Chinese officials took advantage of Sony's willingness to please. The country asked Sony and the other studios to support its bid to join the World Trade Organization—a request they all accommodated. They asked Sony to sponsor a table at a Los Angeles event honoring the Chinese prime minister—a request it accommodated. To demonstrate her commitment toward honoring their culture, Boonshaft hosted a Mandarin tutor in her office each week. The cultural attaché had given her a Chinese name: Hen Ping. It meant "the relentless one."

DISNEY CEO MICHAEL EISNER AND his team huddled to figure out what to do with their inherited mess. Like *Seven Years in Tibet*, Scorsese's *Kundun* portrayed the Dalai Lama as a rambunctious toddler and typical teenager caught in a war with an imperialist China. But *Kundun* went even further, saying the country was "trying to rewrite history" when it insisted Tibet belonged to them. Scorsese even dared to portray Mao on-screen as a belittling elder. The camera pauses on the smooth fingernails and shiny shoes this "man of the people" managed to maintain. In a scene depicting a state visit:

> MAO ZEDONG
> Religion is poison. Like a poison, it
> weakens the race; like a drug, it retards
> the mind of people. . . . Tibet has been
> poisoned by religion and your people are
> poisoned and inferior.

Releasing a movie that so blatantly threatened Disney's ambitions in China offered no perfect solutions or even good ones. Eisner and his team needed to find the least bad option. They had weighed shutting down the movie before the situation had gone public but knew doing so would risk Scorsese's wrath. The director would tar them in the press as bowing to a totalitarian regime, and the rest of the industry would rally against Disney for silencing the director. China's threats challenged a core tenet of Hollywood, especially of filmmakers like Scorsese who'd been inspired by the European auteurs of the midtwentieth century. Movies were a business, to be sure, but they were also a vehicle of American expression, an industry where filmmakers were unafraid to take on—were even celebrated for taking on—politically charged topics.

Disney ultimately decided on a Goldilocks option: they would release the movie, but as quietly as possible. They would spend as little money as possible to market the film in a limited release. Once that dearth of marketing led to lousy returns in its opening weeks, Disney would have justification to tell Scorsese that it wasn't worth expanding to theaters nationwide. Still, no one in Hollywood could argue that Disney had censored it.

Murphy flew to DC to explain Disney's decision to the Chinese. He brought Kissinger with him. The diplomat didn't say much, under-standing that his role was to sit and lend some gravitas to the situation. He joined Murphy on one side of the table; more than half a dozen Chinese officials faced them. Murphy told the Chinese that the limited release for *Kundun* was good for them, since it would avoid any critics saying China had censored a Hollywood movie.

"You do not want us to kill this film. It's not good for either of us," he explained, parsing his words to avoid using the word *apology*. He expressed regret for "the situation we find ourselves in"—not for making the movie. But the Chinese didn't understand.

"How can a giant company let something like this happen without Michael Eisner and the board green-lighting the movie?" one official asked.

It was a scene laying bare the Chinese way of doing business, a top-down system in which any major decision comes with sign-off from the CEO—or from the president. China's command-and-control economy was predicated on the bosses knowing *exactly* what every bureaucrat was approving, on every decision moving in concert with orders from the top. As top-down an organization as Disney was under Eisner, he and the board did not know when cameras started rolling on every project in development. After doing their best to explain they really were in the dark on the decision to make *Kundun*, Murphy and Kissinger left, looking at each other, unsure of how it had gone.

RICHARD GERE WAS NOT HELPING THINGS. Since his Academy Awards riff on Tibet, he had become Hollywood's most outspoken advocate of the Dalai Lama. "The reason the Chinese hate me so much is they have spent billions of dollars creating this wonderful PR image in America, and with my one speech at the Oscars, I destroyed it all. I would not be surprised if they wanted me dead," he boasted. On press junkets, he displayed an uncanny ability to turn any question into an opportunity to expound on his Buddhist philosophy. Asked about his on-screen nude scenes, Gere responded, "It was like being in a monk's cell. It was what I've been trying to do in my life, to strip away all conventions, like the clothes, the fame, all the exterior things that aren't important."

As Murphy and Boonshaft were managing their own angry officials, Gere supplied China with a *third* film to cause a geopolitical maelstrom in 1997, this one produced by storied Hollywood studio Metro-Goldwyn-Mayer. In *Red Corner*, Gere stars as an entertainment executive in China attempting what Disney was trying to do in real life: sell TV shows to air on Chinese stations. His plan is foiled, though, after he spends the night with a local woman and wakes up to find her dead in his room, his body covered in her blood. Gere then takes moviegoers on a two-hour tour of China's terrifying judicial system, one that sees him denied due process, poked with a cattle prod, and forced to watch videos of Chinese executions. With the help of a rebellious defense attorney (Bai Ling), Gere discovers that he is the victim of a vast conspiracy designed to keep Western entertainment out of China—a scenario that casts him as the First Amendment savior, bearing American TV shows as the democratizing force China needs. "Once the system opens up, there's no going back," his character says of letting Western values into China. By the end of the movie, Gere gets out, but the viewer is convinced China is a medieval place where no one who questions the state is safe.

The hope of *Red Corner*—that Western business and culture would have a democratizing effect on China's Communist regime—was one shared by executives and politicians selling a wary public on letting the country into the global economy. The movie's release coincided with reminders of China's outreach to the world, coming around the time of a state visit from Chinese president Jiang Zemin, the first U.S. visit of a Chinese leader since Jimmy Carter had hosted Deng Xiaoping in 1979. Jiang dined with President Bill Clinton, spoke at Harvard, and walked the grounds of Colonial Williamsburg. Chinese officials visited the MGM lot to let executives know they were not pleased to see *Red Corner* coming out in theaters during the visit. For China, the movie and its star were tarnishing the perfect image China wanted to project on the trip.

In this, MGM and China shared a common problem with *Red Corner*: the star of *Red Corner*. Where Jiang went, Gere was not far behind, picket sign in hand. When Clinton hosted Jiang at an October 29 state dinner at the White House, David Geffen and Steven Spielberg attended alongside Disney CEO Michael Eisner, the latter hoping his attendance would win him some favor as the *Kundun* mess shook out. The crowd at the White House watched as the Harlem Globetrotters spun basketballs, John Denver sang "Rocky Mountain High," and Yo-Yo Ma performed, his stature as a Chinese luminary overriding any radioactivity he may have picked up from his cello solos appearing on the soundtrack of *Seven Years in Tibet*. Gere was in DC, too, but not at the White House. He was across the street on the rooftop of the Hotel Washington with fellow Buddhists Uma Thurman and Sharon Stone, hosting a "stateless dinner" in protest.

The escalating trouble at Sony and Disney had leaked to the press, putting both studios on watch. Spike Lee, Barbra Streisand, and others signed an open letter to Chinese ambassador Li Daoyu "to actively and publicly oppose any and all attempts by your government to censor or intimidate." Pro-Tibet activists prepared pamphlets to hand out in movie theaters screening *Seven Years in Tibet*. But no one took the cause more seriously than Gere.

While Brad Pitt responded, "Who cares what I think?" when asked about Tibet, Gere used every opportunity he could to position the film as a political statement, setting up a routine call-and-response with MGM executives and others trying to downplay his comments. Years later, the statements together offer a portrait of a divided Hollywood, where only some constituents grow troubled by the prospect of angering China.

RICHARD GERE: *"Red Corner* is a far more important film to me, because it has the catalyst for change in the world."

MGM PRESIDENT OF WORLDWIDE MARKETING GERRY RICH:
"We're not pursuing a political agenda. We're in the business of
selling entertainment."

RICHARD GERE: "When you're talking about the judicial system
in China, you're clearly talking about the judicial system in the
colonies. If it's that bad in China, imagine how bad it is in Tibet."

GERRY RICH: "There are bad guys [in the movie], but with every
thriller there are bad guys."

When Gere hosted that "stateless dinner" in DC, Rich was quick to
note that the event was "not an MGM-sponsored stateless dinner." In
case the point wasn't clear, he added that "MGM is not joined at the hip
with Richard Gere in those efforts."

The biggest takeaway from Jiang's visit, though, was that it allowed
Americans, in the words of one news account, to see that "today's Chinese wear business suits instead of Mao jackets." Four years earlier, President Clinton had gathered forty Chinese dissidents and Tibetan activists
to sign an order calling on China to improve its human-rights record
before it could enjoy freer trade with the U.S. But during this visit, Jiang
and Clinton signed trade deals. Boeing scored a $3 billion agreement to
sell commercial airliners to the country. The money under China's mattress was starting to come out, and certain uncomfortable political truths
would have to go away if America wanted a chance at it.

GIVEN THE DRAMA THAT HAD already unfolded, it was easy to forget
that only one of the movies in question had come out at the time of Jiang
Zemin's visit to the States. *Seven Years in Tibet* had premiered a few weeks
prior, in October 1997, to a so-so critical reception. The controversies and
Brad Pitt's star power didn't fill seats; the movie collected a middling

$38 million, the worst wide-release performance of Pitt's career until that point. In China, officials prepared their own cinematic counterattack to Sony's movie: *Red River Valley*, a government-sanctioned retelling of the 1904 British invasion of the region that would serve as the country's own Tibet-focused feature. To help cast and edit the film, they called in Mike Medavoy, the longtime studio chief who had run Orion Pictures and TriStar, where he'd presided over hits like *The Terminator* and *Sleepless in Seattle*. His China debut was praised by the critics who matter there.

"The best I have seen in my post," said Sun Jiazheng, China's minister of radio, film, and television.

In Hong Kong, distributors were scared to show *Seven Years in Tibet*. Great Britain had handed over control of the former colony to China three months earlier, and while it was supposed to maintain a democratic distance, they knew better than to anger their new ruling country. "We don't want to get into trouble," said Tony Wong, owner of Cinemation Films International. "I'm only interested in action films, not politics." Those who did distribute the movie found that the controversy had helped in one way: it made the movie so well known to audiences that they didn't need to translate the title. (Cantonese translations of movie titles around that time had included *Boogie Nights* becoming *His Powerful Device Makes Him Famous* and Oliver Stone's *Nixon* released as *The Big Liar*.)

Red Corner debuted two days after Jiang Zemin's state dinner, and the reviews were brutal. It was the biggest release that weekend, with no significant competition, but no one but Gere himself wanted to spend an afternoon contemplating China's corrupt judicial system. It came and went with a dismal gross of $22.5 million.

Few Americans were seeing the movies, and other territories had backed off showing them, but Hollywood was still bracing for impact. Jack Valenti, the head of the Motion Picture Association of America, tried to calm nerves. "The Chinese aren't going to close the window on the future because of two or three films. They are drawing a line in the sand and saying, 'You have gone too far.' That's about it." But on November 1, 1997, a memo from China's State Administration of Radio, Film, and Television went out. None of the efforts had been enough.

"Those three American companies are still pushing out the above films. In order to protect Chinese national overall interests, it has been decided that all business cooperation with these three companies [is] to be ceased temporarily without exception," the memo read.

"All of our business in China stopped overnight," Eisner said. *Kundun* was on the release calendar and there was nothing Disney could do to stop its premiere two months later. It's a wonder anyone saw the released movie at all, though. It opened on Christmas. The other releases that day included a remake of *An American Werewolf in Paris*, which opened on 1,728 screens; a reboot of *Mr. Magoo*, which opened on 1,857 screens; and *The Postman*, a Kevin Costner sci-fi thriller that opened on 2,207 screens. *Kundun* opened on two screens. It would eventually expand to about four hundred, but tepid reviews and Disney's efforts to have it disappear as quickly as possible had worked. The movie collected $5.7 million. Disney executives didn't consider it a big loss. *It's not like we're burying* Raging Bull, Peter Murphy thought to himself.

Collectively, the three movies that angered China grossed $66 million, or about one tenth the haul made by that year's juggernaut, *Titanic*. Hardly anyone had seen them. China's leaders didn't care.

ANNAUD WAS BANNED FROM CHINA. Brad Pitt was, too. Sasser called Boonshaft with advice on how to deal with the escalation. She needed to go to the embassy in Washington and meet with the Chinese ambassador if Sony wanted the ban to be lifted. Sony could not apologize for making the film, she thought, since that would further alienate actors and directors, who would refuse to work for a studio that didn't defend free expression. But Boonshaft thought she could thread the needle and get the officials on her side. Finding the right blend of words to defend the studio was what she was paid to do. She flew to DC, packing a crystal bowl from Tiffany.

Boonshaft entered a room in the embassy where a small table with flowers stood, and took a seat next to the Chinese ambassador, Li Daoyu. She didn't let on that she knew some Mandarin, hoping she might eavesdrop before it was translated. At one point, the ambassador made it clear this would not be an easy conversation.

"Well," he scoffed, "the Japanese never did know how to apologize."

Boonshaft dug her fingernails into the palm of her hand. The Chinese ambassador was interpreting *Seven Years in Tibet*, a movie released by a Tokyo-based company founded in 1946, as a further affront in the decades-long animosity between China and Japan. He was asking Boonshaft to account for years of acrimony—not to mention alluding to a body count in the hundreds of thousands. Boonshaft responded with words she still has memorized years later.

"Mr. Ambassador," she said, "Sony Pictures is an American company, and we do know how to apologize. If we caused any offense to the people of China, we are sorry, for that was never our intent."

The room was silent. The ambassador leaned across the table. He burrowed into Boonshaft's eyes. He had just heard the classic Hollywood apology—saying sorry if any offense was caused by the action without apologizing for the action itself.

And it worked. The tension in the room broke and Boonshaft kept the meeting at a pleasant hum until it was over. Walking out, a Sony lobbyist in the room asked Boonshaft how she'd thought of the comeback to the ambassador's dismissal so quickly. She had no idea, and though the meeting had ended well, she couldn't tell whether it would ultimately work. But at that moment, she felt like a miracle worker.

Boonshaft was back in her office in LA when she got another phone call, this one summoning her to the consulate general. It was January 1998—the *Seven Years in Tibet* ordeal had stretched nearly a year. The Chinese officials asked her to bring Bob Wynne, the company's chief operating officer. They headed across town, along with a gorgeous Tiffany glass bowl. Once inside, the consul general turned to Boonshaft's boss.

"Mr. Wynne," the consulate general said, "I want to tell you that you are once again free to do business in China, due to the efforts of Hen Ping."

It was one of the few times in her life she was completely speechless. The months of screenings, favors, embassy showdowns, and gifts presented in baby-blue boxes had worked. She and Wynne floated to the car and called Stringer with the news.

"You can just go home for the rest of the year," he told Boonshaft.

Instead, she got a bonus and a bigger office, but her work wasn't over. To seal the deal and smooth relations, the company later organized what the executives called an "apology tour" across China, taking twelve executives and their wives from city to city and meeting officials in each one. Boonshaft slipped briefing papers on each official under hotel doors at night. As a gesture of goodwill, they brought *The Mask of Zorro* with them to screen as a sneak preview for officials. They brought that, and other offerings. "Can any of us carry any more fucking presents?" asked one executive as they lugged gifts across China.

A year earlier, it had looked like Sony's future in the country was in jeopardy. Now the executives were singing karaoke with Chinese officials. The Chinese authorities never missed an opportunity, even in good humor, to bring up *Seven Years in Tibet* and remind Sony just how perilous it had made the situation. Sony's response: "It's behind us." But it would be clear, even years later, that it was not behind the Chinese.

Hearts and Minds

The men sitting across from one another in Beijing's Hall of Purple Light had more in common than they might have thought. Zhu Rongji, a descendant of a Ming dynasty emperor who ruled from 1368 to 1398, joined the Communist Party as a young electrical engineering student in 1949, the same year as the founding of the People's Republic of China. His life was interrupted when he gave a speech criticizing Mao's economic policies, saying they would lead to "irrational high growth"—three words that were enough to get him purged to the countryside, where he raised livestock for years. He got a second life after Mao's death, when Deng Xiaoping named him mayor of Shanghai, and Zhu started making up for lost time.

Michael Eisner had also been born into his country's elite circles, growing up in a Park Avenue family that socialized with the Lehmans and the Loebs. He couldn't trace his ancestors to the fourteenth century, but his paternal great-grandfather had started a company with two sewing machines and built a manufacturer that eventually supplied uniforms to the Boy Scouts of America, and his mother's family had founded the American Safety Razor Company. Throughout his childhood, Eisner attended Camp Keewaydin, a Vermont enclave for boys that espoused Horatio Alger lessons of self-reliance and teamwork. Eisner started his career in television programming at ABC, working on shows that fondly recalled American history (*Happy Days*) and laid it bare (*Roots*). In 1976, in only his midthirties, he moved to Hollywood to become president of Paramount Pictures, then the top studio producing movies that shaped the collective imagination, like *Grease* and *Saturday Night Fever.* After jumping to Disney, Eisner fended off board coups to become the rare corporate celebrity, stopped by children for autographs at the company's theme parks.

Eisner met with Zhu at what may have been the apex of the executive's career. As CEO of Disney he had overseen a revitalization in animation that brought *Beauty and the Beast, The Little Mermaid*, and *The Lion King* to the screen and turned Disney from a movie studio with $1.5 billion in revenue in 1984 to a multimedia conglomerate with $23 billion in revenue just fourteen years later.

Eisner traveled to China in October 1998, ten months after *Kundun* had premiered, to win over Zhu, a man also charged with navigating a daunting and unpredictable twenty-first century. Nearly two years had passed since that call to Peter Murphy's office, but Disney was still banned in the country. Eisner needed to fix the problem.

"We made a stupid mistake in releasing *Kundun*," Eisner told Zhu. "This film was a form of insult to our friends."

If he wanted his company to do business in the world's most important new market, Eisner needed to acquiesce to Chinese leaders in ways many in Hollywood's creative community had feared. The two men were meeting just months after the release of *Mulan*, the studio's retelling of a Northern Dynasties myth, a new movie that Eisner hoped would bring more Chinese children into the Disney fold. Eisner assured the premier that they had all achieved the best possible outcome with *Kundun*.

"The bad news is that the film was made; the good news is that nobody watched it. Here I want to apologize, and in the future, we should prevent this sort of thing, which insults our friends, from happening. In short, we're a family entertainment company, a company that uses silly ways to amuse people," he said.

If throwing a company's creative mission under the bus was the price of regaining access to the Chinese market, Eisner was willing to pay it. And it worked: several months after Disney's meeting with Zhu, Chinese officials announced that the ban had been revoked. But it was more than Eisner's politicking that got Disney into China. It was a hundred years of history that made such a conversation between Disney's top executive and a Communist Party official even possible.

EISNER WAS APOLOGIZING HIS WAY into the one major country that—well into the 1990s—had only just recently been reintroduced to American entertainment. Audiences in Bangkok, Buenos Aires, and Berlin knew Hollywood movies, a cultural juggernaut unlike any other. As Hollywood executives and American politicians almost immediately came to realize, the movies were hardly just silly ways to amuse people.

Though Hollywood would become the global epicenter of entertainment, the world's first moviegoers were largely concentrated in Europe, and they didn't see much in those early days. In 1894 and 1895, an evening at the movies featured an early clip of a baby being fed. Another was descriptively titled *La sortie de l'usine Lumière* (*Workers Leaving the Lumière Factory*). The most famous of these first moving pictures—of a train coming into a station—caused moviegoers to leap from their seats, convinced they were watching a locomotive racing toward them. Everywhere, the shock of recognition, the play of light and shadow, and the thrill of possibility turned the experience of seeing ordinary life on-screen into an ecstatic experience.

It wouldn't be until World War I broke out that American cinema got its chance to catch up to the European filmmakers. When fighting spread across Europe, bombing raids leveled production and distribution houses. Film-stock factories shifted their assembly lines to other goods needed for the war effort. Theaters closed. Overnight there was a short-age of movies, and America, where bombs did not fall, was one of the few places that could supply them. Hollywood studios distributed their movies in Europe, Australia, New Zealand, and Latin America. Putting forth something of an insensitive metaphor, the publication *Motion Pic-ture World* in 1914 declared, "Demand for American films in Europe will be large enough to justify a greater 'invasion' than Europe has ever known before." Less than a decade after its founding, Hollywood had become a factory town, shipping its products around the world.

World leaders saw something else on the big screen: a capacity for unprecedented political influence. In Washington, Woodrow Wilson re-alized that his country's newly embraced art form was a worthy conveyor of the American brand of liberal democracy that soldiers were fighting to protect in World War I. "Western ideas go in with the western good," he said. In a 1916 speech titled "Men Are Governed by Their Emotions," he instructed his country's filmmakers to "make this world more comfort-able and more happy and convert them to the principles of America." Two years later, Wilson would deem the movies an "essential industry," mean-ing that their production would continue if a war broke out in the States. Indeed, the following decades would cement Hollywood as a crucial ally in the war efforts to come, and, in the words of one scholar, in an "un-declared war" for hearts and minds around the world.

Soon after Wilson's remarks, movies about American manufacturing were commissioned, and audiences learned how the U.S. made items like fountain pens. The U.S. Committee on Public Information fought to keep films from enemy countries like Germany out of international markets so American movies had the advantage, turning the theater into another territory to occupy. When it came to those American movies that would be shipped overseas at this time, George Creel, the head of the CPI, paid careful attention to the reputation that certain movies might grant his home country. "What we wanted to get into foreign countries were pictures that presented the wholesome life of America, giving fair ideas of our people and institutions," he said. "Film dramas portraying the exploits of 'Gyp the Blood' or 'Jesse James' were bound to prejudice our fight for the good opinion of neutral nations."

Creel had arrived at a key distinction to draw when assessing what movies were appropriate for overseas audiences. Americans could watch gangster flicks and seedy dramas in their hometown auditoriums, but those were not to be the movies shown to foreign audiences. America had to put its best face forward.

THE NEW FOREIGN REVENUE that came with the World War I–era expansion "was like picking up unexpected money in the street," said Carl Laemmle, the founder of Universal Pictures. With foreign audiences in play, producers approved filming in exotic locations, hoping they would draw in international viewers. That, in turn, caused the budgets of Hollywood movies to jump and the stories on-screen to grow more sophisticated. A bigger budget meant greater revenues would be needed to turn a profit, beginning a cycle of reliance on the overseas crowds. In China, operas were adapted for the big screen, and opera stars became movie stars in features produced by new studios popping up in Shanghai. France and Italy had been leading the pack in film quality and technical prowess; with their industries out of commission during the war, American directors focused on the *making* part of moviemaking. Milestone movies like D. W. Griffith's *The Birth of a Nation* and Charlie Chaplin's *The Tramp* emerged from this period; silent-era actors such as Lillian Gish and Rudolph Valentino became America's biggest celebrities.

Movie theaters sprang up in American cities to meet the growing demand for these better films and bigger stars, further weaving the practice into the country's economy. Sears, Roebuck and Co. owner Julius Rosenwald invested in new movie theaters so he could build them near his stores, generating foot traffic from customers heading from one to the other—a strategy that explains why so many theaters are in malls today. The Wrigley Company invested in them so their chewing gum could be sold at the concession stand (and remain on the auditorium floor for decades hence). The air-conditioning introduced in the 1920s was advertised as healthy for pregnant women or those with lung disease. The stars were aligning for the American cinema industry in the 1920s: not only were cities filling with potential customers, but as soldiers returned home from the front, they found a workplace dominated by assembly lines that reduced hours and gave them more free time.

By the late 1920s, foreign audiences composed between 30 percent and 40 percent of studio revenues. In 1927, when Al Jolson in *The Jazz Singer* exclaimed, "You ain't seen nothin' yet!" and introduced sound to the movies, Hollywood was so bullish on its global appeal that MGM studio chief Louis B. Mayer proclaimed his industry could turn English into the universal language. In certain countries, a language was taking shape, but not the one Mayer had in mind. Through movies like *La grande illusion* in France and *Cabiria* in Italy, Europeans were using film "as a means of reminding them of their cultural identity," writes David Puttnam, a former studio executive and film historian. In America, the amalgamation of immigrant cultures meant filmmakers "used the movies as a way of *forging* a cultural identity."

The same phenomenon occurred in China, where filmmakers of the 1930s tapped into a new kind of national self-conception that was forming, especially once Japanese aggression on the continent offered an enemy against which the country could define itself. Filmmakers and writers supporting the Communist revolution taking shape under Mao Zedong formed organizations like the League of Left-Wing Dramatists to produce leftist art. Chiang Kai-shek and the Kuomintang (KMT) Nationalists, Mao's rivals in the Chinese civil war waged primarily between 1945 and 1950, had also identified the political power of film. In the early 1930s, the Nationalists banned the martial arts films that had been popular and replaced them with feudal dramas that focused on everyday Chinese people and their struggles. From some of its earliest days in China, the cinema was a classroom.

As the American brand of moviemaking proved most popular, foreign governments eyed such cultural intrusion warily. In Germany, officials implemented a quota regulating the number of foreign films released in the country so it wouldn't tip the box-office balance away from their local productions. France tried to do the same thing before theater owners protested, arguing that the American movies were so popular that such measures would strip away too much of their revenue. What Americans today consider classic, harmless iconography like Charlie Chaplin's *The Tramp* was in Europe a threat to local traditions like literature or opera. America, when it came to culture, was a place for counterfeit books and other subpar offerings, not high art. Furthermore, these stories coming out of Los Angeles, in the eyes of skeptics, were piping pro-American messaging directly into their auditoriums.

But just as the movies sometimes generated cross-cultural tensions, they also became a way to mend them as an "adjunct of our State Department," as Will Hays, the first chairman of the Motion Picture Producers and Distributors of America, described it. In 1922, Mexico banned certain Hollywood movies due to their stereotypical portrayal of its citizens as criminals. The move would deprive studios of a sizable foreign market and create headaches for leaders in Washington. The MPPDA passed a resolution at its first board meeting prohibiting any movie demeaning to Mexico from being produced. Voilà—the country quickly agreed to distribute American films again. Positive portrayals in exchange for market access: it was a trade-off Hollywood would come to know well.

THE FIRST RECORDED MOVIE SCREENING in China is believed to have taken place on August 11, 1896, when audiences in Shanghai watched a film by early cinema pioneers the Lumière brothers. A robust filmmaking industry arose in the 1920s, but by the midcentury, as Hollywood was establishing its role in American culture and politics through a mix of patriotism and opportunism, Mao Zedong was drafting his country's artists into his revolution. Whereas American movies unconsciously transported Western ideals around the world—and would even embrace the propagandistic in times of war—Mao made no bones about what role he saw literature and art playing in a Communist society.

"There is, in fact, no such thing as art for art's sake," he said. Art was to be reflective of and produced for the masses and their political values. Without it, they could expect their burgeoning movement, still years away from victory, to fail. Art and literature must complement his efforts to rid China of the Japanese invasion and assume power, or else "we could not carry on the revolutionary movement and win victory." This philosophy, articulated in a series of lectures delivered in 1942 in Yan'an, would define his nation's output—and what it would accept for import—for decades to come.

Approximately fifty years before *Kundun* and *Seven Years in Tibet*, Mao foresaw the creation of the film bureau censorship board when he said that internal or external art that undermined the party's efforts should be censored and rejected. "We must adhere firmly to principle and severely criticize and repudiate all works of literature and art expressing views in opposition to the nation, to science, to the masses, and to the Communist Party," he said. A two-pronged approach was necessary: China could make movies that extolled its leaders and their political philosophy, but just as important was influencing the messaging produced and disseminated in other countries that threatened Chinese interests.

Several decades later, it was this kind of harsh response to art deemed dangerous by the Chinese that Michael Eisner was trying to circumvent as he groveled to Zhu Rongji. He reminded him of the $1.2 billion Disney had already invested to produce consumer products in China, and the company's plans to continue distributing movies about the wonders of the country's growth.

"I very much admire your courage in correcting mistakes and the efforts you've made to promote Sino-American friendship. This also proves that you're a very far-sighted businessman, and it's also an important factor in ensuring the success of the Disney Company," Zhu replied. *Nice company you've got there. Shame if something happened to it.*

Eisner pressed his case for a Disney Channel on the mainland, saying his team had considered the "chicken or egg" question of whether to pursue a channel or a theme park first before deciding on the former, believing it was the first step toward introducing characters that drove people to a theme park in a worthwhile way. Every conversation leading up to this one had included this tension: Disney executives arguing for a Disney Channel; Chinese officials saying they wanted a Chinese theme park. Communist regimes tend to be prickly about their airwaves, and officials had expressed fears over ceding so much cultural influence to a Western company. A theme park, on the other hand, fit into the government's plans to develop their countryside—and turn China from a manufacturing economy that produced Disney trinkets into a service economy that hosted Disney tourists. Eisner stuck to his argument that the channel-first playbook was the economically prudent way forward, telling Zhu that a park would be useless unless it could draw between twelve million and fifteen million guests each year.

When it came to economic leverage, Zhu reminded him that China was entering an era in which it would always have the upper hand.

"There are 1.2 billion people in China, so to us, 12 million to 15 million is not a big deal," he said.

"Once you decide to build in China, everything is easily open to discussion," Zhu said. Start building a Disneyland today, and maybe some other Disney products could come into the country during construction. More than fifty years after Mao's speech on the role of art, China had economic leverage to support the boundaries it set on foreign companies distributing messages that it did not want others to learn. Zhu reminded Eisner that Disney's goal—a TV station—might be realized only once China's goal—a theme park—was ensured.

"Having both chicken and eggs together makes for a very tasty dish," Zhu said.

As WORLD WAR II escalated overseas, Hollywood entered its golden era. In 1939 alone, MGM produced *Gone with the Wind* and *The Wizard of Oz*, the American frontier was defended in *Stagecoach*, and Jimmy Stewart assumed the mantle of the American Everyman in *Mr. Smith Goes to Washington*. These movies set box-office records and played in auditoriums for months on end, cementing Hollywood as a commercial force. But political considerations quickly superseded economic ones after the Pearl Harbor attack forced the U.S. into the war, and every frame of every movie was inspected to make sure it was helping the Allied campaign. "An otherwise harmless feature picture of 'boy meets girl' might have them saying good-by on a strip of coast line which had suddenly become of military importance," Hays explained in his memoir.

During World War II, Hollywood went from being an adjunct of the State Department to a subsidiary of the Defense Department. As Mark Harris details in his book *Five Came Back*, Hollywood's biggest directors joined the war effort. John Ford, director of *Stagecoach* and *The Grapes of Wrath*, filmed the Battle of Midway alongside soldiers in the Pacific Ocean, keeping a camera steady amid the bombing to provide an up-close perspective on American heroism so powerful that President Franklin Delano Roosevelt declared, "I want every mother in America to see this film." Ford was also deployed to shoot D-Day. It wasn't all battlefield fanfare for the director: he also made a movie for soldiers called *Sex Hygiene* on how to avoid gonorrhea.

Inside a Los Angeles studio relabeled "Fort Fox," Frank Capra assembled a group of screenwriters to work on features that laid out the stakes presented by fighting the Nazis. The director of *Mr. Smith Goes to Washington* rallied his team to use cinema to preserve the on-screen American dream his movies had come to symbolize. It was an amped-up version of Woodrow Wilson's mandate.

"Some carping individuals will accuse you of fighting 'the Battle of Hollywood,'" Capra told his crew. "Don't argue with them. This is a total war fought with every conceivable weapon! Your weapon is film! Your bombs are ideas! Hollywood is a war plant!"

The war plant made sure its war heroes were as inspirational as possible. The screenwriters for John Huston's *Sergeant York*, a 1941 film about decorated World War I soldier Alvin York, embellished the title character's battlefield heroism so much that the studio had to pay off his fellow soldiers to keep the secret. It still became the most profitable movie in Warner Bros. history at the time.

In a kind of inward-facing propaganda, directors were also charged with acclimating Americans to new wartime realities. The rising number of soldiers deployed overseas meant more black Americans would be filling jobs that hadn't previously been available to them, and so studios were encouraged to place black actors in the background of scenes—"in the stands of ball games, in stores, restaurants, and hotels," Harris notes. If American moviegoers grew accustomed to seeing more diversity in everyday life on-screen, it might help them accept that reality off-screen. Several decades earlier, those first moviegoers had been amazed at street scenes they could have viewed by stepping outside the theater. A couple of decades later, politicians understood that the movies could also inspire the outside world, not just the other way around.

Around the same time Mao was outlining his vision for art's role in supporting the state's campaign against Japan, Hollywood was fighting the Axis powers as well. Japanese characters appeared in American movies "often as grotesque stereotypes baring their buck teeth in phony smiles," Harris writes. Filmmakers grimly presented Japan's imperialist designs on China to engender outrage among American moviegoers. In *The Battle of China*, a propaganda piece directed by Capra, the country was presented as a likely next step in Japanese world domination.

The movies overall contributed to a casting of Asia as a region that "has helped to define Europe (or the West) as its contrasting image, idea, personality, experience," wrote critic Edward Said in 1978. Until quite recently, white actors commonly played Asian roles. Charlie Chan, the Hawaiian detective featured in more than three dozen movies over two decades beginning in 1926, was played by four actors, none of them Asian. Boris Karloff, best known for the title role in Universal's *The Mummy*, also played the title role in *The Mask of Fu Manchu*, putting on-screen one of the region's most gratuitous stereotypes—that of the mustachioed evil Asian man, said to be "Yellow Peril incarnate" and conceived by author Sax Rohmer after he asked a Ouija board how to make his fortune and the board answered C-H-I-N-A-M-A-N. Genghis Khan made several appearances in films, including in 1956's *The Conqueror*. He was played by John Wayne.

Chinese audiences would not learn of these offensive portrayals. After the People's Republic of China formed in 1949 under Mao Zedong, the pockets of Shanghai that had been under British control and included theaters on Nanjing Road were closed. Politburo members could watch movies at home and attend screenings held in unmarked buildings, but the Western entertainment sweeping the world would not enter China for decades. Mao, true to his word, banned American movies in 1950 and nationalized the Chinese film industry by 1953, bringing it under the control of officials also in charge of their country's crops and military. City residents watched state-approved movies in theaters, but Mao wanted to reach the peasants in the countryside, too. Traveling projectors roamed the land with movies that extolled the Communist revolution and its leader. Between 1949 and 1966, when the Cultural Revolution began, Chinese officials in control of the country's film industry made several hundred movies—and several thousand documentaries. The best thing to see on the big screen was the glory of Mao, not the martial arts movies and opera adaptations that had been popular. Movies were particularly useful vehicles for revolutionary thought in a country where millions were illiterate, noted Communist Party leader Qu Qiubai, who called on the Chinese creative class to suffuse movies with Communist ideology—"new wine in old bottles," as he put it.

The only American movie believed to have breached Chinese borders between 1951 and 1981, in fact, was a little-known 1954 drama about a workers' strike at the Empire Zinc mine in New Mexico called *Salt of the Earth*. Chinese authorities praised the collective heroism of its protagonists standing up to the capitalist structure. Few Americans had the chance to see the movie. Its director and writers had been blacklisted by Senator Joseph McCarthy's House Un-American Activities Committee for sympathizing with Communists. In the 1950s, such allegiances could get the same movie banned in the U.S. but embraced in China.

THE MOVIES' POWER IN SHAPING how Americans would process the war and its atrocities arrived almost immediately following the armistice, when Hollywood director George Stevens accompanied troops sent to liberate Dachau, the concentration camp roughly fifteen miles northwest of Munich. Stevens, who had directed Fred Astaire and Ginger Rogers sashaying in *Swing Time*, raised his camera to record the sunken eyes and blank stares of emaciated Jewish prisoners. It was among the first recordings of what was found behind Dachau's gates.

"We went to the woodpile," Stevens said. "And the woodpile was people."

Stevens's footage of the camps would eventually be submitted as irrefutable evidence during the Nuremberg trials, which convicted Nazis as war criminals.

The Nazis had lost, and the U.S. wanted to get Germany back on the side of democracy. If Germans needed to be deprogrammed, Universal and Warner Bros. would be there to help facilitate the rebuilding of democratic ideals. The State Department pledged to cooperate with Hollywood to ensure movies that "reflect credit on the good name and reputation of this country and its institutions" were sent abroad. "Donald Duck as world diplomat!" was how one Hollywood producer described the coming peacetime campaign.

It began in June 1947, when U.S. secretary of state George C. Marshall outlined a plan to repair the postwar economy in Europe, where a breakdown in the division of labor had led to a continental food shortage. As part of this European Recovery Plan (later known as the Marshall Plan), Western directors produced films to convince Europeans of the continent's strength as an interconnected entity. Five percent of the plan's funds were allocated for these public-information efforts. The recovery plan could help Europe's ailing economy; the movies, the organizers said, could help its mood.

The movies lifting Europe's mood were stories of by-the-bootstraps heroes, docudramas about the new life afforded by the Allies' victory, and anti-Communist narratives that portrayed a life in East Berlin as no fun at all. The titles included *Aquila*, about a man who is arrested for theft but who is given a job in a Marshall Plan–funded refinery after authorities realize he's stealing to feed his family; and *The Shoemaker and the Hatter*, in which two characters debate whether to make fewer hats at a higher profit or lots of shoes through a model of mass production and free trade. The shoemaker wins the argument.

More than 250 Marshall Plan films were produced and shipped

across Europe, a cinematic complement to the $13 billion in U.S. assistance flowing to the continent. These films aimed to convince the European viewers of the importance of European interdependence; they were instruments of an "American campaign to create a European 'melting pot'—whether as a mirror of the ideal American democratic society or as a bulwark against Soviet hegemony, or both," writes Sandra Schulberg, the daughter of a Marshall Plan director and an independent filmmaker who has worked to preserve the era's films. A Cold War mentality, in which beating back the spread of Communism was the U.S. government's chief foreign priority, had taken hold. This counteroffensive would be waged in the feelings and allegiances of everyday people.

Though some of the films' plots may seem on the nose, the Marshall Plan movies overall tread carefully for a European audience still reeling from the aggressive efforts of the Nazis and their chief propagandist, Joseph Goebbels. There was an unwritten rule among Marshall Plan filmmakers that the plan itself not be mentioned "more than twice in a one-reeler and three times in a two-reeler," Schulberg notes. "If Americans . . . feel that the 'message' is under-played, let them remember that Europeans have still not recovered from the sledge-hammer blows of Herr Goebbels." The filmmakers learned a key lesson in using the movies to change minds: the most effective propaganda doesn't feel like propaganda at all.

IT WOULD BE DECADES before China, with the help of Hollywood, learned the same lesson. On the mainland, strict artistic control defined the years following the end of World War II. Mao's wife, a former actress named Jiang Qing, mandated that only eight types of "model dramas" be performed on Chinese stages. Approved fare included shows like *The Red Detachment of Women*, featuring a dozen Chinese women in matching bob haircuts, wearing baby-blue uniforms as they stand *en pointe* and dance while aiming a rifle—ballet with ballistics that left no doubt that this was a propaganda piece. The restrictions extended beyond plays. Within China, artists were told to stick to the glorious present day of Mao's China. Since paintings of landscapes could be interpreted as images of the society that Mao's reforms were replacing, artists might paint a tractor or power lines into the vista to indicate it was a scene set in the new China, where productivity was booming.

Mao became a fixture of Chinese propaganda art, a fascinating collection of which is housed in the basement of an otherwise nondescript apartment building in Shanghai. Taken together, the images become a three-room tour of China's shifting political priorities, told through impossibly cheery faces painted in bold colors. "No other leader in human history has been able to generate as much artwork as Mao did," the museum's welcoming remarks note. In the West, Andy Warhol would feature Mao's countenance in a famous series of colorful silk screens, placing him alongside Jacqueline Kennedy Onassis and Elizabeth Taylor. Of course, Warhol's ironic distance is nowhere to be found in China's propagandistic treatment of the leader.

The Chinese posters begin at Mao's ascension and continue through his death in 1976, articulating a series of government priorities that progress from selling this new China to the Chinese ("A Glorious Future Is Ahead!") to highlighting foreign relationships (Chinese and Soviet citizens lock arms) to depicting the Cultural Revolution like a trip to Disneyland (happy children ride trains out to the countryside). China has too many people, and posters extolling birth control are put into production. China wants to be a world leader in science, and posters show smiling Chinese children crammed into a space shuttle, zooming through the stars. The propaganda posters illustrate how Chinese art can become a direct mirroring of the state's priorities, a dynamic the country would also deploy in the resurgence of its film industry beginning in the early 2000s.

America makes curious cameos in the artwork. When China positions itself in the 1960s as a proud Communist nation, it makes delib-

erate reference to U.S. politics to point out that life in the democratic
America isn't bliss for certain kinds of people. Black Americans fight
against the police billy club. Antiwar protesters—exercising a right certainly not seen in Mao's China—find a common cause and ask China to
support their efforts to end the conflict in Vietnam. The most overtly
anti-Hollywood element, however, makes an appearance in 1951, the year
of *A Streetcar Named Desire* and *The Day the Earth Stood Still*, in a mul-
ticast image titled "The U.S. Is a Rotten Imperialist Country, Central
Headquarters for All the World's Reactionaries." In this poster, a fat-cat
businessman sits atop the U.S. Capitol dome and throws coins to a man
with a large, stereotypically Jewish nose. In the courtyard of the Capitol
is gathered every practitioner of American lasciviousness and corruption:
A white man beats up a black man lying on the ground. A hooded
KKK member shoots a capitalist businessman. A young blond boy reads
an issue of *Life* magazine, ogling a bikini model. And a portly movie director stands behind a camera, filming a cowboy and a vixen galloping
on a horse, her long legs exposed above white high heels. When it came to
reasons why China should avoid an American future, Hollywood ranked
as low as the KKK.

Mao's Cultural Revolution, a reset of the country that banned art and
expression that went against the state, began in 1966, and filmmakers,
actors, and storytellers of all stripes were consigned to the countryside
and often publicly castigated. Many were killed. Others killed themselves. The Cultural Revolution treated certain expression as a form of
treason. To ensure that political enemies wouldn't shout revolutionary
statements before their execution, their tongues were sawed off. Forget a
novel or screenplay that explored untoward themes—citizens were jailed
if their diaries were confiscated and found to include antigovernment
sentiment. In one case, a young woman was shot for writing such an
entry, and her mother was charged for the bullet. Another man was
placed under house arrest for saying foreign can openers worked better
than Chinese ones. Affiliation with the wrong kinds of storytelling was

contaminating: a scientist who happened to have the same name as a spy in a Chinese thriller was arrested, along with 166 of his colleagues. Pianists had their fingers broken.

IN POSTWAR AMERICA, suburbanization emptied cities of young moviegoers and widespread adoption of television kept them at home. The competition from the smaller screen was so threatening that MGM banned reference to TV sets in all scripts. The baby boom and consumers' reallocation of money to suburban amenities like cars and washing machines proved just as detrimental. By the early 1970s, the situation had grown so dire at Paramount that its owner, Gulf and Western, considered selling the back lot on Melrose Avenue to a developer who wanted to turn it into a graveyard. Then the struggling film industry was given new life by a generation of film-school graduates who took their cues from European auteurs like Jean-Luc Godard and Bernardo Bertolucci, directors who, just as China was suppressing individual expression, were elevating film as a primary vehicle of it. In America, Francis Ford Coppola, Steven Spielberg, and Martin Scorsese brought a purity of vision—and record-setting grosses—to their industry.

Movies like Spielberg's *Jaws* fit the bill. Universal opened the movie on 460 screens, then a record. The studio typically opened a new movie in a few markets and relied on word of mouth to boost interest before expanding nationwide. With *Jaws*, Universal had marketed the movie *before* its release, building buzz that exploded into a domestic gross in 1975 of $260 million—$1.3 billion in 2021 dollars, and the template for a new mainstay: the summer blockbuster. Studios began focusing on such "event movies," which cost more to produce but could generate ever-larger paydays. If, like *Star Wars*, they also sold tie-in clothing and toys, all the better. Such movies—called "tentpoles" because they lifted all of the others up—began accounting for a greater share of the box office, and the studios concentrated more heavily on the handful of movies that could pull in all kinds of audiences everywhere.

From the late 1970s well into the 1990s, these American spectaculars traveled the world not because they carried deliberate messaging of the Woodrow Wilson style but because they were becoming a form of global entertainment. In 1977 three classic American movies—*Star Wars*, *Close Encounters of the Third Kind*, and *Saturday Night Fever*—were all huge hits overseas, with *Star Wars* generating 39 percent of its worldwide gross from foreign audiences and the other films each collecting 60 percent abroad. By 1982, it wasn't just *E.T. the Extra-Terrestrial* pulling audiences in around the world; the first *Rambo* movie, called *First Blood*, made $78 million of its $125 million gross from foreign audiences who wanted to see a U.S. soldier get his revenge. Five years later, six of the top ten movies that year made at least 40 percent of their revenue overseas, and some, like *Dirty Dancing*, made 70 percent.

These were distinctly American movies pulling in audiences of all nationalities. Some portrayed teenage life in America, like *Dirty Dancing*, or romanticized its past, like *Back to the Future*. The country evoked as a "shining city on a hill" by President Ronald Reagan wanted to project that image in auditoriums around the world. American aptitude in the space race was celebrated in *The Right Stuff*, while the U.S. military helped Jerry Bruckheimer make the navy commercial *Top Gun*. Of the one hundred top-grossing films released around the world in 1993, eighty-eight were produced in America—Hollywood's contribution to a theory popular around this time that an "end of history" was upon the world, and liberal democracy the inevitable mode of governance following the dissolution of the Soviet Union.

Chinese audiences largely missed this rah-rah era of American filmmaking. When *Top Gun* premiered in 1986, Chinese citizens were still watching propaganda movies and only the occasional Hollywood import. That same year, *Superman*, starring Christopher Reeve, was released in Chinese theaters eight years after its American release, but it lasted on screens for only a month. America's most famous superhero, according to Chinese officials who removed it from circulation, was "a narcotic which the capitalist class gives itself to cast off its serious crises."

IN 1990, POLITICAL SCIENTIST Joseph Nye put a name to the phenomenon in which Hollywood had played a major part for the past eighty years. Hollywood movies and the American ideals they symbolized were introducing Western values to audiences. Nye called the diplomatic tool generated by Hollywood and a host of other entities "soft power." As opposed to "hard power," which took the form of military might, soft power, which took the form of entertainment—or diplomacy or philanthropic efforts or institutes of higher education—allowed America to fashion a prestigious brand that often greased the wheels of more aggressive intervention. Citizens around the world flocked to the U.S. and the values it exported: democracy, free speech, open markets. Its gravitational pull allowed America, in Nye's words, to become an "empire by invitation."

Nye was defining the political power inherent in those overseas grosses. Americans knew that audiences around the world recognized Demi Moore and Chewbacca. American culture, Nye argued, was worthy of consideration alongside the atomic bomb and foreign aid as a vehicle of American influence. Better yet, the power came disguised not as political agitprop but as popcorn entertainment. America made a lot of movies showing off how great America was, but the greater power was likely in the movies about more ordinary life in the U.S. Through planning and happenstance, the American movie became simultaneously a harmless form of entertainment, a way to process traumatic historical events, an artery of free expression, and a manufactured product capable of generating profits in the hundreds of millions of dollars.

Critics of Nye's thesis say he puts too much stock in the allure of

American culture, arguing that Levi's jeans and *Top Gun* are no match for religious fanaticism or political rage. "Somewhere in the Middle East," wrote political scientist Samuel Huntington in 1996, "a half-dozen young men could well be dressed in jeans, drinking Coke, listening to rap, and, between their bows to Mecca, putting together a bomb to blow up an American airliner." Huntington's view gained more credence five years later, when a group of young Middle Eastern men flew planes into the World Trade Center, a Pennsylvania field, and the Pentagon. Some Americans have grown rightfully skeptical of the concept since the "hearts and minds" campaign during the invasion of Iraq, when Vice President Dick Cheney and President George W. Bush presented democracy as an intrinsic need that cannot help but sweep a nation.

By the time of Nye's thesis, China was a country torn between two impulses. Officials who had risen in Mao's revolution had spent years controlling what their people saw and guarding against that Western soft power. But by the end of the twentieth century, leaders knew there were economic bounties to be found by engaging more directly with the U.S. and the West it had defined itself against for decades.

Premier Zhu Rongji's career was a capsule lesson in that evolution. He had started his political career in a country that rallied against Western imperialism; now he was a top-ranking official in a party determined to import Western capitalism's most well-known brands to its own people. Eisner escaped his 1998 meeting with Zhu by shrewdly navigating the ultimatums for a Disney park. But he ended the meeting by introducing Zhu to the man who would ultimately deliver the castle: Robert Iger, then the president of ABC and already considered a likely successor to Eisner as CEO. The two Disney executives had no idea how much of what had transpired over the past two years with *Kundun* previewed what was to come. Though China had been relatively absent from Hollywood's global domination of the last eighty years, the events of the country's twentieth century had formed a different attitude about the role of art and who had control over it. China now had something it didn't have before—money—and a country full of people who wanted to see the same movies the rest of the world did. In keeping with Mao's call to police the artistic output of others, *Kundun* would not be the last time China used its economic power to retaliate against studios for movies that challenged Chinese politics. Hollywood would soon awaken to this new China, a place of seemingly limitless revenue and opportunities for cultural exchanges, but also a place fraught with necessary concessions that contradicted the free-speech ideals and patriotic sheen that had molded the industry since its founding.

No, Eisner and Iger didn't know any of that. Instead, with apologies out of the way, the two men were eager, Eisner said, to play a role in "how China greets the new century."

THREE

Opening

Chen Kaige was fourteen years old when he publicly denounced his father. It was 1966, and Chen and his father, a film director named Chen Huaikai, were two victims of the Cultural Revolution sweeping their country. The elder Chen made movies about the Peking Opera, an outpost of bourgeois culture that Mao was replacing. Pressured by teachers to stand on the right side of the revolution, the younger Chen labeled his father an enemy of the state and left soon after for the countryside, where he was to learn from the peasants the values of the new China.

More than a decade later, despite seeing his father punished for his artistry, Chen Kaige decided to become a filmmaker himself. By the time he enrolled in the Beijing Film Academy in 1978, he would join an entertainment industry that reflected a new change across his country. Many of his classmates were, like him, recently returned from their time in the fields—one cinematography student recalled feeling like she had just come back from another country, only to later realize she had been only fifteen miles away. The only reason she had applied to the film academy, she told me, was because moviemaking was one of the few careers in China that offered some travel.

The Beijing Film Academy was the country's most prestigious film school, and it had primarily been a place to learn how to make propaganda films. Chen and his contemporaries, though, arrived with years of life experience that would make for powerful stories, the kind that lay decidedly beyond the state's propagandistic boundaries. The school had closed under Mao, but his successor, Deng Xiaoping, would reopen it as part of a countrywide campaign to revive the arts.

Mao Zedong founded the People's Republic, and Deng Xiaoping modernized it. The son of a wealthy landlord and his concubine, Deng was a young revolutionary alongside Mao who had been banished from his party twice before assuming power in 1978. Deng, who'd once encouraged the peasantry to kill their landowners—saying it would further endear them to the cause—presided over economic reforms that opened the country in ways unheard of in Mao's day. He had watched as Mao's push for agricultural communes had left tens of millions of people dead of starvation, and he advocated for individual production and the introduction of economic pragmatism. His actions led to many Chinese using a telephone or watching a television set for the first time and laid the groundwork for the torrent of economic growth that has defined China in the twenty-first century. He even danced with Mickey Mouse at Disney World during his visit to the U.S. under President Carter. The experience sent him home more determined than ever to revitalize his country's economy.

Deng inherited a traumatized country. Mao's Great Leap Forward, a five-year plan that aimed to rebuild the country from an agrarian state to a Communist industrial power, had resulted in mass starvation. The public excoriations of the Cultural Revolution had turned neighbors against each other. In the years following Mao's death, China was a nation beset with nervous tics and depression, its people flocking to acupuncture treatments for respite; the field of psychology—a "bogus bourgeois science," in the words of the government—had been replaced with prescriptions to read the Dear Leader's speeches when feeling blue. The reflex in the U.S. to process what had occurred during World War II through cinema—the dramas about returning soldiers, the concentration camp footage—was also evident in China, where Deng encouraged filmmakers to explore the traumatic events of the past several years in movies that came to be known as "scar cinema."

Chen's timing at the film academy was fortuitous. It only took a year for Deng's ambitions for the country to be reflected in the academy's curriculum. In 1978, the students watched state propaganda movies about Chinese history and Japanese aggression. In 1979, Hollywood movies from the 1930s, Italian movies from the 1950s, Francis Ford Coppola, and *The Deer Hunter* were on the screening schedule. The overseas movies remained largely off limits to everyday Chinese people, but instructors played them for the academy students twice a week in double features. By the 1980s, commercial filmmaking had returned in a limited capacity to China. Outside the academy's classrooms, China modernized, but echoes of Mao's exhortation on the role of art lingered. In 1987, Teng Jinxian, the head of China's film bureau, called on filmmakers to focus on what he called "main-melody" films: movies that explored themes that were a priority to the state, that contributed to a harmonious society. It was a softer definition than the one set out by Mao in 1942, but it signaled that the government would continue assigning filmmakers a designated role. Over the next decade, main-melody narratives would celebrate China's collectivist society and Communist government while also demoting the values of capitalism and the individualism that was held up as a nonnegotiable ingredient of liberal societies.

The mid-1990s in China would be characterized by reforms that formally brought commercial Hollywood movies to the country for the first time since Mao's revolution. Chen and his classmates would introduce more honest forms of Chinese storytelling that officials would have to reconcile with their system of surveillance and control, all while watching as movies like *True Lies* turned Guangzhou residents into Arnold Schwarzenegger's newest fans. But as Hollywood movies came into the country, would the soft power that had worked everywhere else work here? Onlookers interpreted the opening-up as a sign that China might become the world's biggest democracy, yet the artistic output of both countries—and how those films were received—reminded everyone of the drastic gulf of difference before them in politics and storytelling taste.

The events of 1989 proved that. Even as images of their new leader touring America in a ten-gallon cowboy hat served as a surreal contrast to Mao's gray-suit era, Chinese people were reminded of their government's intolerance for dissent and instability that year when Deng ordered a crackdown on student protesters in Tiananmen Square. Any goodwill he might have built up in the West thanks to his reforms and global tours was eradicated as thousands of young Chinese people were shot or assaulted. For the country's filmmakers, it was a rude reminder of the response any discordant narrative might receive in their authoritarian society.

In the years after the Tiananmen Square massacre, Deng thought the TV sets and individual farming plots his regime had introduced would win over skeptics to his cause. "If we can reach a comfortable standard of living by the end of the century, then that will wake them up a bit. And in the next century when we, as a socialist country, join the middle ranks of the developed nations, that will help to convince them," a state outlet quoted him saying in 1991.

For Chen and his film-school classmates, their material was the history they'd lived through, the decades of trauma and seismic change. The stories they wanted to tell did not fit the melody. Chen would mine his personal history in his best-known work, *Farewell My Concubine*. The film tells the story of a gay Beijing Opera singer's career ascension amid Mao's Cultural Revolution, during which he is increasingly expected to perform for the authoritarian regime. It was aesthetically beautiful storytelling, a reckoning with the Chinese twentieth century told through the eyes of performers celebrating the country's most traditional art form. Those who knew Chen's regret over denouncing his father could see his personal story on-screen, as would-be lovers and friends weaponize the revolution and speak out against one another as class enemies.

The movie won the Palme d'Or at the Cannes International Film Festival in May 1993. That July, though, its interrogation of such history led Chinese officials to ban it, a ruling that made it clear Deng's economic reforms were not eroding some of the core ideological defenses Mao's regime had erected. The movie was a triple threat: it featured a gay romance, harrowing scenes of Cultural Revolution executions, and a climactic suicide. The movie's fate was rescued only when China's international reputation was on the line. Soon after the rapturous reception of *Farewell My Concubine*, China bid to host the Olympic Games in 2000—an honor that, like opening a Disneyland or membership in the World Trade Organization, would signal its arrival to the modern world order. But to be chosen, China needed to show it was a country that practiced free expression, that treated its citizens in a way befitting an Olympic host. *Farewell My Concubine* was put in theaters, with some of the offending scenes removed.

"We face a lot of pressure because some people abroad try to link the issue with China's human-rights situation," an official said at the time. "So we had to let it show." The move necessitated a political counterweight, though, lest filmmakers interpret it as permanent reform. The movie's showing in China coincided with a new directive from the film bureau promising to ban any movie that ran "contrary to the Party's principle on art and socialist spiritual civilization." The warning was prompted by a recent spate of films that "mixed up justice with injustice" or more generally had "attitude problems."

The films made by Chen's classmates similarly agitated the authorities. Another Academy graduate, Zhang Yimou, directed *Ju Dou*, about a young woman who must raise a love child as her husband's heir. In 1991 it had been the first Chinese movie nominated for an Academy Award for Best Foreign Language Film. This cadre of Beijing Film Academy graduates, known as the Fifth Generation because they represented the fifth distinct Chinese filmmaking approach since the early cinema days, had quickly established themselves as a force in global cinema.

But Chinese leaders didn't want this kind of attention. When authorities learned about *Ju Dou*'s Oscar nomination, they postponed its release. It was an early indication of the inherent tension in China's entertainment ambitions, the constant balancing of overseas recognition with the fear that the movies might present a complicated picture of the country's past and present. The nudity and morose ending of *Ju Dou* presented an unflattering view of their country, and they wanted it to disappear. Officials even petitioned the academy to remove it from the list of nominees.

Hollywood was aghast at the interventions. "Even more disturbing than the fate of Zhang Yimou and his film is the Government's new policy of strict censorship," read an opinion piece in *The New York Times* by Steven Spielberg and producer Kathleen Kennedy. In a bit of foreshadowing, the writers asked, "Will China next disqualify itself from the Olympics because only the Chinese can judge the merits of Chinese athletes?" No one watched *Dances with Wolves* and interpreted it as the U.S. government's modern-day position on Native American reservations or watched *Goodfellas* and thought all American kids grew up to be gangsters. The movies about China that audiences wanted to see—and even reward with Oscars and Palmes d'Or—did not conform to what authorities thought was best for their citizens and the world to watch. Every time there was an opening toward the outside world, the government would reflexively rush to close it.

AMONG THE FIRST EXECUTIVES TO navigate this tightrope was Ellen Eliasoph, who first traveled to China seven years after Nixon's trip there in 1972. Eliasoph went as a student at Yale Law School, thinking she might go into diplomacy after graduation. Her student exchange program was one sign that relations were warming between the two countries, a reality that authorities signaled to their people via the propaganda posters popping up in Beijing that showed players from both nations playing Ping-Pong.

Eliasoph had grown up in Massachusetts in a family of artists and writers; her uncle, William Gibson, had written *The Miracle Worker*, the hit Broadway play about Helen Keller and her tutor, Anne Sullivan. In the 1950s, Gibson was a Communist, and many of his friends were targeted by Senator McCarthy's raids. Eliasoph wasn't politically drawn to the People's Republic of China, but she was fascinated by the pictographic Chinese language—she loved that its characters were like little pictures, each of which told a story. The word for "man" was a combination of characters that mean "power" and "rice field," she learned, signaling that land and dominance characterized the masculine in Chinese society. The character for "home" showed a roof with a pig under it, while "peace" showed a roof with a woman under it. The cultural values of the country were encoded in the written language, she realized.

But when she got to China, what struck her was the silence. When she and the other students rode the thirty-six-hour train from Hong Kong to Beijing, all she saw were long stretches of dark, silent farmland. In the morning, she'd see farmers in the field. But for the most part China seemed like a country with the lights turned off. Cabbage was piled on the street to last residents through the winter. Foreigners, however, soon understood China's ability to cast the state of the nation in a new, suddenly sunnier light when the time called for it. Anytime a parade was held to mark the anniversary of the founding of the party, flowers replaced cabbage heads. Trash disappeared.

The movies were expected to do their part. On the Fourth of July in 1987, when American audiences were watching *Full Metal Jacket* and *The Lost Boys*, the Chinese Communist Party created an oversight committee that would produce main-melody films. Their work would truly begin two years later, when the protests—and subsequent massacre—in Tiananmen Square led party officials to counter the rebellion with a slew of movies they hoped would reprogram the masses and quell any insurrection. As scholar Wendy Su notes, the main-melody movies typically fell into one of three categories. There were retellings of Communist Party history and the creation of the People's Republic. Other movies explored stories of the decades of war against the Japanese and other colonizing forces that had tried to take over China since the Opium Wars, two conflicts in the midnineteenth century that resulted in France and Britain acquiring territory and lopsided trade deals. Then there were the endless tales of the members of the Communist Party who served their fellow countrymen, often released in conjunction with a special anniversary to fuel patriotic fervor. "Main-melody films help convince people of the inevitability and validity of a socialist China, maintain the legitimacy of the ruling party, and contribute to the establishment of a national identity that serves the best interests of the ruling party—an identity that is red, socialist, and communist, anti-imperialist and anticapitalist," Su writes.

In 1990, Eliasoph took a job as general counsel in the Tokyo office of Warner Bros., the Hollywood studio that had been kicked out of Shanghai during the revolution in 1949. Eliasoph was based in Japan, then the world's second-largest theatrical market after North America, but she detected the focus would eventually shift toward China. With economic deals sprouting up in energy and banking, she sensed that movies might follow as an acceptable import. Not only were Chinese officials approving more U.S.-China deals, but their nation's theatrical business was bleeding money.

The surge in moviegoing following the reopening of theaters after the Cultural Revolution had not lasted through the 1980s, when only 30 percent of Chinese releases broke even or made a profit. By the end of the decade, a third of studios and theaters were sinking in debt, and attendance had plummeted. With television, video rental stores, piracy markets, and karaoke salons available to them, the Chinese people had little reason to go to the movies as they once had. As foreign movies seeped into the country via the black market, they'd also learned that there were better things to watch than the state-fed main-melody propaganda shown in rundown and neglected theaters.

With the domestic film industry struggling, Chinese authorities turned to Hollywood for help bringing its attendance back to life and rescuing its ailing companies. Eliasoph lobbied theater owners like Wu Mengchen, who operated a well-known chain called Shanghai Paradise. As joint ventures in other sectors continued to be announced, it felt like the winds were shifting in Hollywood's favor, especially after laws passed in the 1990s better protected intellectual property. Wouldn't Hollywood movies jump-start China's ailing business? she asked.

Eliasoph and Warner Bros. continued the campaign by asking Arnon Milchan, a producer known to Chinese audiences who'd watched his film *Pretty Woman* on pirated copies, to come and address aspiring filmmakers. The students asked him how to make a movie like that, one that audiences around the world want to watch. Milchan explained that he came from a small country, Israel, and that the key to telling such stories was to think small. A story that is touching or funny on a human level can resonate in any language, he said; it cannot be manufactured. For Warner Bros., his visit was a signal to Chinese authorities that the studio was committed to bringing talent and investment to the country if the government allowed it. Then Wu Mengchen was named head of China Film Group, a government-run authority with the sole right to import foreign films, placing him in a position to advocate more seriously for the importing of Hollywood movies to invigorate China's business. At Wu's request, Eliasoph and her team at Warner Bros. began drafting a distribution agreement.

China was allowing ten imported movies a year, with studios keeping 13 percent of ticket sales. That was an exceptionally low percentage going back to the studios, which typically collected around 40 percent from foreign markets and up to 65 percent in the U.S. on major releases. In this case, all of the other box-office revenue would go to Chinese entities like China Film Group, the state-run film office. Studio accountants weighed the pros and cons. Under the deal, China Film Group would pay for expenses related to the movie's release, including import taxes, prints, and advertising. That meant the 13 percent was essentially pure profit for the studios—making it, as Carl Laemmle called those early foreign grosses, "unexpected money in the street." More important, a theatrical release could serve as an alternative to the rampant piracy networks that were costing the studios far more money. Among other requirements, censorship was codified in that first contract. Chinese officials would screen every movie prior to its release. The studios negotiated the right to substitute another cut of a film if it didn't pass muster after the first screening.

It would not be the first time that films had been allowed in since Mao's death, but the deal formalized an agreement that would split box-office revenue between partners in both countries and release films in China soon after their global premieres. Warner Bros. chose the first movie shipped over: *The Fugitive*, a critically acclaimed drama starring Harrison Ford as a man who's wrongly accused of killing his wife and hunts the one-armed criminal who actually committed the crime. When Eliasoph reviewed recent releases to find one for China, *The Fugitive* had been an obvious choice. It was an action movie that was relatively easy to follow, and it featured a big star whom Chinese fans knew through pirated copies of *Raiders of the Lost Ark*.

She flew back to Los Angeles and picked up the half dozen heavy canisters of film reels containing the movie, hauling them onto the plane so she could keep her eyes on them the entire flight. When she arrived in China, an official from customs and another from China Film Group arrived with paperwork to process the luggage, which was then taken directly to the government film bureau for a censorship screening. *The Fugitive* might raise some thematic red flags among censors, since it involved a man fighting the police to right a wrong that they brought on, but it was kosher since it was taking place in America, where such things could happen. It was approved and released on three hundred screens in November 1994.

The Fugitive had made $184 million in the U.S., making it the second-highest-grossing movie of the year, behind *Jurassic Park*. It sold more than $3 million worth of tickets in China, making it an absolute blockbuster. Moviegoers went back to see it five times, paying $1.25 per ticket and cheering at the iconic scene in which Ford escapes a U.S. marshal by leaping down a waterfall.

Other Hollywood releases streamed in behind it—*True Lies*, starring Arnold Schwarzenegger and Jamie Lee Curtis as a married couple caught up in a game of spy versus spy, then *Broken Arrow*, starring John Travolta and Christian Slater as air force pilots fighting over stolen warheads. Soon six to ten Hollywood movies were screening in China each year under the 13 percent agreement crafted by Warner Bros. attorneys, now known as "the master contract." More than fifteen years after she'd arrived in the silent country, Eliasoph had brought it the movies.

One Chinese distributor, upon receiving the film reels of *The Fugitive*, said he felt like "an underground agent protecting secret materials." He had good reason to find the canisters radioactive. The movies he was carrying were financially necessary but politically troubling to China's leaders. It was less than two years after *The Fugitive* premiered in China that Hollywood had its first conflagration with the country in the form of *Seven Years in Tibet*, *Kundun*, and *Red Corner*. The same tension evident in its leaders' reaction to those films and those of their country's own

Fifth Generation—a response that revealed both a desire to open and a reflex to close—would quickly rule over Hollywood's best-laid plans.

WITH HOLLYWOOD MOVIES now regularly screening in China, viewers there were treated to the same on-screen romanticism and charm that countries around the world had embraced for decades. When Dan Glickman, a former secretary of agriculture who would eventually serve as the head of the Motion Picture Association of America, visited the country, he saw a generation of young people going into the theater and coming out with new ideas. It reminded him of an old World War I song about American soldiers who are treated to the bright lights of European capitals, only to return to their homes when the fighting stopped. "How ya gonna keep 'em down on the farm (After they've seen Paree?)," the lyric goes.

Corners of Chinese Communist leadership had the same fear. Years of attacking the capitalists of the West had deepened instincts that not even Harrison Ford and Tom Hanks could sweep away. In response to the American movies, Chinese writers reminded readers how European and Latin American countries had successfully beaten back a total monopoly of U.S. films in their marketplace, recycling the strategies born out of skepticism toward Hollywood's messaging half a century prior. Other pieces made sure Hollywood's new fans in China knew the industry's sordid history, including the scandals that had turned the Catholic Church and conservative politicians in the midcentury against the business—Chinese audiences who had never seen a Marilyn Monroe movie learned of her suicide. The blacklisting of Communist sympathizers in Hollywood was regurgitated as another reason Chinese Communist Party members should look askance at the new arrivals.

Chinese critics reviewed Hollywood movies through a collectivist lens, interpreting the messages of even the most patriotic of American movies to fit their Communist cause. Often the messages they took away were similar to the ones American audiences had processed, too, though

China's state media proved more willing than journalists in the U.S. to spell out their core lessons for viewers. *Saving Private Ryan* and its story of a group of soldiers retrieving a comrade from the battlefield was about self-sacrifice and the preservation of the family. *Braveheart* showed the power of campaigning for freedom against oppression. *Twister*, with its earth-rattling tornadoes, and *Deep Impact*, with its earth-destroying asteroid, demonstrated the resilience of the human spirit in the face of environmental disaster. *Forrest Gump* introduced a character who remained loyal and good-natured despite the cynicism around him. These interpretations could change in response to superseding political events. Following America's accidental bombing of a Chinese embassy in Yugoslavia in the summer of 1999, state critics ruled that *Saving Private Ryan* now played as hypocritical sanitizing for a country that clearly did not care about the lives of non-U.S. citizens. American movies were banned from Chinese theaters for six months in retaliation.

Despite the skepticism and political entanglements, the import of American films served its purpose. Box-office grosses surged more than 50 percent, and American movies were accounting for a majority of the yearly tally. By 1998, eight Hollywood movies alone accounted for a 45 percent rise in box office. The American movie had accomplished in China what it accomplished in countries the world over: it got people to show up.

China wanted to put the new money to good use. In 1996 authorities established a quid pro quo system that combined officials' political goals with studios' economic priorities. If a Chinese studio produced a main-melody film, it would be given the distribution rights to one of the Hollywood imports that were generating so much money. A quota had been set: fifty main-melody movies must be produced and released between 1996 and 2000. If a state-owned studio didn't meet that requirement, it wouldn't receive the rights to distribute the Hollywood films. The box office of all movies became a Chinese subsidy when the government then mandated that 5 percent of all theatrical revenue get funneled to a program supporting Chinese movie production. China's leaders had planted ideological and financial counterweights to Hollywood influence in their distribution deals with the studios.

None of this was a secret. As film bureau director Liu Jianzhong said less than two years after *The Fugitive* first hit screens in his country, the guiding philosophy of the new opening of the Chinese market should be *yi wo wei zhu*: China's national interest takes precedence.

JUST AS CHINESE LEADERS WERE coming to terms with the economic necessity of opening their country up to Hollywood, executives in the West were eyeing the new market and seeing a sequel to the Cold War–era battle of ideas. Rupert Murdoch, CEO of News Corp and holdings that included the Twentieth Century Fox film studio, moved aggressively into China after purchasing Hong Kong–based Star TV in 1993. But the satellite dishes ran channels that chafed Chinese officials, like MTV with its salacious music videos, or the BBC with news reports that weren't filtered by the state. Murdoch worsened relations considerably when he articulated a core assumption driving some Western politicians and business executives toward China: that economic reform would give way to political reform.

"Fax machines enable dissidents to bypass state-controlled print media; direct-dial telephone makes it difficult for a state to control interpersonal voice communications. And satellite broadcasting makes it possible for information-hungry residents of many closed societies to bypass state-controlled television channels," Murdoch said in 1993. Telecommunications technology was nothing less than "an unambiguous threat to totalitarian regimes everywhere."

After his comment, China outlawed private satellite dishes. Murdoch began making several concessions to regain favor, including flipping his portfolio toward Beijing-aligned interests. The BBC was off the air. Murdoch sold his ownership stake in the *South China Morning Post*, a respected news outlet based in Hong Kong, to a businessman sympathetic to Beijing. Instead he invested $5.4 million in *People's Daily*, a mouthpiece of the party. Elsewhere in the Murdoch empire, a separate News Corp division would publish a rosy biography of Deng Xiaoping—written by his daughter—while its publisher, HarperCollins, pulled out of a deal to release a book by Chris Patten, who had served as governor of Hong Kong before the handover and was a well-known critic of Beijing. The supplication worked: within years, Murdoch would have a greater stake in the mainland China TV market than his rivals.

Disney had similarly spent money to repair relations following its *Kundun* fallout. The studio's movies were still not granted entry into China following the November 1997 ban until February 1999, when *Mulan*, the myth about a Chinese girl who disguises herself as a boy to fight in her father's stead, was finally allowed onto screens. In the intervening months, Disney had done far more than send Michael Eisner over to apologize. The company bought the rights to release *A Time to Remember*, a love story that tugged at the heartstrings and stirred patriotic fervor, which was produced by Forbidden City Film Co., an outfit closely linked to the very officials who would decide whether *Mulan* was allowed in. When Disney was accused of using distribution deals to curry favor, the company presented it as a run-of-the-mill agreement not unlike any of the many others it made with foreign partners. That didn't quite explain why they'd also decided to sponsor a Chinese acrobatic troupe that toured Europe. But its strategy proved successful when *Mulan* was eventually allowed into China, ending the country's boycott of Disney.

Murdoch had been punished by China for commenting on its totalitarianism and responded by placating the regime. But the prediction he'd made about democracy following the dollar did not fall out of fashion. "Liberty will be spread by cell phone and cable modem," President Bill Clinton said in early 2000, in the midst of negotiations on a landmark trade deal with China. "We know how much the internet has changed America, and we are already an open society. Imagine how much it could change China." Trying to regulate what users could access on the internet was "like trying to nail Jell-O to the wall," he added. In these estimations, Deng Xiaoping's reforms represented not only a lucrative investment opportunity but also a chance to spread Western ideals to the country feared as a Communist superpower since the 1940s. *Forrest Gump* playing to sold-out crowds in Beijing seemed to justify this optimism. Where capitalism might go, democracy would follow. In the late 1990s and early 2000s, China offered the most promising opportunity available for both forces.

WHILE WESTERN LEADERS LIKE Murdoch and Clinton were hoping that the American influence would travel to China, Chinese leaders were hoping that they could export some of their values abroad, too. From its earliest interactions with Hollywood, China had harbored an ambition to ship its culture around the world, just as the U.S. had done throughout the twentieth century. The holy grail, even in the 1990s, was a Chinese-produced movie that made audiences in both countries swoon.

The best shot after China's opening-up came courtesy of Ang Lee, who by the late 1990s had made a handful of acclaimed movies for Hollywood studios, including *Sense and Sensibility* and *The Ice Storm*. Born in Taiwan in 1954, Lee was the eldest son of parents who had fled the civil war in China. The trauma of the Cultural Revolution threaded through his family; his father's parents were killed because they were landlords when Mao assumed power. Growing up in Taiwan, Lee had ready access to American movies that his counterparts in mainland China did not. His mother often went to the movies when she was pregnant with Lee, initiating his love of films in the womb, he joked. While his contemporaries in mainland China were being sent to the countryside, Lee watched Billy Wilder, Frank Capra, and Woody Allen, a case study in Woodrow Wilson's hopes for the form.

Hollywood "told the world what to dream," Lee told me. "Somehow it just captured that world, established that dream, of an American narrative. It's fantastic. We all dream and look up to it. That's how me and most of the world—at least the free world—is dreaming." In the movies of the Cold War 1960s, America was also "big brother" on-screen, he said, protecting the "little guys" like Taiwan.

Still, the idea of coming to America to direct movies himself was a remote proposition, certainly one his parents didn't support. When Lee failed Taiwan's college entrance exams—a particularly ignominious result for the son of two scholars—he enrolled at a local arts academy. After that, he moved to the U.S. in 1978, entering the theater program at the University of Illinois and then the master's program at New York University.

"When I first came to America, it felt like I was walking onto a set. All those people were really there," he said. "If you grow up with American movies, you tend to romanticize them, [thinking] that's how Americans see themselves, beautiful. It's a romanticized version of themselves, lush and colorful. . . . They're having fun, very open, just fantastic. You cannot help but idolize them." After some time in America, he realized the reality was not the filtered version delivered through a script and soft lighting. "The people are not as pretty. They have to go to the bathroom. It's not like in the movies."

After years of frustration and some acclaim from screenwriting competitions, Lee directed *The Wedding Banquet*, a comedy about a gay man who must hide his partner and marry a woman ahead of his Taiwanese parents' visit, a comedy-of-errors decision that culminates in a giant, traditional wedding banquet for the wrong couple. It was his second feature, and Lee was already lampooning the wedding banquets that were a staple of his culture. It was named best film at the 1993 Berlin International Film Festival and became the most successful movie in Taiwanese history. His father only then started to reconsider his son's line of work, an indication of the generational resistance to art as a viable career. "I love stirring things up rather than sticking to the Chinese ideal, which is to appeal for calm," Lee said at the time.

Soon afterward, Lee got his first Hollywood assignment: an adaptation of Jane Austen's *Sense and Sensibility*, starring Kate Winslet and Emma Thompson as the novel's lovelorn sisters. Oscar nominations followed. Next was *The Ice Storm*, about unsatisfied swingers in 1973 Connecticut. Friends were confused: How was a man who'd grown up in Taiwan making such good movies about patrician England and patrician New England? These movies, and later his masterpiece *Brokeback Mountain*, he explained, all focus on something his post-Mao generation knew well. "People asked me, 'How did you do *Sense and Sensibility*? It's so British.' Look, for a repressed Chinese director, repression was easy."

After *The Ice Storm*, he would return to Asia for inspiration and adapt the novel *Crouching Tiger, Hidden Dragon* into a film. It was an updated take on the *wuxia* film, a classic Chinese genre of martial arts stories. Chow Yun-Fat and Michelle Yeoh star as former martial arts partners and possible lovers battling a mysterious young politician's daughter and her master, the Jade Fox. The movie's theatrics were unlike anything seen by most Western audiences. In the middle of dramatic, grounded sword fights, the fighters would leap into the trees, run up walls, and glide in the air through a combination of muscularity and the suspension of gravity. Sony bought the distribution rights.

Hope Boonshaft, just a few years removed from her Tiffany gifts and DC showdown over *Seven Years in Tibet*, traveled to China for the premiere as part of the Sony delegation. The film was beautiful, she thought, but the more lasting impression came at the after-party, where Triscuits and Cheez Whiz were served. A few weeks later, she was in a theater in Los Angeles's Century City neighborhood over the 1999 Christmas break when she saw a line forming at the box office. What was everyone seeing? she asked the cashier. *Crouching Tiger, Hidden Dragon*, he told her. Boonshaft called her colleagues at Sony. They had a hit. *Crouching Tiger, Hidden Dragon* ended up making $128 million domestically, by far the most ever made by a foreign film in the U.S. The movie received ten Academy

Award nominations and won four, including Best Foreign Language Film. Though it was a Chinese coproduction, the submitting country was Taiwan, depriving China of the Oscar it would grow to covet.

Lee wanted to make *Crouching Tiger, Hidden Dragon* as a movie that was by China, for China, while the country was at this turning point. But though it was embraced around the world, it failed to meet that criterion of the holy grail production, since it was of little interest to audiences in China. There, moviegoers were watching *True Lies* because it was the kind of action-packed spectacular their own country's filmmakers couldn't produce. *Crouching Tiger, Hidden Dragon*, which had seemed so novel in America, was old hat to Chinese moviegoers reared on kung fu. Furthermore, while Chinese citizens were flocking to Hollywood movies, they found that the two storytelling modes could mix like oil and water. Michelle Yeoh, a new discovery in America, was a generation older than younger, hipper actors in China. Lee had made the film to a different rhythm than traditional *wuxia* movies, opting not to open with a fight scene—the first one comes about fifteen minutes in—and ending on a melancholic note, not a climactic battle. The action scenes, when they did occur, were slower, not head-spinning, and they focused on the actors' faces so that the movie was suffused with Western-style drama and character, not just stunts. In America, audiences "did not have that cultural burden" of knowing exactly what a *wuxia* movie should be, Lee said, so they were not constantly comparing it with tropes they knew. *Crouching Tiger, Hidden Dragon* turned in a disappointing showing at the Chinese box office.

A movie beloved by audiences and authorities in both countries felt like an impossibility. The Chinese authorities could place all the restrictions they wanted on the American movies they had just allowed in, but no set of strictures could completely overrule taste. In the first decade of new American movies in China, Chinese audiences returned to the cinema and wanted to see what the West did best.

FOUR

Development Hell

or children born in the years following the Cultural Revolution, foreign entertainment in China was largely confined to a few hours on Sunday night, when the state broadcaster aired a Bollywood musical or Mexican telenovela. Ben Zhang loved watching these shows with his mom, commenting on the big eyelashes of the Indian stars while his dad ignored the television set. Zhang was born in a tiny fishing village two hours southeast of Beijing in 1979, three years after the end of the Cultural Revolution, one year after Deng Xiaoping's economic reforms began, and the exact year that the one-child policy ensured that he and his contemporaries would have no siblings. In middle school, when he wanted a VCR to watch more movies, Zhang convinced his dad to fork over $500. "I was the only kid. We get our ways," he said.

Zhang excelled in school, and his teachers encouraged him to become a physicist so he could work on one of China's top priorities: advancing its science industries. He was sent to a larger town to go to a better high school and was walking to class one day when a friend rushed up to him.

"Do you know," she said, "that there's a movie coming out about this huge ship—*and they built a ship to make it?*"

The buzz for James Cameron's *Titanic* had spread to rural China, building to a point that otherwise dutiful students skipped school to see it on opening day. Zhang was among them. It was not the first movie he saw in a theater, but it was unlike anything he had ever seen.

The visual effects were overwhelming enough: the giant ship, the giant iceberg, the third-act destruction and slow sink into the ocean. But Cameron's movie was also a three-hour introduction to Western narrative devices: the Romeo-and-Juliet romance, the vengeful mother and conniving fiancé, the tragic ending. It was old-school storytelling: Leonardo DiCaprio played a young man who finds himself in a world and station he never could have imagined, and Kate Winslet played a debutante fighting her country's and family's expectations. Zhang went back to see it again two days later, along with pretty much everyone else from school.

Moviegoers like Zhang powered *Titanic* to $44 million at the Chinese box office—not just the highest gross of all time in the market but a number beyond what executives considered mathematically possible for a country that still operated with such a slim screen count and cheap ticket prices. *Titanic* alone composed 20 percent of box-office grosses in China that year.

The movie—and its gargantuan success and frenzied fandom—might seem like just the kind of Western influence President Jiang Zemin, who assumed office in 1993, would keep from his people. But he saw the movie and was moved by its evocation of class struggle, watching as the musicians on board famously played as the ship sank. Jiang viewed these men as examples of good citizens looking out for their comrades in the face of despair, and he praised how the movie demonized the rich and exalted the poor. More generally, he wanted his fellow political leaders to study it. Speaking at the National People's Congress, Jiang said that—even though the movie's $200 million budget was an example of the excesses of capitalism—his country could "learn from capitalism. . . . I invite my comrades of the Politburo to see the movie—not to propagate capitalism but to better understand our opposition, the better to enable us to succeed." In an extraordinary acknowledgment of the West's allure, Jiang said *Titanic* and the fever it inspired must remind Chinese officials, "We should never think that we are the only ones who know how to persuade people." Few could watch *Titanic* and not feel something as the chords of "My Heart Will Go On" played and the credits rolled—Jiang realized this emotional appeal could have great power.

His endorsement meant that the movie would play in Chinese theaters with no resistance, and when Zhang and his classmates went to the theater, they passed posters for the film emblazoned with Jiang's praise. After the release, Rupert Murdoch, whose Fox studio had released *Titanic*, traveled to China to thank Jiang for his support of the film. The meeting was a coup for Murdoch, coming only a few years after his poorly received call for democracy in the country. This meeting, hosted in rooms where Mao and his men had governed, was polite and friendly. *Don't go into the basement*, one executive in the delegation thought to himself. *There are probably still bloodstains on the walls.*

The Fugitive had opened the door four years earlier, but Chinese grosses had remained a pittance. *Titanic* and its $44 million convinced Hollywood executives who had otherwise left it to local players like Ellen Eliasoph that this new market might be worth their time. Simple math explained how China could be an enormous moneymaker. There were a billion people there, discovering how much they liked Big Macs and DiCaprio. But there were entrenched problems that Hollywood would need to solve if it wanted to access the market. On that victory-lap trip after *Titanic*, a Fox executive named Michael Werner asked a classroom of students at Beijing Film Academy how many of them had seen the movie. Everyone raised a hand. He then asked how many of them had seen it in a movie theater. Barely a third kept their hands up.

· · ·

HOLLYWOOD'S ONWARD MARCH INTO MARKETS around the world had done little to prepare it for China. Expanding to China felt in some ways like entering a futuristic frontier and in others like opening an office in the developing world. No metric logically followed the other: China had the world's largest population, but tens of millions of its citizens lived more than one hundred miles from a movie theater. It had a moviegoing population hungry for Hollywood but a government guarding against its influence. The early 2000s were the early days of the courtship, with both sides getting to know each other, awkwardly misinterpreting intentions and setting boundaries. Through it all, Hollywood would learn that the cultural monopolization that followed its arrival in nearly any country would be kept in check by China's way of communicating with its people. In the half decade following the release of *Titanic*, Hollywood executives would learn the dance this country required—one that presented some problems they could solve and others they would have to tolerate.

First, there was the problem evident in the classroom Werner had visited. Piracy was not merely widespread in the country—it was the preferred mode of consuming entertainment. A sophisticated supply chain had formed in the 1990s, beginning with video copies recorded in American theaters that were then subtitled or even dubbed by Chinese pirates. Chinese officials had cracked down on the system in the past, usually to avoid tariffs and other economic sanctions, but to no avail. The pirates moved fast: copies of Universal's 2000 adaptation *Dr. Seuss' How the Grinch Stole Christmas* sold for $1.20 within a week of its release in the U.S. The pirated films were a welcome alternative to the propaganda movies produced by the party—but even those were pirated, too. When *Titanic* premiered on video, the country's largest legitimate distributor sold about three hundred thousand copies, a record at the time. But that was dwarfed by the number of customers who bought cheaper copies sold by pirates—more than twenty million.

The piracy sucked the studios dry of possible revenue—though alarming as it was, it also was what caused Barry Meyer, then many years into his tenure running Warner Bros., to pay attention to a market he had otherwise ignored. When Meyer took over the studio in 1999, the international markets to watch were the United Kingdom, Japan, and Western Europe. When it came to China and its massive population, Meyer had a refrain: "China has a lot of potential," he would say, "and it always will."

Since Warner Bros. had released *The Fugitive* in Chinese theaters, the box office was still generating tiny grosses—in part because there were so few screens, in part because tickets cost so little, and in part because the movie would be pirated almost as soon as it played in a Chinese auditorium. Inevitably Warner Bros. executives would return from trips to China with stories of seeing the studio's most popular movies—*Miss Congeniality*, *Ocean's Eleven*, *Batman Begins*—for sale on the street, usually for the equivalent of one U.S. dollar. Knockoff poster art adorned the VHS covers, making the aisles of city stores resemble an off-kilter Blockbuster Video.

Ben Zhang had used the piracy shops to acquaint himself with the twentieth-century entertainment he had missed. After college, he went on a buying spree, soon owning more than a thousand DVDs he purchased from a dealer who made regular trips to his apartment with a book bag full of selections. Zhang watched a season of *Friends* in a day. He didn't have access to film reviews, so he had no way of knowing whether a movie was considered any good or any actor was a notable star; "Meg Ryan was just some blond chick," he said. Favorites emerged: James Bond, *The Prince of Egypt*, *The Sound of Music*. Zhang might have been having a lovely time, but people like him were Meyer's worst nightmare.

FOR YEARS, CHINESE OFFICIALS HAD turned a blind eye to the piracy networks, some of which were supported by government divisions

themselves. But in the late 1990s, they had a new motivation to sophis-
ticate their country's movie-watching habits. China was mounting a bid to
join the World Trade Organization. Membership would open China up to
trade deals with other world powers, another validation of government
reforms that had generated the fastest-rising GDP in history and transformed an expanse of farmland into a global economic powerhouse. Private companies in China would be able to rise to the level of the state-run
firms, further realizing Deng's decision to integrate some free-market
elements into his country. It was not just Zhang's family who were suddenly able to afford to send a son to a better school or buy him a VHS
player. Across China, Deng's reforms had led to troves of Chinese citizens
taking new jobs in urban areas, helping lift hundreds of millions of Chinese people out of poverty. The percentage of Chinese workers making a
living in agriculture plummeted as a result, while the service and industry sectors grew. In 1960 about 85 percent of people lived in rural areas,
a share that stayed stagnant until the late 1970s, when it began a sharp
decline. By 2015, only about 45 percent still lived outside cities.

In order to gain acceptance to the WTO, China needed a U.S. endorsement, which meant it needed to change how it conducted business
with a host of American industries. The deals and concessions that China
made would eventually fill hundreds of pages of an agreement. Hollywood, like the carmakers and farmers of America, didn't waste the opportunity. Studios lobbied for intellectual property protections that
would curtail the piracy operations—and called for an increase in the
number of movies let into Chinese theaters each year, then still capped
at ten.

In November 1999, the U.S. and China reached an agreement that
cleared the way for China's entry into the WTO in 2001. President Bill
Clinton hailed it as a transformative moment for the world economy. The
agreement opened a once-impenetrable market to dozens of industries—
crops, cars, telecom—eager for a share of that new Chinese disposable

income. Hollywood's win in the agreement: the number of movies permitted into the country each year would double from ten to twenty.

Chinese leaders accelerated their urbanization campaign soon afterward, making over their country from one of rural hamlets to one of shiny new cities. But new cities required new attractions if they were going to lure folks from the countryside. Grocery stores, parks, and hospitals sprang up. So did movie theaters, which Meyer decided, in an effort to get those fans of Hollywood to pay Hollywood, he was going to build himself.

The strategy had worked before. Meyer's team would identify a foreign market with potential and seed a theatrical ecosystem to boost their overseas grosses. In Europe, for instance, Warner Bros. analysts had noticed that the prime moviegoing season was not the summer, as it was in the U.S. Why? European theaters were big boxes in city centers, often with no air-conditioning or concession stands. Warner Bros. moved in with a multiplex of its own, exporting the big-seat, big-auditorium, air-conditioned model that was sprouting up in American neighborhoods. Moviegoers started showing up—to watch Warner Bros. movies and those of its competitors. Once the better, Warner-branded theater stole business, other owners would start adding amenities to match the new competition. Soon a habit of moviegoing would form. Warner Bros. was in the movie business, not the theater business—so it didn't mind where the films played, as long as the improved theaters increased the number of tickets sold overall. In fact, once tickets were selling at a regular clip, Warner Bros. would sell its original theater, leaving in its wake the moviegoing culture it had created.

In 2003 the studio decided it needed to build theaters in China that were appealing enough to counter the ease and ubiquity of pirated-video shops. For decades, Chinese citizens had associated moviegoing with watching a party-promoted video projected onto a screen in a field, surrounded by neighbors summoned for the experience, or in dilapidated auditoriums devoid of concession stands or comfortable seating. Warner Bros. would bring the goods. Per Chinese rules, they would need a local partner to do business in the country—a rule put in place to ensure that no foreign entity grew too powerful or capitalized on Chinese citizens without some benefit flowing back to China. Warner Bros. found the perfect partner in a real estate conglomerate then riding high on the expansion of China's cities.

Dalian Wanda Group was the country's biggest developer of that quintessential symbol of an ascendant middle class: the shopping mall. As Chinese people moved into metropolises, a Wanda mall would often greet them—a multistoried attraction that included shops, restaurants, and grocery stores. Adopting the strategy of the Sears, Roebuck & Co. founder, most Wanda malls included a movie theater to provide a steady stream of foot traffic. Under the terms of the agreement with Warner Bros., Wanda would pay for the construction of these new theaters, while Warner would provide the technical know-how it had used to construct multiplexes in other countries. Once the theaters were built in Wuhan, Beijing, Zhengzhou, and other cities, they would be branded Warner Wanda Cinemas, their designs including the iconic Warner Bros. shield logo and characters from its Looney Tunes brand. It was an easy trade-off: for its knowledge of how the theater business worked, Warner Bros. would gain unique access to the moviegoers it wanted to adore its movies—and finally get them to pay to see them.

Under the deal, announced in early 2004, Warner Bros. shared with Wanda a trove of data and information. Building a movie theater was more complicated than just setting up a giant room. The studio had developed algorithms that determined the best location for a theater based on factors like population hubs or access to public transportation. It knew the technical specifications for an auditorium with the perfect screen-to-seat ratio and picture quality. Concession stands and surround sound, which had proved appealing in other countries, would be included, too.

If the theater strategy worked, it would be a game changer for Hollywood. The Chinese box office was growing but still operated at a fraction of its potential—in 2005 its annual box-office grosses matched those of Switzerland. A "hit" in 2005 was a movie like the disaster flick *The Day After Tomorrow*, which made a whopping $10 million. The next year, the adaptation of Dan Brown's *The Da Vinci Code* took off, making $13 million on its way to passing *Pearl Harbor* as the country's second-most-successful import after *Titanic*. The government hastily pulled the movie from theaters after realizing that it would eat into the box-office share of several party propaganda films on the schedule. No film was going to replicate the performance of *Titanic*.

Building more theaters that sucked business from the pirates' market might help change that. But the deal Wanda had signed with Warner was going to give the studio a 51 percent ownership stake after seven years, at which point it would likely sell the venture to another firm at a profit. The Chinese government, however, had rules against foreign companies taking a majority position in domestic companies, one of several protectionist measures in place that executives said created an unfair playing field. Soon after announcing the partnership, Warner Bros. executives learned that the terms had changed, and the new conditions were not up for negotiation. Warner would not be the majority owner but instead a minority stakeholder.

Wanda wasn't kicking Warner out of the agreement, but it was making it nearly impossible for the studio to continue doing business with it. If Warner Bros. couldn't manage the locations, it had no way of ensuring that the theaters didn't operate in a way that damaged its reputation. Some theaters in China were home to fishy ticket-buying schemes. Others played pirated movies in their auditoriums. The last thing Warner Bros. wanted was to be called out by another studio for profiting off pirated movies in its theaters. As with many similar situations in China, it was always unclear whether the decision to alter the arrangement originated at the company or with the government.

As they weighed what to do, executives wondered whether the American rush toward China was going to come back to haunt them. A clash of values was inevitable. Was the prospect of billions of dollars in new revenue blinding American executives to the fact that they were getting the raw end of the deal—always having to find ways to benefit Chinese partners, and without any guarantee they would emerge unscathed?

Warner backed out of the theater deal. Wanda's chairman, Wang Jianlin, though, already had Warner Bros.' blueprints and business plans for building better movie theaters. It was a galling turn of events, one that would have immediately led to arbitration and lawsuits in the U.S. Some Warner executives, however, were quietly relieved to see the deal dry up. Their ultimate goal was supporting a legitimate theatrical business in the country, and that would happen now whether they were involved or not. Besides, getting out of the messy business of managing theaters halfway around the world was going to save them some headaches. Still, the brazen theft, as some characterized Wanda's actions, aggravated them. It would continue to bother them when they saw just what Wang Jianlin was able to do with the goods.

IT WAS NOT JUST THE financial terms of Chinese deals that were new and confounding to Hollywood. If American studios were going to enjoy access to Chinese moviegoers, executives would need to reframe their thinking about what was allowed in the country and what of their output ran ideologically counter to the motives of the state. In these early days, confusion reigned about what exactly the Chinese took issue with. No one in Los Angeles planned on shipping the next *Basic Instinct* over for approval by Chinese censors, but innocuous movies were getting rejected. Studio chiefs appealed to Glickman at the Motion Picture Association of America. His job was maintaining warm relations between his studios and foreign markets, much as his predecessors had done as the industry wove its way around the world.

In 2004, Universal Pictures had failed to get a forgettable comedy called *In Good Company* into Chinese theaters. This was not the kind of film the studio expected to see rejected. *In Good Company* starred Topher Grace as a young business executive who climbs the corporate ladder and becomes the boss of an older colleague who happens to be the father of his new girlfriend—a classic tale of upstart ambition, complicated by love and an ignorance of work-life balance. Glickman approached a Communist Party contact. This movie, he explained, was rated PG-13, with no excessive violence, drug use, or graphic sex scenes. Its plot hardly challenged China's worldview in the ways that *Kundun* had. It didn't have anything to do with the Communist Party or even Communism. Why weren't the Chinese people allowed to see it?

"You don't understand," the official told Glickman. "It's not that you're challenging the Chinese Communist Party. It's that so many American movies have a basic premise of a little guy taking on the system, and that is at the heart of what we worry about."

"The system" could be the principal at the local high school or the chairman of the company. If the narrative that the Chinese official described was going to present a problem to Chinese censors, then studio executives had to reevaluate core structural aspects of their films. The underdog narrative has underlaid much of American cinema, from the American origin story of rebel colonists fighting the British Empire to any David-versus-Goliath story, and has deepened Americans' reflexive support for the outsider, the rebel with or without a cause: James Dean, Norma Rae, Ferris Bueller.

"When you show things that are critical of the state, even implicitly, or even challenging the authority of a mayor, that really triggers their belief that this could break apart this need for stability," Glickman said. "Stability drives their thinking"—so much so that a Topher Grace rom-com was seen as a possible fissure.

For Glickman, it was an awakening to another core dynamic of the China-Hollywood relationship, one that would undergird every decision made by officials in charge of controlling their country's cultural spigot. Even if Hollywood movies gained an entrance onto Chinese screens in order to lift its theaters out of near bankruptcy, there would be a check on their power through quotas and censorship that went deeper than cosmetic edits on racy material. As much as Deng Xiaoping's reforms had opened China to this most American of products, China's leaders did not lose sight of the greater priority.

MORE THAN ANYTHING, Chinese officials made sure to stop American movies from monopolizing the marquee. Not only was there a cap on the number of Hollywood imports allowed in each year, but there was still a prolific output of Chinese propaganda or main-melody features required to play in auditoriums. American movies would need to exist alongside these Chinese anthems—a check, not unlike those seen in France and other protective markets, on Hollywood simply sweeping away all of the business and cultural cachet.

The career of actor Michael Gralapp offers a sense of what this arm of China's entertainment industry produced as an alternative to Hollywood blockbusters. Gralapp was a Sioux City native who moved to China in his forties to take advantage of its post-WTO growth. In the early 2000s, Gralapp was managing a shopping program on Chinese TV. For fun, he acted in English-language productions at the Beijing Playhouse, breaking out in his most famous role: Oscar Madison, the slob of *The Odd Couple*. After one of his performances, a Chinese agent asked Gralapp to audition for a main-melody movie, a genre that was often in need of non-Chinese actors. Gralapp got the part and in 2007 made his big-screen debut, playing George Marshall in a Chinese drama about the country's victories in World War II. It was merely a prelude to his signature role: Winston Churchill.

No topic then consumed Chinese propaganda producers more than the battles of World War II and Japanese atrocities, so simply existing as a balding, jowly white guy in China had given Gralapp the most unlikely of moonlighting gigs. He soon lost count of how many times he played the British prime minister. Though he isn't British, Gralapp wanted to do right by the hero of Western history. He scrutinized his mannerisms and studied his speeches, watching videos to mimic how he sat or held his cane. The director's degree of investment in his preparation varied.

"Some don't even ask for a British accent," he said.

The World War II parts forced Gralapp to consider the morality of such roles. One fellow actor always passed on the parts, worried they might jeopardize a desired future in American politics. Gralapp himself tweaked the language of the scripts, never delivering lines written in broken English, and turned down roles he called "Down with America!" parts. The main-melody movies he made, usually timed to a Communist Party anniversary, were like Hollywood films about Americans at war, he told himself. It was just that here, audiences were following Chinese soldiers and rooting for them instead of American ones. The only difference was the pervasive family-friendly tone these Chinese films struck. Gralapp always led the only soldiers in history who didn't curse.

Gralapp got to know the fraternity of white American actors who had moved to China and suddenly found themselves in demand by casting agents. One of his acquaintances was the guy producers knew to call when they needed a Hitler. Many others were like Nathaniel Boyd, a Los Angeles native and air force veteran who studied abroad in China and got himself jobs playing every conceivable part a white man might play in a Chinese movie set in China: backpacker, missionary, soldier, businessman. After a while, he realized that to be a Western character in these movies required growing accustomed to playing the corrupting influence: "I'm either a guy who tries to chase a Chinese girl and I don't get her, or I get her and something terrible happens to her," he told me. In one movie, he wooed a Chinese woman whose father had fought in the Korean War and was devastated to see his daughter fall for an American.

Gralapp was a small player in a much larger infrastructure of production

that churned out pro-China messaging with new fervor in the decade following Tiananmen Square, the ultimate break in the stability Glickman's
associate had described. Though *Top Gun* or *Rambo* can be called American propaganda, often by critics in America, the term was embraced by
Chinese authorities, who had a heavy hand in producing such movies. Like
an early Hollywood studio chief with a list of players under contract, these
officials, as much today as in the 1980s and 1990s, have access to directors, writers, and actors who have little choice but to agree to the job. The
movies are often tied to a prominent anniversary that the party wants to
celebrate and use as a chance to boost national patriotism. It could be the
founding of the party, or the army, or the People's Republic. When a director is contacted to helm such a feature, there is little room for negotiation—
in the euphemisms of China, the directors are "requested" to make such a
film, or "given the opportunity." Even onetime state agitators like Chen
Kaige take the gigs. A political currency system takes shape, one that rewards participation in propaganda features with easier approvals for commercial films down the line—a "one for you, one for me" model that savvy
Chinese directors have perfected.

On the set of such films, Gralapp would watch producers phone government officials with dialogue changes, tweaking the language in real
time until it was approved and the scene could be filmed. It's understandable, then, that the propaganda features are so closely linked with
the ruling authorities that they are interpreted as reflections of shifting
Beijing policy. After *The Founding of a Republic*, released in 2009 to commemorate the sixtieth anniversary of the founding of the People's Republic, portrayed Mao in consultation with other politicians before arriving
at decisions, American officials stationed in Beijing told the CIA and
secretary of state's office it signaled "an effort to recast the image of the
CCP as a party with a long history of openness." A more sympathetic
portrayal of Chiang Kai-shek, the Chinese Nationalist who in past propaganda films had been a "heartless villain," could be designed to appeal
to audiences in Taiwan, where he had fled following Mao's overthrow.

As his filmography grew, Gralapp came to understand the divide forming between the new moviegoers of China and the old. In these new cities, in the newly built Wanda theaters, audiences were catching *National Treasure* and familiarizing themselves with stars like Nicolas Cage. His young assistant at his day job was one such Chinese moviegoer. She didn't even know her boss was an actor who'd starred in numerous Chinese films.

Her mother, however, lived in a rural town where CCTV remained the dominant entertainment, and she recognized him immediately. If Gralapp left Beijing—where he could walk down the street uninterrupted—and traveled to the countryside, fans in restaurants would send over free peanuts and drinks. A generational and geographic split was forming between those who were opting out of Chinese-produced propaganda for the entertainment of the West and those who held fast to the features made for them by the state.

But this was not a free market of appeal, where the movie desired by the most people secured the biggest stars or best release date. Propaganda movies were the government's priority, and Beijing officials had levers in place to ensure they had an unfair advantage. This was evident in an exchange that IMAX chief executive Richard Gelfond, whose premium auditoriums were sprouting up in the country, had in 2010 with Han Sanping, then the head of China Film Group. Despite board members warning him that China was a "sinkhole," Gelfond was among those Hollywood executives most bullish on China's prospects, especially since his megascreen auditoriums specialized in the superhero spectacles that collected the biggest box-office grosses there. On the advice of Chinese associates, he had already moved his company's Asia headquarters from Singapore to China to show officials he was serious about doing business with them. His conversation with Han was another case in good business politics.

The two men spoke at a sound stage where *The Founding of a Party* was filming. Produced for the ninetieth anniversary of the founding of China's Communist Party, it was a state-sanctioned ode to the country.

Han called Gelfond to a pair of director's chairs outside the facility and showed him some footage of the war epic being filmed inside.

"We're doing this movie, *The Founding of a Party*. Would you be interested in showing the film in IMAX?" Han asked him.

This is like the pope saying, "Would you be interested in being a Catholic?" Gelfond thought to himself. There was only one right answer if he wanted to keep his company in good standing with China Film Group, the country's top state-run distributor.

But Gelfond needed to play a part. He needed to pretend that a high-ranking Chinese official asking you to show his movie on your screens was not a fait accompli—it was a negotiation.

"Mr. Han, tell me something about the movie," Gelfond said. "Who's the star?"

Han said a name Gelfond didn't recognize.

"Is it going to have big, epic scenes?" Gelfond continued.

Of course, Han said. But that was as far as he was going to let this charade go.

"Mr. Gelfond," Han said. "You and I both know you are going to do this movie. Can we make this conversation go any quicker?"

"You're absolutely right, Mr. Han," Gelfond said. "Where do I sign up?"

Hollywood had conquered the world's movie screens with relatively little resistance, but in China, where the economic opportunity was greater than any before, a simple upload of its product would not work. The Communist Party operated by its own rules, with its own priorities, and with more leverage than even Hollywood could match. Protectionist conditions ensured China always had the upper hand. And these were still early days. The confidence that Chinese leaders felt in demanding what they wanted would only grow as their nation's presence on the world stage reached new heights.

FIVE

Spielberg in Beijing

On September 22, 2004, a giant clock went up in Beijing's Tiananmen Square. The city blocks are home to a giant portrait of Mao Zedong—and to Mao Zedong himself, entombed in a casket—but the plaza remains best known to the world as the site of the June 1989 massacre. The government has largely scrubbed the event from Chinese history. There is no mention of it in the country's textbooks, and iconic images from that day of a "Tank Man" holding grocery bags and staring down a line of tanks are blocked. On this day in 2004, however, Chinese leaders wanted to turn the square from a representation of suppression into one of openness, engagement, and newfound power.

When the clock switched on, it began counting down the 1,417 days until China's capital city would host the 2008 Summer Olympics. By bringing the world to Beijing, Chinese leaders had accomplished a mission decades in the making: the Olympics would represent the culmination of Deng Xiaoping's economic reforms, the recovery from global banishment in the wake of the Tiananmen murders, and the start of a new era for China, one that might reinstate the country's central position in the world as the Middle Kingdom. The hopes for a Disneyland in China seemed quaint by comparison. Chinese leaders ordered their country's taxi drivers to learn English so they could accommodate visitors. Even weather was tamed: silver iodine and other tools were deployed to the clouds to either flush them of moisture before the ceremony or shrink droplets to make sure it wouldn't rain on the day of the opening ceremony.

In Hollywood, another clock was ticking. Cracks were forming in once-solid business plans. The cultural conversation was moving toward television. Superhero movies were teaching Hollywood that its future lay in bigger, more expensive titles. A distribution plan predicated on cheap discs was eroding by the day. In the time between the mounting of the clock in Tiananmen Square in 2004 and its final tick in 2008, Hollywood would go from looking at China with curious interest to needing it to survive.

Several months before the Olympics, the promise of Chinese revenue and the growing ambition of Chinese leaders led to a breakthrough in Disney's negotiations to build a theme park on the mainland. In early 2008, Robert Iger, now the company's CEO, met with Shanghai Communist Party chief Yu Zhengsheng and made two major concessions that would give his company entry into China. First, Disney would drop its campaign to get a Disney Channel onto Chinese airwaves, an abdication of the first step in its multipronged approach to justifying a theme park in the country. Second, Disney agreed to give up a majority stake in the park. Chinese companies could own a 57 percent stake in the Shanghai Disney Resort, which would also include revenue generated from every hotel room booked, dinner eaten, and set of Mickey Mouse ears purchased on the grounds. Chinese officials didn't stop there. They also wanted to approve rides at the park before they were constructed, and they requested a garden be built in the middle of the grounds for their older citizens.

Still, for Disney, China was worth it. The way Iger saw it, Shanghai Disney Resort represented "the greatest opportunity the company has had since Walt Disney himself bought land in Central Florida."

WALL STREET HAD PRIMED HOLLYWOOD for the moment when a massive market like China would be required to keep shareholders happy. The 1980s and 1990s had seen a surge in corporate appetite for Hollywood studios, and nearly every year brought a new deal that placed a major studio inside a bigger and bigger conglomerate. The 1980s began with Coca-Cola buying Columbia Pictures and ended with its sale to Sony. Matsushita Electric, now known as Panasonic, acquired MCA, which owned Universal Pictures, in 1990 and sold its stake in 1995 to Edgar Bronfman's Seagram, the beverage maker that had turned down *Kundun*. Five years after that, the studio went to Vivendi, a French water utility and media firm, where it lasted for four years before a handoff to General Electric, which already owned NBC, rendering the new unit NBC-Universal. In 2011, General Electric sold a majority stake in the studio to Comcast, the cable giant. Paramount was gobbled up by Viacom Inc. in 1994, putting it under the same corporate umbrella as MTV and Nickelodeon. In 1989, Warner Communications merged with Time Inc. to become Time Warner, and in 2000 executives announced the ill-fated AOL–Time Warner deal—then the biggest in history at $165 billion. This head-spinning sequence of transactions altered the stakes for Hollywood executives; turning once-mighty studios into small fish in larger corporate ponds ratcheted up the pressure to release moneymakers. Studios that once had to please family owners or independent boards now had to worry about contributing to the stock price of a publicly traded company.

At no point was this new dynamic more apparent than in 2008, which for Paramount was the year of *Iron Man*. The first movie in the Marvel Studios cinematic universe of superheroes wasn't a one-off hit—it was the first episode in a franchise series that would offer a new model of how to produce blockbusters. Starring Robert Downey Jr. as the metal-suited Tony Stark, it was chosen as the first cinematic adaptation by Marvel because a focus group of young children had gravitated to the doll. When it opened to $99 million and went on to gross $319 million domestically and another $267 million overseas, the business plan of every major studio changed. Now the most important asset in a studio portfolio was a franchise, a series that could spawn interconnected sequels, action figures, theme-park rides, and dozens of consumer products: Iron Man fanny packs, watches, Lego sets, and single-serve coffee makers were all available for purchase. For studios trying to please shareholders, a franchise offered that magic word: *synergy*. But these movies were the most expensive in history. They often needed to sell $1 billion in tickets around the world to pull in a profit, meaning about two thirds of all grosses would likely come from overseas audiences. A new megamarket like China would be welcome.

At Sony, the studio's television operation had successfully pitched *Breaking Bad*, the AMC drama about a high school chemistry teacher–turned–meth dealer. The show would go on to win a host of Emmys, run for five seasons, and send Sony a surge of revenue from licensing deals. But it would also, alongside *Mad Men* and *House of Cards*, be held up as a case study in a new wave of prestige television series best binge-watched on streaming platforms. Indeed, *Breaking Bad* was a critical favorite, but it became a cultural phenomenon when new fans discovered it on Netflix. A-list directors and actors had seen television as a cultural backwater for years, but they now had to admit that the better stuff was on TV. Consumers agreed, especially as the price of flatscreen TVs fell drastically and turned living rooms into mini theaters. If *Iron Man* and its type were for teenagers, TV was for grown-ups. In 2008 this cultural shift contributed to stagnation in U.S. movie-ticket sales, which would rarely register more than the slightest annual growth for the next decade.

Then the DVD market collapsed. It can be hard to remember in the streaming age, but the thin discs were once so popular that they underwrote much of Hollywood for years. Cheap to produce and $20 to buy, DVDs were among the studios' most profitable earners, capable of turning all but the biggest theatrical flops into profitable performers. As household collections grew, Walmart and other retailers would buy DVDs at $17 from studios and sell them for $15. They'd lose $2 on every sale, but they made up for it just from the foot traffic that the DVDs brought into stores. In 2000, the year of their major entrance into the marketplace, sales for DVDs totaled $2.5 billion. That number would nearly triple the next year and increase nearly tenfold to $21.2 billion in 2004. In 2006, sales hit a peak at $24.1 billion. Forget finding money in the street—these were numbers that kept the lights on.

But in 2008, the recession hit American households, leading many consumers to opt to rent DVDs rather than buy them. Netflix sent them through the mail, making ownership of a physical disc unnecessary. Disney had once enjoyed a time when more than eight million DVDs of *Finding Nemo* were sold on its first day of release. By 2008, DVD sales had fallen 33 percent, dragging the film studio's operating income down by 64 percent.

Now Disney, and every other studio in Hollywood, needed to find new money fast.

IN 1908 A CHINESE GOVERNMENT-LED campaign asked citizens, "When will China be able to invite all the world to come to Peking for an International Olympic contest?" They would meet their goal exactly one hundred years later.

If some Americans thought China was jumping the gun by positioning itself as a world power as it prepared to host the Olympics in 2008, the reality was that China was merely filling the role of the new-century upstart that the U.S. had once occupied. When St. Louis hosted the

Olympics in 1904, critics said an immature America was not worthy of the platform. But the U.S. was flexing its muscles abroad and wanted a global stage on which to announce itself. The president of the International Olympic Committee, summarizing Europe's response to the global power shift toward America, disparaged the country as "utilitarian." The utilitarians were happy to show off their utility: in St. Louis, town leaders touted their extravagant new train stations.

The shiny new attraction of the Beijing Olympics would be the Bird's Nest, a round structure of interwoven beams built in a newly developed portion of the city and designed by Ai Weiwei, a Chinese artist who had become famous worldwide for defying his country's leaders. Ai's father, a poet, had been banned from publishing his work for nearly two decades during the Mao era. In accepting the Bird's Nest job, Ai took pains to clarify that he was working for a Swiss architecture firm, not the Chinese government. In fact, he was revolted by those who were helping Beijing plan the opening ceremony.

"All the shitty directors in the world are involved," he said.

The targets of his scorn—those "shitty directors"—were no less than two of the world's most acclaimed moviemakers: Zhang Yimou and Steven Spielberg. Nearly twenty years after their lives had intersected over Chinese censorship of Zhang's Oscar-nominated movie, they were tapped by Chinese leaders to direct and advise on the opening ceremony. For friends of Zhang, it was a sign of the steady absorption of filmmaking talent into the Communist Party apparatus, similar to those who accepted propaganda-film jobs as a way of currying favor with officials. Outside of his Olympics duty, Zhang had joined the country's top political advisory committee and made films that critics said were veiled endorsements of authoritarianism. As his cooperation with the government grew, his movies were given plum release dates that boosted box-office sales.

Beijing's organizing committee for the games then announced that Ang Lee would also consult on the ceremony, as though the party had hired a headhunting firm that specialized in Chinese figures who lent prestige but carried political baggage with the government. Less than a year before being named to the post, Lee won an Oscar for directing *Brokeback Mountain*, his 2005 Western about two closeted cowboys in love. After he won the prize, the government played his acceptance speech on television but edited it so Chinese audiences who hadn't caught a pirated version of the film wouldn't know the gay plot of his winning film. Furthermore, Chinese media held him up as "the pride of Chinese people all over the world," not mentioning that he was from Taiwan.

Political issues soon consumed Spielberg's involvement. Actress Mia Farrow and her son Ronan Farrow published an opinion piece in *The Wall Street Journal* criticizing China's support for the government of Sudan, where a genocidal campaign had killed more than four hundred thousand people in Darfur. The Olympics were only emboldening China's regime, they said. "Does Mr. Spielberg really want to go down in history as the Leni Riefenstahl of the Beijing Games?" they asked, referencing the Hitler propagandist's recording of the 1936 Olympic Games in Berlin. Spielberg immediately requested a meeting with Chinese president Hu Jintao. Two weeks later, with attention mounting, a Chinese official traveled to Sudan to lobby the government there to accept a UN peacekeeping force—illustrating the specific blend of publicity and political pressure that can draw attention to events that years of diplomacy cannot. But when months passed and the situation in Darfur had not changed, Farrow called again for Spielberg to drop out, and about a week later, he did. Backlash against the director was swift. His decision to quit, another Chinese critic noted, was "aligned with imperialist assumptions bred by living in the United States. . . . Spielberg claims that China is not 'using its influence' with Sudan to 'end the suffering.' However, the notion that a 'great power' should 'use its influence' to control the internal affairs of other sovereign nations arises from the U.S., and not Chinese, assumptions." In the narrative most Americans accepted, such standard-bearing was the duty of a world leader. Even then, China wanted to reset the terms.

Inside China, Ric Birch was helping a team of Chinese nationals on the opening ceremony. A former television producer, Birch had parlayed a gig producing the Commonwealth Games in his native Australia to become a veteran orchestrator of opening ceremonies. By now, Birch had spent several weeks working with this group of young Chinese people in Beijing, even as the Spielberg controversy engulfed the press. As they'd brainstormed ideas, he'd arrived at a sense of how this was a different process from the opening ceremonies he'd designed in Barcelona and Torino. During one concept review, Birch and his partner proposed constructing a giant tree in the middle of the stadium that would have its leaves fall, symbolizing the changing eras of Chinese history. They were met with silence. The Chinese workers hesitated to say what the problem was, until one spoke up: "In 1644 the last emperor of the Ming dynasty hanged himself from a tree," he said. "People will think this is that tree."

Birch was confused.

"No, this is a different tree," he said.

It didn't matter if this fictional tree wasn't the historical tree. Some people might think this tree was that tree, his colleague said. They abandoned the idea. Birch thought of his friends overseas, who had not updated their mental image of China beyond rice paddies and chopsticks. *Just you wait*, he thought. There were thousands of years of history that lived in the hearts of contemporary Chinese citizens, who were eager to share it on the world stage.

"You could just about hear the sound of China beating their chest," he said.

At the ceremony itself, every detail was timed for an auspicious start. Eight is a lucky number in Chinese culture, so the opening ceremony started at 8:08 p.m. on August 8, 2008. Drummers at the opening ceremony—2,008 of them—moved in such unison their clothes blurred together to look like a magic-eye drawing. A catalog of China's cultural

landmarks followed, reminding the world it was the country that had
invented paper and movable type, the latter demonstrated by human-
controlled blocks rising and falling in perfect symmetry. Puppeteers performed a Beijing opera. A dancer gallivanted across a giant scroll held aloft
by hundreds of her countrymen, flitting across it in a hearkening to the
country's history as a trading hub on the Silk Road.

Other opening ceremonies had been a series of performances; this one
was a narrative that combined ancient Confucian ideals with the bombast of the eighty-one-year-old People's Liberation Army, all in a ceremony whose central narrative was the magnetism that had drawn other
countries to China for centuries—and a reminder that the past several
centuries of Western hegemony had been an exception to world history,
not the norm. Television announcers, sticking to the script distributed to
networks by China's state-run media, commented on how it was all "a
natural expression of China's reverence for the traditions and great men
of the country's past." At the ceremony, every compromise was made for
China to look its best. The seven-year-old girl who was hired to sing a
patriotic song had missing teeth and a severe haircut, so a pretty nine-
year-old in a red dress and pigtails lip-synched while a recording of the
other one played through the speakers.

U.S. president George W. Bush watched from the Bird's Nest. In the
years leading up to the ceremony, his war in Iraq, and in particular its
failure to spread democracy as promised, had called American hegemony into question. Just six weeks after the bombastic opening ceremony,
Wall Street would suffer the worst collapse since the Great Depression, a
damning indictment of capitalism that came just as China produced a
spectacular Olympic Games that doubled as a commercial for an alternative system. A Pew Research Center poll conducted the next year asked
people in twenty-five countries whether China would supplant the U.S.
as the world's top superpower. A majority of respondents in thirteen of those
countries said yes. The global narrative of American supremacy appeared
more and more vulnerable.

. . .

Two months before the opening ceremony, Hollywood had presented China with a particularly embarrassing example of how effective the movies could be in supporting a nation's rise. DreamWorks Animation had released *Kung Fu Panda*, introducing audiences to Po, an overweight, clumsy panda who dreams of learning kung fu. The movie had combined China's unofficial mascot with a centuries-old tradition and made a global blockbuster, pulling in more than $600 million.

Though the movie came out at a time when Hollywood had awoken to China's economic power, it had not been conceived as a strategic play for those grosses. In December 2004, Jeffrey Katzenberg, the chief executive of DreamWorks Animation, had gone on a holiday break with homework, flipping through coffee-table books and photography for inspiration. Was the next *Shrek* or *Madagascar* in this random collection?

Working over the holidays was more or less a given if you worked for Katzenberg. Since skipping college and arriving in Hollywood in his twenties, he had defined himself as the industry's top hustler, maniacal in his work ethic. He woke at 5:00 a.m., starting the day with an exercise bike routine while he read several newspapers before leaving for three back-to-back breakfast meetings each morning. At Disney, the studio where he made his name, his motto to workers was "If you don't come in on Saturday, don't bother coming in on Sunday."

The books passed out to DreamWorks employees included a collection of stills from old kung fu movies, showing masters like Bruce Lee with high kicks and devastating palm strikes. Another featured panda photography, displaying the black-and-white mammals in various states of repose, munching on bamboo or climbing trees. After Katzenberg said he was newly obsessed with pandas and a colleague said he was interested in kung fu, an animator said, "Well, let's just do *Kung Fu Panda*."

Big idea, Katzenberg thought.

From that postholiday meeting, Po, one of DreamWorks' most famous creations, was born. His father, a goose named Mr. Ping, operates the noodle restaurant where Po works. His chance at heroism comes when an evil snow leopard escapes prison—and Po is called upon to defeat him. First he must master the art of kung fu, training under a wise red panda named Master Shifu. Jack Black would voice Po; Dustin Hoffman played his teacher.

The filmmaking team immersed themselves in Chinese film history and philosophy and studied classic battle scenes and ancient Chinese painting. The result was animation far more sophisticated than what DreamWorks typically produced—not a lampooning of kung fu movies but an homage to them. One of its directors, Mark Osborne, pulled from Zhang Yimou's color theory. Producer Melissa Cobb hired consultants to guarantee that the architectural detail of the Chinese homes and towns was precise and the flora and fauna of each animated region correct. They were not going to do "generic China," she said.

After almost five years of development and animation, *Kung Fu Panda* premiered in the U.S. in the summer of 2008, opening to a robust $60 million and going on to collect $215 million domestically. DreamWorks had another franchise on its hands. But its overseas numbers made Katzenberg sit up: the movie had grossed $416 million from international theaters, an amount on par with the second *Madagascar* installment and third *Shrek* film, both sequels with characters that had the benefit of having already been introduced to audiences.

Most startlingly, the movie had made a healthy $26 million in China. Cobb had still thought of it as a market with limited imports and a vast piracy network; if Chinese moviegoers were going to meet Po, she had thought, chances were they would do so on illegitimate DVDs.

Oh good, we didn't screw it up, Cobb thought when the returns came in. *They don't hate us.*

On a trip to China after the movie's release there, she took a tour of the Shaolin Monastery, a Buddhist temple constructed in the fifth century. One of the monks guarding the burial ground discovered his guests were the team behind *Kung Fu Panda*.

"I've seen it three times!" he told the group. Cobb took in his saffron robe and shaved head.

How does this monk who is guarding a temple in the middle of nowhere see Kung Fu Panda *three times?* she thought to herself. It may have been in a theater or on a pirated disc, but at a moment of national pride, Chinese audiences yearned to see themselves on-screen, so much so that a CGI panda had made it to a 1,500-year-old temple.

WHILE *KUNG FU PANDA* DELIGHTED Chinese moviegoers, it immediately threw Chinese leaders into an existential crisis.

"The film's protagonist is China's national treasure and all the elements are Chinese," said Wu Jiang, president of the China National Peking Opera Company. "Why didn't we make such a film?"

No movie occupied the minds of Chinese authorities trying to learn commercial cinema quite like *Kung Fu Panda*. American filmmakers had conceived of Po as an adorable vehicle of Chinese culture. The animation, which featured scenes of shadow puppetry and kinetic kung fu sequences, was a top-notch representation of the culture they in 2008 wanted to show the world.

Years later, Chinese animators would quiz Cobb on the mechanics of the movie. This is an iconic figure of China, they told her, our most respected animal. Why did you make him tired, embarrassed, shy, a creature who stress-eats like the rest of us? *Kung Fu Panda* had humanized an icon in a way that Chinese moviegoers embraced—but in a way in which Chinese filmmakers would not have thought to do, they said. "We would have been afraid to take a revered animal and make fun of him," Cobb was told.

When Katzenberg later traveled to China, he tried to learn more about how China's censorship affected its storytelling approach—and would in turn be bombarded with questions revealing the nation's hope of reverse-engineering *Kung Fu Panda.*

Take the absurdist decision to make Po's father a goose named Mr. Ping. Would Chinese officials have approved the film with this unexplained mash-up of characters? Katzenberg asked.

The Chinese officials homed in with intense curiosity about the motivations that would lead to such a choice.

"Is it subversive?" one official asked of the goose-panda relationship. "Was it a commentary on mixed-race families?"

It's just a goose! Katzenberg would respond.

The Olympics had given Chinese leaders their biggest modern-day chance to experiment with controlling their nation's narrative. Translated copies of Joseph Nye's theory of "soft power" had been passed around Beijing government circles. Andre Morgan, a producer who worked in the country, recalled leaders quizzing him about the notion: "That's why we feel that way. We see American movies, American TV. That's why we want to go to Las Vegas." The barrage of questions continued: "How does this apply in a Communist society?" "What in Chinese culture and history could we use?"

With *Kung Fu Panda*, officials feared America had beaten them to it. "I cannot help wondering when China will be able to produce a movie of this caliber," lamented Chinese director Lu Chuan. Lu was no slouch himself. Two years before the *Kung Fu Panda* release, he had been hired by Chinese authorities to produce his own animated film—one made specially for the Olympics. But his "producers" wouldn't stop trying to shape what the movie should say. "I kept receiving directions and orders on how the movie should be. . . . An important part of the instructions was that the animation should promote Chinese culture," he said. The project was eventually dropped.

Even before the release of *Kung Fu Panda*, optimistic executives in Glendale were plotting the second installment. Chinese authorities got to work, too. To get their filmmakers to begin thinking more like those who had produced *Kung Fu Panda*, they took the approach they knew best: legislating to make it so.

They had been laying the groundwork for such an effort. The year before *Kung Fu Panda*'s release, the 17th Communist Party Congress—where China's leaders delivered a broad annual proclamation of country-wide priorities—designated animation as an area to support. Tax breaks encouraged animated production; construction started on office parks where animation studios could be housed; copyright laws were strengthened to convince creators their work would remain theirs. In that same summer of *Kung Fu Panda*, a document from an advisory panel called the Chinese People's Political Consultative Conference went further than party leaders and suggested the country ease its restrictions on filmmaking, internalizing that the best creative industries emerge from a sense of chaos.

"Although there is no secret ingredient to film-making success, the government ought to relax its oversight," the advisory panel wrote. "Opening more space for Chinese artists would allow more innovation, ultimately giving China great cultural influence abroad."

The aspects of American culture seeping into China were not the beacons of democracy that U.S. politicians had hoped for and Chinese officials had feared, but creative freedom that leaders in Beijing registered as valuable. The chest pounding that Ric Birch had observed in the Olympics rehearsals would not be enough to grant China the global influence it sought. Some influential people in China were acknowledging more openly than ever before that the control that defined their system of government was holding back their country's creative class—and therefore China's ability to sell itself to the world.

SOON AFTER THE OLYMPICS, a blast as loud as any drum line rippled through Hollywood when *Avatar* premiered. The Chinese box office had never seen anything like it, and the studio chiefs in Los Angeles—many of whom still categorized China as a place of novelty hits like *Kung Fu Panda*—woke up to the grosses it could generate. Moviegoers waited in line for six hours. Tickets were scalped for $100 apiece. Members of the politburo closed an auditorium so they could watch it in private.

The story of blue-skinned aliens fighting colonizing forces to save their home planet was a universal allegory, one cited as a metaphor for the shrinking Amazonian rainforests and strip-mined Navajo reservations. It was another example of director James Cameron's singular ability to transpose classic storytelling tropes—the sacrificial savior, star-crossed lovers, David versus Goliath—to blockbuster entertainment like *The Terminator*, *Titanic*, and now *Avatar*. For Chinese audiences, the Na'vi fighting to save their land with the help of a rebellious soldier recalled the rural residents across the countryside who had been forced out of their homes to make way for their government's mass urbanization campaign, the invading spaceships on-screen standing in for the bulldozers they'd watched demolish their villages.

Anticipating its success, executives at Twentieth Century Fox had lobbied Chinese officials to build more 3D screens in the country, knowing the technological leap of the movie's effects would be a draw. On a per-screen basis, Chinese theaters were outperforming any location in the world. It was the kind of attendance driver that Chinese authorities had wanted when they loosened the import restrictions back in the days of *The Fugitive*. But like most Hollywood successes in China, this one quickly came with a correction. Less than two weeks after *Avatar*'s release, Chinese authorities pulled it from most of its screens. Out went *Avatar*, the highest-grossing movie of all time. In went a biopic about Confucius.

Chinese authorities were still finding a way to balance popular imports from the West with the priorities their country had established for

Chinese art. If the state needed to intervene so that Chinese moviegoers didn't get too swept away by the new competition, so be it. As a concession to Fox, China Film Group kept the movie playing on the country's nine hundred 3D screens.

The move spoke to the tension within China's top ranks about which movies were good for their people. Officials were skeptical of the loosening up that had followed the *Kung Fu Panda* self-reflection. Tang Linxiang, a party secretary in Anhui Province, told an American official in 2009 that most Chinese citizens were so poorly educated that without "tight controls" the country could devolve into "chaos." If an independent filmmaker made a movie that aggravated the Chinese citizens, they would be so unable to process it that they could respond in "unpredictable (and dangerous) ways." The box-office success of *Avatar* the next year might tip the economic balance in favor of American movies and grant the Americans a degree of cultural influence that conservative parts of the Chinese government had warned against since *The Fugitive* and those first Disneyland negotiations.

In dropping *Avatar* from two thirds of its screens, China's film authorities weren't just reusing a tactic deployed against *The Da Vinci Code*. They were calling on a playbook established decades earlier by the Soviet Union's efforts to gin up excitement among moviegoers for the films its leaders wanted them to see. In the winter of 1926, *Battleship Potemkin* premiered in the Soviet Union, the government ready to embrace the story of a heroic mutiny on a Russian battleship. Ushers dressed as soldiers at the premiere.

The Soviet empire had threaded its cinematic propaganda efforts into the nation much as China would decades later. By 1925, the country had installed 75 percent of cinemas in workers' clubs, a direct pipeline into the proletariat groups. But due to the expansion of Hollywood movies during World War I, *Battleship Potemkin* had pesky competition from lower-brow Hollywood fare. The year before, imported movies had accounted for 79 percent of the annual box office. Soviet officials yearned for a film industry of their own, one that would entertain their people and inculcate them with Soviet ideals. *Battleship Potemkin* was their chance. But Douglas Fairbanks in *Robin Hood*, a United Artists movie notable for being the first Hollywood release to hold a glitzy premiere, was drawing in audiences when *Battleship Potemkin* hit screens. Fairbanks and his merry men were sent to theaters outside the city centers to make way for *Battleship Potemkin*. Twelve days after the release, Soviet officials published attendance figures showing their movie beating Hollywood's— despite the fact that they were manipulating those sales to make it appear that moviegoers preferred *Potemkin* to a swashbuckling Fairbanks. It was yet another case of Soviet officials finding it acceptable to steal from the rich.

China's attempt at the *Potemkin* playbook only dented what was still a gargantuan haul for *Avatar*. It grossed $2.7 billion at the global box office, a record it would hold for a decade, with an eye-popping $202 million coming from Chinese theaters. More than $200 million, at a time when *Kung Fu Panda* was considered a hit at $26 million. It was four times the record set by Cameron's *Titanic*, and it embodied a solution to the problems that had converged for studios in their home market the year before—the demand for higher grosses, the stagnation in the U.S., the new competition on TV, and the lost revenue from DVD sales. China to the rescue.

BY 2010, THE NUMBER OF theater screens in China had more than doubled to thirteen thousand. The box office had nearly doubled in the same time. Wang Jianlin was driving much of this growth. The chairman of Wanda had been busy since dropping Warner Bros. from his theater plans. The country's urbanization campaign and the growing middle class of consumers had supported Wang as he built cinemas, malls, and hotels across China.

It was a different story in America, where theaters were struggling.

Gerry Lopez, the CEO of AMC Entertainment Holdings, knew this better than anyone. At the demand of the private-equity firms controlling his company, potential acquirers started coming through the Kansas City headquarters of AMC, then the nation's second-largest movie theater chain. Executives grew accustomed to the dog and pony show: the NDA signing, the financial audit, the negotiations that never went anywhere. Following the 2008 recession, few wanted to get into the movie theater business—in America, at least.

Lopez was in Hong Kong a couple of years after the 2008 financial meltdown when one of AMC's owners told him to detour to Beijing and meet a billionaire interested in buying the company. He needed one thing ahead of the meeting: a tie. Few people in Hong Kong meetings wore them, so Lopez hadn't packed one. He got word that things were a bit more formal with Wang, a wealthy man whom everyone knew as simply "the Chairman." Lopez bought a tie—at a nearby Wanda mall.

Wang had identified companies for sale that would help him dominate certain sectors. Wang told Lopez he wanted to be number one in four areas of business: movie theaters, commercial real estate, department stores, and hotels. After becoming number one in those sectors in China, he would become number one in the world.

Say what? Lopez thought to himself. *That's ambitious. This guy wants to be bigger than Marriott and Starwood? He wants to buy AMC and be the biggest movie-theater operator in the world?* AMC wasn't even the biggest movie theater chain in the U.S.

"By 2020, we should be listed among the top 100 worldwide companies," Wang said at the time. Buying an American company and taking it public soon afterward would signal to the world that he—and his country—meant business.

Lopez's story was quintessentially American. He was born in Cuba in the months after Fidel Castro's revolution, the grandson of a Cuban businessman and landowner who saw trouble ahead and sent his family

away. Lopez, then just one year old, flew to Miami in 1960 before settling in Puerto Rico. Some members of his family stayed in Cuba, convinced things would calm down. The Lopezes who had escaped talked
about freedom constantly; it was literally the dinner-table conversation
every night. "There is a love of something you have lost that can only be
understood when you lose it," Lopez said. His mother barred him from
wearing red, the color of the Communists.

The company he ran had been founded in Kansas City in 1920.
When American moviegoers moved to the suburbs in the years following World War II, the chain met them there. Decades of growth and
innovation—the armrest cup holder, the multiplex housing several screens
under one roof—followed until the company had a national profile. A
"bigger is better" arms race in the 1980s led to overbuilding into the
1990s and early 2000s; in the thirteen years between 1988 and 2001, the
number of screens in the U.S. jumped 61 percent to nearly thirty-five
thousand. The boom days quickly gave way to a third-act calamity. Exhibitors took on monumental debt to keep erecting gargantuan multiplexes, cannibalizing their own business by building new complexes too
close to old ones. Bankruptcies followed. By 2006, AMC was owned by
five private-equity firms.

When a delegation of Wanda executives traveled to Kansas City, they
crammed more than two dozen advisers into an overheated conference
room for that road show. The only difference this time was in the choice
of restaurant: instead of the usual barbecue joint, Lopez treated the
Wanda team at a local Chinese spot.

Wang's visit to the Kansas City suburbs may have offered a crystal-
ball vision of what he wanted to see in China: towering theaters anchor-
ing strip malls lining endless parkways. Wang had been the beneficiary
of a construction boom similar to the midtwentieth-century growth that
had allowed AMCs to sprout up in suburbs across America. In China,
Wang wanted to build more Wanda Plazas. Like the Sears, Roebuck &

Co. founder before him, Wang knew it was all about the anchor tenant: the movie theater.

ON MAY 20, 2012, WANDA announced it was buying AMC for $2.6 billion. Even if China was struggling to figure out how to match Hollywood creatively, it could at this point outspend just about anyone.

It was among the biggest acquisitions of a U.S. company by a Chinese company in history, and it had come not in semiconductors or airplanes or any of the many other industries weaving themselves into China's post-WTO economy. Until this point, Hollywood had been going to China with its business, not the other way around. Those working in the movie industry were confused: Why would a Chinese billionaire invest in the U.S. theater business? Ticket sales were flat, Netflix was advancing, and the business itself operated on thin margins.

In Washington, officials with an oversight body called the Committee on Foreign Investment in the United States (CFIUS) had their own questions. The group included officials from the Treasury Department and Department of Defense. Their job was to monitor such investments for undue influence in American affairs, often scrutinizing deals with military overlap, like aerospace. The AMC acquisition, in their eyes, was a soft-power threat. Could Wanda force AMC to show Chinese propaganda on its screens?

They certainly could, Lopez said. But only if they wanted to kill their business.

The committee's line of questioning was treating AMC theaters like a radio station that broadcasts for free, he argued to officials. With movie theaters, patrons decide with their spending what to watch, making it difficult for Wanda to use the locations as messaging systems. America's capitalist system acted as a control on any desire on China's part to turn AMC screens into propaganda venues.

U.S. authorities approved the deal. It closed on Labor Day. Much of the $2.6 billion of the deal was in acquiring debt, but Wanda still needed to transfer some $700 million in cash to complete the sale. The money would travel from a Wanda office in Beijing to a Citibank in Beijing, and then from the Citibank in Beijing to a Citibank in Hong Kong, and then from the Citibank in Hong Kong to a Citibank in New York.

Even after more than a year of negotiating and meeting Wang in China and the U.S., Lopez asked his team to update him each time the funds reached their next stop. "We want to make sure the money is real," he told his bankers.

Wang traveled to Los Angeles to commemorate the purchase at two events. Gelfond from IMAX introduced him at the first one. Katzenberg introduced him at the second one. With his eye on building a studio in China, Katzenberg studied Henry Kissinger's *On China* and told the heads of Warner Bros. and Disney to do the same. The book did not discuss Hollywood or the movies in China, but its study of the country's history, culture, and political strategy through the dynasties might prove helpful. The executives would have done well to read the part of the book that concerns the fate of those who had come before them, conquerors who throughout history have believed China was theirs for the taking.

"When foreign dynasties prevailed in battle, the Chinese bureaucratic elite would offer their services and appeal to their conquerors on the premise that so vast and unique a land as they had just overrun could be ruled only by use of Chinese methods, Chinese language, and the existing Chinese bureaucracy. With each generation, the conquerors would find themselves increasingly assimilated into the order they had sought to dominate," Kissinger wrote. "They would find themselves pursuing traditional Chinese national interests, with the project of conquest effectively turned on its head."

Katzenberg printed up new business cards—English on one side, Chinese on the other. The DreamWorks Animation logo, of a boy fishing off the edge of a blue crescent moon, was localized too. The boy became a panda. The moon went from blue to red.

The word was out: China wanted to be a global player, which meant it wanted to be a player in global entertainment, and it had billions of dollars to spend to get itself there. Producers with movies that might hit in the country like *Kung Fu Panda* did could expect unheard-of windfalls. Even companies in the most dire straits thanks to the DVD collapse were now eyeing Chinese grosses as a replacement revenue—or thinking they could be takeover targets like AMC. Studios hungry for new eyeballs and under pressure for those $1 billion worldwide grosses need not look further. There was a reason that executives in Hollywood were fighting for the chance to schmooze the Chinese billionaire.

China's ambition was clear, and its wallet was open. As one studio distribution executive, at the end of a long conversation about the concessions Hollywood made to maintain access to that wallet, put it: "I would not see myself as the standard bearer of Western democracy. I'm here to make money!"

Censorship

n the original cut of 2006's *Mission: Impossible III*, Tom Cruise chases villains through the streets of Shanghai. A global movie star in a major Chinese city taking down the bad guys—this was the kind of scene usually cheered by Chinese officials who wanted to see their country on-screen. But there was a detail that threatened to ruin the whole thing. In the Shanghai scenes, Cruise's heroics take him past apartment buildings where underwear dries on clotheslines, a typical sight in the city. But Chinese officials thought the drying clothes might make their country appear backward. At the request of China's film censorship board, Paramount Pictures cut the clothes from the movie. The censors made sure no one could see China's dirty laundry.

In the spring of 2013, Paramount was months away from premiering *World War Z*, based on a novel by Max Brooks about a virus outbreak that turns the world's citizens into hungry zombies. The movie, starring Brad Pitt, was near completion when a scene was scrutinized. Early in the film, scientists speculate that the zombie outbreak originated in China. Brooks had thought that such an outbreak could fester in a country like China, an authoritarian regime that maintained strict control on the press and tried to project a certain image globally. But what made sense in his book would not fly in a movie that needed a global box office. Paramount executives removed the plot point from the finished film before sending it over to the censors, who took in its gory scenes and still rejected it.

Several years later, Sony Pictures was readying the Chinese release of *Men in Black 3*, starring Will Smith and Tommy Lee Jones as federal agents hunting down undercover aliens on Earth. Each time an everyday citizen sees an alien reveal itself, the agents have a particular tool at their disposal: a small contraption that wipes clean the eyewitnesses' memories. Before the movie could be released in China, that plot device had to be cut from the film. In a country where officials control how history is remembered, the memory-erasing device became a metaphor for authoritarian control.

In the years immediately following the Beijing Olympics, it was clear that the Chinese box office would become the number one movie market in the world. Projections varied as to how quickly it would get there, but North American ticket sales had stagnated, and Chinese receipts were clocking double-digit annual growth. Studios dependent on pleasing shareholders and justifying ever-larger production budgets needed to access it if their companies wanted to stay afloat, never mind grow.

As the Chinese box office grew, then, parts of movies started to disappear. They had to if their creators wanted access to the market. For Hollywood studios, dealing with Chinese censors would be a crash course in political, economic, and cultural concerns—and the most important foundational element of doing business there. Censorship was the first concession that made it all possible, the core concern of Chinese officials opening their country up to outside influence, and the most frequent way Hollywood executives dealt with the country. China was going to be the top market, and its box office became blackmail.

Xi Jinping warned in 2013 that "the disintegration of a regime often starts from the ideological area." Since Hollywood began exporting movies to China in 1994, protecting the country's ideological barrier has fallen to a clandestine group of party leaders, retirees, and film studies professors who inspect every movie before it plays for Chinese audiences. Before studios can access the hundreds of millions of dollars in box-office grosses, they must first demonstrate that their movies have no adult themes (violence, nudity, drugs), political third rails (Tibet, Tiananmen), or even problematic metaphors (rebellion, resistance, questioning authority). As Hollywood's studios began shipping more and more movies to China, they learned that while their industry had catered to the tastes of foreign markets since its founding, none of those countries had ever had the economic muscle China had now.

This went deeper than Mexico complaining that all on-screen Mexicans were criminals or Japan boycotting movies critical of monarchies. *Pirates of the Caribbean: At World's End*, starring Chow Yun-Fat as a ship captain, trimmed scenes of the Chinese actor because he portrayed a malevolent force. A scene in the James Bond movie *Skyfall*, in which a Chinese security guard is shot and killed, was cut from the film since it showed a Chinese character at a moment of weakness. A gay love scene was among the thirty-eight minutes stripped from the Warner Bros. adaptation of the novel *Cloud Atlas*. Chris Pratt's bare butt was taken out of the space drama *Passengers*.

The censors keep China in a perpetually PG-13 world, one where drug use, naked bodies, and violence do not exist. Gay people stay in the closet or off-screen. Whiffs of spirituality—including the cinematic portrayal of ghosts—do not abide in the People's Republic. Even time travel, with the creative license it brings to the historical record, is forbidden. A list published by the State Administration of Radio, Film, and Television in 2008 had nineteen codicils that illustrate the rules movies must follow to be shown in Chinese theaters, a cinematic update to the edicts laid out by Mao decades earlier on molding art to the regime's purpose. Together, these requirements help ensure that the version of China shown on-screen is the one its leaders want people to believe exists off-screen. Under these strictures, China is a country where residents do not display a "passive or negative outlook on life," participate in "bad habits," or advocate harming the environment or animals. China is a country where residents do not masturbate. It is a place where rape and murder do not occur in grisly detail—or if they do, it is a place where there are no "deliberate expressions of remorselessness" in committing such crimes. No one in China disparages the police. In China, you will not find religious extremism that causes "disharmony in the community." China is a country where no one threatens the territorial definition of its borders. China is also a country where no one "defames the superiority" of Chinese culture.

Avoiding scenes of masturbation and excessive drinking is easy enough for writers and directors, but how exactly was a studio chief supposed to interpret what in a movie constitutes a threat to Chinese national security, as rule 3 requires? It falls on studio representatives in Beijing to divine what will be acceptable by lobbying China's film bureau and reading the cues from cuts made to other movies. Chinese producers making movies in their country often have changes of their own to make in the days before a film's release, too, even though all Chinese scripts have to be approved before shooting can begin. Hollywood studios have a trickier road to navigate, since they are often submitting a film for review after production and editing have finished, leaving little time for major changes.

By examining what doesn't pass muster, we gain an understanding of what Chinese officials are scared their citizens may learn: that the afterlife gives people faith, that time travel gives them hope. In the context of China's history of propaganda films, the rule that controls how the past is portrayed makes perfect sense. For decades, the country has churned out movies about the Communist Party's glorious history, often in baldly revisionist ways that present a government-sanctioned view of history. In China, it's known colloquially as "the Oliver Stone law," since it rules out the director's interpretive treatments of historical events, such as the presidential assassination in *JFK*. It has also, according to some directors, contributed to a nation that refuses to reckon with its greatest historical demons. If film helps a nation process its past, China has left massive portions of its history unexamined.

Chinese leaders not only control what comes into their country; they have also managed to dictate what moviegoers in other territories can see. This reality was made clear in 2004, when Sudhir Nandgaonkar was programming the Third Eye Asian Film Festival, an annual celebration of the region's cinema in Mumbai. Prior to the festival's start, he received word from the Chinese consulate in Mumbai to reconsider two programming choices: *Seven Years in Tibet* and *Kundun*. It had been nearly a decade since the movies had premiered, and Chinese officials were still on guard against them.

"We decided to play safe," Nandgaonkar said. The movies came off the schedule.

If audiences at the Third Eye film festival in Mumbai had been allowed to see *Seven Years in Tibet*, they would have watched a scene more prescient than anyone could have known in 1997, one that would ask a question answered as the new economic reality for Hollywood took shape. It comes early in the film, when the young Dalai Lama is watching newsreel footage of British royalty, a display of power and wealth that prompts him to consider the arc of empires. He turns to his tutor and asks: "Do you think someday people will look at Tibet on the movie screen and wonder what happened to us?"

AUDIENCES IN CHINA ARE REMINDED every time they go to the movies that what they are about to see has been approved by their government. When the lights go down in an auditorium, a green screen first appears bearing the golden dragon seal of the state's film bureau. A trumpet blare accompanies it, enveloping the auditorium in a cinematic gaze like few others in the world. The political class is a phantom presence in the auditorium, since all viewers know that what they are watching has been deemed acceptable by those in power.

Acquiring the seal involves a lobbying process that Hollywood studio employees learned to master as the scale of the post-*Avatar* box office came into focus. It starts early in a major movie's life cycle, when international distribution executives meet with Chinese film bureau officials to build buzz for the titles they think have the best chance of becoming blockbusters. In a presentation given to officials, these studio executives walk the film bureau through each movie's plot or stars. If the studio has secured an on-the-ground Chinese company to help market the movie or finance it, it makes sure to relay that crucial information, since it could give the title a leg up in the market. Each movie gets its own spin— perhaps the message of the movie about a superhero rallying troops and allies against an intergalactic enemy will resonate in a country where bureaucrats are expected to fall in line behind party leadership.

Studios have layers of Chinese bureaucracy to navigate before a movie appears on-screen. Officials assess the movie's economic prospects, as well as any censorship issues. To prepare for the examination, a studio's China-based office runs reconnaissance on the censors' reactions. Did anyone have a guess as to why Sony's reboot of *Ghostbusters* wasn't allowed in? (Ghosts and other supernatural entities aren't permitted on-screen.) How many minutes of gore had Fox removed from the *X-Men* spinoff *Logan?* (Fourteen.) What had producers of *Pixels* done about that scene in which the Great Wall gets destroyed? (The Taj Mahal was blown up instead.) Despite the published set of rules, the film bureau didn't need to worry about consistency with its decisions, since the requested cuts are never publicized or formalized. With little feedback from the censors, studios are trapped in a guessing game. Warner Bros. tried three times to get its 2017 Stephen King adaptation *It*, about a sewer-dwelling killer clown called Pennywise, into China. The studio recut the film—twice—and even added text that ran ahead of the movie explaining the clown to be an alien from outer space, hoping this would avoid tripping up the country's no-ghost rule. It still didn't convince censors to let *It* in.

Very few directors in Hollywood have the power to question the studio's response to censor requests. Christopher Nolan is one exception. In 2008 his blockbuster *The Dark Knight* was up for release in China but would first need to cut dialogue that pertained to a subplot involving a Chinese mobster. Nolan refused, saying his movie and its plot must be preserved. The movie never did cross China's borders, likely costing the studio tens of millions of dollars.

Tricks of the trade have emerged over the years. Occasionally studios will substitute softer lines of subtitled dialogue in the version sent to censors and hope no one notices the difference when the movie ultimately comes out. A studio's recent record at the Chinese box office may work in its favor; Disney is widely known to get the best release dates and most consistent approvals. Politics can also work against a studio's chances: when tensions are high between China and Japan, Sony executives remove their company's logo from the opening credits of a film before it screens for the board. Another psychological ploy: leaving more offending material in the movie than the studio expects to get past the bureau so the censors focus on cutting the obvious scenes or details and unwittingly preserve other parts of the movie.

If Chinese citizens view most movies as two-hour diversions, Chinese censors view them as two-hour threats—most of the time. It might sound like a fun job, getting to see some of the movies the rest of China cannot, but censors often complain to friends that it can be a bit of a drag. They can zone out during parts of a movie they know won't be a problem.

Occasionally things do go wrong, as they did with Quentin Tarantino's *Django Unchained*. The director's 2012 historical drama starred Jamie Foxx as a slave who becomes a bounty hunter—hardly the kind of movie that typically passes the Chinese censors. Its studio, Sony Pictures, wanted to get it through to build credibility with other directors, figuring that if they could get Tarantino past the censors in Beijing, they could make a case to others that their movies would gain entry. Their campaign started early, when they hosted an official from China Film Group on the movie's plantation set in Louisiana.

When it came time to submit a cut for censorship, executives trimmed about ninety seconds from the version of *Django Unchained* sent to the board, sanitizing some of the violence and trimming a scene in which Foxx hangs upside down in a barn, completely nude. The lighting on the scene is dark, making it difficult to see more than his naked silhouette. This required some intense scrutiny from the distribution executives, who spent hours hunched over a laptop examining Foxx's body frame by frame, compiling a list of time codes where the outline grew too detailed. Knowing the hands-on Tarantino would revolt against any major changes being made to his movie, the executives kept most of the edits a secret.

The movie was, miraculously, approved for release, after Tarantino agreed to darken the color of the blood to make the movie's gore appear less gratuitous. About eight hundred screenings of it had gone off without a hitch in its first weekend when a call came in to Sony that the movie was being pulled from theaters immediately. This was not another case of Chinese officials trying to make way for a Confucius biopic. An associate of a Communist Party official had seen the movie, they explained, and sworn she could see Jamie Foxx's penis in the barn scene. She called her husband, who had the film bureau's decision reversed. The Sony executives cutting the movie had parsed the barn scene over and over again. Nonetheless they'd have to go back to the editing room and take more seconds from the movie, losing precious time as they did. By the time *Django Unchained* returned to theaters, a pirated version of the movie had proliferated through the country and killed any theatrical market it had.

WORD THAT CHINA'S CENSORSHIP BOARD did not approve movies about time travel or ghosts was distressing to screenwriter Ryan Condal, who was writing a script about a time-traveling ghost. It was 2011, and Condal was a working writer in Hollywood who had made his name on some screenplays that were sold but never produced. Executives at the Legendary production company, seeing the growing box office, wanted to produce "Western-made movies that have a distinct cultural resonance in China" and hired Condal for the job. He soon became a case study in the absurd lengths Hollywood writers would go to in trying to read the minds of Chinese censors.

Condal started by finding a centuries-old book to update: Sun Tzu's *The Art of War*, the fifth-century BC military strategy guide that has since been adopted as a self-help and business bible. The camera opens on a young Sun Tzu: talented but a hothead. Condal loved studying Roman history, so he had Sun Tzu cameo in the Julius Caesar era, advising Caesar on invading Gaul. The movie showed his immortal Sun Tzu serving multiple Roman emperors, making it clear he had a major, previously unknown hand in several major battles throughout history—a war-tourist Forrest Gump. Rather than follow white characters into China, Condal's script would take the Chinese character out of China. More than that, Condal would make the Chinese character a leader among the Europeans.

Then the script notes started coming in from executives learning on the fly what kinds of stories weren't getting past the Chinese censors. "It can't feel like time travel," he was told. He overhauled the script, killing off Sun Tzu at the beginning of the film so he is then brought back by the gods to help mortals avoid war. This new version emphasized the fact that the Chinese character here was the wise one, and the West was full of buffoons who didn't listen to him. *They're going to love this thing*, Condal thought to himself.

Then he was sent a list of guidelines on what doesn't pass Chinese censorship. It didn't look like an official document, more a list of terms that had been drafted by someone in Hollywood interpreting what China wanted. Time travel was on there, but he'd avoided that problem. Then Condal read that ghosts weren't allowed, either. He made more changes to emphasize that Sun Tzu had come back to life and was a living, breathing form.

An outsider might assume the Chinese censorship board would be more accommodating to a screenplay that focused on their country's military hero, but placing Sun Tzu in a fantasy film might also anger officials unhappy to see any appropriation of their cultural touchstones. Hoping for the best wasn't an option when more than $100 million was about to be spent on a movie that would lose money if it didn't get into China. As China's box office got baked into Hollywood balance sheets, studio executives became as risk averse as the Chinese bureaucrats who weigh whether it's worth it to let a questionable movie into the country.

Condal's movie went nowhere. If a plot detail has even a small chance of taking the China market off the table for an expensive project that needs it to turn a profit, why risk it at all?

CHINA'S ALLERGY TO SUPERNATURAL THEMES can cause the most confusion among studio executives. When Warner Bros. was about to release *Harry Potter and the Sorcerer's Stone*, the studio knew that getting the first movie into China would clear the way for the other installments. It also knew that wizards and sorcery made the censors nervous, adjacent as both were to the supernatural elements they routinely shunned.

The censors watched the movie. It's fine to screen in China, they told executives, so long as Warner Bros. did one thing: strip the movie of references to the words *wizard* and *sorcerer*. This is not the easiest request for a movie about a wizard called *Harry Potter and the Sorcerer's Stone*. The British title of the book had been *Harry Potter and the Philosopher's Stone*, but *philosopher* was considered discouragingly highbrow for American audiences. The studio and the censors settled on a third interpretation for China, where Harry Potter would be described as having more earthly powers when the film's dialogue was dubbed. When the evil, soul-sucking

Dementors were introduced later on in the series, their screen time would be cut because they were considered too disturbing for Chinese audiences.

The country's resistance to on-screen acknowledgment of homosexuality has clashed with Hollywood's elevation of such stories. More than a decade after censorship of Ang Lee's Oscar acceptance speech for *Brokeback Mountain*, attitudes had not evolved by the time *Bohemian Rhapsody*, about the rock band Queen, premiered. The movie had already been criticized by Western audiences for focusing more on Mercury's brief relationship with a woman than on his long relationships with men. The U.S. version of the movie had put him back in the closet for most of the film. China's version locked the door. Before the movie was released in China, three minutes of *Bohemian Rhapsody* were removed at Chinese censors' request. Those three minutes included a scene in which Mercury comes out to his fiancée, and then another that introduces his male lover. At the moment that Mercury reveals he has AIDS, the audio on the film went out altogether. These moments added up to 2 percent of the movie, yet they removed entirely the representation of a gay character in the lead role.

Distribution executives performed a similar reframing on the Best Picture winner *Green Book* during a scene in which one of the main characters, a black pianist portrayed by Mahershala Ali, is discovered naked with another man in a YMCA. In the Chinese version, the shots tightened to focus on the actors' faces so it wasn't apparent that they were nude. In a way, this decision—to tighten the shot, limit the exposure—mirrors the Chinese attitude toward its own gay and lesbian citizens. While traveling in China, I've met with gay men who describe a relatively open life among their friends in the city, going to gay bars and texting in gay WeChat groups. But when I would ask whether their families knew they were gay, they would look at me as though it were crazy to think that was even a possibility. Still, the presence of gay people and gay-rights groups speaks to the disparity between the country the censors live in and the reality they want to portray on-screen.

Oftentimes the solution is to make the unseemly disappear when it's con-
venient. One summer in Shanghai, I tried to go to Lucca 390, a popular
gay bar, during Pride Week. When I arrived, I found it temporarily closed,
a common occurrence during a week when citizens might get some ideas.
A sign on the front door said the bar was shut down due to a utility issue,
but the notice's clunky English translation let slip an unintentional truth
that revealed the dynamic at work. The bar was closed, it said, due to an
issue of "power allocation."

FOR DECADES, HOLLYWOOD KEPT ITS movies as inoffensive as
China does today. The industry had become a favorite target of parents
and preachers in the midtwentieth century, so it recruited a moral arbi-
ter, someone with the virtuous rectitude of a Midwest mother and the
backbone of a Washington pol. They found their man in Will Hays.

Hays was an Indiana Protestant who knew the movies could be a morality tool as surely as Woodrow Wilson had known they could be a
political asset. A high-ranking Republican in his home state, Hays managed Warren G. Harding's successful presidential campaign before becoming postmaster general in the administration. Only one year later, he
was recruited to head the newly founded Motion Picture Producers and
Distributors of America, an industry group representing Hollywood's
major studios. If a postmaster general who didn't drink or smoke until
age twenty-one—because his mother had told him she'd give him $100
if he promised not to—seemed like an odd choice to helm Hollywood's
leading industry group, it was because the industry was intentionally casting against type, worried that celebrity scandals and agitation among religious authorities would spell the end of their business.

He was soon greeted by other constituents realizing the power of a
good or bad cinematic portrayal. The Yellow Cab Company asked Hays
to limit the number of taxis in cops-and-robbers movies, worried the
public might think criminals always escaped in their cars. The National

Billiard Association hated to see scuzzy poolrooms on-screen. The American Hotel Association didn't like movies that showed people smoking in bed. Teachers asked producers to stop portraying class-clown characters as stammering fools—impressionable children, they said, were imitating the characters and might develop a stutter. (Adults are sensitive to how entertainment plays with children in China as well. When the *High School Musical* franchise was taken to the country, writers had to find creative ways to incorporate musical numbers that did not take place in the classroom. The film bureau wanted kids to know that school is for studying, not jazz hands. The characters break out in song after the bell rings.)

Hays's main objective, though, was to eliminate "modern" or "pagan" elements from the movies, enlisting a reverend to help craft the rules that would define the limits of cinema for the next several decades and become his most lasting legacy: the Hays Code, an industry-wide set of guidelines that made every movie family-appropriate.

Under the Hays Code, profanity was out of the question—and *God*, *Lord*, and *Jesus Christ* permitted only if "used reverently." There would be no nudity, "inference of sex perversion," or on-screen use of illegal drugs. Women in labor had to smile through the ordeal. Romantic relationships between white and black characters did not exist on-screen. In short, "no picture shall be produced which will lower the moral standards of those who see it." Hays even suggested Rhett Butler's most famous line in *Gone with the Wind* be revised to "Frankly, my dear, I don't care." (Producer David O. Selznick refused and accepted a $5,000 fine for the transgression.)

In China, several of the top rules implemented by the film bureau concern preserving the reputation of the government, its leaders, and its history. The American instinct to censor movies of "pagan" elements in the twentieth century derived its rules from a religious conviction—Pope Pius XI thanked Hays on behalf of the Catholic Church for cleaning up the movies. The censorship of a country reveals its character—in this case, the different priorities of a Christian nation and a Communist one.

In the first year of the censorship program, sixty-seven plays or novels were blocked from cinematic adaptation by Hays's team due to inappropriate material. But then the number of problematic projects started to fall as Hollywood absorbed the rules and came to understand the limits of what writers could put in a script. Soon producers did the Hays committee's work for them, changing scripts ahead of submission.

"The best way to avoid censorship was to produce pictures that did not need censorship," Hays noted.

The Hays Code dissolved in the late 1960s, after provocative films like *Who's Afraid of Virginia Woolf?* forced new warnings for audiences and led to the creation of the movie-rating system still used today. When its enforcement fell, Hollywood filmmakers in the 1970s became known as the boundary pushers of American culture, the industry that said the unsayable.

WHEN ASKED ABOUT ACCEDING TO Chinese censors, Hollywood executives will often say they change movies for many foreign countries—and that's true. Yet none come with the economic leverage China does, or its ability to change not only the movies shown within its borders, but the ones made outside them. In fact, China's system of censorship follows a playbook established by another totalitarian regime that once mandated what audiences around the world saw and what Hollywood producers created, and continues a lineage of Hollywood acquiescence to the almighty market.

The troubling precedent to consider begins on a winter evening in December 1930, when a crowd gathered at a Berlin movie theater for an opening-night screening of *All Quiet on the Western Front*. In the U.S., the adaptation of Erich Maria Remarque's novel was a breakthrough in Hollywood sophistication and storytelling. In Germany, it was an indictment of the country's part in the Great War. No audience member watching this movie was unsure of its jaundiced view of recent history—with its cynical soldiers, lying lieutenants, and unvarnished acknowledgment that war is hell. But to the moviegoers assembled in Berlin that Friday night, the movie also dared to rebuke the central historical animus of their new leader, Adolf Hitler.

Brownshirts in the audience yelled as the film appeared on-screen. Pro-Hitler moviegoers assaulted Jews in the crowd. The projectionist soon gave up and the movie was stopped. Joseph Goebbels, a failed novelist a few years away from becoming the most famous propagandist of the twentieth century, addressed the crowd. Hollywood had come to Germany to sully its reputation, Goebbels told the faithful. This movie was an opening blow in a coming clash of ideals, and they would not stand for it. Then some Nazis in the crowd released stink bombs and mice into the auditorium.

By the time the crowd had dispersed from the aborted movie screening that December night, German officials had set into motion a system of censorship and coercion that for years would force Hollywood to trade moral qualms for market access, keeping the stories of vulnerable Jews and Europeans off-screen at the Nazis' request. It is an uneasy parallel to draw, but the Nazis' approach to regulating film following that 1930 screening bears alarming resemblance to the one China would adopt a half century later.

In the eyes of Germany's censorship board, *All Quiet on the Western Front* showed the world an unflattering portrayal of Germans, and allowing it to screen with no repercussions would convey a weak Germany. The choice was clear: the movie was banned. "Victory is ours!" shouted a Nazi-run newspaper.

Universal, the studio behind *All Quiet*, began scrubbing the film of any scene that might offend Germans. Eight months later, they resubmitted it. German censors approved this version, but only if Universal agreed to an extraordinary demand: the edited cut must be the version shown not only in Germany but in cinemas *around the world*. The Germans did not simply want their own people to think that their country

had an unblemished war record; it wanted the rest of the world to believe it, too. Moviegoers everywhere would see a sanitized version of *All
Quiet on the Western Front*—one in which the German soldiers weren't
dunked in mud so often and one missing the dialogue about the kaiser
causing the war. German consuls stationed in overseas offices went to
the theater to confirm Universal had kept its word.

In 1932 the German government, riding a wave of nationalist sentiment, introduced Article 15, a provision that gave Germany the right to
cancel distribution agreements with any studio that produced a film it
found offensive. It didn't matter if the offending film had shown in
Germany—if Nazis or German honor were disparaged on-screen anywhere,
the studio behind that movie could have its future releases banned from
Germany and German-occupied territories. The outsize reach of an Article 15 infraction gave the Nazis disproportionate power—power that
meant the party would rise without significant cinematic pushback from
the most powerful cultural force on earth.

Hitler had watched in frustration as Hollywood won the war for
hearts and minds. After assuming the chancellorship of Germany in
1933, Hitler ordered his Supreme Command to create Universum-Film
AG, a film company that produced propaganda movies that reflected
the values of the regime. The Reich's ownership stake in Universum-
Film AG was kept secret so audiences wouldn't receive its movies suspiciously. Hundreds of actors, directors, and producers joined its ranks.

Controlling imported films was just as crucial. German authorities
oversaw a quota system limiting the number of foreign releases allowed
into the country. German censors approved films only after screening for
"moral, political, and eugenic" infractions and kept a blacklist of Hollywood offenders whose projects would not be imported. Soon Hollywood
was making changes at the root level of production. After the German
backlash to *All Quiet on the Western Front*, Universal delayed production
on a sequel and Paramount scrapped a project about the sinking of the
Lusitania, an ocean liner taken down by a German U-boat in 1915.

Germany was also unique in the degree of its on-the-ground pressure campaigns. Georg Gyssling, by then a member of the Nazi Party for two years, moved to Los Angeles and became Hitler's ambassador to Hollywood, overseeing a currency system that rewarded good behavior and punished bad. He urged Warner Bros. to remove moments of German indignity from a POW film called *Captured!*, like when a German prisoner complained of thirst. Warner Bros. complied with the requested cuts, but Germany rejected subsequent movies for release anyway, including the musical *42nd Street*, which was expected to be a box-office smash in musical-loving Germany. The official reason, the censors said, was that the movie was "too leggy." (There are a lot of kick lines.) Yet when MGM canceled a screening of an anti-Nazi movie called *Are We Civilized?*, a dozen of its movies were approved for release in Germany a week later.

Gyssling looked for public examples, specifically protesting portrayals of World War I where Germans looked weak. Loud public protests taught everyone a lesson and convinced others to avoid anything incendiary. Eventually, studio executives took it upon themselves to volunteer changes to the censorship board. Could they substitute a different score for *Give Us This Night*, since the original was composed by a Jew? The director of *All Quiet on the Western Front* later directed *The General Died at Dawn*. When the latter film was rejected, Paramount offered to cut his name from the credits. On a 1938 adaptation of another Remarque book, *Three Comrades*, Louis B. Mayer himself looked at a political speech delivered in the script: "There's more to fight for—better than food— better than peace. Democracy—freedom—a new Germany! Isn't that worth fighting for?"

The studio chief's notes: "Delete references to 'democracy.'"

Such rules and accommodations did not register as bizarre—the German rigmarole for screening a movie was "no more or less onerous than the edicts handed down by the Chicago Board of Censors," as scholar Thomas Doherty writes. Countries were known for idiosyncratic demands. The British didn't like to see married couples sleeping in the same bed or to see the mistreatment of horses. The Chinese were sensitive to portrayals of the racial stereotypes common at that time. France had warned Warner Bros. against making a movie about a French penal colony. Making a movie that kept all of those customers happy wasn't kowtowing. It was business.

But no one in Chicago or France was screening films for reasons the Nazis were. Shirley Temple was beloved the world over, but one movie that showed her befriending a Native American boy demonstrated too much comingling of the races for German eyes. Chicago did not reject *Tarzan*, but German censors did, because its romance between Tarzan and Jane ran afoul of the Nazis' thoughts on racial purity and "the highest sense of responsibility in the selection of a husband," as the Propaganda Ministry ruled.

Even more crucially, no foreign market was exerting as much pressure on studio chiefs to avoid scripts altogether that would anger a foreign power, and the Hollywood aversion to ruffling feathers created a marketplace in which the only way to see a story about Nazis on-screen was through obscure documentaries or independent films. Much like China today, Germany had built a system of economic punishment for political crimes, one that combined vocal outcry, retaliatory tactics, and the preemptive obedience of Hollywood executives to keep certain stories off-screen. That is, any narrative that challenged their version of history, their national sovereignty, or their strength.

When *The Mad Dog of Europe*, among the first major attempts to dramatize Hitler's rise, was submitted for review at the U.S. Production Code Administration, the group advised against making the movie. The PCA explained its rationale, which ran counter to Goebbels's idea of cinema's role: "While it might serve a good purpose from a propaganda angle, it might likewise establish a bad precedent. The purpose of the screen, primarily, *is to entertain* and *not* to *propagandize*." Whereas Goebbels was trying to conscript his nation's film industry into making entertaining pro-Nazi propaganda, the American officials had prioritized keeping the

movies a conflict-free zone. More *42nd Street*, less *Mad Dog*. Behind the
scenes, Gyssling appears to have threatened studio executives and government officials, saying the release of *Mad Dog*—written by *Citizen Kane*
screenwriter Herman Mankiewicz—could lead to a ban in Germany of all
American films. Studio executives and Will Hays leaned on the film's
producers to abandon the project for the good of the industry, and the
movie, which would have been the first to tell the story of Hitler's perse-
cution of the Jews, was never made. The cancellation "occurred in the first
year of Hitler's rise to power," writes scholar Ben Urwand, "and it defined
the limits of American movies for the remainder of the decade."

STATESIDE CRITICISM OF DOING BUSINESS in Germany intensified
as the Nazis rose in power. Some studios had left Germany, but others
fell back on familiar defenses: Paramount claimed, "It is only logical for
us to do business wherever profitable as an obligation to our shareholders." MGM pled ignorance, too, saying it "will make pictures without re-
gard to politics and with only box office and entertainment in mind."
Those studios that continued working in Germany were subject to new
rules requiring overseas businesses to reinvest their profits locally. MGM
set up a loan business, lending money to companies in the German ar-
mament industry.

Gyssling, the Nazi ambassador to Hollywood, appeared to overplay
his hand, though, when he tried to stop an *All Quiet on the Western Front*
sequel called *The Road Back*. When Universal began preparing production of the film in 1936, Gyssling sent a letter to the sixty actors who
were to appear in the film, warning that their careers in Germany would
be over. It was a classic scare-the-monkeys ploy, and the entertainment
press, the anti-Nazi groups forming in Hollywood, and the State Department all protested the letter. *The Road Back* went into production
soon afterward, but with twenty-one cuts made in anticipation of any
German objection, including the sanitizing of an ending that went from

being about militarism in Germany to militarism around the world. Germany still kicked Universal out of the country as punishment.

After Kristallnacht in November 1938, Hollywood faced more stringent criticism for doing Germany's bidding. Hollywood's presence in Germany shrank but remained until mid-1940, when the studios still working there began a wholesale retreat. Geopolitics was only one reason for the departure. German box-office receipts were falling, and Hitler's war across the continent had taken several European markets out of distribution. "With all hope of profit gone, we can, at last, become properly indignant and raise our voices in shocked protest without any pecuniary regrets," said screenwriter and director William C. de Mille. And with much of Europe off the table, anti-Nazi movies that tapped into growing anti-Nazi sentiment in the U.S. seemed the better box-office bet. Newly unbound executives embraced a patriotic role, making movies that "sold the American way of life, not only to America but to the entire world," as Fox executive Darryl Zanuck said when he testified before Congress in 1941. People in the chamber applauded at the speech.

FOR CHINA, CENSORSHIP WAS A prerequisite to doing business, and the foundation upon which its larger soft-power ambitions were built. But it would need to grow in stature before it could grow in influence. In 2011 only three years removed from the Beijing Olympics, which had served as a coming-out party on the global stage, Chinese leaders signaled just how seriously they would take their entertainment ambitions by placing cultural industries in their twelfth five-year plan.

No document provided the blueprint for China's economic priorities like the five-year plan. The first Five-Year Plan of the Chinese Communist Party, introduced in 1953 as the initial outline of the country's economic and political priorities, signaled the incredible might of a Chinese government with a mission. China's industrial businesses were essentially nonexistent, but then seemingly overnight production in China grew about 10 percent a year as investors and authorities focused on certain sectors in lockstep. Under five-year-plan outlines, China made textiles, radios, coal, steel and oil, nuclear missiles, and jet fighters. The twelfth five-year plan was the first of the government agendas to mention entertainment. China wanted to produce something else.

A goal was set: culture would be a "pillar industry" of China by 2015, meaning it would account for at least 5 percent of China's annual gross domestic product. To hit its mark, China's culture and entertainment industries would need to grow more than 15 percent per year through 2015. Contrasted with the anything-goes alchemy that had characterized the storytelling of *Kung Fu Panda* and other Hollywood imports, it was an explicitly straightforward strategy that treated a highly subjective industry with the metrics and calculation once afforded textiles and coal.

One year later, China's five-year plan coincided perfectly with a Hollywood desire to milk the market for all it was worth. Greg Frazier, an MPAA official, had been working for years on a case before the WTO that accused China of breaking trade rules by restricting foreign media. Negotiations to settle the case had dragged on, slowing Hollywood's effort to expand access to the market. Studios were hoping to boost the number of movies allowed into China beyond twenty a year but also, more important, get a larger share of ticket sales than the measly 13 percent negotiated in the *Fugitive* days. The terms that had been grudgingly accepted in the mid-1990s, when the focus was also on combating piracy, were woefully out of date now that the market was among the top five in the world.

In February 2012, Frazier had his shot when Xi Jinping, then his nation's vice president and heir apparent, arrived in the U.S. Prior to his arrival, President Barack Obama sent Chinese premier Hu Jintao a letter outlining "deliverables" the two men should work on during the trip. Settling the film-agreement dispute was among them, and Obama's letter reignited settlement talks.

The ultimate breakthrough came at a hotel in downtown Los Angeles, where Xi met with Vice President Joseph Biden during an afternoon of deal signing and photo ops. At one point, Xi and Biden found a quiet moment with Jeffrey Katzenberg, who was by now a Zelig in anything related to China and Hollywood.

"You know, Mr. Vice President," Biden said to Xi, "I'm sure it's not lost on you: you're here in the home of Hollywood. I know this negotiation has been going on for a long time, about this movie quota, and we're coming to a deadline. It would be a matter of face for me if you and I did not resolve this while you're here."

Telling Xi it would be a matter of face-saving was a savvy tactic: now Xi would lose face if *he* couldn't deliver for Biden. The three men outlined the terms they wanted, Katzenberg serving as a de facto representative for Hollywood—or at least knowing to say, "Absolutely, Mr. Vice President" when Biden asked if the agreement sounded fair. Xi said he would call Beijing and get back to them. That evening, Biden and Katzenberg took Xi to a Los Angeles Lakers game at the Staples Center. Frazier had advised Katzenberg to press Xi to accept the improved conditions outlined in the negotiations: thirty-four movies a year, with 25 percent of sales flowing back to studios. While the three men watched the tipoff, Frazier joined a conference call with U.S. officials to go over an agreement that was reached that evening with those very terms.

In the eleven months between the twelfth five-year plan and the quota negotiations during Xi's visit, the chief motivations of China and Hollywood had merged with perfect timing. China's leaders wanted an entertainment industry that would support their new political rise, and Hollywood's executives wanted greater access to a market that would save their business and please their shareholders. Biden and Katzenberg were responding to the call of the markets, not realizing they were slotting into Xi's governmental mandate. Over the next decade, China's plans for its own cultural industry would fall into place as planned, with the help of an American entertainment business that could not believe its luck.

PART II

————— ★ ★ —————

SEVEN

Fakeistan

ollywood loves recycling. In the ruthless assessment of whether a movie will be a good investment, nothing comforts a studio executive more than something that's worked before. Whether it's an old TV show, an old movie, or even a historical figure like Abraham Lincoln, "preexisting IP," or intellectual property, is the industry's favorite crutch.

Metro-Goldwyn-Mayer Inc. desperately needed to retreat to the familiar in 2008. The studio was fending off bankruptcy, and this was not the time to try something risky. It was time to look through the studio's most prized asset—a library of decades of cinema classics—and see what could be remade. Eighties nostalgia was hot, with versions of *Clash of the Titans* and *The A-Team* being resurrected, so MGM found two of its own. The musical *Fame* was one. *Red Dawn* was the other.

The original *Red Dawn* had starred Charlie Sheen and Patrick Swayze as two members of a vigilante band of teenagers who, between practices for their football team, the Wolverines, see their hometown invaded by

Communist forces assembled from the Soviet Union, Nicaragua, and Cuba. The high school students grab hunting rifles and fashion home-made bombs. In another transfer of Reaganism to the screen, the Cold War of the 1980s had created a market for thrillers casting Soviets as the evil-empire threat to America. Across the multiplex around the same time, Rocky boxed a Soviet fighter named Drago and Rambo mowed down Communist soldiers. *Red Dawn* brought the Cold War battle even closer to home by placing it in the Michigan suburbs, where patriotic teenagers furiously fought back.

Red Dawn was a hit, its premise connecting with the teenage audiences of the 1980s. When George W. Bush sent troops to hunt for Saddam Hussein in the months following the invasion of Iraq, they did so on a mission called Operation Red Dawn in homage to the film, then nineteen years old. MGM hoped to tap into that resonance when it dusted off the original and asked screenwriters how they would handle a remake. A new *Red Dawn* wasn't going to save the studio, but it could be—in Hollywood's baseball-inspired lingo—a solid double.

MGM even found a writer uncannily suited to the job. In 2008, Jeremy Passmore was an up-and-coming screenwriter, but in the 1980s he'd been one of those teenagers who caught *Red Dawn* at a sleepover. Passmore grew up in a family of liberals in Bellingham, Washington, but the movie about unapologetically patriotic teens appealed to him in a surprising way. When his friend's dad watched the on-screen murder of a teenager found to be conspiring with the Soviets, Passmore was struck when he heard the adult remark, "Yep. That's what we do to traitors." Passmore was a student who exasperated his teachers by constantly asking, "What if?" in class, and here was the ultimate "what if?" scenario: What if the U.S. got knocked on its ass by another superpower?

Many years later, *Red Dawn* was jostling around in Passmore's head when he moved to Los Angeles with a mathematics degree and aspirations to make it in the movie business. The U.S. had just invaded Iraq, and he wrote a script inspired by the government's misleading campaign

on weapons of mass destruction—proof, as he saw it, of the U.S. government's comfort with lying to the public. In his vigilante story, a community in the Pacific Northwest is quarantined after a viral outbreak
has killed the adults but allowed the kids to survive. When the surviving minors are told to report to the high school for vaccinations against
the virus, they discover that the mercenary defense firm Blackwater—a
top public enemy of liberals during the Iraq War—is planning to kill
them on behalf of the U.S. government, forcing them to band together
and fight back, *Red Dawn* style. Passmore's first draft even paid tribute
to his sleepover favorite.

"Wolverines!" one character shouts in an effort to rally his crew. His
friends are confused by the outburst. "Haven't you seen *Red Dawn?*" he
asks them.

Passmore's story was an R-rated script full of violence that was "uniquely
mistimed," he said. Hollywood refrained from such narratives in the years
after the Columbine school shooting, and the hit *Hunger Games* had not
yet acclimated audiences to narratives about kids killing kids. Nonetheless, everyone in Hollywood needs a brand, and Passmore became known
as the "kids with guns guy."

Then MGM asked Passmore to tackle *Red Dawn*, a classic of the
vigilante-kids genre. But there was the question of the villain. One thing
was clear: you couldn't remake *Red Dawn* with Russia as the invading
enemy, since that country's threat to the U.S. was over. Political sensitivities had struck most depictions of Middle Eastern terrorists since the
September 11 attacks (and few would buy an all-out invasion by Al-
Qaeda into the U.S.). Germany may have loomed large in World War II
but was now a part of the friendly European Union alliance. Japan was
passé.

Who's the villain? Passmore asked the producers.

We're thinking China, they said.

It was the obvious choice. MGM was planning to release *Red Dawn*
in the wake of a 2008 recession that shook faith in the American economy,

a time of high unemployment and a trillion-dollar deficit. China, on the other hand, had just hosted the world at the Beijing Olympics. Chinese manufacturers were building factories in the U.S., a development that was once unthinkable to most Americans. In a Pew Global Research Center poll conducted in 2010, about 47 percent of respondents said they thought China's growing economy was bad for the U.S.; nearly 80 percent said the country's modernizing military was a threat. The drumbeat of those Olympic Games performers echoed in such thoughts, disrupting America's assumption that it was and would always be the world's unimpeachable superpower.

It was a chance for *Red Dawn* to perform a function that many movies, from *Invasion of the Body Snatchers* to *Rosemary's Baby*, had before: to reflect subconscious anxieties back to audiences as popular entertainment. The studio had the concept, the writer, and the novel update. It could have been, against the B-movie odds, a movie of its time in its evocation of American concerns about the viability of the empire. Instead it became a movie of its time for a different reason—one that proved the power of China's booming box office and taught Hollywood what it must do to maintain access to it.

As with most major studio releases, MGM had asked several screenwriters for their ideas on the film. Carl Ellsworth, a journeyman screenwriter who had recently had success with the thriller *Disturbia*, was also brought on board.

Ellsworth had one condition: "I don't want to do Fakeistan invading the U.S.," he told MGM executives. The only country with a military sophisticated enough to mount a physical invasion of the U.S. is China, he told them. Great, the executives replied. That's what we were thinking.

Ellsworth had a friend with connections at the Pentagon, so he went to DC for inspiration. After turning over his cell phone to prevent foreign surveillance of the meeting, Ellsworth outlined his new *Red Dawn*: China attacks Taiwan, forcing a U.S. response. China dumps U.S. debt unannounced, sending the U.S. economy into a tailspin. Chinese paratroopers land on suburban lawns and Chinese generals take over city squares.

Ellsworth felt insecure describing this Hollywood fantasy of Chinese war games to real-world generals. But his schlocky scenario was met with the silence of recognition.

"No one ever said, 'That's ridiculous. That would never happen,'" he said.

Passmore, sticking to his "kids with guns" persona, went all out and even featured scenes of a teenage suicide bomber. Ellsworth, humbled by his Pentagon visit, grounded his plot in the real-life ramifications that could come with a newly aggressive China. The *Red Dawn* scripts came in to MGM, each imagining a Chinese invasion of the U.S. Passmore went back to work at his temp job in quality-control testing for Deluxe, a video technology company, until one day the movie's producers got back in touch.

"You're coming in tomorrow," he was told. "And we're meeting with Tom Cruise at noon."

At this time, Cruise was not only the marquee star of *Risky Business*, *Jerry Maguire*, and *Mission: Impossible*. He was also the head of United Artists, which had a deal with MGM that turned the A-list action star into another Hollywood executive giving notes on a script. Passmore, one day removed from his "survival job" at Deluxe, arrived to a small meeting room that included two producers, the director, Cruise, and Mary Parent, a longtime Hollywood executive serving as MGM's co-CEO. They would meet from noon to 5:00 p.m. for several days straight. Their task: to take the scripts and suture them into one.

Passmore arrived with a vision for *Red Dawn* that didn't shy away from the pessimistic reality of war and occupation—a chance to challenge moviegoers' ideas of U.S. hegemony in the guise of a silly action movie. Cruise dissected that vision line by line and translated it into a different language, one that Passmore soon understood as American cinematic justice.

In an early scene, Cruise pointed out, a minor character is shot and killed in the initial invasion. He's so minor that Passmore didn't give him a name. But Cruise zeroed in on the man. Passmore should introduce a brief moment in the story before the man dies that makes it clear he's not a good person—someone who, if not deserving of death, isn't going to bum the audience out too much in his demise. They added a few shots earlier in the screenplay: The man is pulled into a truck to safety as the Chinese invade. But once inside the truck bed and safe himself, he's reluctant to pull others in after him. A few shots and some wordless action were added, and the unnamed character had an arc. More than that, Cruise taught him: the audience had the sense of justice they go to the movies to see reaffirmed.

Every such granular detail was debated except for one: no one asked if casting China as the invader was a bad idea. Cruise cautioned that the movie couldn't be racist, but even that remark was an aside. Cruise's *Mission: Impossible* sequels would eventually collect hundreds of millions of dollars in the country, but at this moment he wanted only to get the audience on the side of these patriotic teenagers telling China to back off.

In fact, the new *Red Dawn* script—put together by some combination of Passmore, Ellsworth, Parent, Cruise, and yet another uncredited screenwriter hired by the studio—would have gained the approval of the proud-patriot dad at Passmore's sleepover. The leader of the Wolverines is a high school quarterback and the son of a police officer. His girlfriend drives a Mustang. His older brother is an Iraq War veteran who downs Rolling Rock. Do you need to ask if an establishing shot shows an American flag flying outside their home?

Chris Hemsworth, a beefy Australian not yet known as the actor who plays Thor, and Josh Hutcherson, a diminutive heartthrob not yet known

as a lead in the *Hunger Games* franchise, were cast as two of the teen soldiers. The budget was set at $60 million. The movie was ready to shoot.

MGM EXECUTIVES WHO MIGHT HAVE remembered the studio's *Red
Corner* imbroglio had left years earlier. But before long, the studio had a
sequel of the worst kind on its hands. When photos from the *Red Dawn*
set leaked and spread throughout China, the country's state-run newspapers got to work trashing a movie that their readers would likely never see.

"Tempers here will probably explode like kernels of movie house
popcorn" when it comes out, *China Daily* wrote in an April 2010 editorial, calling it a "ticking time bomb." Once again, Chinese officials considered a Hollywood movie to be an interference in their internal affairs,
and their loud protests were turning MGM into a very public example
for other studios watching.

MGM executives quietly told crew members they could take their
names off the *Red Dawn* credits if they feared retaliation by China. One
editor whose wife was Chinese took the offer. He was worried about her
family being targeted in the mainland because he'd worked on the film.

Chinese critics were only one issue facing MGM executives at the
time. The studio had filed for bankruptcy protection during the filming
of *Red Dawn*, and the studio was paying about $300 million in annual
interest on an outstanding $3.7 billion loan. Its chief executive was
ousted and replaced by a turnaround pro best known for leading Enron
after its implosion. To raise money, MGM sold off films sitting on the
shelf.

Universal Pictures and other studios came in to take a look at *Red
Dawn* and determine if they wanted to buy it for distribution. But something had changed between the moment Passmore was told to cast China
as the villain and when the movie was ready for release. Work on the
script had started in the summer of 2008, and filming wrapped in late

2009—days before *Avatar* would awaken Hollywood to China's economic potential. By the time editing finished in mid-2010, no Hollywood executive would touch a movie that turned their most important new customer into the villain, especially after China's early response. Yet if MGM held on to the movie and released it unchanged in the U.S., China could retaliate by refusing to show the studio's more lucrative James Bond movies in its market—a strategy straight from the *Kundun* and *Seven Years in Tibet* days of punishing a company however it could.

Those movies were never scheduled or considered for release in China; it was their very existence that threatened the other divisions of their studios and their parent companies. The same went for *Red Dawn*. If Universal, for instance, released a relatively small movie about teenagers fighting China, chances were the likes of its $250 million *Jurassic World*— a movie put into production on the promise of hundreds of millions of dollars in Chinese grosses—would get a second look by the film bureau in Beijing. When it's the *Jurassic World*–type movies that dominate a studio's balance sheet, free expression comes at a price. None of the potential buyers of *Red Dawn* wanted to take on the risk.

For the producers of *Red Dawn*, that meant the only solution was a drastic one: changing the enemy of the completed film.

It would not be China invading the U.S. in this *Red Dawn* remake, MGM executives decided, but North Korea. The movie was finished, but extensive editing would change every scene in the film depicting Chinese villains—from the expository montage to the teenagers' ultimate victory— to show the football players fighting North Korean troops. No actor would be recast; those who had filmed scenes as Chinese invaders would now just play North Korean soldiers.

Even these changes were risky. Were they putting themselves at risk with North Korea, too? one executive worried. Kim Jong-un was a big fan of the movies, and he might hear about it and cause a stink. But the movie had been shot with East Asian actors as the invaders, and options were running out—no one was going to buy a South Korean or Japanese invasion. North Korea was a real-world antagonist of the United States. And most important, Hollywood didn't sell tickets in North Korea.

Red Dawn went from being a B-movie update to a case study in the second form of censorship taking root at studios: anticipatory censorship. After numerous negotiations with censors and examples of the response China's leaders had to certain films, executives in Los Angeles had absorbed what would fly and what wouldn't in China. They had seen the fallout of scare-the-monkey moments like *Kundun*. Soon they had enough intelligence that they started doing the work themselves.

MGM NEEDED TO FIND A special-effects company that could pull this off. Once it did, the geopolitical crisis moved from the executive office to the side-by-side computer monitors of employees working in a two-story block of concrete on a residential street in the San Fernando Valley, next door to a Physicians Diagnostic Reference Library. Custom Film Effects was located on a road of worn-out Burbank bungalows, in a squat building with a blacked-out front door appropriate for a company Hollywood considers best kept hidden.

CFE's visual-effects team specialized in what workers there called the "oh shit" jobs: erasing floating boom mics from the shot, smoothing out the back acne of a shirtless action star, erasing underwear worn by Jessica Alba so it looks like she's fully nude. Under CFE's brush, askew wig lines disappeared. Splotchy makeup blended. When the director of *The Notebook* filmed a romantic scene in a rowboat over several days—only one of which had featured the rain needed for the full heart-swelling effect—the team at CFE took the dry-weather clips and digitally created fake rain to match. At CFE, footage became fantasy.

The work was called "hidden effects," the kind no audience member registers if it's done well. Most jobs at CFE were done in a week or two, delivered with nondisclosure agreements signed and no fingerprints to be found. The *Red Dawn* job immediately took over the office with its demands. Here was the ultimate "oh shit" job. Chinese flags appeared throughout the movie on trucks and on the arms of soldiers' uniforms. Chinese banners hung off the sides of buildings and Chinese propaganda posters were displayed on nearly every outside wall. Even the epaulets on the soldiers' uniforms had to be changed, since they were Chinese military medals and not North Korean ones.

"The flags are one nightmare unto themselves, and then there are all these subnightmares," said Jamie Baxter, the lead CFE illustrator.

The difficulty was not just in the sheer number of frames that had to be changed. Flags on-screen are not static images; they wave in the wind. Flags on arm patches shift when the actor's arm moves, creating a complex interplay of shadows that registers as movement to the human eye. This would not be a copy-paste operation of swapping in one nation's flag for another. It would require erasing the Chinese flag and painting the North Korean one in its place, changing it frame by frame so its movement registered as realistic. From a collection of cubicles in small offices darkened by window shades so they could better see their computer screens, the workers dragged their mouses across the footage frame by frame until China's red-and-yellow stars were replaced with North Korea's red, white, and blue horizontal stripes. China was out of the picture.

Baxter led the effort, arriving each day after a ninety-minute commute to an office that looked like any nine-to-five routine: worn mouse pads, packed lunches, Post-it notes attached to cubicle walls, souvenir liquor bottles balanced atop computer monitors. He was an Ohio native who'd moved to Los Angeles to be an illustrator. Baxter's boss, Adam Gass, had managed a limousine service before coming to Los Angeles. Now they were key players in an international incident.

To Baxter, the whole North Korean mess felt like a waste of money. Wouldn't the effort be better spent on making it a better story? *Whatever*, he thought. At the time, he was already putting in extra hours to make money for his new wife and stepson.

I'm a cog, he thought to himself. A cog charging overtime.

The whole thing took Baxter and his colleagues two months. When the revised movie was turned over to MGM, CFE was paid $1 million and didn't take a credit.

CHANGING *RED DAWN'S* VILLAINS REQUIRED more than just cosmetic swaps at CFE. That opening montage about China invading the U.S. because of Taiwan and debt obligations had to be excised from the film, and new lines of dialogue would need to explain that it was North Korea invading and not China.

"This is the most ridiculous thing I've ever heard in my life," Ellsworth told executives when they informed him of the plan.

He'd written the film only after being told it wouldn't be a "Fakeistan" plot. China invading the U.S. was already farfetched but not crazy—his meeting at the Pentagon had taught him that. But North Korea was a bridge too far.

Hollywood was losing its balls, he thought. *Red Dawn* wasn't Truffaut or even Spielberg, but this was one country censoring another country's art. What had happened to freedom of expression? Was anyone going to speak up here? Would he?

Then Ellsworth started to weigh his own financial concerns. The movie's release meant a cash payment for him, followed by residuals for DVD sales and cable-TV deals. He'd live off those checks for a while, supporting his wife and two kids. And it was in his best interest to be an agreeable writer, not a difficult one, if he wanted to keep working. Moral outrage over the decision wasn't going to do him any good. So he went in to help salvage the movie.

Sitting in the producers' offices off Sunset Boulevard, Passmore and Ellsworth shoehorned as much logic as they could into this new version of *Red Dawn*. The opening sequence went away, replaced by generic news reports of geopolitical buzzwords: Markets! Depression! Cyberattacks! The invading soldiers' leader, Kim Jong-un, was introduced in a montage of North Korean military parades showing soldiers marching in lockstep.

Ellsworth and Passmore added lines that alluded to a plot involving more countries than just North Korea, a detail they thought made it somewhat more believable. Hemsworth and the other actors recorded these new lines, one of which sounds like the writers channeling their own frustration into the characters.

> MATT ECKERT
> North Korea? It doesn't make any sense.

Audiences didn't think so, either. The revamped *Red Dawn* was purchased by FilmDistrict, a small company with no business in China, and came out in November 2012. The movie made about $45 million at the U.S. box office—not a bomb, but certainly not enough to recoup MGM's investment. Still, it was a crisis averted, better than the losses MGM might have realized if it had released the movie itself and faced a retaliation that kept its bigger, more expensive movies out of Chinese theaters. The story of *Red Dawn* spread throughout the studio lots, a lesson immediately absorbed by everyone working on Hollywood's biggest productions.

The *Red Dawn* revamping came at the start of a new decade for the industry and China, one of increased entanglement. China had a box office built up since the early 1990s that demanded attention, but any partnership would soon be complicated by clashing values and motives from both countries. By the time of its release, studios had employees on the ground who could explain what topics or themes to avoid. Studio chiefs had heard of the box-office losses associated with movies that didn't get onto Chinese screens and ingested the editing changes required for others. They realized it was better to present China's censors with acceptable movies rather than rush to address their concerns after the fact—

preemptive obedience that could avert a repeat of what MGM had experienced.

When *Red Dawn* hit theaters, critics cited the villain switch in their critical pans of the movie—often noting, to Ellsworth's frustration, how implausible the story now was. But the public response to MGM's decision was surprisingly muted. Among the few constituents to criticize MGM's decision at the time were Michigan militia members who loved the original film. They called the changes a "copout."

It was a bigger story in China, where state-run publications bragged about MGM's panicked edits. It was a movie most Chinese citizens would never see, and yet it had been changed at their government's behest. One state-run outlet reminded readers that the edits came "without a single word from Chinese authorities."

EIGHT

Transformed

While *Red Dawn* and *World War Z* were teaching Hollywood what to remove from a movie to avoid angering China, the revenue opportunities there were prompting producers to take this appeasement strategy one step further. After China was stripped from movies where its presence or portrayal could pose a problem, producers started asking a recurring question each time a new idea was pitched: How can we work China into this?

With Chinese box-office riches in mind, they began stuffing characters, scenes, and products they thought would appeal to Chinese audiences into their films. A Chinese city, actress, or energy drink, which producers referred to as "Chinese elements," became selling points for a film. More appeal, more box office, the thinking went, and it made sense, since sizable returns were no longer the *Avatar* exception. By 2012, they were becoming the norm. At Sony, *Skyfall*—absent its dead Chinese security guard—made $59 million in China. At Disney, *The Avengers* made

$86 million. At Warner Bros., *The Hobbit* made $50 million. At Fox, an *Ice Age* sequel made $68 million. At Universal, *Battleship* made $48 million.

Michael Bay wanted to share in the bounty. As the director of Paramount Pictures' biggest franchise, *Transformers*, he was responsible for the only series the studio had that could go head to head with the Avengers and Spidermen of the world. By the time he directed the first one in 2007, Bay was already known for unabashed patriotic fireworks (*Pearl Harbor*) and destroying large portions of Planet Earth (*Armageddon*). Now he had in his hands a case study of Hollywood's new franchise strategy.

The Transformers toys manufactured by Hasbro enjoyed a heyday in the 1980s as a Japanese cartoon embraced by young boys drawn to its ingenious combination of cars and robots. Transformers toys raced on carpets like Hot Wheels but had car doors and hoods that flipped open to reveal a second configuration of a robot hidden inside the car. These robot-cars were members of dueling robot armies; the heroes were led by an alien sentinel called Optimus Prime. For Paramount, the movie was a chance to hook original Transformers fans, then in their twenties, and bring on younger kids new to the franchise. They'd all buy tickets, they'd all buy toys, and they'd all ride the Transformers attractions coming to amusement parks—a franchise trifecta.

Trolling the toy aisle for inspiration proved profitable. *Transformers* was the third-highest-grossing movie of 2007, at $319 million. It collected an additional $390 million abroad—with a respectable $36 million coming in from China. Then the sequel machine started up, and *Transformers: Revenge of the Fallen* came two years later: $402 million in the U.S., $434 million abroad—including $66 million from China. *Transformers: Dark of the Moon* followed that—a dip domestically, with $352 million, but a huge boost abroad: $771 million. Of that total, an eye-popping $165 million came from China, nearly tripling its predecessor's performance. Chinese audiences had been showing up to see the special-effects spectacles that Hollywood specialized in, but *Transformers* struck a deeper chord: the original *Transformers* cartoon had been one of the few imported entertainment options available in the country in the 1980s. "These are our superheroes," middle-aged Chinese men would tell Bay.

It was easy to see where the trajectory of the franchise needed to go, as Americans grew fatigued but more and more Chinese moviegoers kept showing up. For Bay, preserving that Chinese box-office growth was essential to his bottom line. His contract stipulated that he received a percentage of all ticket sales, and China's box office was necessary for it to cross the symbolically important $1 billion mark.

He had reason to wonder whether the country would allow it to happen. Though the grosses were rising, China was not making it easy to export a movie and watch the money roll in. In addition to blacking out popular moviegoing seasons and abruptly pulling top-performing titles from screens, officials' protectionist measures included "stacking" Hollywood movies atop one another, releasing them on the same day so they cannibalized one another's grosses. It appeared to be yet another ploy that ensured that Hollywood movies never accounted for more than half the country's annual grosses and therefore that it never looked to the world as though Chinese citizens preferred Western entertainment over their country's own.

If China decided his next *Transformers* movie—to be called *Age of Extinction*—would open on top of another major Hollywood release, it would inevitably underperform relative to the last installment. Distribution executives had learned the consequences of this trick when two of Hollywood's biggest releases in 2012, *The Amazing Spider-Man* and *The Dark Knight Rises*, were both to be released in China on August 28, 2012. In the U.S., studios had given a three-week buffer between the two films. The China office of Warner Bros., which released *The Dark Knight Rises*, hurriedly paid a local entertainment blogger to trash Sony's *Spider-Man* ahead of their simultaneous release. When Sony discovered the deal, representatives visited the blogger with an ultimatum: retract the *Spider-Man* criticism or be outed as a compromised outlet. A rave of the movie was published soon after, but it didn't move the needle. *The Dark Knight Rises* grossed $53 million in China, slightly ahead of its Australian showing but behind the United Kingdom. *Spider-Man* collected $48 million. Both movies trailed other Hollywood imports that they were expected to outperform. It was a "who, us?" strategy that Chinese officials could explain as a simple coincidence.

Rob Moore, then Paramount's vice chairman, shared Bay's concern. Moore had a reputation as an entertainment executive drawn to the industry not by a love of the movies but by a love of power, and he was such a micromanager on the Paramount lot that colleagues joked that he even valeted cars. His studio was struggling, and Moore thought that an edge in China might give Paramount an advantage among the six major studios in Los Angeles. Some of his counterparts still treated the Chinese box office as found money they need not chase too hard. But Moore reasoned that the makers of any movie with a budget of $80 million or greater—that is, any movie that was a priority for the studio—should not only avoid creative choices that jeopardized a theatrical run there but also consider making overt choices that could draw in bigger Chinese audiences.

Transformers was the best chance he had. Paramount, once known for producing Hollywood classics like *The Godfather* and *Chinatown*, was withering as a division of Viacom Inc., a media conglomerate that also included movie theaters, Nickelodeon, Comedy Central, and MTV. Paramount was a crown jewel in that portfolio, given its pedigree. The lot off Melrose Avenue felt like old Hollywood, with its gated entrance and sun-soaked sound stages. Like the lead character from another one of its most famous movies, *Sunset Boulevard*, the studio was still trading on its glory days. *Transformers* was a case study in the movies that now dominated studio strategy, a series based on a toy that was one of the few billion-dollar assets Paramount had to offer to the corporate overlords.

Moore needed to keep the franchise upswing going—a bigger world-wide gross with each installment. He also needed to keep his director happy. Together, the men would devise a strategy for *Transformers* to hold special appeal for Chinese audiences and authorities.

If *Red Dawn* was the extreme example of a studio anticipating China's concerns and removing parts of a movie that might anger officials, *Transformers* became the opposite: a kind of reverse censorship in which a studio would stuff as many "Chinese elements" into a script as possible in the hope that it would appeal to bureaucrats and audiences there. For the first time since Hollywood's founding, creative decisions at the root level of moviemaking—casting, story lines, and dialogue—were being made with China, not America, first in mind. Audiences watching outside China barely registered the subtle ways that the tastes of moviegoers thousands of miles away were changing the American blockbuster. The quota deal had significantly increased the amount of money a studio could expect to generate in China but also flooded the market with more titles, making it all the more important to stand out in a competitive field. Whereas there had once been twenty movie slots split among the studios, now there were up to thirty-four. Not everyone could get out with a guaranteed good performance. Furthermore, Chinese releases were pulling in audiences on their own, forcing Hollywood executives to acknowledge they didn't have a monopoly on the tastes of the country's moviegoers. The years following the 2012 film-quota expansion were marked by trial-and-error attempts across Hollywood to secure those ticket sales. No strategy was too silly.

BEFORE A MOVIE GOES into production, top-ranking studio executives gather for their most important task: the "green light" meeting. Finances for the project are scrutinized—not only the budget required to make the film but also what accountants can expect it to gross in every major market, based on similar movies that have come before.

These projections are later used to judge whether the movie succeeded or failed—and in the eyes of corporate parents, whether the executive who approved it with such finances in mind made a good call. For movies with large budgets, like *Transformers*, the expected Chinese box-office gross is usually included, even if its release in China isn't guaranteed until the movie is completed and approved by Chinese censors.

What Moore needed more than anything, then, was certainty— certainty that the movie would be released in China and certainty that its release date would be optimal. Once Paramount executives had as much of a guarantee as was possible that their movie would get into China on a preferred date, they could begin pursuing partnerships and deals that boosted their chances of drawing millions of Chinese moviegoers to the theater. Without a guaranteed release date, it became difficult for studios to secure tie-in deals to splash movie characters onto concessions-stand cups or manufacture Happy Meal toys. There was only one place to go that would promise such certainty.

In a massive meeting room near the Forbidden City, Moore, vice chairman of Paramount Pictures, sat next to Tong Gang, the vice minister of the State Administration of Radio, Film, and Television of the People's Republic of China. The rest of the *Transformers* team filled one side of the table and a row of more Chinese officials lined the other. The Chinese officials had already read the script and listened through translators as Bay gave more detail on the plot of his fourth *Transformers*. They had heard of the movie's hero, Cade Yeager, an overprotective Texas dad who tinkered in his garage and policed the length of his daughter's shorts until one day he acquired a beat-up pickup truck that was actually Optimus Prime and became a soldier in an intergalactic war.

Bay hadn't even outlined how this purchase dragged Yeager into the robot war—or even how the movie's action would shift to China in the second half—when the officials cut him off. They had heard enough and wanted a deal. Their enthusiasm was about not only the plot, Moore realized, but also the benefits accrued to both sides if a deal came together. The success of previous installments made it an economic no-brainer. *Age of Extinction* would not be an official coproduction between the two countries but a new model that afforded Paramount perks in exchange for filming in China and signing partnerships with Chinese companies.

There was only one thing standing in the way of final approval. There was a scene toward the end of the film when Hong Kong is getting demolished in robot warfare. The heroes are down when Optimus Prime and the Americans arrive to save the day in the nick of time. The movie would be better, the film bureau said, if China's good guys showed up first instead. Beijing, and not the U.S., would rush to rescue Hong Kong.

This never happens, Moore thought to himself. From *The Day the Earth Stood Still* to *War of the Worlds*, American screenwriters have made sure Americans are called in no matter where first contact is made or the giant robots have landed. But why did that have to be the case here? he considered. The Beijing fighter jets would be physically closer to Hong Kong, for one thing.

No one watching the movie will be like, "What just happened?" Moore thought to himself. For the people he wanted to do business with, he sensed it was about "showing that image—that there are other countries that care about protecting you." That was more important to China's leaders than a slight tweak in a script was to him, especially one that made logical sense. New dialogue was written, a scene was added, and Paramount got its release date.

Sensitivities about Hollywood's portrayal of China's military had been brewing. While *Age of Extinction* was filming in the summer of 2013, another robot spectacular was released: *Pacific Rim*. Directed by Guillermo del Toro, it starred Charlie Hunnam and Idris Elba as soldiers fighting a war in the Pacific with gigantic sea monsters. The movie has since become a critical favorite for its homage to Japanese filmmaking, but American audiences didn't take to it. *Pacific Rim* made $102 million in North America, a financial failure. In China, however, it was an immediate hit, opening to $45 million, a record for Warner Bros. Subsequent weeks were equally successful, and the movie had crossed the $100 million mark when a very important critic weighed in.

In a piece published by the *People's Liberation Army Daily*, a Communist Party officer named Zhang Jieli warned his countrymen that *Pacific Rim* was American propaganda designed to "[export] the U.S.'s rebalancing of its Asia-Pacific strategy." At the end of the film, when the soldiers take on the sea monsters in the coastal waters adjacent to Hong Kong, "the intention was to demonstrate the U.S. commitment to maintaining stability in the Asia-Pacific area and saving mankind." The choice to set a battle in the South China Sea—and then allow America to emerge victorious— was deliberate, he wrote, a big-budget effort to show the West winning in the disputed region where China's trade routes and sovereignty meet to become one of its most fiercely protected borders.

"Soldiers should sharpen their eyes and enforce a 'firewall' to avoid ideological erosion when watching American movies," Zhang wrote.

Inside Hollywood, the original *Pacific Rim* was one of a handful of movies around this time that were performing better in China than in the U.S., the first signs of a balance in power shifting. But Zhang's editorial made it clear that the country's officials still watched every movie through a political lens. Chinese officials would mention the *Pacific Rim* problem to the executives behind *Transformers*, a casual aside that ensured they knew not to make the same mistake.

THE MOST POPULAR FORM OF "Chinese element" quickly became the Chinese actor hired for the American movie. Massive stars in their home country, these actors were largely unknown to U.S. audiences, but studios cast them in their biggest franchises, hoping the familiar faces would pull in crowds. The casting of such parts typically began with calls to the talent agencies in search of a Chinese star. Producers often didn't care whether the Chinese actor being sourced would play a male or female character—sticking a Chinese face into a cast was thought to be enough. Suddenly the appeal of a certain actor relied less on acting ability than on English-language skills or on the logistical ease brought to the role. "He's a Hong Kong passport," agents would say, or "She's a dual citizen in Canada," they'd note hopefully, knowing it would help their chances if producers didn't need to worry about the paperwork associated with Chinese visas.

Chinese faces—most often those of beautiful young actresses—popped up in major summer releases as ambassadors of China's new celebrity class. Few could have imagined the stars of older Chinese propaganda films having much use in Hollywood, but here was Angelababy, an actress and pop singer from Shanghai, as a fighter pilot in Fox's *Independence Day: Resurgence*. Jing Tian, a Chinese actress from Xi'an, struggled through Warner Bros.' *Kong: Skull Island*, at one point getting such bad feedback on her acting that she was replaced in some scenes by a substitute who did not resemble her. For the new *Transformers*, Moore cast Chinese star Li Bingbing as a Chinese executive who partners with an American businessman (Stanley Tucci) on harvesting a powerful element called "Transformium." Her character embodies old and new tropes about China, equal parts mysterious Orient and contemporary challenger to the West. At one point, Tucci's character introduces her as his "delicate flower." At another, she saves him by beating up CIA agents.

But none of the actresses getting these roles had the crossover potential of Fan Bingbing, the biggest and most ambitious star in China. She was born in 1981, the daughter of artists conscripted into serving the party during the Cultural Revolution. After a car accident in her teens left her bedridden, Fan watched a Taiwanese drama about a Tang dynasty empress that inspired her to attend a performing arts school in Shanghai, where she was discovered by a producer. She quickly became a star, at sixteen years old the walking embodiment of the capitalist allowances introduced to modern-day China in a single generation.

Fan was part of a celebrity class blossoming in Xi Jinping's China, ubiquitous as the face of Adidas, Louis Vuitton, and Moët champagne. Young women paid plastic surgeons to break their jawbones, rearrange their skulls, and suck out cheek fat so it healed in the form of her V-shaped face.

She would also, in 2013, be tapped by Disney to sell *Iron Man 3* to the country. An additional four minutes of footage was added to the movie, including a scene of the suited superhero surrounded by adoring Chinese schoolchildren.

Fan's big moment came in a scene opposite Wang Xueqi, a Chinese actor hired to play a doctor who rescues Iron Man (Robert Downey Jr.) after he is injured. The doctor's assistant, played by Fan, retrieves the surgeon just as he happens to pour himself a glass of Gu Li Duo, a drink produced by Yili, a Mongolian manufacturer that was on an image rehabilitation campaign after distributing milk formula with elevated levels of mercury the year before the film's release. The doctor treats Iron Man with a combination of Western surgery and Eastern acupuncture, and the hero is saved. In the middle of this otherwise ordinary American superhero movie, China had a cameo—as a place of world-class doctors, beautiful actresses, and safe milk.

Kevin Feige, the head of Marvel Studios, thought it would be obvious to any American viewer that the filmmakers were pandering to another country, and the scene was only approved for release in the Chinese edit. He made an understandable assumption in doing so. Chinese audiences, he figured, were the ones who wanted to see their stars on the big screen. He was wrong.

The scenes of Iron Man with his Chinese fans and Chinese saviors were not agreed to by Chinese officials and executives so their own people would feel included in a global blockbuster. They were agreed to so audiences *outside* China would see the country in a new light. Any thrill that a moviegoer in Guangzhou might have in seeing Fan Bingbing alongside Robert Downey Jr. was unimportant compared with the imprimatur of first-world-nation status granted by having the country play a heroic role in an American movie's plot. When word spread of the two-version solution, Chinese partners on the movie and fans on social media responded in outrage.

Feige and his team prioritized the integrity of the American cut over the economic concerns of angering Chinese audiences. But their mistake was well timed for the Paramount team on *Transformers*. Officials sent word to the producers: there must be only one global version of *Age of Extinction*.

Hollywood executives were also learning that their strategy of blindly introducing Chinese elements did not guarantee a warm reception among Chinese audiences. Hollywood executives around this time, many of whom had never traveled to China, viewed the country's hundreds of millions of moviegoers as a monolith, warming to any acknowledgment the West would give them. But the Chinese audiences were more sophisticated than that. They saw right through the pandering, which they called "getting soy sauced." They quickly diagnosed the bait and switch being pulled by the studios, which would highlight scenes with the local actors in online advertisements, only to have fans show up and find those actors relegated to nothing more than glorified cameos. The Chinese coined a term for the actresses who took such jobs: "flower vases."

Transformers would try to avoid such criticisms by dedicating a significant portion of the movie to its Chinese subplots. Roughly a third of *Age of Extinction* would trade the cornfields of Texas, where a light never stops shining on the American flag in Cade Yeager's garage, for the cityscapes of Hong Kong and mainland China. But before the location switch, other appeals to China start to appear on-screen. Yeager and his daughter raid a convenience store for food and pick up Chinese protein powder sold, for some reason, in Chicago. When he needs to track the enemy's location,

Yeager uses an ATM operated by China Construction Bank—somehow located in the middle of Texas. These brands wanted to boost their credibility within China, and putting their products in the hands of Western movie stars was seen as the best possible endorsement.

IN 2012, WHILE MOST IN Hollywood were focused on China's calendar-stacking shenanigans, a few started noticing a trend that would recalibrate the balance of box-office power by the end of the decade—a trend that was also driving Moore's decision to make his movie as Chinese as possible. It had occurred in the case of a movie called *Lost in Thailand*, a late-2012 *Hangover*-style farce about three Chinese men gallivanting around Thailand. The movie was directed by Xu Zheng, who happened to be the first client signed by Jonah Greenberg, a Los Angeles native and third-generation Hollywood professional who had been hired to run the Beijing office of the Creative Artists Agency talent representation firm, known for managing megastars like Meryl Streep and Beyoncé. Greenberg, who had first traveled to China in 1994 on a study-abroad trip, was tasked with signing Chinese directors emerging in their country's growing commercial cinema business—for the agency, a growth market at a time of stagnating star salaries in the U.S.

Lost in Thailand premiered with Hollywood bombast—it was released on December 12, 2012, and the date, 12/12/12, was used as a marketing ploy that broke through the party-produced releases and Western competition. Its plot was nothing special by Hollywood standards, a typical road-trip romp. But it included jokes that only Chinese audiences would appreciate, about always being in a hurry to get somewhere, or the difference between cultures and generations. It collected more than $200 million, a record for a Chinese title at the time and second only to *Avatar* on the all-time list.

Greenberg suspected some other force besides savvy marketing was at work and asked Xu why audiences had responded so passionately to a comedy about Chinese buffoons. For years, Xu told him, Chinese moviegoers have been eating French cuisine in the form of art-house films, hamburgers in the form of American blockbusters, or broccoli in the form of state-produced propaganda.

"It turned out all Chinese people wanted was a bowl of noodles," he said—cinematic comfort food from their own culture. No one in Hollywood at this time could have known how prescient his observation was.

BAY RETURNED TO HONG KONG with his stars for the *Transformers* premiere, mounting a massive, attention-grabbing red-carpet affair on Kowloon Bay, with a giant Optimus Prime looming over the water. Li Bingbing walked the carpet in a black-and-white gown with a sheer skirt; Mark Wahlberg signed autographs for fans. "I didn't think I'd ever have celebrities like this so close to me," said Jorden Bhavnani, a thirteen-year-old Hong Kong student who went to the autograph line after a day of studying. "I'm really excited to see Mark Wahlberg. Hong Kong hasn't had this type of thing before."

Everyone was on their best behavior thanks to a separate controversy involving a Hollywood star. One week earlier, Angelina Jolie had been in China promoting her new Disney movie, *Maleficent*, when she was asked a question about her favorite Chinese directors—a question typical of Chinese interviewers.

"I am not sure if you consider Ang Lee Chinese, he's Taiwanese, but he does many Chinese-language films with many Chinese artists and actors, and I think his works and the actors in his films are the ones I am most familiar with and very fond of," said Jolie.

That comment—and its implication that Taiwan was a separate country—inspired headlines across China and outrage in selected corners. One Weibo user called her a "stupid laughingstock" and another a "deranged Taiwan independence supporter." In Taiwan, fans said the comment made her a "brave and brilliant woman."

A Disney spokesperson said, "That was her own personal opinion."

Jolie's husband, Brad Pitt, had traveled to China with her on the publicity tour in an attempt to mend relations still sensitive seventeen years after he had starred in *Seven Years in Tibet*. In interviews, Jolie told the media that Pitt was taking dim-sum classes to pass the time in the country. That flattery faded in the glare of his wife's gaffe.

After Jolie's snafu, the *Transformers* actors who had resisted media prep before sitting down to Chinese interviews now wanted to know what topics to avoid. Executives split up the cast and filled them in on dos and don'ts. Beijing's curriculum was spreading across Hollywood.

Keeping quiet about Tibet and Taiwan was already on the list of talking points from Paramount's public relations department. Talk about the movie, your career, what you think of the *Transformers* series, they suggested. No politics. No references to geography or the history of nations. In interviews, Wahlberg and the others followed the rules.

"The food was fantastic, so I was eating way too much," the actor told reporters.

When it was released in the U.S., *Age of Extinction* followed the trend of diminishing domestic returns, opening to $100 million and eventually grossing a franchise-low $245 million, behind that year's hits *Guardians of the Galaxy*, *Captain America: The Winter Soldier*, and its latest competition from the toy aisle, *The Lego Movie*. But thanks to full auditoriums in China, it was a different story overseas. The product placement, casting decisions, and Beijing acquiescence had worked wonders. The movie set an opening-weekend record, collecting $92 million.

Chinese exhibitors showed *Age of Extinction* on up to 70 percent of their screens, putting the movie on its way toward a new record for the country: $301 million. That was more than it made in the U.S. and more than any Hollywood movie had ever made in China. The franchise was among the most popular of all time; farmers in Shandong Province began finding spare car parts of their own and constructing fifty-two-foot-tall Transformer replicas, sold as public sculptures for $16,000 apiece.

The robust returns of *Transformers*, *Pacific Rim*, and *Iron Man 3* helped set new records at the Chinese box office in 2013 and 2014. By the end of 2013, the first full year under the Biden-Xi quota agreement, the number of screens in China had risen 30 percent and the box office was up more than 25 percent. Because of the terms set by the 2012 quota agreement, only $75 million of the *Transformers* ticket sales flowed back to Paramount—as opposed to the $150 million or so the studio got from its $245 million made in U.S. theaters. Still, if the movie hadn't overperformed in China, chances are it wouldn't have crossed the $1 billion mark worldwide. Most important for Moore and the Paramount executives pleasing their corporate bosses, Viacom would report its quarterly earnings a few months later, and revenue for the studio would rise 12 percent on the strength of the *Transformers* performance, driving the parent company to a record profit. Most important for those officials in the Forbidden City, the movie's global haul of $1.1 billion meant that millions of moviegoers around the world watched Beijing's heroism.

NINE

The Rise and Fall
of China's Richest Man

D alian Wanda Group took AMC public far faster than many had expected. On a Wednesday morning in December 2013, executives from Wanda flew in to ring the opening bell at the New York Stock Exchange, joining Gerry Lopez and his colleagues from Kansas City. On the floor of the exchange, representing the American Multi-Cinema chain with his new Chinese owners, Lopez wore a red tie.

He had reason to be bullish. Shares opened at $18 and closed up 5 percent. Chairman Wang Jianlin had put around $800 million into an 80 percent stake in AMC in August 2012 that was worth nearly $2 billion by early 2014. The IPO financing funded a growing trend of replacing stadium seating with cushy recliners in AMC auditoriums. AMC was the first chain to execute the recliner model on a mass scale, and the refurbished auditoriums performed so well that rivals installed their own. It was the biggest trend to hit American moviegoing since the multiplex, and it was made possible by Chinese money.

For a bunch of Communists, these guys make pretty good capitalists, Lopez thought to himself.

Lopez still struggled to get a handle on his new boss. Even after Wanda coughed up $2.6 billion for his company, Lopez had little idea where Wang—then said to be the second-wealthiest man in China—had gotten his money.

"Oh, he used to be in the army," his Chinese associates told him.

"Okay," said Lopez. "But what does that mean?"

Across Los Angeles, producers and recently fired executives—suddenly seeing Chinese money dangled before them—asked similar questions about new benefactors who, like Wang, showed up out of nowhere with billions to spend and dreams of making it in the movie business. Then again, the times quickly got so good that they didn't want to ask too many questions. For decades, the film industry had attracted the savings of businessmen with abbreviated acting careers or heiresses who wanted to meet the stars. Executives called it "dumb money," marveling at how the prospect of attending a movie premiere could drive even the most rational investor to part with millions. China wasn't just coming to the rescue on-screen—the country's billionaires were the saviors of the entertainment industry off-screen as well.

In 2013 the booming box office yielded another unexpected gusher of cash: Chinese financiers following Beijing's orders to build their country a cultural industry, a "salute and march" that transformed Hollywood executives into retrievers chasing new riches. At first, China's billionaires were written off as another group of suckers. Eventually, Lopez and other executives would learn that these new backers arrived with support from a government that could shut off the cash flow overnight, leaving a trail of broken hearts and abandoned deals. But for a moment, it was the absolute best of times for a movie industry desperate for a bailout. No one seemed more committed to fulfilling his country's five-year plan and turning culture into a major Chinese industry than Wang

Jianlin, the most prominent of the potential saviors whose rise in Hollywood coincided with a new eagerness to find stories that would generate *Transformers*-level boosts at the box office.

WANG JIANLIN WAS BORN IN 1954, the scrawny son of a soldier who had participated in Mao's Long March. He served for sixteen years in the People's Liberation Army until the mid-1980s, joining the government in the city of Dalian after he was decommissioned. Rather than rise through the ranks of provincial government, he pursued a career in real estate, renovating slum housing by adding a bathroom to every apartment, a novelty at the time. From the start, Wang had an eye on the government allies one needed to cultivate to rise in China's post–Deng Xiaoping economy. He became known for "Wanda Speed," turning around renovation projects quickly enough for politicians to get their victory lap before they left office or were shifted to a new job. In 1994 he took control of the Dalian soccer team and renamed it after his company so the team's championship tournaments doubled as brand building. In 2015, *The New York Times* exposed how far Wang would go to keep the government happy, reporting that relatives of Xi Jinping and other top leaders had been given early stakes in Wanda that totaled more than $1 billion.

But when people asked, he attributed his success to the Confucian ideal of focusing on the long term and a sense of Chinese national pride, pledging to build a company that could stand alongside American and European multinationals. His timing cannot be denied. Wang built a career catering to the new consumer life emerging in 1990s China, beginning with flashier apartment buildings and growing to include his malls, hotels, and office buildings sprouting up across the country, all often clustered together in a Wanda Plaza built on former farmland.

Wang had a flair for the dramatic, on display at an annual company meeting for high-ranking employees, where he serenaded subordinates with patriotic anthems and pop ballads. Each business unit would then perform sketches or songs prepared over the previous year. Energetic workers at AMC's headquarters in Kansas were recruited to choreograph a routine and flown over to perform it. To new employees, it appeared Wanda employed startlingly talented workers. Then they would hear the whispers: in order to impress the chairman at these yearly shows, divisions were said to hire beautiful singers as receptionists, telling them that they could work the phones part-time and rehearse for the annual meeting the rest of the time. Pleasing Chairman Wang was worth it.

Wang was once asked how his parents—Mao-aligned Communists— felt about their son's exorbitant wealth. His father was retired, Wang explained, and had been living in a home for elderly military officers with poor accommodations. Wang hired his dad a driver and moved him to a better facility.

"So later, I asked my parents which is better: relying on the institution or relying on your son? They said it themselves: relying on their son was better. Although their goal in the past was to undermine the rich, now they wholly feel having money is better than not having it," Wang answered.

Wang Jianlin's shopping-mall empire made him China's richest man in 2016, with an estimated fortune of more than $30 billion. Despite having billions of dollars, Wang insisted that his only lavish expense was his $2,000 suits. In reality, Wang had a number of flashy spending habits. He bought a Picasso for $28 million, the Atlético Madrid soccer team for $54 million, and the Ironman competitions for $650 million. He added more cinema chains to his portfolio in Australia, the UK, and Sweden, spending $5.9 billion on movie theaters—including a deal to buy Carmike Cinemas, the number four theater chain in the United States, headquartered in Columbus, Georgia, to become the top theater operator in the world. His son became a tabloid fixture as a key member of the *fuerdai*, the name given to the second generation of China's nouveau riche. In these three generations, China's shifting relationship with consumerism is on display: the Communist father bent on destroying the rich, the son who becomes the modest billionaire, the grandson best known for buying his dog two gold Apple Watches—one for each front leg.

Wang moved into film production with a $3.5 billion deal to buy Legendary Pictures, the company that had kicked around Ryan Condal's time-traveling-ghost script but was better known as a passive investor in fanboy favorites like *The Dark Knight* and *Jurassic World*. The Legendary deal of early 2016 turned Wang from a movie theater owner to a player in production. But he didn't want to merely take over Hollywood. He wanted to beat it, and his self-effacing start gave way to Los Angeles self-promotion. In China, he visited Shanghai Disneyland and vowed to build his country its own beloved theme parks. To give himself a head start, Wang dispatched researchers to Disney parks in the U.S. to come back with their secrets. At Walt Disney World in Orlando, park workers discovered Wanda employees measuring the bricks that lined Main Street and scrutinizing the keyholes on shop doors. They took countless photos, trying to copy the colorful details that Disney hides in its layout. Finding the competitor's blueprints was a trick from the days of the Warner Bros. deal. As in most endeavors, Wang pledged to outspend and outbuild his way to the top. Disney had one park in mainland China. He would build twenty.

"One tiger is no match for a pack of wolves," he said.

WANG MAY HAVE BEEN THE flashiest investor cutting the biggest checks, but he was merely one of several Chinese billionaires who decided, at various points around this time, to follow their government's suggestion and invest in show business. The five-year plan in China was making unemployed executives in Hollywood very, very happy.

The new Chinese benefactors had millions of dollars and a playbook:

Find a recently fired studio chief. Put him in charge. Believe him when he said that the key to success was making the kinds of movies his former employers had fired him for making. What could go wrong?

In 2015 four such men controlled $660 million in money committed by China to re-create a Hollywood that didn't exist anymore. The executives leading these four ventures all came from high-powered gigs running film operations at studios like Disney or Warner Bros. Another former executive, Adam Goodman from Paramount, soon joined this class with money from LeEco, a Chinese conglomerate whose vice chairman, Zhang Zhou, once told me he invested in movies so they could be integrated into self-driving cars his company was developing.

On the surface, the LeEco venture looked like the perfect marriage of Hollywood expertise and Chinese financing. "This is really one of the first true Chinese movie studios in Hollywood," Goodman said. "It's a creative partnership taking the best of where we came from and where they're going." Together the partnerships would bring the market everything from live-action family films to smaller character dramas, each focusing on the genres Hollywood was abandoning in pursuit of ever-bigger franchises.

China's box office, meanwhile, had grown 188 percent from 2012 to 2016. By the end of 2016, China's box office would be larger than the combined box offices of Japan, India, and the United Kingdom.

Movies went into production solely on their box-office potential in China. Legendary, seeing the successful reception of *Pacific Rim* in China, approved a sequel that would double down on the market. This one was filmed in China at Wanda's studios and cast several Chinese actors in leading roles as part of the movie's Pan-Pacific Defense Corps. The sequel didn't make the mistake of the original and avoided any plot detail that could be interpreted as a case for American aggression on the South China Sea. Instead, at the end of the film, the heroes must fight at a volcano that is giving rise to evil monsters. The volcano housing the monsters is located in Japan.

Other strange patterns started to take shape. In the summer of 2016, a movie adaptation of the popular video game *Warcraft* was released. The story of orcs and magic portals failed to translate any popularity among gamers into box-office sales, grossing a dismal $47 million in the U.S. on a $160 million budget. In China, however, it was a smash, collecting $221 million. Two months later, a streaming service paid a record $24 million for the rights to distribute *Warcraft* online.

For it and other U.S. flops, China was becoming a bailout, and the final assessment of a movie's success had to account for how it had done in that market. With this evidence in mind, no one believed that China was a "developing" market anymore, making it that much harder to stomach the fact that studios received only 25 percent of ticket sales from it. Warner Bros. had negotiated a 13 percent rate for *The Fugitive* when the box office was seen mostly as a solution to cutting back on piracy in the country, and China got away with looking generous when officials nearly doubled the rate to 25 percent. Distribution executives griped that China had become the world's second-largest market while insisting on terms typically seen in a much smaller one.

For producers trying to wring every possible dollar out of China, there was a solution at hand. Movies that really leaned into Chinese themes or settings could apply for the official designation of coproduction, signaling that the film was equal parts American and Chinese. It would take more than the product-placement deals or flower vases seen in *Transformers*. The movie must film in China and have Chinese stars in front of the camera and Chinese financiers behind it. Only then would China Film Bureau bestow coproduction status—and suddenly that 25 percent box-office share rose to 43 percent.

At this moment in Hollywood's relationship with China, deep in the honeymoon phase, the coproduction offered a holy grail of riches. Suddenly there were multiple projects in various stages of development about the Flying Tigers, the group of American pilots who bombed Japan and protected China during World War II. Agents dusted off old scripts and sent them to producers with notes attached, explaining how a once fully American script could go the coproduction route.

"Pretend London is Shanghai!"

"Imagine the girl is Chinese!"

Studios engaged in such overreach to avoid the fate of movies like *Iron Man 3*, which thought it could hire some Chinese actors for a day or two and collect that bigger coproduction share. "We want films that are heavily invested in Chinese culture, not one or two shots," Zhang Xun, president of China Film Co-Production Company, advised a gathering in Los Angeles.

Jeffrey Katzenberg green-lit a second sequel to *Kung Fu Panda*, this one coinciding with DreamWorks' partnership on the "Dream Center" in Shanghai, conceived as a forty-acre entertainment and retail campus built on the site of a former airport and cement factory. A sister operation, Oriental DreamWorks, would be housed alongside eight massive event spaces and the requisite shopping and dining developments. Modernizing that part of Shanghai, the city's deputy mayor noted in an echo of Zhu Rongji's Disneyland prediction, was part of the government's twelfth five-year plan, and if a cement factory was the old China, then a Dream Center featuring an animation studio and high-end boutiques was the new. In 2011, a second *Kung Fu Panda* film had set records in China that were eventually bested by *Monkey King: Hero Is Back*, a children's film about a classic Chinese character that brought fans to tears, another "bowl of noodles" for audiences. The director of *Monkey King*, Tian Xiaopeng, though, displayed none of Katzenberg's bombast in response to his success; his reaction was a study in Confucian humility. "Frankly speaking," he said, "there are so many problems in the movie, especially technical details. It would be better if I worked harder. So I felt quite ashamed when audiences praised our work."

Kung Fu Panda 3 would be the first animated coproduction between China and the U.S. The original film was made without the Chinese box office in mind; by the time of the third installment, it factored into major decisions. Screenwriters placed a scene on Mount Qingcheng, a mountain known as a Taoist landmark, as well as other subtle nods that would mean nothing to most American viewers but carry heavy symbolic resonance for most Chinese ones. Dubbing the movie wasn't enough; artists reanimated the mouths of Po and others in 60 percent of the shots so their cartoon lip movements matched the Mandarin being spoken. Katzenberg was so bullish on the film that he predicted Chinese moviegoers might see it twice—once in English, and then once again in a Mandarin version where they could focus on the precise lip movements. With a gross of $154 million, *Kung Fu Panda 3* beat the record set by *Monkey King* one year earlier and became the highest-grossing animated movie in Chinese box-office history. The records were volleying back and forth between U.S. and Chinese releases, but *Kung Fu Panda* had won. Katzenberg, who had overseen a renaissance of American animation, appeared to have a business sequel on his hands.

DURING ONE VISIT TO LOS ANGELES, Wang met Hawk Koch, then the president of the Academy of Motion Picture Arts and Sciences, the organization behind the Oscars. At the time, Koch was fundraising to build an academy museum in Los Angeles that would house Dorothy's ruby slippers, the teeth-baring extraterrestrial headpiece of *Alien*, and other classic Hollywood artifacts. Koch, whose producing credits included *Chinatown* and *Wayne's World*, knew what to do when a rich potential donor showed up asking for a meeting. He grabbed the extra Oscar the academy kept on hand for selfies and went to meet Wang. Everyone got a picture with the statuette and headed to lunch at Mr. Chow. For the second time in his American acquisition journey, Wang was hosted in an American Chinese restaurant.

Wang told Koch of his newest grand plan, the largest ambition yet in a year of major China-Hollywood dreams.

"I want to build the Hollywood of the East," he said.

He outlined plans for a real estate explosion of sound stages, auditoriums, and editing facilities in an unidentified Chinese city, so state-of-the-art it would attract stars and craftsmen from every country. Serendipity and strategy had turned undeveloped farmland in Southern California into America's entertainment hub. Wang was plotting the same for his country, though without any serendipity. Every move would be orchestrated.

Three months later, Koch had just landed in Beijing to give an address at the city's film festival when he arrived at the hotel and saw a note waiting for him from Wang. His presence had been requested. A car took him back to the airport he'd left hours earlier, where he was whisked away on a whirlwind visit to scout a province that might house this Hollywood East. It was a surreal twelve hours that started on a Gulfstream and ended with dinner around an O-shaped table with live fish swimming in the center cavity.

"Do you like karaoke?" Wang asked Koch as they flew back to Beijing.

Koch, still fighting jet lag, found himself in the presidential karaoke suite at a Sofitel hotel in a Wanda Plaza, complete with flat-screen TVs and a live DJ. Then six young women showed up.

Oh my god, where are the cameras? Koch thought to himself. He could see the headlines now: ACADEMY PRESIDENT BUSTED WITH UNDERAGE GIRLS IN CHINA.

But his worst fears were avoided. They were students from a Beijing performing arts school, brought to entertain Wang and Koch with song and dance. Wang took a turn himself, performing a Chinese anthem in a strong voice and ending each song with the fist-bump gesture Koch had taught him. If there were ever a scene that encapsulated the happy marriage forming between China and Hollywood, it might be this: the president of the academy sharing the microphone with China's richest man at a karaoke lounge in Beijing, where the soundtrack alternated between Johnny Mathis and hits from the People's Republic.

Toward the end of his trip, Wang flew Koch to see another candidate for his plans, a city of eight million people on the eastern coast called Qingdao. Qingdao was larger than all but a few U.S. cities but merely a third-tier metropolis in China. A former German settlement known for brewing Tsingtao beer, the city hosts an annual festival in which waitresses wear Bavarian outfits and pour more than three hundred brews, much like the Oktoberfest celebrations hosted in Germany and other Western countries. State officials had allocated acres of land along the water outside the city center for development, the kind of open expanse early studio chiefs saw when they looked out over the Southern California valley in the 1920s. Seeing a part of China with no snow, typhoons, or pollution, Koch told Wang that Qingdao was an appealing location for Hollywood East.

When it came to land development in a country where private land ownership doesn't exist, Wang's ambitions were subject to his government's desire to build China's cultural industries. Though the marketing focal point of Qingdao would be massive sound stages where movies film, Wang had his eye on the development that could spring up around it— the hotels, malls, and apartments now justified by their proximity to this government-backed cultural effort. This real estate strategy had worked before. When China's government signaled that it wanted to develop its native car industry, real estate titans started building auto factories. When renewable energy was a priority, developers suddenly discovered solar panel factories. If culture was a centerpiece of the five-year plan, Chinese firms would build sound stages.

These twin goals—China's cultural priorities and Wang's endless appetite for real estate expansion—would converge in a new part of Qingdao built by these ambitions. Production couldn't start for years, but Wang turned the ground-breaking itself into another signal to Hollywood of his seriousness. Leonardo DiCaprio and Nicole Kidman flew to Qingdao to attend the ceremony, alongside Harvey Weinstein, Catherine

Zeta-Jones, John Travolta, and other stars. Some of the celebrities were paid more than a million dollars apiece to appear on the red carpet and pledge their support.

"It is the beginning of a new era," Travolta said.

"I am hoping to come to Qingdao to make a Chinese movie," added Zeta-Jones.

Wang promised the world. Thirty foreign films would be made at Qingdao each year—alongside a hundred Chinese titles! A film festival would be held every September—and within five years, it would rival Cannes! The biggest sound stage was ten thousand square meters, three times the size of the biggest one on the Warner Bros. lot, and the world's biggest water tank was nearby!

Across the water from the production facilities, though, would come the real moneymakers: a six-star hotel, two performing arts auditoriums, rows of restaurants and shops. Wang had even gotten a yacht club approved in a country where officials had once banned them along the coastline, worried they might inflame tensions with Taiwan or between their own country's rich and poor. The perimeter of the development was perpetually ringed by construction cranes, expanding its borders.

Above the sound stages, Wang installed a permanent reminder of his ambitions. On a hillside above the Wanda sound stages, white Chinese letters were erected on a grassy hillside—the area's own Hollywood sign. This one translated to "Movie Metropolis of the East." Of course, Wang made sure his version stood taller than the one in Los Angeles. And it lit up at night.

It didn't take long for the lights to start to flicker.

BEHIND THE SCENES, STUDIO CHIEFS were questioning whether Wang could deliver on his ambitions. His shtick came off as so performative—and possibly too good to be true. There was the time he told executives at one studio he wanted to buy their operation and then didn't seem to understand that that would require cutting a deal with their parent company, not the people in the room. Or the time Gerry Lopez was at a Wanda dinner in China and left the table to go to the restroom. When he walked into the wrong door, he discovered some Wanda employees pouring cheap wine into the empty bottles of more expensive labels.

Wanda's $3.5 billion deal for Legendary had drawn gasps of disbelief in Hollywood, since the production company's own track record of making movies was so lousy. By investing millions of dollars into each production, Legendary had helped make massive hits like *The Dark Knight*. When it produced movies on its own, the track record shifted to middling performers like a *Godzilla* remake or bombs like the gothic horror story *Crimson Peak*. The library Legendary actually owned—and that it had sold to Wanda—was filled with movies not nearly as popular as those it had merely co-financed. Was it possible, rivals at other production companies wondered with a bit of arrogance, that Wanda was buying Legendary without quite realizing what it was getting, or at least drastically overpaying for it?

Then Washington got involved. In October 2016, John Culberson, a Texas Republican and House subcommittee chairman, called on the Justice Department to review Wanda's acquisitions in Hollywood, which he said amounted to "foreign propaganda influence over American media." The month before, Culberson had joined fifteen other House members in calling on the Government Accountability Office to consider expanding the power of the Treasury Department to review such deals. Chinese hard-liners had been skeptical of letting American movies into their theaters, fearful of a westernizing influence. Now U.S. politicians were questioning influence moving the other way, their concerns tinged with fear over a future in which China assumed the world-leader role long occupied by America.

Concerns about a foreign agent hijacking American entertainment had hit Hollywood before. In the 1980s, a wave of Japanese investment rode into the industry on the strength of VHS revenue. Japan had experienced an incredible economic rebound after the destruction of World War II, and the country's investors, taking advantage of a strong yen, bought marquee assets like Rockefeller Center, the Hotel Bel-Air, and the Pebble Beach Golf Links in short order. Smaller production companies in Hollywood had sold stakes to Japanese firms, but it was Sony's 1989 acquisition of Columbia Pictures that cast the trend in a new light.

JAPAN INVADES HOLLYWOOD, blared the cover of *Newsweek*. Underneath the headline, Columbia's iconic symbol—a redheaded woman bearing a torch in her right hand—was dressed in a kimono. The outcry revealed the fear the acquisition had evoked in everyday Americans. In 1989 American cinema was still arguably the most influential cultural force in the world. To cede that power to a country the U.S. had fought just four decades earlier constituted an existential threat. And what would follow? America's core industrial and manufacturing businesses? And would even that be as powerful as control of Hollywood, the industry called the "dream factory" for a reason?

Concerns about Sony owning Columbia quickly proved overblown. The new owners axed a movie about sumo wrestling out of cultural sensitivity. Other than that, a sushi bar was installed on the lot, but that was about it. When similar fears were raised by China barnstorming into Hollywood, many executives would remind me of the Japan scare in the 1980s, predicting that this new red-scare bombast would also fade.

AT THE BOX OFFICE, the actual grosses were being manipulated by Chinese theater owners, who sold tickets for Hollywood movies but registered the sale as a ticket bought for a Chinese propaganda picture. Auditors working for the MPAA had also discovered Chinese theaters were underreporting American grosses by 9 percent. The manipulation was glaring, as was China's insistence on maintaining the illusion of

Chinese moviegoers warmly receiving government-produced propaganda. When Paramount's *Terminator Genisys* had been released, moviegoers who went to see the film noticed their ticket stubs were for *The Hundred Regiments Offensive*, a nationalist movie produced by China Film Group for the seventieth anniversary of Japan's surrender in 1945.

Neither these revelations nor Culberson's letter slowed down the wave of Chinese investment that Wang had been leading. On November 13, an outlandish tie-up in a sea of outlandish deals was announced: a Chinese copper-processing company called Anhui Xinke New Materials was going to buy an 80 percent stake in Voltage Pictures for $345 million. Voltage was best known then for Oscar-winning movies like the Middle East war thriller *The Hurt Locker* and *Dallas Buyers Club*, starring Matthew McConaughey as a Texas man dying of AIDS who slips black-market drugs to his fellow patients. Xinke said it wanted to diversify its holdings as commodity prices softened. Still, for those watching in Hollywood, the Xinke-Voltage deal offered a case study in how irrational Chinese money flowing into Hollywood had become. A Chinese firm that made its profits processing copper was going to own a majority stake in a West Hollywood company that won Jared Leto an Oscar for playing a trans woman.

Marching onward, Wang spoke of plans to buy a U.S. studio, starting talks to pay $4 billion for a 49 percent stake in Paramount, a deal spearheaded by Rob Moore three years after his *Transformers* success. While the Paramount deal churned, Wang pursued an acquisition of Dick Clark Productions, the namesake company of the *American Bandstand* host best known for producing awards shows, including the Golden Globes. Wanda wanted to pay $1 billion for it, which came as a welcome shock to its investors, who had recently valued the company at about a third of that. Members of the Hollywood Foreign Press Association, the organization that puts on the Globes, privately wondered if certain actors would be barred from getting nominations if a Chinese owner was in charge.

They need not have worried. The copper company buying Voltage, the Wang Jianlin bombast about buying a studio, the overinflated Dick Clark deal—it had gone too far in the eyes of a Chinese government that had viewed such deals suspiciously. When a Chinese firm paid three times the reported value of an American company, authorities found it hard to believe these deals were just about fulfilling the five-year plan to expand China's cultural industries. They were deals that got money out of China and converted it into the safer U.S. dollar, a trend that illustrated shaky confidence in China's currency and posed a potential threat to the country's economy.

Politicians in Beijing ordered a twist ending and told businesses to invest at home, not abroad. Beijing authorities announced they would examine "irrational" outbound investments in which a company was operating outside its core business—specifically citing film-related acquisitions—as well as deals totaling more than $1 billion. Wang and his counterparts were on notice.

Suddenly the executives at Voltage realized the timing of their early November 2016 payday could not have been worse. On December 20, five weeks after the Xinke deal had been announced, the acquisition was canceled. By early 2017, others would join the deal graveyard. A Chinese media firm called Recon Holding had said it would pay $100 million for a majority stake in Millennium Films, maker of movies like *The Expendables*. That would be dead by August. Wanda's purchase of Dick Clark Productions dragged on until it was declared over in March 2017. That group of five companies founded by former studio executives collectively produced a handful of movies before most of the entities dissolved. By the end of that summer, Beijing's intervention had caused Chinese outbound investment into entertainment for the first seven months of 2017 to fall 79 percent from the prior year. A separate deal to finance Paramount movies with $1 billion from Shanghai Film Group and Huahua Media forced studio executives to get on a plane and fly to China looking for the cash. They came home empty-handed.

. . .

MEANWHILE, THE COPRODUCTION STRATEGY that was supposed to mint money for Hollywood producers had turned into a nightmare of paperwork and second-guessing, marked by postproduction editors frantically removing American-themed scenes and stuffing Chinese ones in, following instructions by producers who were desperately trying to strike the balance required to secure the coproduction status that boosted box-office share. The decision was ultimately in the film bureau's hands, and the answer—even after the script rewriting, casting calls, and editing frenzy—was oftentimes no.

Achieving an acceptable balance of Eastern and Western elements wasn't expected to be a problem for *The Great Wall*, the biggest U.S.-China coproduction in history, to be directed by Zhang Yimou. It would be the perfect marriage of the two cultures. Matt Damon starred as a mercenary who travels the Silk Road to China, where he joins a group of soldiers to fight a species of aliens trying to breach the Great Wall. America's A-list actor would star alongside Jing Tian, China's A-list actress. The financiers would include Universal Pictures and Wanda. More than one hundred translators on set would coordinate production for a blended crew working from several locations in China.

Jonah Greenberg at CAA had helped put the movie together, having established an office in Beijing that had signed China's A-list directors with the promise of getting them work in the U.S. On a visit to Los Angeles, he drove Zhang across town in a rental car to meet with studios and producers, many of whom still had little idea of the legend in their midst. After traffic kept them from arriving at Warner Bros. in time to discuss a retelling of the character Quasimodo from *The Hunchback of Notre Dame* that Zhang wanted to make, the two men had met Jon Jashni, an executive at Legendary, for drinks at the Beverly Hills Hotel. It was there the seeds would be planted for Zhang to join a project in development at Legendary called *The Great Wall*.

Zhang soon wished Greenberg had driven off the road. The *Great Wall* crew landed in China and immediately started choking on smog. "How do I look Matt Damon in the face when he's the only one not wearing a mask?" one producer asked in a meeting, worried about bringing a Hollywood star to polluted Beijing. Most of the movie filmed at Wanda's new studios in Qingdao, where an unofficial caste system emerged between the Western and Chinese crew, Hollywood safety protocols requiring harnesses and limits on toxic sealants on set were disregarded, and Zhang had to veto producer ideas to have Damon's character sleep with Jing's.

When it came to appealing to audiences in both countries, producers on *The Great Wall* would have done well to observe what had happened after *Kung Fu Panda 3* set a record for animated movies in China. The movie, with its reanimated lip movements and beloved central character, held its box-office record for only six weeks. It was unseated by Disney's *Zootopia*, a movie about a city populated by anthropomorphized animals. Its hero: Judy Hopps, a young bunny who leaves her rural hometown of Bunnyburrow to work in metropolitan Zootopia, where she must team up with a con-artist fox to investigate the disappearance of more than a dozen predators throughout the area. Compared with *Kung Fu Panda 3, Zootopia* made the tiniest of creative choices to appeal to the Chinese audience. In one scene involving a newscaster, American audiences saw a moose version of Walter Cronkite, while Australians saw a koala and the British got a corgi. In China, a panda in a black suit and red tie was swapped in for the scene.

That one character in one scene hardly explains the massive business *Zootopia* did in China—$236 million, a 58 percent increase from *Kung Fu Panda 3*'s record. Studio executives looked at the results to understand what had driven Chinese audiences to *Zootopia* in such numbers. It had nothing to do with Mandarin lip-syncing or Mount Qingcheng. The answer they arrived at: Chinese moviegoers saw—and deeply related to—a character who had moved from the country to the city in pursuit of her dreams. The painstaking effort that *The Great Wall* was undergoing to work in both countries reinforced the lesson of the flower vases. Rather than make decisions that were best for the story, *Great Wall* producers were trying to plant appeal in a way that looked to Chinese audiences like a "white savior" narrative and to Western audiences like a bizarre cultural mash-up.

In China, far more people wanted to see Judy Hopps in a story that resembled their experience than a movie that tried so transparently to cater to them. *The Great Wall* made $171 million, far below Legendary's expectations. In the U.S., the movie was even more flatly rejected, grossing only $45 million.

The measly performance was just salt in the wound for Wanda, which had once represented China's limitless potential but now embodied a fall from grace. Xi, amassing his power, personally barred China's state-owned banks from giving Wanda loans for its overseas pursuits. Xi and his associates had studied the Japanese outbound investments of the 1990s that had so worried lawmakers, a trend that allowed Japan's economy to grow but ultimately led to sour deals that rippled through its banking industry. "When private entrepreneurs take their money out, it's gone. It's no longer something that China can benefit from or the Chinese government can get a handle on," explained one Chinese attorney. When selling AMC, Gerry Lopez had observed how the Communists could make good capitalists, but it took only a few months in 2016 and 2017 for Hollywood to learn which side was ultimately in charge.

Among the more unusual casualties was Wang's maniacal ambition to win his country an Academy Award. He called it "the O Project," a secret campaign that paid his karaoke partner Hawk Koch a six-figure salary to find him a production that would get him onto the Dolby Theatre stage. Wang had Koch buy the adaptation rights to nonfiction books that screamed Oscar bait. He tried to enforce payouts from studios if their Wanda-backed movies didn't receive a nomination. Such hopes evaporated after the government crackdown forced Wanda to go from a shopping spree to a government-mandated fire sale.

In the summer of 2017, only a year after Wang had ordered Hollywood to heed his warnings of China's rise, Wanda sold a collection of its holdings for more than $13 billion to another developer, Sunac China Holdings Ltd. The "Hollywood East" facilities in Qingdao went with it. Less than five years after he'd brought Nicole Kidman to mark the development's auspicious start, Wang was left with a 9 percent stake in the Qingdao Movie Metropolis. On signs erected around the development, *Wanda* was covered by *Sunac*, the original lettering faded but still visible.

TEN

Magic Kingdom

The patriarch of the Tang family was born in 1945 in Zhaohang village, a community twenty miles southeast of Shanghai's city center, and he spent much of his life there creating more space for himself and his family. He worked in a garment factory but, like many of his neighbors, raised crops on his farmland to subsidize his income. Tang owned only about three fourths of an acre in Zhaohang, but he and his wife were able to expand their bungalow into a two-story home in 1985 for a modest amount. They bought the steel, cement, and bricks needed to build the addition themselves. Later, he constructed two-story homes for both of his sons, realizing they would never find wives if they didn't own property. It worked: today he has two grandchildren.

Tang is one of millions of Chinese residents who have lived on what feels like several different planets in their lifetime. He was a small child at the dawn of the Communist revolution, a young man during the Cultural Revolution, and a middle-aged man as Deng Xiaoping's reforms opened up the economy. Like so many Chinese families, the Tang family history mirrors the country's history. Tang worked in a garment factory and farmed the land. Both of his sons work at the Pudong International Airport in Shanghai, which opened in 1999 and was the world's ninth-busiest airport by 2018.

In 2009, after sixty-five years in Zhaohang, Tang received word that his life was changing once again. He was moving. His entire village, in fact, was going to be leveled, and he would be sent for the first time in his life to live in the city. He had not realized it, but the world's largest entertainment company would soon be building its first-ever theme park on the mainland of the world's most populous country. Tang's land would account for three fourths of an acre for a park covering nearly a thousand of them.

To secure that land, CEO Robert Iger had been on a Chinese charm offensive since Eisner had introduced him at the *Kundun* apology tour. When Iger had learned that Xi's father had visited Disneyland in 1980, he had his staff hunt down a photo of the man, shaking hands with Mickey Mouse while wearing a Maoist uniform. Three years after ceding majority ownership of the park to Chinese businesses in the spring of 2011, Iger and some of his top lieutenants flew to China for a ground-breaking ceremony. Confetti blasted across the room and a children's choir sang. Seventeen years after Shanghai mayor Zhu Rongji had looked at acres of rural farmland and promised, "This is where Disneyland will be," construction on the park began not far from the very fields he'd identified.

Residents of the villages on that land visited the office of the demolition authority to sign an agreement offering forty square meters of new real estate per family member. The Tangs received four hundred square meters across five apartments, already under construction in Shanghai's Pudong New Area. Villagers were frustrated to learn that they would be required to pay various amounts, including up to 200,000 yuan, to the demolition authorities to make up the difference between the value of their rural homes and the brand-new apartments. To many, it wasn't fair that they should have to pay even a dime, given that the national government had decided that Disney was taking over their land. Some homeowners refused to leave, erecting signs outside their doors challenging the authorities to make them go. Others were hired to work at the resort that was forming atop their lands. But either way, they had little choice. Tang and his neighbors left behind their farming tools, figuring they wouldn't need them in their new homes in the city. More than 1,200 tombs would be moved from under the land designated for the Magic Kingdom. Officials moved fast: Ding Guojun, the cemetery's general manager, reported that 400 urns had already been relocated in the six weeks since Iger had announced the park, many choosing to move their relatives according to a Chinese custom of maintaining a favorable burial spot as a way to bring good luck to future generations.

As the demolition authority cleared the area, Disney executives conceived a park already years in the making. Design and engineering teams gathered focus groups of Chinese consumers. They covered a wall with photos of castles from around the world, asking the group to place stickers on the images they thought best symbolized a castle. The stickers ended up on all kinds of structures, but the focus group agreed on one thing: China's should be the biggest of any Disney castle in the world.

Iger, the man in charge of getting it built, was a former television weatherman who had something in common with Xi Jinping: he was an heir apparent who wasn't expected to pursue a strategy that deviated from that of his predecessor, but upon assuming office, he had made an unexpected and entirely transformative impact. Iger oversaw a collection of acquisitions that turned Disney into the entertainment industry's undisputed leader in storytelling. Under his watch, a quartet of acquisitions—Pixar Animation, Marvel Studios, Lucasfilm Ltd., and Twentieth Century Fox—made Disney the studio of *Toy Story*, *Captain America*, *Star Wars*, and *Deadpool*. Suddenly, no box-office record was out of reach. Even if it was considered one of Hollywood's five major studios, the sense around town was that the industry was Disney and then everyone else. Its strength in Hollywood extended to China, where Disney's long game made it the one studio capable of weathering the tumult of the Wanda era, when billionaires were reined in by Beijing, promised funding never materialized, and audiences rejected anything that reeked of pandering. In the background of Hollywood's ups and downs with the country over the previous decade, Disney was steadily amassing more power in China than any American rival. By the end of the decade, Disney's future success would depend to a large degree on maintaining the peace there.

CHINESE MOVIEGOERS HAD LARGELY MISSED the Disney renaissance of the 1990s. Pirated versions of older titles like *Cinderella* or *Snow White and the Seven Dwarfs* might have been available on a street corner, but they weren't in circulation in elementary school classrooms and birthday parties as they were in other parts of the world. Even worse: pirates often slapped the Disney logo on any animated title, not just legitimately Disney-produced ones, so Chinese consumers had little idea which princesses were Disney ones, or that the company's brand represented the best in family entertainment. The government's rejection of the Disney Channel years back had deprived the company of its main vehicle for introducing itself to kids.

To make up for lost time in this crucial market, the company hatched an ingenious business strategy: Disney English. In 2007, Disney hired Andrew Sugerman, an executive with a background in education, to open a collection of English-language schools for children—with a branded twist. Disney English, as the program was called, took over storefronts in Chinese cities, converting them into classrooms. In Disney English schools, young Westerners would instruct Chinese children in the language of the upwardly mobile class, teaching vocabulary and sentence structure using its characters and story lines. *A* is for *apple*, as in "Mickey wants an apple." *D* is for *dress*, as in "Cinderella wears a pretty dress." *F* is for *friend*, as in "Lilo is a good friend to Stitch." The kids would learn English, and they would learn Disney.

Three-year-olds would learn the alphabet and numbers one to twenty. Four- and five-year-olds would learn verbs like *have* and *want*. Eight-to-ten-year-olds would take on grammar. This was all standard enough. But the lessons ran on a digital whiteboard produced by Disney with each day's lesson. When students broke into groups to practice, they role-played as Disney characters, "acting in much the same way as paid Disney employees do when embodying these characters in the company's theme parks," as scholar Aynne Kokas has noted.

Sugerman and other executives who crafted Disney English curricula saw two objectives: introducing young Chinese people to Disney characters and introducing the Disney brand as one of safety and reliability to Chinese parents. In China, they had a willing base of customers: parents who, now with some disposable income to spend, wanted their children to learn using Western models of education. If Disney was one symbol of American soft power, Harvard was another. Chinese parents who considered the American education system the finest in the world rushed to enroll their kids, even lying about their ages to start early. The one-child policy, enacted in 1979, had resulted in a younger generation with two parents and two sets of grandparents who could help finance one child's education. By the time Disney English was concocted, nearly thirty years had passed of Chinese families having only one child. Any Disney accountant sizing up the situation could see the "identifiable market."

The emphasis on education was another remarkably fast leap forward in Chinese society. In 1980 only about a quarter of Chinese babies and young children were enrolled in nursery schools and kindergarten. The education push repudiated Mao, who'd eliminated college-entrance exams and targeted teachers in his public shaming. A true education, he'd maintained, could be found as much in the field as in the classroom. Those who did make it into school had been fed a curriculum that toed the party line. One question: "What is the root cause of the inevitable crisis of capitalism?" Answer: private property.

As a consequence, Chinese parents sending their children to Disney English schools may have been accustomed to the use of targeted messaging in the classroom. Now their children would be taught a distinctly American mythology—the princesses and princes, mermaids, and lion cubs who had taught generations good and evil and love and valor, all set to catchy soundtracks. As insidious as it may sound to some, early engineers of Disney English insist that the initiative was not intended as commercial brainwashing. But that appears to be what it became.

Teachers were often drawn to the program by a love for Disney, and the company recruited instructors from their theme park ranks. Others were like Ivan Encinas, an El Paso native who'd applied for the position after growing fascinated by a time-lapse video on YouTube of Chinese megacities popping up out of nowhere. He was living at home, selling men's shoes at Dillard's, when a recruiter contacted him. Two Skype interviews later, he had the job. Disney handled the paperwork and paid him 15,000 yuan a month, or about $2,000. Encinas didn't speak any Chinese, but the classes were total English immersion, and a Chinese assistant was on hand for emergencies.

Encinas was soon immersed in the Disney way. The company provides an extensive set of rules for its employees, whom it refers to as "cast members" who must preserve "brand integrity." In the Disney parks, women portraying princesses must maintain a certain weight to match the silhouette of their animated counterparts. Outside the park, they are not allowed to publicly acknowledge their roles, for fear that will break the illusion by revealing that there are actors in those costumes to begin with. Before he started, Encinas was told his scruffy look was banned— he'd have to either shave every day or grow a full beard. He was told to smile every time he saw a parent—or, as they were referred to internally, a "customer." Encinas is a friendly guy who smiles easily, but he didn't like being told to smile.

The real cynicism set in when the announcements were introduced. Parents would come into the room at the end of every day, part of an effort of the schools to show them more of what their children were learning. The cast members were fed scripts to relay to these customers, often about new Disney movies or events. When a new *Star Wars* movie was coming out, for instance, the Disney English teachers gave the parents a flyer that they encouraged their kids to read at home. If the parents took a video of their child reading the flyer—and reciting dialogue along the lines of "Use the force, Luke Skywalker"—they could upload it to Chinese social media for a chance to win a *Star Wars* Lego set or free passes to the Shanghai park. The videos would promote the schools to other parents and the movies to other kids. Annual class renewals came with a Disney toy.

Encinas's location in Beijing had nine separate classrooms, each one highlighting a different Disney movie: a *Cars* room featuring automobile characters; a *Lion King* room that re-created the savanna. (No character mixing from room to room was allowed, per the "brand integrity" rules. A colleague of Encinas's was once reprimanded for bringing the wrong princess doll into the wrong room.) When he left his job in 2018, the school was converting one of the classrooms to a *Frozen* theme after that newer movie had proven so popular in China. Encinas wasn't surprised. In the Disney English classrooms, students chose English names, and every class he taught had an Elsa in it, maybe two. The company's goal of introducing such characters to Chinese children was working. "That's soft power at its finest," he said.

Soon after meeting with him, I walked by one of the Disney English classrooms in Shanghai, located in a courtyard of shops that included a White Castle and a yoga studio. Posters on the wall inside featured *Peter Pan*, *Monsters Inc.*, and *Dumbo*. That week, Disney's *Toy Story 4* would open in theaters. All of the English teachers wore T-shirts advertising the new movie.

THE CHARACTERS ENCINAS AND HIS colleagues taught to Chinese children are the envy of Hollywood, all assembled under one roof thanks to a string of crafty acquisitions. Soon after taking over the company, Iger negotiated with Steve Jobs for the $7.4 billion purchase of Pixar Animation, the family entertainment company behind *Toy Story*, *The Incredibles*, and *Up*. Six years later, he bought Marvel Entertainment, then the producer of a handful of successful superhero movies like *Iron Man*, for $4 billion. The comic book adaptations would become the most successful string of movies in Hollywood history—twenty-two films grossing more than $21 billion worldwide. In 2012, Iger bought a company no one knew was even for sale—Lucasfilm Ltd., the house that *Star Wars* built, for another $4 billion—so that Disney could produce and release a new collection of movies in the space Western saga.

Each of these new holdings went into the Disney franchise machine. A movie like *Toy Story*, for instance, was more than just a box-office moneymaker. It was a sequel generator—three other films over twenty-four years. It was a toy commercial—Woody, Buzz Lightyear, and other dolls sold at a premium in Disney stores. It was a theme park attraction—Toy Story Lands in Orlando, Paris, Hong Kong, and Shanghai.

But no division of Disney has matched the success of Marvel. The studio had enjoyed fortuitous timing with the 2008 premiere of *Iron Man*, a movie that arrived just as China's screen count began to grow. Over the next decade, grosses for Marvel movies in China would steadily grow, too, routinely drawing in hundreds of millions of dollars—totals that were second only to North America. After a screening of *Captain Marvel* in Hong Kong, I spoke with a young college student trying out his rudimentary English. He knew only a few words but could say clearly the words *Easter egg*—known to fans as the clues planted in Marvel movies for eagle-eyed viewers.

The production budgets routinely topped $200 million, meaning they would require significant Chinese grosses to turn a healthy profit. After acquiring Marvel, Disney took pains to nurture those grosses in China, with outreach like its ham-handed *Iron Man 3* scenes of the heroic Chinese doctor. But in one of the most blatant attempts at placating Chinese authorities, the American superhero factory also made sure to keep a Tibetan character off-screen when the time came. It occurred in 2016, when Marvel was on its fourteenth movie in the superhero series. Benedict Cumberbatch was starring in a comic book adaptation called *Doctor Strange*, and Disney had every reason to believe it would pull in Chinese audiences. But *Doctor Strange* posed a problem that threatened all of it, much as *Kundun* had. Once again, a peace-promoting Tibetan character had to be dealt with. The movie's title character, in the original comic books, is counseled on his powers by a Tibetan monk called the Ancient One. The original artistry of the books shows a bald, long-goateed man with Asian features, an Orientalist, Fu Manchu–type rendering that would be unacceptable to most contemporary audiences.

Disney's solution, though, was to make the Ancient One not a Tibetan man at all but a Celtic woman played by Tilda Swinton—a mystic presence, to be sure, but not an Asian one. The decision allowed Disney to avoid any consternation among Chinese censors who would refuse a movie that glorified Tibetans, but it angered several constituencies in the U.S. Critics called it whitewashing, evidence that Disney would cast white actors over minorities in major roles. Supporters of Tibet registered it as the latest in a string of scrubbings. The movie's writer, C. Robert Cargill, made no bones about what he believed was behind the choice.

"The Ancient One was a racist stereotype who comes from a region of the world that is in a very weird political place," he said. "He originates from Tibet. So if you acknowledge that Tibet is a place and that he's Tibetan, you risk alienating one billion people and risk the Chinese government going, 'Hey, you know one of the biggest film-watching countries in the world? We're not going to show your movie because you decided to get political.'"

In a sign of its shifting priorities, Disney was willing to endure a small controversy in its home market to avoid a bigger controversy in an overseas market. *Doctor Strange* hit Chinese theaters in November 2016 and grossed $109 million there, the most in any market outside the U.S.

THE POWER OF THE MARVEL narratives can be found in fans like Lawrence Zhou, who in 2020 was a twenty-four-year-old master's student studying history in a northern Chinese city. Zhou found *Iron Man* by accident soon after starting college. He was looking for something to watch on his phone, and this was different from his usual Hollywood favorites like *Pirates of the Caribbean* or James Bond movies. He quickly caught up with all the movies in the series, growing to understand how they were interlocked into one unifying storytelling universe.

Going to see a new Marvel movie in a theater, he said, is like "participating in a carnival. For the first time, I would scream, applaud, and interact with the strangers who are sitting next to me." Marvel movies were linked to favorite memories: *Doctor Strange* was his first midnight premiere. When Captain America lifts Thor's hammer in the climactic battle of *Avengers: Endgame*, a bending of the comic book rules of physics, Zhou cried.

Along the way, these American superheroes came to represent more than popcorn entertainment. Captain America has been his favorite since *Captain America: Civil War* was released in 2016. Zhou was drawn to the brawny good guy, who made his comic book debut months before Pearl Harbor would pull the U.S. into World War II. Captain America was the alter ego of Steve Rogers, a son of New York City immigrants who enlists to fight the Axis powers but is turned away because of his frail frame. After officials inject him with a serum, Rogers emerges as a hypertrophied specimen, using an indestructible shield and patriotic motif to take on bad guys the world over. Captain America always stayed a moral step ahead of everyone else. In his first-ever comic, published in 1941, he punched Adolf Hitler. An adult in the 1940s, when his body and personality are preserved, he is a throwback warrior who represents Greatest Generation ideals while taking on Communists, corrupt businessmen, and international terrorists.

"He is like the orphan left in the last era," Zhou said.

Like many growing up in a changing China, Zhou felt a deep connection to the most American of superheroes. Executives at Disney and other studios privately wondered what exactly had drawn audiences so consistently to these superhero movies and turned them into one of the few examples of a monocultural offering in a fragmented entertainment market. They are called the Westerns of the twenty-first century, trading the cocky cowboy for the suited superhero who flies into town to take on the villain and restore a sense of justice. Others say they offer a clear-cut contrast between good and evil—an idealized version of a post-9/11 society, where uncomplicated good always prevails, even after skyscrapers are blown up. For Zhou, Marvel—and Captain America specifically—offered a blueprint of behavior for living in an authoritarian state where he feels he must acquiesce to cultural norms or governmental expectations.

"I have grown up in the context of collectivism and have always been an obedient one," said Zhou. Captain America "chose to say no to the mainstream opinions of the society. It is so attractive to me."

One scene in *Captain America: Civil War* cemented Captain America as his hero. A main tension in *Civil War* is between Captain America and Iron Man, who are split over the Sokovia Accords, a government initiative that would register superhumans and bring them into the fold of the state. Iron Man argues that registering is the responsible thing to do, since it will ask the government to control their powers and avoid the needless destruction of cities and loss of innocent lives. He wants to go to the government for help. Zhou's hero disagrees.

```
                    CAPTAIN AMERICA
          If we sign this, we surrender our right
          to choose. What if this panel sends us
          somewhere we don't think we should go? What
          if there's somewhere we need to go, and they
          don't let us? We may not be perfect, but the
          safest hands are still our own.
```

For Captain America, a superhero born from a sabotaged state-sponsored experiment, and who has seen his friends framed by officials for crimes they did not commit, cooperating with the government would abdicate freedom. Iron Man has seen his uncontrollable power level cities and considers government enforcement inevitable, so he wants defined parameters. Marvel fans debated who was right in this civil war. Zhou watched Captain America advocate for personal choice instead of voluntarily being subsumed into the state and saw his everyday life in contemporary China projected back at him.

"Captain America is not just a superhero, but also represents the spirit of freedom and democracy that the United States has always promoted," he said. "My love for him is also in line with my fantasy of liberalism."

Marvel superhero movies are the most global films made today, the only franchise able to draw audiences from every country every time. But as Zhou's interpretation of the movies and their characters shows, they remain inherently American narratives, not only in their characters but in the themes of individualism, triumphalism, and personal freedom they explore. It's just that Iron Man gets operated on by Chinese doctors sometimes, and even Captain America uses a Chinese-made Vivo phone. In the case of Captain America and his biggest Chinese fan, the movies convey the Western good in ways that would likely concern

Chinese officials who want the box-office grosses these blockbusters provide but chafe at the Western values they promote.

IF MARVEL IS THE HOLLYWOOD cinematic universe with the best timing in China, then *Star Wars* is the one with the worst. Much like the approach taken by the live-action remakes of 1990s animated classics, Disney's *Star Wars* strategy trades heavily on nostalgia for the original trilogy, which premiered in 1977. After buying Lucasfilm, Disney began planning a trio of films that would combine new actors with Mark Hamill, Carrie Fisher, and Harrison Ford, alongside other props and characters made famous by George Lucas's first installment. The first movie in the new series, *Star Wars: The Force Awakens*, introduced new characters like Rey (Daisy Ridley) and Poe (Oscar Isaac). Like *Transformers* before it, *Star Wars* would hit at the box office by drawing in several generations.

With a price tag of more than $250 million, Disney wanted *The Force Awakens* to win over fans in China to the franchise—especially since it would be one of several *Star Wars* movies coming in the next decade. They had a Chinese-Korean boy band make a music video for a song called "Lightsaber." They had five hundred miniature storm troopers stand in formation on the Great Wall, their iconic white helmets a modern addition to the 2,700-year-old structure. Director J. J. Abrams traveled with the movie's stars and new droid, a Creamsicle-colored roller ball called BB-8, for a premiere in Shanghai.

Ahead of the movie's release, though, most publicity Disney could generate was unwelcome. The studio had radically changed the makeup of its *Star Wars* cast, introducing black, Asian, and other ethnicities to what had been a largely white space force. The changes earned praise in the U.S., where a conversation about on-screen representation had pressured studios to make sure their movies reflected the countries watching them. *The Force Awakens* included a black actor from the United Kingdom,

John Boyega, as a renegade storm trooper named Finn, alongside Latino actor Oscar Isaac as Poe. Disney released an overstuffed poster showing these new actors alongside the 1970s players.

When the poster appeared in China, however, local executives in Disney's Beijing office had made some conspicuous changes. Anticipating local pushback against actors of color, they shrank Boyega's image on the poster so that he was about as prominent as BB-8, the droid. Chewbacca, the dark-haired Wookiee, also got reduced billing, and Isaac disappeared altogether. The controversy exposed a sensitive topic in Hollywood circles, where some executives believe Chinese audiences are less receptive to lead actors of color than American ones are. In China, where many residents may have never seen a black person in their everyday life, the unfamiliarity can read as racism—or at least give executives another risk to avoid. Disney's office in Beijing confirmed these fears, unfounded or not, when it tried to trick audiences into thinking they would be seeing a movie with largely white stars.

When *The Force Awakens* opened in the U.S., it sold out theaters around the clock and went on to gross more than $900 million, a new record. Yet in China, the movie petered out fast, eventually grossing just $124 million, when Disney accountants had projected $200 million. The biggest franchise in Hollywood wasn't appealing to the industry's most important foreign market.

Lucasfilm sent longtime executive Howard Roffman to China to figure out why. It wasn't a poster fracas that was keeping audiences away. Roffman started interviewing fans and nonfans across China, soon discovering that the generational appeal of *Star Wars* in the West had no analogue in China, which was only a year out from the Cultural Revolution when the original movie premiered in 1977. Those going to the new movie in theaters around the world were revisiting their childhood and introducing their children to it. Without a drive to shepherd children into the saga, the movies needed to have stand-alone appeal. And in that respect, Chinese audiences felt left out. Lucasfilm had incorporated in-jokes and callbacks to the thirty-eight-year-old film, and without that base knowledge—the Death Star, Yoda, "I am your father"—dialogue that caused American fans to go into paroxysms of bliss just confused Chinese viewers. When Harrison Ford's Han Solo first returns to the *Millennium Falcon* and says, "Chewie, we're home," moviegoers in China thought he might live there with the giant ape. The disparity in appeal lays bare a critical vulnerability in Hollywood's reliance on mining studio libraries for inspiration. Chinese moviegoers had caught up on a lot of entertainment they'd missed before the theater count began to grow, but this new approach in Hollywood of leaning on nostalgia revealed what blind spots persisted.

Roffman's second discovery, however, had more to do with the new China than the old *Star Wars*. China in 2015 looked a lot more advanced than this supposed future on-screen. When moviegoers noticed Han Solo piloted the *Millennium Falcon* with button controls, it looked less sophisticated than anything available on the smartphone in their pocket. The future was supposed to be a place of holograms and virtual reality, they said. Who pushes buttons?

"It's this very gritty, dirty, shopworn thing, and in the West it got great praise for looking like a lived-in universe," Roffman said. "But in China it was like, 'Ew, why would anybody want to live there?' The Jedi knights wear monk robes; the planets look like junkyards."

Disney did not give up. For the studio's next *Star Wars* feature, a spin-off called *Rogue One*, the company went the flower vase route, casting two Chinese actors in supporting roles. Donnie Yen, a well-known kung fu actor, had an idea to make his character blind, a deft combination of the Chinese blind swordsman trope and Lucas mythology that elevated the part. But his Chinese costar, Jiang Wen, didn't help matters when he admitted, days before the movie's premiere, that he had never seen a *Star Wars* film. "I know nothing about them," he said. *Rogue One* disappointed by grossing a tepid $69 million in China.

Disney then tried seeding the *Star Wars* mythology among young

Chinese children, publishing a line of manga comics on the Skywalker saga. Those failed to develop a critical following. The new movies' grosses kept falling. *Star Wars: The Last Jedi* collected $42 million. Lucasfilm executives wondered if they should make a spin-off movie based in China in an all-out effort to win over consumers. It went nowhere. The last of the new trilogy, *Star Wars: The Rise of Skywalker*, made only $20 million in China—or about as much as it had made in Spain.

Instead, a different story of resistance appeared to Chinese audiences the weekend *The Rise of Skywalker* premiered and collected nearly six times its gross—a financial symbol of Chinese tastes deviating from Hollywood offerings and toward their own stories. It was the fourth installment of the *Ip Man* movies, a series about a real-life Chinese martial arts master best known for training Bruce Lee. Playing Master Ip was Donnie Yen, the Chinese actor who had been cast in *Rogue One* to pull in Chinese audiences. In this film, Master Ip arrives in 1960s San Francisco, a city teeming with suburban mothers, city cops, and drill sergeants united in their hatred of the Chinese. A young Chinese girl is attacked by a pretty blond cheerleader and her pack of jock protectors. They cut off her hair and declare, "In America, people like you follow and don't lead."

In the climax of the film, a racist marine declares the U.S. the best country in the world—"a land of supremacy"—and challenges the Ip Man to a fight, karate versus kung fu. "You're nothing but another yellow chink," he tells Master Ip, standing underneath the U.S. Marine Corps flag. The American villain is a stand-in not unlike the Russian antagonists of 1980s American movies. The fight goes as expected—one man up, one man down, then reverse—until Master Ip lands a solid punch that bloodies the marine's right eye, kicks him in the groin, snaps his right arm, and, in classic kung fu fashion, delivers a punishing three-finger jab to a pressure point in his neck that sends the marine to the ground and then to the infirmary. The group of marine soldiers watching start to applaud. Black soldiers, Asian American soldiers, white soldiers—all of them cheer for the Chinese hero. Before the credits roll, text on the screen tells the viewer the U.S. Marine Corps has incorporated kung fu fighting into its training program since 2001. The entire movie becomes an origin story for an American reliance on the Chinese. When the lights came up in the theater, I asked my Chinese guest what he thought of it. He told me he was close to crying. Even as moviegoers like Zhou flocked to Captain America, some others in China didn't want to see Donnie Yen helping the rebels win in *Star Wars*. Judging by my guest's reaction, this was the movie China wanted to see Donnie Yen in.

Soon after the fizzle of *Rise of Skywalker*, though, Lucasfilm announced it wasn't giving up yet. In late 2020, it began publishing *Star Wars* web novels, a popular form of online literature released in installments and shaped in real time by audience feedback. The first release, *The Vow of Silver Dawn*, takes place two hundred years before the Skywalker saga and is populated by Wookiees and humans who stew their meat in soy sauce and go by names like Zhang San. This was in addition to the forty preexisting *Star Wars* novels that Disney was translating into Chinese to try to bring the Chinese up to speed. With more than a dozen TV shows and movies planned for the next several years of *Star Wars*, the company could not afford to give up hope that China would come on board.

WITH TANG AND HIS NEIGHBORS out of their homes, migrant workers traveled across the country to fill the construction jobs needed to build a Tomorrowland, a Fantasyland, a Toy Story Land, an Adventure Isle, a Treasure Cove, Gardens of Imagination, and Mickey Avenue (as opposed to the Main Street, U.S.A., found at most other Disney parks). Ahead of its opening, some officials raised alarms about Disney's corrupting influence that echoed those Mao-era concerns about Western art infecting Chinese brains.

"I suggest that we shouldn't allow too many Disneyland theme parks to be built. . . . If children follow Western culture when they are little, they will end up liking Western culture when they grow up and be uninterested in Chinese culture," said Li Xiusong, China's deputy head of culture.

But the forces in Li's government that wanted a Disney park in their country won out. In June 2016, Iger and his deputies traveled to China for the opening of Shanghai Disney Resort, a $5.5 billion attraction covering those one thousand acres, with room to grow beyond the theme park, two themed hotels, dining and entertainment district, and nature park that opened the attraction. A subway station was built just to ferry guests to its gates. Iger hosted journalists on walks through the park and promised it would be "authentically Disney, distinctly Chinese." In the first days of its opening, some growing pains emerged. Chinese patrons weren't accustomed to lining up for rides the way Western visitors were, and they had little understanding of how "dark rides," or coasters built indoors, operated. But for the most part, the opening of Disney's new outpost in mainland China had gone as preordained.

I visited Shanghai Disneyland in the summer of 2019, riding the subway out to the park on a weekday. The landscape visible through the train's window grew increasingly desolate as we rode out of Shanghai, the Magic Kingdom castle blurry in the distance through expansive fields, greenhouses, and endless power lines. Three stops before our arrival, two men got on board to sell counterfeit Mickey Mouse ears out of a plastic bag. As the train grew closer to the park, unruly greenery gave way to Disney order: clipped bushes and hedges that make the Shanghai subway start to feel like a theme-park tram. The Shanghai Disneyland subway stop had been completely taken over. Silhouettes of Goofy and Donald Duck struck jaunty poses on the wall, and primary colors had replaced the palate of gray and off-white that the other stations have. Baby-blue stars hung above the security guards scanning bags and the facial recognition cameras that log visitors on their way out of every train station.

In the years since opening, annual attendance at Shanghai Disneyland has hovered around eleven million visitors, enough to place it in the top ten theme parks by attendance anywhere in the world. (It still trails attendance at Disney's parks in the U.S. and Tokyo.) The experience of the Chinese park wasn't much different from visiting an American one. Tickets cost about $58, or about half the price of a ticket to Disneyland, but that's considered overpriced by most Chinese parents. Soon after the opening, visitors, like their American counterparts, complained that food prices were inflated—a steamed bun that cost 20 cents on the street was $1 inside the park gates.

On my visit, an orchestral arrangement of "Go the Distance" from *Hercules* played outside merchandise stores selling Disney enamel pins and Disney coffee mugs. Fake storefronts were interspersed among the real ones, including B.B. Wolfe & Co. Demolition, a riff on the Three Little Pigs rhyme. Its slogan: "We'll blow your house down." A Chinese worker at the front door of a restaurant waved goodbye wearing a giant Mickey Mouse glove on her left hand, making it appear as though she suffered from a brand-specific version of elephantiasis. I walked through a sea of bubbles being dispersed by an Iron Man claw worn by a young boy also wearing a Donald Duck canteen and a *Pirates of the Caribbean* eye patch. His mom was in mouse ears.

TODAY, TANG AND HIS WIFE live in a cluster of thirty high-rise apartment buildings reached by a fifteen-minute car ride from Disneyland. Four such communities, totaling about 6,500 apartments, were built for the Zhaohang village families. Tang lives on the second floor of a sand-colored high-rise, one of several identical structures. The area has the feel of a retirement village at certain parts of the day. In the mornings, Tang takes a walk on a two-lane asphalt road lined with camphor trees. There's a playground that fills in the evenings and an on-site kindergarten for the children of the relocated families. After dinner, Tang dresses in gray pants and a striped shirt to smoke and catch up with old Zhaohang neighbors downstairs.

Many of the families have realized considerable wealth thanks to the relocation. Since they lived in multigenerational housing on their farmland, they qualified for multiple apartments in the new buildings, many of which they did not need. Several families rented out those additional units, collecting monthly rent far beyond their old farming income. The gas stoves took getting used to—some residents say the old clay and iron pots of Zhaohang made better food.

For his part, Tang is happy in his new home. It doesn't leak when it rains, as his old place did.

"I think being a farmer was my hardest time ever," he said. "Now I'm old, but it's also the age when I can enjoy my life."

He and his wife have been to Disneyland three or four times—he can't remember the exact count. He thought it was fantastic. It struck him as particularly good for tourists who come to China or Shanghai and want an unparalleled experience. But all in all, he thought the tickets and food were too expensive. He does not feel the need to go back.

ELEVEN

Hollywood's Translators

The 1995 movie *Cutthroat Island*, about buried treasure and sword fights on the high seas, was cursed from the start. Michael Douglas quit the lead role eight weeks before filming. The shoot dragged over schedule by months. A writer parachuted in for a $100,000 last-minute script rewrite. The crew got food poisoning.

Then audiences actually saw it. PIRATE MOVIE'S SO BAD, IT SHOULD CUT ITS OWN THROAT, went one representative headline. A $10 million gross on a $100 million budget earned the movie an unwelcome distinction: a Guinness World Record for the biggest flop of all time.

Renny Harlin, the director of *Cutthroat Island*, found it hard to recover. The biggest movie of his career became industry shorthand for "colossal bomb," an unmitigated mistake of the 1990s alongside Beanie Babies and Y2K anxiety. The life Harlin had constructed up until that point—the car (Ferrari), the house ($9 million), the movie-star wife (Geena

Davis)—disintegrated. People averted their eyes when they saw him at restaurants.

Cutthroat Island had been Harlin's seventh movie after a decade-long career specializing in proudly mainstream entertainment: *Die Hard 2*, starring a bloodied Bruce Willis saving the day; *Cliffhanger*, with a brawny Sylvester Stallone doing the same. The chances of getting work like that again evaporated, but jobs still came in sporadically. In 1999 a B movie about hyperintelligent sharks chasing LL Cool J called *Deep Blue Sea*. Seven years after that, *The Covenant*, about four male witches with flip phones. A remake of *The Exorcist* that no one wanted. A 2014 Hercules movie that opened the same year as another Hercules movie, that one starring Dwayne Johnson. Harlin's starred Kellan Lutz, the sixth-billed star of *Twilight*, and the box-office tallies correlated accordingly.

It was a few months after *The Legend of Hercules* bombed that Chinese producers halfway around the world started hunting for a Hollywood director who could come to their country and make a movie. Someone who could lend the production some Hollywood flair, maybe teach them a thing or two along the way about moviemaking. Harlin was just the guy for the job.

As Hollywood was chasing riches at the box office from Chinese audiences and in financing from Chinese billionaires, China's domestic film industry had been growing in size and producing hits, but it needed to get better at nailing the subtler aspects of effective cinematic storytelling, such as pacing, dialogue, and tone. After years of state-run propaganda features, the nation's commercial entertainment was underdeveloped, with relatively few directors making the romantic comedies, action adventures, and quiet dramas that fill out a studio slate beyond the franchise tentpoles. It was just those kinds of midlevel movies that were falling out of favor at American studios, where they were considered a waste of time and money compared with putting together another superhero epic that would sell tickets everywhere. Within China, producers backed by government ambitions and eager financiers wanted to build a more diverse industry and not just cede Chinese audiences to foreign competition. The future of China's film industry lay in its domestic market, making "bowls of noodles" for its own people, but it needed help getting there.

Since the earliest days of Warner Bros.' failed partnership with Dalian Wanda Group, a teacher-student dynamic had pervaded Hollywood's relationship with China. Warner Bros. gets an early foot in the Chinese exhibition market; Wanda gets the theater blueprints. The term was *technology transfer*, and it informed every American venture in the country regardless of industry. American businesses eager to get into the country would agree to hand over their know-how, and China's market leverage was allowing the country to skip a few grades. On the set of *The Great Wall*, Western crew members noticed that their Chinese counterparts took cell phone photos of scaffolding plans and other schematics that they could replicate on local productions. The American instructors would not only rewrite scripts to turn sidekicks into romantic interests or infuse winking humor into action scenes. They would, in some cases, try to capture the more ineffable attributes of moviemaking—such as when Bruce Feirstein, a writer of James Bond films like *GoldenEye*, explained to the Chinese actor Xin Baiqing on the set of a low-budget comedy called *Hutong Days* the subtler power of cinema. Feirstein was a producer on the movie, in which Xin played an architect whose wife is out of town when he meets an attractive twenty-eight-year-old maid.

"A man of my stature would not be interested in a maid," he huffed to Feirstein.

"You're absolutely right. An architect might not be interested in a maid," Feirstein responded. "But do you know who that housekeeper is in real life?"

Xin had no idea where this was going.

"She's every one of your fans across China," Feirstein said. "It's not about class. It's about hope." He had made his name in Hollywood writing scripts for the biggest-budgeted action movies, starring one of cinema's indelible creations. But in this lesson, Feirstein cut to the heart of the challenge of anyone trying to manufacture appeal in the form of soft power. In successful films, there was nothing more powerful than an audience that saw itself on-screen—or what it hoped to become.

Learning from other nations had been a core instruction of Mao Zedong's speech on art in Chinese society in 1942. Decades before Hollywood screenwriters and directors would travel to China to help make movies, Mao said the country should "on no account reject the legacies of the ancients and the foreigners or refuse to learn from them, even though they are the works of the feudal or bourgeois classes." The only thing to keep in mind, he added, was not losing sight of the core purpose of Chinese art: to serve China. When Ellen Eliasoph first started putting together Hollywood-China deals in the 1990s, she learned a dialectic that dated to the nineteenth century and had since guided Chinese leaders who wanted to retain their society's Confucian outlook while learning from the outside world: "Chinese learning as substance, Western learning for application." The philosophy initially emerged following the Second Opium War, when leaders within China advocated replicating the military and technology strategy of their country's foes.

In 2017, at the height of his new career in China, Harlin would be at the vanguard of a class of Hollywood hands serving as one-man instructional manuals. But what to do when the technology being transferred was not blueprints of set scaffolding but the tools of storytelling? It was one thing to hire Western visual effects artists or sound designers, which many Chinese productions during this time were doing. It was another to find the writers and directors who could take a Chinese story and alter it, lending its Eastern approach a Western arc or character development. And it wasn't like Christopher Nolan or Spike Lee had time on their hands to do this. The directors who were available would not have been Hollywood's choices for ambassadors of craft. But in November 2017, three years after he'd been hired for that first Chinese job, I met Harlin on a sound stage outside Beijing. I've rarely seen someone so happy.

. . .

HE ARRIVED ON THE SET of *Bodies at Rest* at 7:50 a.m. Hundreds of crew members were already preparing in a two-story morgue populated by rubber cadavers, jars of fluid, and posters displaying the central nervous system. Trailed by two translators and his girlfriend, Harlin greeted the crew in Mandarin. He was done directing his first shot by 8:22.

Bodies at Rest is, essentially, *Die Hard* in a morgue. A coroner, played by Hong Kong actor Nick Cheung, has teamed up with a young intern (Yang Zi) to fight back a band of criminals who have broken into the office on Christmas Eve to retrieve an incriminating bullet lodged in one of the bodies. If it sounds like a textbook Hollywood action movie— an unassuming good guy is conscripted into fighting the bad guys in a confined space to save himself and a woman he's growing to love—that is because *Bodies at Rest* started as a Hollywood script. Harlin came in and "China-fied" it for a production backed by Alibaba Pictures and Dalian Wanda Group.

"Renny has prestigious credits," Peggy Pu, a producer from Wanda, told me. "That's why we chose him."

The movie that brought Harlin to China also shared DNA with his older films. *Skiptrace* paired Jackie Chan with Johnny Knoxville, a comedic actor best known for the MTV prank show *Jackass*, to form an unlikely duo who team up to avenge the murder of Chan's partner at the hands of a mob boss known as "the Matador."

Harlin was used to dealing with rules—in Los Angeles in recent years, he told me, he'd been forced to keep violence in every movie at a PG-13 level to maximize the number of potential moviegoers. Action movies in China had different parameters. He'd wanted to film a scene in *Skiptrace* involving a helicopter but was told that helicopters can be used only by employees of government agencies, so his character couldn't take the controls. In Hollywood, *Skiptrace* would have ended with Chan killing the Matador on behalf of his fallen friend, and his individual heroism would have been celebrated. In China, *Skiptrace* had to end with the Hong Kong Police Department coming in to save the day, rather than a rogue agent. The Matador died, but by sacrificing himself, not at Chan's hands.

According to Chinese censorship rules, the coroner in *Bodies at Rest* must maintain a similar moral distance, since he is not a cop or authority figure who can kill with no compunction. This movie, too, culminates in a showdown in which the head criminal dies by his own hand—in this case, by tripping and falling to his death. Forget a gunshot—even a push by the Everyman hero would be morally suspect in a country that wants every movie to achieve a moral equilibrium. In a Chinese *Silence of the Lambs*, Clarice Starling would apprehend Hannibal Lecter before he could escape to the tropics. Requiring a corruption-free cinematic reality can twist producers into all kinds of logical knots. I met one American producer who was trying to make a Chinese version of *Serpico*, about a police officer who exposes corrupt colleagues. The protagonist's actions were laudable in a country where Xi has rooted out corruption himself, but the movie's very premise relied on corruption existing in the first place. The producer called it "a metaphysical quandary." He thought he might get away with it by setting the story twenty years in the past, before Xi was in charge.

"Go against the system and prove yourself. We celebrate that. That arc doesn't exist in China," Harlin says.

Bodies at Rest is filming in Huairou, a district an hour's drive north of Beijing that has been home to the state-run China Film Group sound stages for decades. A giant statue of three party members anchors its main courtyard, and the back lot includes replicas of Chinese villages that can be refashioned as ancient China for countless costume dramas or propaganda movies about historical events.

The town outside the sound stages feels like a concerted effort to commercialize China's film industry beyond that historical fare. A sign welcomes guests to CHINESE FILM FAMOUS TOWNS. Harlin lives across the street in a two-story suite at the Cineaste Hotel, a sixteen-story establishment with a Hollywood theme and an Oscar logo. No opportunity for cross-branding is overlooked. To mark the men's room, a photo of Clark Gable hangs outside; Vivien Leigh is across the hall. The handicapped stall is graced by a picture of Jimmy Stewart from *Rear Window*, the movie he spends in a wheelchair. The fact that few Chinese stars could prove as recognizable on a bathroom sign gets to the root of why Harlin is here, a problem CFG chairman Yang Buting defined in 2012: "China boasts a long history and a rich culture. But we must see that compared with the American film industry, we still have a long way to go in terms of screenwriting, production, marketing, and distribution."

China's technology transfer strategy has a long and controversial history—one that has put American companies at odds with their government, where officials are weary of handing over trade secrets so readily. The examples range from a fracking company based in Fort Worth, Texas, that entered a joint venture with a state-owned Chinese firm and taught its drillers how to access the reserves themselves to General Electric, which signed an agreement with a state-owned Chinese firm that included handing over blueprints for the communications and navigational tools found in the Boeing flagship 787 Dreamliner. That same year, General Motors agreed to share with a local Chinese firm the battery technology that made its electric cars run. Chinese leaders embraced the pollution-cutting technology, and within the decade, GM was selling more cars in China than in the U.S. In each case of technology transfer, critics warned that China's controlled economy could quickly take over, holding on to the lesson plans while forcing out the Western competition through cheaper prices or forced renegotiations. But it was often the only way in, since doing business in China often required finding a local partner, who was likely affiliated with the government. Executives in each industry can tell the same story: China lures them there with the incredible market power, then learns their ways and doesn't need them anymore.

. . .

HARLIN TAKES SERIOUSLY HIS ROLE in helping China's entertainment industry. After a 4:00 a.m. workout and breakfast in the hotel restaurant, Harlin is driven across the street to the sound stage. He stands more than six feet tall and wears an intimidating amount of heavy jewelry, but he projects a softer authority on set, sipping from his thermos as he gives notes to his translators or cinematographer to relay to the actors.

The stars of *Bodies at Rest* are Cheung and Yang—"the Robert De Niro of China" and an ingenue best known for growing up on a Chinese TV show, respectively. In a scene filmed later that first morning I'm on set, they huddle behind a metal table, conspiring on how to evade the gun-toting madmen. Cheung, born in Hong Kong, is delivering his lines in Cantonese. Yang, born in mainland China, is saying hers in Mandarin. And neither of them speaks the other's version of Chinese.

Since all of the dialogue in the movie will be dubbed before it's released in theaters, it's not a problem. Cheung and Yang have simply memorized all of the dialogue in their scenes so they know how to respond and when. Harlin hardly speaks any Chinese at all.

"Can I tell that they're saying the right words? No. I am just judging their performances on the universal scale of emotions. So far, in three movies, I've never felt a problem," he told me. Two Chinese women who graduated from American film schools translate for him. Harlin's girlfriend, Kay, is an unofficial third. More than thirty years his junior, Kay met Harlin at a Chinese film festival and has been by his side ever since. Her English is so perfect and accent free that Harlin jokes she is a spy.

When the translations don't quite work, directing takes the form of exaggerated gesticulating and onomatopoeia. One of the actors filming was Ming Peng, a former flight attendant not many years out of high school who became a Weibo celebrity after a stranger uploaded his photo to social media and remarked how similar he looked to a K-pop star.

After that, Ming left his job and became an actor, cast in *Bodies at Rest* in the hope he could pull some of his Weibo followers into the theater. He is having trouble responding on camera to a kick to the stomach, so Harlin pulls his own stomach in, contorts his face into pain. Later, he claps out the tempo of a pistol whip because he's learned in Hollywood that "violence has a rhythm to it."

"Run, run, run—they crash through the window—pssh!" he tells Yang ahead of one scene, moving his arms like a jogger, gesturing toward the glass, waving his hands in front of his face to convey the shards that fly everywhere.

To help her prepare for the role, Harlin gave Yang a reel of strong female leads from Hollywood movies: Linda Hamilton in *Terminator 2: Judgment Day*; Angelina Jolie in *Salt*; his ex-wife, Davis, in his own *The Long Kiss Goodnight*. In a set cafeteria between takes, wearing a floor-length Hello Kitty purple poof jacket, Yang told me it was intimidating to work for a famous director from Los Angeles and compare herself to those American stars. "It's not easy for a Chinese woman to act as a superhero on film. I don't know if I can be the ideal image that Renny wants me to be. I feel like my body isn't as sexy as Hollywood."

Yang and her fellow actors were not used to Harlin's morning shot list and ruthless efficiency, telling me story after story of life on set with Chinese directors, who are notorious for keeping plot details a secret— and sometimes showing up in the morning without a clue of what they're filming that day. Harlin, by contrast, arrived each morning with a list of scenes he needed to complete, keeping the set open only from 7:00 a.m. to 7:00 p.m., or about four to six hours shorter than the typical Chinese film workday. Harlin may be best remembered for a movie that went two months over schedule and millions of dollars over budget, but in China he was a model of efficiency.

The disparity between Harlin's approach and his cast's expectations of a director's behavior speaks to one of the central differences in movie-making between China and the U.S., one that technology-transfer filmmakers are helping to bridge. The difference was best articulated to me by Ang Lee's longtime producing partner, James Schamus, who observed how the cast and crew approached Lee on set. When Lee was directing *Eat Drink Man Woman* in Taiwan, crew workers were scared to sit near him during lunch, giving him a wide radius of empty picnic tables. A few years later, Lee was in the UK in rehearsals on *Sense and Sensibility*, an adaptation starring classically trained actors like Hugh Grant, who at one point even wanted to give Lee his opinion on how to approach an upcoming shot.

Lee looked at Schamus. "You know, James, I used to be an emperor, and now I'm just the president," he said. Years later, Schamus hosted a master class for Chinese filmmakers, who asked him which model of governance was the right approach on set. Schamus said moviemaking should be a "constitutional monarchy," where collaboration takes place but the director has the ultimate authority. When a recording of his class was posted online, Chinese authorities removed his reference to "constitutional monarchy."

HARLIN OWES HIS CAREER TO his first movie getting banned. It was called *Born American*, and at the time, it was the most expensive movie ever filmed in his native Finland. Starring Chuck Norris's son as one of three boneheaded college friends who decide to cross the border into Russia, *Born American* was blocked from release in Finland, where authorities feared it would anger Russia by its portrayal of their citizens as bloodthirsty nationalists. The banning gave the movie more attention than it ever would have garnered on its own.

Harlin's parents, a doctor and a nurse, weren't thrilled when their son enrolled in film school at the University of Helsinki. Even worse, he didn't graduate. But Harlin couldn't stand his classmates, a group of art-school snobs smoking cigarettes and "talking about film theory blah blah blah," he told me. On a school trip, he purchased a can of Coca-Cola and they scoffed. "They thought I was kissing America's ass as a lover of capitalism," he said. Even in his earliest days, he thought the movies should focus on entertaining people. While in school he practiced by making commercials for local products like baking soda, viewing such gigs not as selling out but as having the chance to explain, in thirty seconds in a concise narrative, why this woman *loved* this baking soda. Just because a production was commercial didn't mean it couldn't tell a story, he figured.

Then *Born American* turned Harlin into a cause célèbre of the international film community. In the eyes of cinephiles, he was a director kept down by his government, even as he tried to explain himself at the time: "This is an action-adventure film. I am not a politician." The attention got him to Hollywood, though, where he drove around Los Angeles in an MGB convertible with a torn roof for months, interviewing for work. Finally he was hired to direct *Nightmare on Elm Street 4: The Dream Master*, the latest in the Freddy Krueger horror franchise. When it unexpectedly became the most profitable installment yet, offers poured in. Harlin abandoned the broken convertible at a parking meter and bought a Ferrari.

Bigger movies followed, including *Die Hard 2*, the sequel to the 1988 hit and, in Harlin's hands, "pure American entertainment," according to film critic Gene Siskel. Harlin often took only a week off work between productions. Though he pursued more serious projects, like a biopic about the founder of Greenpeace, his output remained commercial, expensive, and loud. He became a symbol of a glamorous Hollywood floating on VHS sales and dumb money, boarding private jets with kilograms of caviar for weekends away with studio executives. At a time when money was rolling in and everyone was getting a cut, "you didn't have to feel guilty about enjoying the spoils," he told me.

With blond hair hanging past his shoulders and the hard-to-place European accent, Harlin had a romance-cover flair and became the rare celebrity director, showing up on red carpets with actresses like Laura

Dern and Geena Davis, the latter of whom he'd marry. Davis was at the
peak of her fame as well, having won an Oscar and starred in *Thelma &
Louise*. The couple became a fixation of gossip columnists ("Tall Director
and Actress to Become Tall Newlyweds") who covered their appearances
at Planet Hollywood openings, where they partied alongside Melanie
Griffith and Danny Glover. Their wedding in Sonoma County featured
confidentiality agreements and a skywriter.

"He got hit by the Hollywood crack pipe," said Bob Shaye, the New
Line Cinema executive who had hired Harlin for the fourth *Nightmare on
Elm Street*. "When you get so high so quick—and then you come down."

Cutthroat Island was that comedown. Twenty years later, it comes up
constantly. "It's impossible to stand up on a podium somewhere and say,
'People, people, quiet down. Let me explain what really happened,'" he
said from the *Bodies at Rest* set. He looked into the middle distance while
his crew readied a scene involving a villain getting his neck snapped by a
roving piece of morgue equipment. He doesn't think the movie is as bad
as people say. It was just a pile-on. "We just looked too much like the
Hollywood dream couple," he added, referring to his marriage to Davis.
"People just wanted to throw up when they looked at us." That married
life would not last much longer; Harlin and Davis divorced three years
after *Cutthroat Island*, when it was revealed he had fathered a child with
her personal assistant.

Even if Harlin hadn't directed *Cutthroat Island*, chances are it would
have been hard for him to find work in Hollywood when studios abandoned the kinds of movies he made. *Cliffhanger* cost $90 million to produce
in 1993, a figure too high for nearly any movie in contemporary Hollywood that isn't based on a video game, comic book, or toy line. Actors
like Bruce Willis and Sylvester Stallone cannot draw audiences in on the
strength of star power alone. By the time China called in 2013, Harlin
had found himself back where he was in Finnish film school, a man
again out of fashion in his country's entertainment industry.

China was a different story. The infusion of capital and the excitement

about moviemaking—both from producers and government officials—
felt like 1990s Hollywood again. Even better, the campy style Harlin
trafficked in, the definition of the "popcorn movie," didn't read as antiquated or cliché to Chinese audiences. Several other middling directors in
Hollywood came over to Beijing to work around this same time. Nearly
all of them left. Harlin broke up with his girlfriend, got a dog, and
stayed. "Like many times in my life, I chose my first love, which is movies," he said. From the set of *Bodies at Rest*, he was brainstorming an idea
for a film about China's impressive space-exploration efforts.

"When I see the Chinese flag in the wind, it makes me feel proud
and good. This is where I live, and I want my audience to feel good
about themselves and their country. It doesn't make me anti-American.
I live here. I'm patriotic about Finland. I'm patriotic about America.
And I'm becoming very patriotic about China as well," he told me.

THE POACHING EVEN PULLED IN directors who never thought
they'd set foot in China, much less work there. Jean-Jacques Annaud,
whose *Seven Years in Tibet* had ignited an international incident, was interrupted in his office one day in 2010 by an assistant who said a Chinese delegation wanted to see him. The delegation asked if he'd read a
book called *Wolf Totem*, about a student who communes with wolves
while living in Mongolia. Annaud had loved it. Would he be interested,
the delegation asked, in directing a cinematic adaptation of it?

"I'm sorry," he said, laughing. "But I'm banned from your country."

Don't worry about that, they assured him. Their company was backed
by the government—if they wanted Annaud, they could get him. They
had already approached Ang Lee and Zhang Yimou, but they needed
someone with more experience working with animals, which Annaud
had from making *The Bear*. If Annaud could come and make the movie,
"we'll study how you do it, and when we understand, we won't need you
anymore," they said. Everyone laughed.

He flew to Beijing, where a town car and a woman bearing flowers greeted him. His first stop: a government office, where politicians made it clear they knew Annaud's movies very well. This shocked Annaud, whose movies—even the ones that weren't about a young Dalai Lama—would never pass Chinese censorship. Chinese women, upon learning that he'd directed the explicit romance *The Lover*, thanked him for their sexual awakening. A top-ranking official at China Film Group surprised him by introducing himself and then saying, "I want you to tell me how you did that second scene in *The Lover*." An alternate universe existed for those who set the rules but were able to circumvent them.

In the eyes of some officials, Annaud had made one of the most offensive films of all time. But it was precisely Annaud's history with controversial movies that made him the right candidate for *Wolf Totem*, which Chinese officials hoped would convey ideas that they did not want to be seen as explicitly backing. If it was a known agitator of the Chinese government exploring charged themes like environmentalism, the message of the film would be more easily received.

"We have a terrible problem with pollution, and we know where your heart stands in terms of protection of nature. If you say things that we cannot say . . . ," one executive explained to him at an early meeting. Understanding the maxim that the best propaganda should not feel like propaganda, the Chinese producers putting *Wolf Totem* together knew that Annaud's reputation could guard against audience skepticism. Not only would they get Annaud's technical filmmaking skill, but he would also provide political cover to Chinese officials who wanted to tout a new open-mindedness.

"The freer I was going to be, the better it was going to be for them," Annaud told me. His Chinese backers suspected *Wolf Totem* could be a contender for the Academy Award for Best Foreign Language Film, and Western audiences would likely be more receptive to the movie if they knew it had been made by Annaud, a man still best known for a movie that China had banned.

Working on the set, Annaud was once again captivated by the culture of an Asian country. He recalled his early days in film school, where one of his professors was a hard-line Communist who screened movies from Russia, Ukraine, Poland, and East Germany. "They all had something in common: they were masterpieces because there was censorship. Censorship usually pushes the artist to say what he wants to say through a parable." Although Annaud was given more freedom than the filmmakers he had studied—the ones who had still been capable of telling a compelling story despite the state parameters in place—he still had to submit the film to China's censorship board, which approved it without any major changes. Critics hailed *Wolf Totem* as one of China's finest contemporary movies, and its Oscar chances looked bright—until, in a cruelly ironic twist, the academy disqualified it for the foreign-film award because too many of its creative players were non-Chinese.

Annaud's stature in China rose all the same. He spoke at film festivals and dined with important officials, getting to know a country whose leaders had denounced him as an enemy of the state. Despite the warming relations, a din of patriotic social media commentators who never forgot *Seven Years in Tibet* followed him everywhere. They called him a Dalai Lama apologist relentlessly, to the point that Annaud had to address it. He went the Eisner route.

"Due to the lack of thorough understanding of Chinese history and culture, I could not predict the adverse effects of [*Seven Years in Tibet*] in China after the broadcast. I apologize for this. In fact, my final intention in this film is to convey the will of peace, but I regret it," Annaud wrote in a blog post circulated by Chinese state media. He is an atheist, he explained, someone whose core beliefs are equality, independence, and freedom.

"I have always respected the provisions of international conventions and recognized that Tibet is part of Chinese territory," he added.

In 2012 he took his defense further while chairing the jury at the Shanghai International Film Festival. The international community held

China to a double standard, he claimed. "What would we think in France if the Chinese were interfering with Corsica? Or what would Americans think if the Chinese were interfering with Puerto Rico?" he asked one interviewer.

Today, Annaud says no country is perfect. "I can be a friend to both sides," he told me.

I CAUGHT UP WITH HARLIN a year after visiting the *Bodies at Rest* set, when he returned to Los Angeles. The trappings of his resuscitated success came with him. A driver waited outside for the entirety of our two-hour dinner at Il Piccolino, a Beverly Hills restaurant that had been a hot spot during Harlin's heyday in the 1990s. For him, it was like returning to a different city. As one of the few directors known to have cracked the Chinese market, Harlin was suddenly indispensable. His schedule was booked.

I saw the finished *Bodies at Rest* when it opened the Hong Kong International Film Festival nearly two years later, in 2019. During a press conference held before the screening, Harlin stood with the practiced experience of having been here before. He spoke in short sentences, pausing to let the translator keep up, and responded to jokes with a tape-delayed laugh. He added a slight bow when he thanked the audiences.

"We have a Hollywood director working with us!" Nick Cheung said to applause.

The movie had followed Harlin's rule of commercial action movie-making: never let ten minutes lapse without an outburst of action. In his American hit *Cliffhanger*, for instance, a woman plunges to her death four minutes into the movie. At fourteen minutes in, a hijacking gone wrong ends in machine-gun fire between two planes before one explodes, and so on. In *Bodies at Rest*, the criminals barge into the morgue at the eleven-minute mark. The employees make their first attempt at an escape twenty-two minutes in, and a fistfight breaks out ten minutes later when the intern throws supplies at one of the accomplices. Another show-down comes at forty-four minutes, continuing until the villain's demise at the final climax.

The movie retained some of Harlin's Hollywood humor. When the criminals break into the morgue wielding guns, the coroner looks at them and drolly remarks, "You know this is not a bank." No one in the audience laughed. Harlin, I saw, had also successfully directed Cheung and Yang to hug convincingly after the villain dies and the shooting stops. On set, he had wanted the two leads to run and collapse into one another's arms, just like Willis does when he sees his wife at the end of *Die Hard 2*. They hadn't been able to nail it, instead filming the scene as though they had just caught up over coffee and not survived blood-shed together. In the finished product, the hug was big, and, in a move straight from the Hollywood playbook, a line of romantic dialogue had been added that allowed the leading lady to show a romantic interest in the man who had become her cofighter.

```
                        LYNN
        Who says it's my last Christmas here?
```

As the crowd left the theater, one of the moviegoers remarked, "All that was missing was 'Yippee-ki-yay.'"

A handful of projects next awaited Harlin's attention. A Chinese science-fiction coproduction might film in Australia, or he might start on *Operation Wild*, a China-India coproduction about ivory poaching that the government was supporting as a means of improving relations be-tween the two countries. He'd been approached about remaking *The Long Kiss Goodnight* for a Chinese audience. The original 1996 film starred Davis as an amnesiac whose criminal past catches up with her. Harlin had lived in China long enough to know he'd have to make some adjust-ments to the storyline, in which Davis's character takes down a nefarious plot involving the director of the CIA. He had a solution at hand.

"We can have the police come in at the end and solve it for every-body," he said.

BY THE TIME HIS CAREER in China came to a close, Bruce Feirstein had realized his onetime students no longer needed him. When he first traveled to China in 2005, he was hired to assess screenplays written by Chinese screenwriters. In those early scripts, he quickly found, a model was followed, one in which a character's fate remained immutable. But as familiarity with Hollywood filmmaking and filmmakers grew over the next several years, the heroes of Chinese scripts changed. That is, they became capable of changing.

"The number of 'fate' stories diminished, and we began to see more narratives where people became the masters of their own destinies. Young women who took charge of their dating lives; athletes who over-came insurmountable odds; nerdy computer geeks who got the girl—or sometimes the guy," he would later write.

At first, he thought the Chinese were copying Hollywood. And then he realized Hollywood had copied these narratives itself. The secret agent who'd bought him the mansion in Los Angeles, James Bond, was not unique to the West. He was merely England's most famous "lone warrior," sent by the king (or spy agency) to save the world, following in the tradition of shogun in Japan or *wuxia* in China, and drawing on cultures that revered their fighters, from Africa to New Zealand. The superhero movies breaking box-office records around the world had ori-gins in Greek, Indian, and Chinese mythology that anyone could tap.

"The beloved Chinese Monkey King alone could make 72 different transformations," he would write. "The only real difference between now and then is that instead of hurling city buses and wreaking havoc on modern municipal infrastructure, Zeus was throwing lightning bolts."

China's filmmakers, he thought, were not simply flying in directors and screenwriters from Los Angeles to learn camera angles and dialogue punch-ups. They were turning to the source material that had inspired narratives in their own country and around the world, long before the projector was even invented. China's entertainment industry had caught up. China was rising above its station, and so were they. To assume these stories were the domain of Hollywood alone was to fall prey to another mythic concept, Feirstein thought: hubris.

TWELVE

The Hero's Journey

n the summer of 2000, executives at Sony Pictures were waiting to hear if their Mel Gibson movie *The Patriot* would play on Chinese screens. It may have been an unlikely draw: the film was about Benjamin Martin, an eighteenth-century farmer who is pulled into the Revolutionary War after his son is killed by a cold-blooded British officer, compelling him to take up arms alongside the colonists. Martin avenges his son and kills the officer. Celebratory soldiers hoist the American flag over their heads in its rousing final minutes. Its effective storytelling—historical fiction grounded in a family story about a father's love for his son—was a hit with audiences, and the movie collected critical praise and $215 million at the global box office. Since it had overperformed in foreign markets, Sony executives were hopeful when they sent the print to Beijing for approval. Then they didn't hear anything for weeks.

A distribution executive called his contact in Beijing.

"We're not going to play it in our country," the official said. "But can we hold on to the print a little longer?"

Sure, the executive said. But why?

"We want others in the bureau to watch it so they can understand how to make a good propaganda film," the official replied.

The Patriot had managed to do what had long eluded Chinese officials: present a patriotic movie that didn't go down like medicine. Few moviegoers in the U.S. watched Mel Gibson slaughter the British and registered it as pro-America propaganda, or as a revisionist historical drama that scrapped nuance for a good-versus-evil telling of the Revolutionary War. To most viewers, it joined the tradition of cinematic American exceptionalism shown through the decades in movies like *The Longest Day*, *Patton*, and *Glory.*

In China there had been countless attempts at making similar movies, but the production was always a nationalized process, starting with culture and propaganda ministers in Beijing who doubled as film producers. The movies they made were not historical lessons wrapped up in family drama—they were uncontested propaganda about China's history, casting A-list actors as Mao and his contemporaries in roles that recreated their country's most glorious moments. There was a reason Michael Gralapp kept playing Winston Churchill. On Chinese screens, the war never ended.

Other countries had looked with similar awe toward America's ability to sell itself so subtly. In the 1940s, officials studied how *Mrs. Miniver*, a 1942 drama about a resolute British family surviving the war, accomplished what their state-backed screenplays could not. Churchill said the movie was "worth a whole regiment." Joseph Goebbels marveled, "There is not a single angry word spoken against Germany," and yet it was somehow a damning indictment of his regime. "I will show this film to German producers to explain how it must be done," he said.

For China, the breakthrough came in 2017. Seven years after IMAX

CEO Richard Gelfond had agreed to play *The Founding of the Party* in his auditoriums, the company's screens were allocated to that movie's follow-up: *The Founding of an Army*, produced in celebration of the ninetieth anniversary of the creation of the People's Liberation Army. More than fifty of China's most famous actors were cast in the film. Teen music idols played generals and other Chinese founding fathers—the equivalent of putting the Jonas Brothers in a film about the Battle of Gettysburg, hoping it pulls the median age of moviegoers out of the grandparent generation. IMAX cinemas were not the only advantage the government-backed production was afforded. It would premiere with sixty-eight thousand screenings, nearly double the number allocated to the other new movie opening that weekend, another sequel called *Wolf Warrior 2*. No foreign competition from Hollywood was allowed in, so Chinese films had a monopoly on the holiday box office.

The Founding of an Army opened to a fine, if not spectacular, $30.5 million in the first four days. But *Wolf Warrior 2* became an immediate phenomenon, grossing $146 million in that same window. By August 8, twelve days after its premiere, *Wolf Warrior 2* was not just the highest-grossing movie of the year—it was the highest-grossing movie in China's history. *Wolf Warrior 2* would run for months, eventually grossing $854 million—then the second-highest amount of money earned by a movie in one country in world history. By 2017, China's box office had grown to a point that Hollywood could regularly realize gigantic grosses, such as the $393 million made by *The Fate of the Furious* months earlier. But *Wolf Warrior 2* made more in China in 2017 than *Thor: Ragnarok* and *Wonder Woman* had made that year *worldwide*.

China's film industry had laid the groundwork for such a breakthrough. In 2017, just thirteen years after that Warner Bros. deal with Dalian Wanda Group to build Warner Wanda Cinemas, the number of movie screens in China surpassed that in the U.S., becoming number one in the world at 50,776. Crucially, this meant that screens had penetrated not only urban areas, but also towns far smaller than China's megacities, where rural audiences were more likely to buy tickets to domestic productions.

Now they had a homegrown blockbuster to show for it. While China had started the decade leaning on the American film industry for revenue and education, the country would end it by not needing U.S. entertainment at all. *Wolf Warrior 2* managed to wrap Xi's propagandistic messaging in popcorn entertainment. It gave Chinese audiences a hero they could put up against the Captain Americas of the world, one who matched the moment emerging across the ascendant country. Other made-in-China blockbusters followed, putting on Chinese screens versions of the Americana classics that filled auditoriums in the U.S. in the 1980s. Hollywood studios turned to Chinese partners who could identify what themes would resonate among these discerning audiences no longer content to flock to whatever Los Angeles sent them, the incumbent global industry becoming the student for a change. Soon even Steven Spielberg, a decade after his Olympics controversy, was turning to China's richest man for help. China, on-screen in *Wolf Warrior 2* and off-screen at the box office, was winning.

The past decade had been kindling; *Wolf Warrior 2* was the first match. Stories emerged of audiences spontaneously bursting into the Chinese national anthem as the credits rolled. China had a blockbuster that its people could cheer. What were they cheering?

THE ORIGINAL *WOLF WARRIOR* HAD premiered in 2015 and introduced audiences to Leng Feng, the supersoldier portrayed by Wu Jing, a Hong Kong kung fu star who also wrote and directed both movies. The sequel sent the hero to Africa, where he is called to rescue residents from extremist terrorists threatening their country. Wu Jing offered China a heroic family man–soldier—the guy who, faced with incompetent bosses and a dangerous situation, has no choice but to go it alone and save the village, defuse the bomb, rescue the kid held hostage on the top floor.

This is a narrative Americans have come to know well—call it the Bruce Willis template. *Wolf Warrior 2* opens with Wu Jing's character defying authorities razing the home of a fellow soldier's family, an altercation that lands him in prison for two years. The action picks up when Leng is released and travels to a nameless country in Africa, where Wu Jing does his best approximation of Sylvester Stallone heroics to save the local communities from terrorists and mercenaries running over the land. Machine-gun bullets spray toward him, but not a one grazes him. He dispatches dozens of bad guys with switchblades and martial arts moves. He consoles young children and outdrinks the other men. When a soccer match breaks out, he scores a goal and flexes his biceps for the women. Deprived of most resources in one battle, he fashions a deadly arrow using poisonous sap extracted from a desert cactus.

Though he is ostensibly saving the day in Africa, a phantom opposition pervades the film: the United States. "There's our hero!" shout American sailors after Leng—and not their own military—rescues them from Somali pirates. When a fight breaks out, he and a woman drive to safety. She suggests going to the U.S. consulate, where the marines are stationed.

> LENG FENG
> You think the U.S. Marines are the best in
> the world?
>
> That may be true, but where are they now?

Later, she calls the U.S. consulate from a cell phone and gets the answering machine. The UN helicopter comes to help. It crashes soon after taking off.

While Hollywood studios were stripping their movies of Chinese villains, Chinese filmmakers were not extending the same courtesy. The main adversary in *Wolf Warrior 2* is Big Daddy, leader of the mercenary soldiers. Big Daddy is a disgusting caricature of American ego and entitlement. He looks at the African villagers whom Leng wants to save and assesses them as worthless lives, a one-man representation of China's main argument to the continent: America has abandoned you, but we are here to help.

During their final battle, Leng gets to show Big Daddy who is boss, the moment where he can beat him not only physically but metaphorically. The two men have exhausted themselves in battle.

```
                    BIG DADDY
     People like you will always be inferior to
     people like me. Get used to it. Get fucking
     used to it.


                      LENG
     That's fucking history.

     Leng repeatedly stabs Big Daddy in the neck.
```

Leng ends the movie with his character hoisting a Chinese flag above his head and riding through the African countryside. "Hold your fire! It's the Chinese," the villagers shout. In the movie's closing credits—played as some sold-out auditoriums sang or burst into applause—a pronouncement appeared: "Citizens of the People's Republic of China, when you encounter danger in a foreign land, do not give up! Please remember, at your back stands a strong motherland."

A TWENTYSOMETHING LEAVING a screening in Beijing remarked, "It feels good to be on the side of justice." The swagger was a balm after decades of humiliation—one Xi couldn't have written better himself.

Shortly after taking office, Xi had said that "after more than one hundred and seventy years of struggle since the Opium War, the great renewal of the Chinese nation can finally glimpse a bright future." Elementary school classrooms had once displayed posters reading WU WANG GUO CHI—"never forget national humiliation"—a pervasive insecurity rooted in the Opium Wars, yet here was a Chinese hero proudly waving the country's flag and stepping in when other countries fled, a cinematic incarnation of Xi's promise in 2017 that "no one should expect China to swallow anything that undermines its interests." Wu Jing was not unlike John Wayne, who, Joan Didion wrote, became an American star in the 1940s because he was a "perfect mold" for "the inarticulate longings of a nation wondering at just what pass the trail had been lost." Wu Jing soon became a perfect mold into which Chinese officials and moviegoers alike could pour their ambitions. Yet unlike with Wayne, there was no wistfulness or examination of the nation's past sins clouding the bravado, only a newfound identity as a nation on the world stage: unapologetically patriotic, strong, and ready to call America on its bullshit.

Or as Wu put it: "Why do only foreign nations get to have superheroes?"

He had come of age in the new China. He was born in Beijing in 1974 and sent away as a young child to learn martial arts at the Beijing Wushu Academy, as men in his family had done since the Qing dynasty. He studied Bruce Lee movies and decided to follow his lead. In 2008, he says in an often-cited origin story, he visited Sichuan villages destroyed by an earthquake and watched Chinese soldiers rescue victims. "Their machismo and selflessness truly touched my heart," he said. He decided to make a movie honoring them. Wu took out a second mortgage to pay the $12 million it cost to produce that film, the original *Wolf Warrior.* It did modestly well, grossing $81 million—hardly an amount that a producer could expect to increase more than tenfold with the sequel. But *Wolf Warrior 2* met the moment, and it was easy to understand why Chinese audiences, after years of being fed Western heroes, would grow emotional at seeing their own.

The company that produced *Wolf Warrior 2* with Wu, Beijing Culture, had arrived at a magic formula at the box office: patriotic movies that do away with the textbook approach of state-produced propaganda and place the pro-China messaging in the vessel of a commercial action flick. When it was founded in 1997 as Beijing Tourism, the company's real estate portfolio consisted of a couple of temples, a handful of parks, and some hotels. When Xi began encouraging companies to pursue entertainment deals, Beijing Tourism—like Wanda and the other firms that had flocked to Hollywood—acquired several production companies. Beijing Culture was born, an entertainment company with a self-professed mission to "spread Chinese culture" with movies.

To make *Wolf Warrior 2*, Wu relied on freelance help from the West that had shaped some of Hollywood's biggest blockbusters of all time. The creation of Leng Feng, China's own superhero, had come with help from the superhero creators of Marvel Studios, Joe and Anthony Russo, brothers known for helming two *Captain America*s and a two-part *Avengers* epic. As thanks to Beijing Culture for investing in their production company, the brothers offered filmmaking advice in a meeting held at the Disney studio lot (Wu showed up in camouflage). They encouraged Wu to hire Sam Hargrave, a stuntman and action coordinator who had choreographed Chris Evans's fight scenes in *Avengers: Infinity War.* At the Russos' recommendation, Frank Grillo, a character actor whom they had directed as a villain in *Captain America: The Winter Soldier,* would be paid $1 million to play Big Daddy. The Russo brothers themselves, though, declined an executive producer credit, deciding it wasn't worth the risk to their reputation to put their name on the movie. Beijing Culture's model kept the story's theme and characters Chinese but outsourced some of the components of a movie that can signal sophistication to audiences: special effects, fight choreography, music.

"Though we should learn from our foreign counterparts, such as Hollywood, we should also preserve the unique 'Chinese flavor' by focusing on stories featuring the lives of Chinese people," Wu said.

At the time of the release of *Wolf Warrior 2*, China established its first overseas military base in Djibouti, the small country in the Horn of Africa, perhaps not far from the unnamed African country Leng Feng rescues in the film. *Wolf Warrior 2* reflects these foreign policy initiatives. African soldiers lower their guns when they hear that "China and Africa are friends." The local emergency room is located at the "St. Francis Chinese-invested hospital." Chinese embassies on the continent hosted screenings, but audiences there soured on the antiquated stereotypes of the film, in which villagers dance around garbage-can bonfires and an office is decorated with posters of zebras and cheetahs. In the case of *Wolf Warrior 2*, Wu was more successful at internal messaging, convincing Chinese moviegoers that their country's investments in Africa were justified, than he was at selling African viewers on their new benefactors.

China, meanwhile, submitted *Wolf Warrior 2* as the nominee for the Best Foreign Language Film award. Americans working in China could only shake their heads. This was like trying to get the academy to announce, "And the Oscar goes to . . . *Commando*." Wu Jing campaigned in West Hollywood, getting drunk with Vin Diesel and befriending Dwayne Johnson, who tried to get him into a *Fast and Furious* movie before a scheduling conflict made him promise to make it happen in a sequel. "Just imagine what that would be like for the world—Hobbs and Wu Jing, unstoppable!" Johnson said. But when the nominees were announced in early 2018, movies from Chile, Lebanon, Russia, Hungary, and Sweden were represented. *Wolf Warrior 2* would win the box office but not the Oscar.

Undaunted, the Chinese movie industry produced other treatments of Chinese heroism at a clip, many inspired by real-life efforts by Chinese soldiers to save their countrymen overseas. *Operation Mekong* retold the story of an attack on Chinese ships near the border of Burma and Thailand. *Operation Red Sea* dramatized efforts by Chinese soldiers to rescue Chinese citizens stuck in Yemen during that country's civil war. Even though the movie was produced in cooperation with the Chinese navy, the film added a propagandistic sheen to the real-life stories. Its soldiers fired slow-motion bullets and made impossible shots to the target's cranium. When a soldier in *Operation Red Sea* is injured in battle, he recovers in—where else?—Djibouti. Both movies performed phenomenally at the box office, but *Operation Red Sea* was a particular hit. It grossed $580 million, becoming the fifth-highest-grossing movie in Chinese history. Decades after Qu Qiubai had called for "new wine in old bottles," China's filmmakers were grafting propagandistic impulses onto commercial storytelling.

MICHAEL GRALAPP STARTED TO NOTICE a change in the kinds of stories China wanted to see, too, when he stopped getting hired to play World War II figures. China's film industry had expanded far beyond official "red movies," and Gralapp started auditioning for Chinese producers experimenting with new genres. One day he was being called in to audition for Winston Churchill parts, the next he was reading for a different jowly icon of the West: Warren Buffett.

Gralapp played Buffett—or at least an obvious version of him called Warren Luffett—in the 2018 blockbuster *Hello Mr. Billionaire*. The movie starred Teng Shen as a soccer goalie who must, before inheriting $30 billion, prove that he can bear the wealth responsibly by spending $1 billion of it in a month. If it sounds familiar, it's because *Hello Mr. Billionaire* is a Chinese remake of *Brewster's Millions*, the 1985 Richard Pryor comedy about a minor league baseball pitcher who must, before inheriting $300 million, prove that he can bear the wealth responsibly by spending $30 million of it in a month. (Apparently $300 million wasn't much in contemporary China.)

A movie released in America in 1985 made perfect sense for China in 2018, for a similar reason that the country's rising nationalism had helped fuel the *Wolf Warrior 2* phenomenon the year before. The story of overnight wealth and the responsibility of new power might resonate for the millions of Chinese who'd seen their country go from farm rations to Starbucks rewards programs in the span of a generation.

The appetite for such "bowls of noodles," as Xu Zheng had put it in 2012, blew Hollywood returns out of the water. *Hello Mr. Billionaire* made $367 million in China when it was released, more than all but four American films had in their home market that year. And it was still only number four at the Chinese box office at the end of 2018, behind a Chinese military action movie similar to *Wolf Warrior 2*, a Chinese detective comedy in the vein of *Beverly Hills Cop*, and a medical drama that had echoes of *Dallas Buyers Club*. Each of these movies made at least $400 million, more than any Hollywood movie imported into Chinese theaters that year. Older Chinese moviegoers might want to see Gralapp in his Churchill movies, opposite Mao and other historical figures. Younger ones wanted to see him as a hero of the investing class in a commercial comedy.

It shouldn't have come as a shock that Chinese people wanted to see movies that reflected their lives, but it did in a Hollywood where decades of dominance had built an arrogance that assumed U.S. movies would be the preferred product by default. *Wolf Warrior 2* had its fantastical appeal, but movies about more grounded heroes—and particularly about situations that might speak to the experiences of contemporary Chinese—would give China new kinds of cinematic catharsis, told in stories that had grown more sophisticated in their telling after years of watching Hollywood movies and training with the filmmakers who made them. As the nationalism of China in the 2010s defined the Xi Jinping era, the country's moviegoers needed what Hollywood gave America in Ronald Reagan's 1980s, when commercial cinema specialized in sentiment, adventure, and stories of everyday citizens who find themselves in extraordinary circumstances. They even called on the same director to do it.

. . .

IN 1981, STEVEN SPIELBERG FORMED Amblin Entertainment, the production company where he would go on to direct his most iconic films—*Jaws*, *E.T. the Extra-Terrestrial*, *Raiders of the Lost Ark*—and produce others in a similar vein, like *The Goonies* and *Back to the Future*. In the 1980s, an "Amblin movie," with its logo of a young boy bicycling E.T. across the moon to safety, became shorthand for a kind of nostalgic storytelling that put ordinary people (and often children) in the hero's role, rooted in a clear understanding of good and evil, swept up in forces beyond the imaginative limits they had when the story started.

The West has long embraced the classic "hero's journey" template, described by scholar Joseph Campbell as the scaffolding of countless myths updated into popular Hollywood movies. The journey begins when the hero is forced to venture out and overcome adversity, emerging from the challenge transformed internally and victorious externally. A station at the beginning of the film is not permanent—indeed, the lack of a fixed point enables the story entirely. Frodo treks across Middle Earth to destroy the One Ring. Simba traverses the African desert to avenge his father's murder. Neo rejects a life inside the matrix and kills the suited agents keeping it a secret. Together these movies tapped what Campbell called the "private, unrecognized, rudimentary, yet secretly potent pantheon of dream." And many of the movies that resonated with audiences in this Amblin era did not need mythic characters. They often found their protagonists in the American suburbs; these unsuspecting heroes functioned as the audience's surrogate.

In the decade after he'd quit the Beijing Olympics, Steven Spielberg's career oscillated between the popcorn entertainment he'd started with, like *Indiana Jones and the Kingdom of the Crystal Skull*, and the highbrow films he'd graduated to, like *Lincoln*. After raising $800 million in equity and debt with a trio of investors, he restarted his company as Amblin Partners. The new Amblin identified a need that its 1980s iteration hadn't had to address. Spielberg's new backers left a stake in the company for a Chinese partner that could ensure that their movies got a piece of the country's box office. Spielberg's reputation after the Olympics controversy hadn't taken a hit, and other studios had demonstrated the power of partnering directly with a Chinese business in the years since Rob Moore's contract-signing spree on *Transformers*. After the catchall approach that Wanda had taken, a smarter strategy emerged: targeted one-off deals between studios and Chinese partners operating in their government's good graces. These were not the joint ventures required to do business in China by the bureaucrats in Beijing but rather a way for Hollywood to navigate the challenges of new competition and discerning audiences.

The new backers came from the country's booming internet industry, all massive conglomerates that made Google look quaint by comparison: Baidu Inc., a search engine; Alibaba Group, an e-commerce platform; and Tencent, the owner of social media giant WeChat. Collectively called the BATs, they ruled China's internet, which had largely skipped the home-computer stage and gone straight to smartphones used to hail cabs, order food, and pay for just about everything. When I'd travel to Shanghai and try to use cash instead of a smartphone at the register, cashiers looked at me like I was a time traveler. Even homeless people were known to seek donations by holding up signs bearing a QR code passersby could scan to send a few bucks over.

The biggest of these companies was Alibaba, which was responsible for a majority of online purchases in the world's most populous country. Its founder, Jack Ma, replaced Wang Jianlin as China's wealthiest man in 2017—as much a symbolic changing of the guard as a monetary one, since Wang had made his fortune in physical retail and Ma had made his by taking it online. His company's mission was to promote "health and happiness," said Ma, who, like Wang, had his quirks. He wanted Alibaba to exist in three Chinese centuries, which would require staying in business for 102 years. Every year, 102 couples gather at the company's headquarters in Hangzhou for a collective wedding ceremony marking the goal, not far from three twenty-foot-tall statues of frail naked men that anchor the campus. Ma installed the men, all standing fully exposed with their heads down and their shoulders slumped, to remind workers to stay humble despite their success.

Ma's love of movies led Alibaba to diversify into entertainment, as stateside tech firms like Amazon and Apple were doing. For Ma, it was a chance to yet again spread health and happiness across his country. His favorite movie, he often said, was *Forrest Gump*, the quintessential example of an American director offering a glossed treatment of American history. Alibaba Pictures formed in 2014 to bring similar kinds of feel-good stories to China. Ma dispatched a deputy to Los Angeles to find them.

WEI ZHANG WAS BORN IN Beijing in the early 1970s, just as the Cultural Revolution was coming to an end. Wei grew up on the campus where her father was a professor, allowing her access to foreign movies that didn't play in regular theaters. Some nights, she and her parents took stools and sat for outdoor screenings projected onto a hanging sheet.

"That state had its own beauty. Everyone was equal," she said. "Everything was simple." In school, teachers spoke with awe of the year 2000, when Deng Xiaoping had vowed China would realize its Four Modernizations, or four pillars of the Chinese economy: agriculture, technology, industry, and defense. In 1990, Wei moved to Greensburg, Pennsylvania, to attend Seton Hill, a small Catholic school located in a tiny exurb of Pittsburgh. Her parents, who made about $50 a month, had sent her with $1,000. She bought a used car and learned how to drive on the Pennsylvania highway, going to work at a local Chinese restaurant or shop at the nearby Westmoreland Mall. The tractor-trailers crossing the state terrified her, looking unlike any kind of vehicle found in 1980s China. When she first returned home after leaving for college, her dad told her he hoped to one day afford a three-wheel moped.

After attending Seton Hill, Wei enrolled at Harvard Business School in 1997, one of ten mainland Chinese students in a class of eight hundred. Beijing had only started allowing student exchanges in the 1970s, and most until that point had decided to stay in the U.S. and not return home after earning a degree. Even more opted to stay out of China following the 1989 massacre in Tiananmen Square. For some members of this so-called Tiananmen generation, the U.S. offered a better shot, and the easy venture capital money of Silicon Valley's dot-com days proved alluring. Others wanted to stay in the U.S. so they could raise more than one child under smog-free skies. Wei's cohort were a close-knit group figuring out which country offered more promise at a time when the answer wasn't so clear.

Wei had journeyed out and was ready to return. "We can't sacrifice the present for the sake of tomorrow," she told her classmates. "We should start doing right now what we really want to do." She had seen the gray hair on her parents' heads, and as their only child, she was the only caretaker they had. She soon after got a job in the Beijing office of Rupert Murdoch's News Corp, where her life became a blend of her two countries and her career a reflection of the seismic changes the post-WTO China was implementing. A poster for the TV show *Friends* hung above her desk, and a Snoopy charm dangled from her cell phone. She got her coffee at Starbucks. Meanwhile, the Four Modernizations that her elementary school teachers had promised were coming true. Her father ditched the moped idea. By the end of the century, he could buy himself a car.

Wei joined Alibaba in 2008 and took over its Los Angeles entertainment office in 2014. To outsiders, Wei arrived on the West Coast with the world's heaviest purse. She came on the heels of Alibaba's record-setting public offering, which valued the company at $231 billion. Rumors swirled that Alibaba would succeed where Wanda had failed and be the first Chinese company to swallow a studio. In reality, Wei had been sent to Los Angeles with a more strategic mandate. The company's first investment was a single movie, *Mission: Impossible—Rogue Nation*, hardly a risk for a country already familiar with the franchise and its star. Alibaba set up merchandise tie-ins with local manufacturers to make toys and products attached to the film. Other one-off investments followed, all in movies that were natural fits in China: *Teenage Mutant Ninja Turtles: Out of the Shadows, Star Trek Beyond.*

Ma had told Zhang to find a different kind of movie to bring back, those that were "small, big, positive." That is, movies about small people with big hearts and a positive impact. Movies that Spielberg had directed into classic Americana. Movies that Wei suspected a changing China wanted to see.

"We grew up during that period where we're all equal on food stamps. Now we're able to dream for bigger things. It's up to us, how to take our own destiny into our own hands. This is a period where people have dreams and want to see the little guy get their chance in the world," Wei said.

Wolf Warrior 2 had given China a superhero. Wei was collecting evidence that other movies would give audiences their Amblin moment. *Dying to Survive* told the true and touching story of the Chinese cancer patient who provided drugs for his fellow patients. It made $453 million. *Detective Chinatown 2* was a cop comedy sequel featuring a sleuth who uses feng shui, among other tools, to solve crimes: $524 million. Two amusement park workers who discover an ET in their midst must figure out what to do with the creature in *Crazy Alien*: $328 million. A troupe of dancers and singers navigate love and life while performing in the People's Liberation Army in *Youth*: $236 million. An unhappy musician wakes up in the body of his teenage self, capable of redoing his adult years and becoming a pop star in the process, in *Goodbye Mr. Loser*: $228 million. The story of a couple's romance is told in sections that alternate between their past in the countryside and their present in Beijing in *Us and Them*: $209 million.

In a matter of three years, the hit movies of China's growing film industry would fill up the list of the country's top fifty highest-grossing films of all time. By 2020, the U.S. accounted for only seventeen of these movies and only one of the top ten, while twenty-seven of the top fifty were Chinese movies released between 2017 and 2020. Such stories were similar to the artifacts of contemporary Hollywood, blockbusters like *The Graduate, American Graffiti, Beverly Hills Cop, Home Alone*—movies about everyday people that outperformed modern-day comic-book adaptations when ticket sales are adjusted for inflation. As China's own movies took over the box office, the only American titles to break onto the list were the absolute biggest franchise movies Hollywood had to offer, like *Avengers: Endgame, The Fate of the Furious,* and *Aquaman.* The American industry, for all its know-how and receipts, could not best China's own directors when it came to putting their own stories on-screen.

The release of *Crazy Rich Asians,* the adaptation of Kevin Kwan's bestselling escapist book about love and friendship amid a pack of jet-setting, Fendi-wearing young people, was a noteworthy reminder. The movie was a smash hit in the U.S., where it made $174 million, and executives expected a windfall when the movie opened in China. But then authorities delayed its release, possibly because of its emphasis on "crazy" and "rich," and social media users decried its portrayal of their people as money-obsessed chronic shoppers. When the movie finally did premiere in the country, the representation that had made it so novel in the U.S.—the first all-Asian cast in a studio film since 1993's *The Joy Luck Club*—was old hat in a China now accustomed to seeing its *own* romantic comedies, starring its *own* actors and actresses. "Some of the things that made such a huge demand weren't as intensely felt," said producer Nina Jacobson. *Crazy Rich Asians* made $1.6 million.

The share of annual top ten releases gradually shifted toward Chinese movies. In 2014, the year of *Transformers: Age of Extinction,* five of the top ten highest-grossing movies in China were from Hollywood. In 2017, three were. In 2019, two were. The growth had always been in China. Now it was in Chinese movies.

In 2016, Wei flew to the London set of Spielberg's film *Ready Player One*. It was a surreal moment for Wei, who had caught up on much of Western cinema while in school in Pennsylvania. She'd watched *E.T.*, crying each time the alien pled to "phone home," since it was too expensive to call her parents in China more than every few months. At a dinner that evening, Alibaba and Amblin agreed to a deal in which Alibaba would take a small stake in the company in exchange for marketing and distribution rights on Amblin titles released in China. Less than twenty years earlier, Wei's classmates at Harvard had stayed in the U.S. to work in Silicon Valley. Now Hollywood's most famous director was coming to her Chinese company for help.

Alibaba executives looked at the Amblin slate and suggested they had a China hit in *A Dog's Purpose*, a saccharine family movie about a reincarnating canine. *A Dog's Purpose* cost $22 million to produce. It had no superheroes or special effects. It starred Dennis Quaid and a photogenic golden retriever. No executive making the movie thought it would "travel" to China, in the industry parlance. Amblin had sought a Chinese partner for its dinosaur movies, not its dog movies.

Wei and her colleagues thought differently. They had seen how Chinese audiences were flocking to family stories, but it was more than just a gut sense of shifting tastes that led to that conclusion. Alibaba had troves of data on more than five hundred million consumers, the Chinese middle class taking shape and living their lives online. Pet ownership across the country was rising, and Alibaba knew this better than anyone. They knew who bought dog bowls and the homes where they used them, thanks to their e-commerce platform. They knew who had watched dog movies on their streaming app in the past year, and their GPS service told them what theaters they passed on their way to work.

A targeted campaign started advertising the movie to those users, and it propelled *A Dog's Purpose* to an $88 million gross—31 percent higher than its total in the U.S. and Canada. Amblin raked in "money in the street" it had never expected.

China's newer commercial film industry was late to the game compared with Hollywood, but this turned out to be an advantage. Marketing *A Dog's Purpose* with such precision wouldn't have been possible in the U.S., since Hollywood remains largely yoked to costly television commercials and billboards, broad campaigns that ignore the fact that moviegoers are most reachable through digital advertising. China's late addition to the marketplace allowed it to absorb what had worked for Hollywood—and ignore what hadn't. When it comes to getting movies in front of the people most likely to see them, Chinese companies have leapfrogged their counterparts in the U.S.

In Alibaba's hands, *Green Book*, the Amblin drama about an African American pianist (Mahershala Ali) touring the Jim Crow South with a New York City bouncer (Viggo Mortensen), became a movie about loneliness. A single line of dialogue about people feeling alone was highlighted on posters, leaning into a sense of isolation that Wei thought pervaded China since the one-child policy had left her and most Chinese people without siblings. It was the kind of perceptive marketing that many Chinese partners might have landed on, but a cultural nuance that few American executives could be expected to intuit. After its studio hadn't even planned on releasing *Green Book* in China, a movie that takes place largely in the Deep South of 1962 America made $71 million there—only $14 million shy of its home-market haul.

SOMETHING WAS GNAWING AT Chinese entertainment leaders. Even as *Hello Mr. Billionaire* and similar titles collected billions of dollars, Hollywood still inspired more affection worldwide than any Chinese movie could. *Wolf Warrior 2* was the first Chinese movie to break into the global top ten at the worldwide box office, but all of the other movies on the list collected grosses from dozens of countries. *Wolf Warrior 2* was there with 99.7 percent of its ticket sales coming from a single market. The homegrown dramas and comedies selling out auditoriums in every Chinese town played only limited runs in Chinese immigrant neighborhoods in the U.S. and Europe, their grosses hardly ever totaling more than a few million dollars.

No one but the Chinese was watching Chinese movies, and everywhere you looked you saw affection for American entertainment: A bored boy on the subway in Qingdao is entertained with stickers of characters from Disney's *Cars*. A Batman book bag sells in a shop outside Renny Harlin's sound stage in Huairou. A middle-aged woman in Shanghai passes the afternoon wearing a black T-shirt with the Paramount Pictures logo across her chest.

At an annual gathering of film industry executives I attended in Shanghai in 2019, soon after those Chinese blockbusters had come out, one question dominated the discussion: How could China go from being a big market to being a beloved market? Though the conversation was about the movies, it stood in for China's larger ambitions around the world—the struggle to turn infrastructure, medical supplies, and unapologetic patriotism into allegiance and goodwill.

"How do we come up with our own narratives?" was how Ren Zhonglun, the head of Shanghai Media Group, put it. Hollywood was obsessed with the "old days," he said, never able to cite movies more modern than *The Godfather* as classics. Nonetheless, "is there a Chinese film that can join that rank?" What Chinese writers needed to understand, Ren said, was that a compelling character kept audiences engaged far more than an overengineered screenplay could. The myth of *Star Wars* or the appeal of *The Avengers* wouldn't persist over a half dozen installments if audiences the world over didn't grow attached to Luke Skywalker or Iron Man.

After the panel, the executives retired to a hotel conference room called Oscar. This Shanghai hotel, like Renny Harlin's lodging in Huai-rou, was movie themed. The shooting scripts of old features sat in glass display cases throughout the hallway. Most of them were party-anniversary triumphalist pictures like *The Opium Wars*, a red movie produced to commemorate the tenth anniversary of National Day, encased not far from the shooting script of *Deng Xiaoping in 1928*, produced to commemorate what would have been the leader's hundredth birthday. Even though these were the pro-party movies given the curated treatment, framed portraits of movie stars hung above the glass cases—not Chinese actors but Michael Douglas, Sean Connery, and Julia Roberts. Their faces, recognizable to any of the Shanghai residents gathered in the hotel that day, seemed to mock the executives who had just voiced their envy of Hollywood's global appeal.

This would be the final hurdle in China's own journey toward building its own Hollywood. No one remembers *Deng Xiaoping in 1928*, but everyone knows Julia Roberts's smile. When would China be able to export something like *that*?

PART III

★ ★

THIRTEEN

Heartland

P aula Dvorchak's mother was always getting the family involved in something like this. Not content to live the small-
radius life of a small-town Iowan family, Eleanor Dvorchak—a
New York transplant with her accent still intact—had taken
her husband and three kids on overseas trips and volunteered for any
cultural exchange their town of twenty-three thousand residents had to
offer. And so it wasn't entirely unexpected that, on a school night in
1985, fourteen-year-old Paula stood at her kitchen counter trying to
make conversation with the two Chinese strangers her mother had invited to live with them for a week.

The tall, smiling gentleman and his shorter, smiling translator were
freshly arrived in Muscatine, a farming town downriver from the Quad
Cities, whose main drag runs parallel to the Mississippi. Mark Twain
had lived there once, writing for the *Muscatine Journal*, run by his brother.
Besides farming, the town's main business then was button making. By
1905, "freshwater pearl" buttons made in Muscatine accounted for 36.6

percent of total button revenue in the U.S., expanding the town into a collection of churches, shops, businesses, and even a small airport. By the 1980s, the pearl button business was a local museum highlight, not a place of employment. Teenagers entertained themselves by driving, and the new McDonald's in town was headline news. The Dvorchak home, at 2911 Bonnie Drive, was a typical specimen of domestic life there: Screen door. Split entry. Four bedrooms.

How weird are these guys? Paula thought to herself. They wore matching black suits, white shirts, and black ties, and though they smiled easily, their teeth were crooked and disfigured. They kept staring at her, taking in her Nikes, neon T-shirt, and blond hair.

Through the translator who had accompanied them, she tried making conversation. When did Chinese students go to school? How long did they stay in school? Then she moved on to pop culture, the common language of any teenager in 1985 who was thrilled to have just gotten MTV. Had they seen *The Godfather*? Had they seen *Indiana Jones*? Had they seen the biggest movie of all, *Star Wars*? They didn't seem familiar with it. Paula suggested they watch it together.

When her mother showed one of the men to his room, he seemed to recognize *Star Trek*'s Spock from a hand-drawn picture that Paula's brother Gary had made, hanging near the models of *The Empire Strikes Back* spaceships he had built with a hot-glue gun. Gary had been away at college for more than a year, but his mother had kept the room perfectly preserved: it was a shag-carpeted ode to one teenager's love of science fiction movies. Starting that night, it would be temporary lodging for the taller of the two men.

Adjacent to his room was Paula's bedroom, adorned with posters of Michael Jackson and Corey Hart, in the prime of his "Sunglasses at Night" phase. That meant she and the man would be sharing the bathroom she used each morning to tease her hair to 1980s heights. On his first trip to the most prosperous nation on earth, Xi Jinping inhaled a ton of Aqua Net.

.   .   .

THE THIRTY-ONE-YEAR-OLD CHEMICAL ENGINEER and bureaucrat was standing at the Dvorchaks' kitchen counter thanks to an exchange program established two years earlier between Iowa and China's
Hebei Province. China wanted to learn agricultural technology; Iowans
wanted to sell their crops to the Chinese market. Long before his country would hire Hollywood hands to teach it how to produce entertainment, it needed help from America to build its farming industry. Xi and
his five companions were the vessels of this technology transfer, charged
with observing the factories and interviewing farmers.

"Come to America and learn how to feed our people," Xi's father had
told him. The Dvorchaks asking Xi about *The Godfather* did not know he
was a *hong er dai*, a "second-generation red" whose father had led a similar
delegation to Iowa five years earlier. They never could have guessed the
years of childhood trauma that had prompted this young man to leave
his country for the first time in the hope of returning and bettering it.

The Dvorchaks did not know that the father who'd told his middle
child to "feed our people" was a former Chinese propaganda minister
and vice premier who'd joined the Communist Party from jail. (He was
locked up as a teenager when he and some friends tried to poison a
teacher whom they suspected of being a counterrevolutionary.) His father's ascendance in the party had been derailed, though, by accusations
in the Cultural Revolution that he was a "class enemy." His infraction:
on a government trip to East Germany, he'd dared to look toward West
Germany with a pair of binoculars.

When his father was in favor, Xi grew up with the luxuries afforded
the children of officials. He went to the August 1st School, an elite institution named for the founding of the People's Liberation Army. In 1962,
when Xi wasn't yet ten years old, his father was sentenced to forced labor
after he endorsed a novel that Mao opposed. Soon afterward, Xi and
other students were among the young people ordered to the countryside

to be "reeducated" by peasants. Working at the farm was a humiliating experience for the teenage boy, who was ranked a six out of ten among laborers—lower than some of the women. During his first days in the countryside, he was seen feeding some dogs a piece of bread. His new neighbors were aghast. They had never before eaten bread themselves, and here was a city boy feeding it to animals. Xi was so miserable that he fled back to Beijing, but he was soon sent back to the farm, where he learned that his half sister had died in what is believed to have been a suicide. According to Xi's often-cited origin story, he then had an epiphany and began to partake in the hard labor of the Chinese countryside and the glory to be found in Communist ideology. Largely self-educated, he worked by day and read by night: *Lenin on War and Peace*, *The Old Man and the Sea*, policy by Henry Kissinger and Erwin Rommel, the originator of the Nazis' blitzkrieg strategy. He was of a "little generals" generation that learned, as one contemporary, poet Huang Nubo, said, that "you had to act like a wolf to survive. . . . The winner takes it all."

What must it have been like for thirty-one-year-old Xi Jinping to see Muscatine, a place where every family lived together under one roof, in houses with yards and so much space, cars to cruise in, parents who threw birthday parties? Paula was asking if he'd seen MTV when he had come from a country where a permit and political connections were often needed to buy a television at all. The Dvorchaks and their neighbors had TVs in the living room, in the kitchen, in the *kids' own rooms*. Xi had arrived in the heart of Amblin America.

The trip exposed him to more than farming know-how. In Muscatine, Xi had a perfect vantage point into a particular brand of American life, one now romanticized by politicians and mined for sentimentality by Hollywood. Xi, who had spent his adolescence in the countryside learning from peasant farmers, was staying in a room brimming with the tastes of an Iowa boy in the 1980s. There were models of *Star Trek*'s *Enterprise* and of Klingon ships and shuttles, a *Star Wars* poster, and books on *Planet of the Apes*. Action figures guarded shelves, and hand-drawn re-creations of Luke Skywalker and other Jedis hung on the wall, otherwise covered in fake wood paneling and wallpaper adorned with illustrations of football players. He slept surrounded by proof of how alluring the right heroes could be to a country's youth.

Xi's room had a large window that faced the street, toward a quiet collection of eight homes that turned into rush hour every day around 3:00 p.m., when students drove home from school listening to Van Halen and AC/DC. The boys wore mullets and played *Back in Black* at every keg party, but Muscatine was so remote that car radios still couldn't pick up the rock station produced out of Davenport, thirty miles to the east.

"It was *American Graffiti* but in real life," said Bill Maeglin, the son of two other Muscatine hosts. One night, his family hosted Xi and his fellow countrymen for Bill's sixteenth birthday party. His German immigrant grandparents shared a vanilla cake covered in chocolate frosting with the Chinese men.

Few in Muscatine thought of their Chinese visitors after they left. Then Xi Jinping, like Mark Twain before him, turned Muscatine into a town best known for a visitor who didn't stay long. The mythmaking started on a return trip to Muscatine he made in 2012 as China's vice president and heir apparent, a stop on the U.S. visit that had included the film-quota negotiations with Vice President Biden. The man who had been astounded to cruise the Iowa streets in a red Mustang arrived in a 747 too big to land at the Muscatine airport.

The Long John Silver's in town hung WELCOME BACK TO MUSCATINE XI JINPING on its marquee. (On the other side: ORIGINAL MENU AVAILABLE, FISH SANDWICH 2 FOR $3.) At the time, farmers were nervous about the purchasing power China had over their soybeans. Xi posed for photos that showed him connecting with the farmers of another country, in the field like his Communist forebears. He climbed up into a giant tractor as Iowans and photographers watched.

"It's kind of propaganda," said Michelle Cacho, the general manager of that Long John Silver's. "But if it helps folks in Iowa, we might as well roll out the red carpet."

An enterprising Chinese businessman turned the onetime Dvorchak home at 2911 Bonnie Drive into the Sino-U.S. Friendship House, a Chinese version of "George Washington slept here," but in America. Inside, the *Star Trek* figurines are gone, but the 1980s interior design has been maintained so that visitors have a sense of what Xi saw when he arrived. A shed still sits in the backyard, a Tot Finder sticker is pasted to a basement window, and all of the homes around it have remained homes, not museums.

Muscatine and its residents have discovered the power any proximity to Xi can grant. Gary Dvorchak was invited to Beijing in October 2019 for the largest military parade in the country's history, thrown by Xi to commemorate the seventieth anniversary of the People's Republic. When another Muscatine guest of the parade told a Chinese flight attendant of her connection to the leader, the woman knelt down and cried, saying "Papa Xi" over and over again like an incantation. Once a month or so, a giant tour bus parks on Bonnie Drive and a few dozen Chinese tourists get out for photos and a look inside. When the China National Peking Opera completes an American tour, they've been known to perform at the Chicago Symphony Center, the Kennedy Center, and the Muscatine Central Middle School auditorium. The school jazz band usually performs afterward. Between the time he slept in Gary's twin bed and when he ascended to a position of power capable of turning that room into a tourist attraction, Xi Jinping's transformation was complete.

WHEN HE RETURNED TO CHINA and began rising through the party ranks, Xi proved a savvy self-brander, frequently referencing the "yellow earth" in his blood, an allusion to the countryside where he lived among the peasants during the Cultural Revolution. It is a region, so named for the color of its soil, with a history anchored to the country's first emperor. "The cave-houses of the yellow earth are the equivalent of log cabins to American presidents," writes Xi biographer François Bougon. Such personal details imbued Xi with an aura of inevitability to some Chinese, as though he had always been destined to lead his country during a century they'd make their own. Ahead of his ascension, politicians and analysts believed he would usher in a new, more democratic China, an update to the optimism expressed in the WTO days. That turned out to be one of the most consequential miscalculations by American officials in the post–Cold War era. Instead, Xi quickly consolidated power like few leaders before him, so much so that he is now considered the most authoritarian ruler in China since Mao. Xi rooted out rivals in an anticorruption campaign; forced millions of Muslims into concentration camps; quashed opposition by jailing dissenters and journalists; and eliminated term limits, effectively allowing himself to serve as president of China for life.

Few industries have aided Xi's consolidation of power quite like China's internet. Bill Clinton and Rupert Murdoch might have believed that the web would inevitably lead to democratic reform, but they turned out to be deeply mistaken. Instead, the Chinese internet has become the most powerful tool of the party's surveillance state. Most of the West's most popular websites—Google, Facebook, Twitter—are accessed only using a VPN service that tricks the computer into thinking the user is surfing from a freer country. On Chinese apps like WeChat—a communication service used for texting, online payment, and other services in modern China—web users risk jail time for any post that "[upsets] social order," according to a 2013 law. Any overseas citizen communicating with friends in China knows what words—*protests*, *coronavirus*—to avoid so that calls don't mysteriously drop midconversation, confirmation that someone is listening. (To circumvent authorities peering over their digital shoulder, online commentators started referring to Xi as "Winnie the Pooh," based on his portly frame, until authorities caught on. When Disney tried to get its 2018 family drama *Christopher Robin*, about Pooh creator A. A. Milne, into the country, it was rejected in the fallout.)

Most troublingly, the state has gamified devotion to the party through an online social credit system that rewards or docks points to an individual based on pro-China behavior. Points go up for activities that speak to China's storied history, such as calligraphy lessons or using your living room to host a Communist Party sing-along. Driving through red lights or not cleaning up after your dog costs you points, and so does hanging around neighbors known to have spoken out against the government.

"In one part of the world, monitoring what citizens routinely do online is used to drive corporate revenues," writes scholar Peter Frankopan. "In another, it is considered a matter of national security."

When it came to the movies, Xi had a remarkable economic force at his disposal. Since the drastic decision to remove Chinese invaders from *Red Dawn*, no major studio release had cast Chinese characters as villains. More than that, no major studio release had portrayed China's government as a bad actor, or life there as anything less than that of world-class megacities, populated by stylish stars and top-notch products. By virtue of the economic leverage at the box office, China had managed to turn American-made Hollywood movies into endorsements for itself.

The potential for big-screen influence was even greater in his home country. The Chinese box office would increase 195 percent between Xi's first year in office, 2013, and 2019. The screen count would more than triple to sixty-five thousand, the most of any country in the world. In 2018 nearly 80 percent of all Chinese moviegoers were between the ages of nineteen and thirty-four years old, younger than audiences in the U.S.—and just the kind of young people a political party might want to influence. The film industry that had been under development in the decade before Xi's reign would be fully operational and sophisticated by the time he was in office, and he knew well the political advantages it could give him.

THIS REALITY WAS HAMMERED HOME for CAA talent agent Jonah Greenberg one winter afternoon in 2014, less than a year after Xi took over as president. At the time, Greenberg was among those in Hollywood taking the most advantage of China's new entertainment riches. He had signed China's up-and-coming directors and gotten Zhang Yimou and others their gigs in Hollywood. He was the representative of the industry's most powerful talent agency in its most important new market. Yet in the midst of this rush toward China, Greenberg had an experience that he would later remember as the first indication that he was working in a country with unique dangers.

Two days after New Year's in 2014, most of Hollywood was looking with envy at the grosses Rob Moore had ginned up for *Transformers*. Greenberg was leaving a screening of Martin Scorsese's *The Wolf of Wall Street*, which he'd caught at an ArcLight theater while visiting family in Los Angeles. He always used the visits home to catch up on R-rated movies the Chinese censors would never allow him to see in their country. His phone rang soon after the movie ended. A client of his, a director based in China, was calling with terrible news.

Li Ming, the head of a film and television production company called Galloping Horse, had been called in by the government for questioning— in the government's words, to "cooperate" with an anticorruption campaign launched by Xi in the early days of his presidency. By this point, Greenberg had spent several dinners and meetings with the "Big Dog," as Li was known, in pursuit of deals for a client. Galloping Horse wanted to expand into feature films, and Greenberg's client list was a shortcut to doing so.

Initial reports said Li had died of a sudden heart attack, but then more details emerged. He had been summoned for questioning in a corruption probe tied to a top-ranking police officer who had been a business associate of his at CCTV in the mid-1990s. That official was connected to Bo Xilai, an imprisoned Communist Party leader and a chief Xi rival. Though details were scant, it appeared that Li had gotten upset during his interrogation and been given a sedative that caused a stroke. His body was released only after his family agreed not to conduct an autopsy. Chinese social media sites banned references to the people involved.

By this point, Greenberg wasn't naive. He knew the sense of awe and fear Beijing could inspire among filmmakers when officials canceled movie releases with little warning or pressured foreign festivals to cut certain films from their lineups. But this was a darker reality—one in which affiliation with a state enemy had led to a mysterious death, a development he found all the more disturbing since Li had been a proud man who'd boasted to him of never breaking when he was called in after the Tiananmen Square crackdown.

Li Ming's case would fade from memory soon enough, but it would resurface years later when other Chinese entertainers disappeared or found themselves on the wrong side of Xi. Greenberg would eventually realize that phone call foreshadowed a change in China's relationship with Hollywood. Yet at the moment, in the courtyard of the ArcLight theater on Sunset Boulevard, Greenberg felt strangely inured to the situation. It was what happened in China, he thought, his place of business.

LATER THAT YEAR, XI DELIVERED a lecture on art's role in the state that was intentionally reminiscent of Mao's May 1942 address at Yan'an, in which he asked Chinese artists and authors to satisfy the masses with state-backed messaging. On the seventy-second anniversary of Mao's address, Xi said, "We must make patriotism into the main melody of literature and art creation, guide the people to establish and uphold correct views of history, views of the nation, views of the country and views of culture, and strengthen their fortitude and resolve to be Chinese."

In numerous ways, Xi would follow Mao's lead in turning his country's entertainment into an expression of the state. When the Chinese Communist Party turned seventy years old, Xi marked the occasion with an elaborate military parade through the streets of Beijing. Within China, locals had been primed for the festivities for weeks beforehand. The state's National Radio and Television Administration released a list of eighty-six approved TV shows and movies that broadcasters were allowed to air in the weeks before the anniversary date. The decree called on broadcasters not to air anything that was "too entertaining"—seeing movies and TV shows as though they should serve a medicinal purpose. The eighty-six sanctioned programs were about "different stages of the Chinese people's road to independence, prosperity, and strength; they praise the country, praise the people, praise the heroes, and praise the times."

The rise of streaming services has given most Chinese smartphone owners movies and TV shows to watch beyond what's on CCTV, but the government has jurisdiction over what they show as well. In late 2018, the iQIYI service announced it would stream *Wolf Warrior 2*, *Operation Red Sea*, and *Operation Mekong* in rural parts of China. The ostensible purpose of the programming was to "alleviate the problem of cultural poverty" in those parts of the country. When protesters in Hong Kong marching against China's extradition law broke out in the show tune anthem "Do You Hear the People Sing?" from the French Revolution musical *Les Misérables*, the movie version of the Broadway hit was taken off streaming sites owned by Tencent and Alibaba.

Under Xi, the country's movie studios fill out their slate with patriotic movies. As China's film industry matured, these patriotic-minded movies diversified beyond narratives of Japanese aggression to include stories of everyday heroism and celebrations of the collectivist spirit. They were movies like *My People, My Country*, an anthology of true, inspiring

stories from across China, such as the Chinese scientist who helped develop the country's first atom bomb and the engineer who built a machine that would automatically raise flags during a ceremony marking
the founding of the People's Republic of China. These movies attract
China's top directors—when the authorities call, they answer. Xu Zheng,
the director of *Lost in Thailand*, that original "bowl of noodles," was
summoned from the set of a sequel to that comedy hit so he could film
an installment of *My People, My Country* about a young boy who joins his
neighbors to watch China's national volleyball team win the gold medal
at the 1984 Olympics. Political points accrued for his trouble.

XI'S EXPANSIONIST AMBITIONS predated the election of Donald
Trump, but they received a golden opportunity with a U.S. president
who had been elected on the promise of retrenching America's reach
abroad. At his own inauguration, Trump said, "We will seek friendship
and goodwill with the nations of the world, but we do so with the understanding that it is the right of all nations to put their own interests
first." Three days later, Xi delivered a speech that would have once been
given by an American president.

Speaking at the World Economic Forum in Davos, Switzerland, Xi
positioned himself as counselor, big brother, and champion of globalism.
"Many people feel bewildered and wonder: What has gone wrong with
the world?" Xi said. The isolationist movements that had taken root in
the U.S. and in Europe could not be reconciled with a global economy
that is "the big ocean that you cannot escape from," he added. A leadership vacuum had formed on the world stage, and Xi wanted to fill it.
"We should strike a balance between efficiency and equity to ensure
that different countries, different social strata, and different groups of
people all share in the benefits of economic globalization. The people of
all countries expect nothing less from us, and this is our unshakable
responsibility as leaders of our times."

This was Xi's ultimate brand play—an exporting of his combination of authoritarian measures and market economics that tacitly offered other politicians the chance to give their people shopping malls and a surveillance state. China's alternative to liberal democracy, which its leaders called "socialism with Chinese characteristics," seemed the ultimate refutation of the long-held belief in American exceptionalism that Hollywood had spent decades selling to the world. China's rise led to conversations among politicians, professors, and policy experts about America's necessary fall—was the world big enough for both? Political scientist Graham Allison foresaw an inevitable clash between the two countries he called "Thucydides's Trap," inspired by the dynamic between Athens and Sparta before the Peloponnesian War, when another rising power threatened an existing hegemony.

Seeds of support for Trump were planted in Hollywood's early entry to China. When officials in the Clinton administration backed China's acceptance into the WTO, an agreement that had significantly expanded the presence of Hollywood and other American businesses in the country, some in the president's party warned it would eventually alienate core members of their political base of Democrats. Steelworkers and teamsters rightfully suspected the agreement would ship their jobs overseas, and human-rights advocates said it was emboldening the regime without requiring it to improve the lives of its citizens.

Nearly twenty years later, Hillary Clinton lost the presidential election to Donald Trump in part because of the WTO agreement and gospel of free trade her husband had championed, the one that had opened the door for movies to stream into Chinese theaters and eventually grow to depend on them. In the 2016 election, Trump performed best in counties that had lost the most jobs after China joined the organization.

Democracy, Chinese leaders wanted to convey, was not the only way. A threat assessment released in January 2019 by the U.S. director of national intelligence found that China wanted to not only export its culture and system of authoritarian capitalism but also "erode norms, such as the notion that the international community has a legitimate role in scrutinizing other countries' behavior on human rights." The Chinese economy, now the second largest in the world, often became the means by which such ulterior motives and Beijing's priorities were realized. In a case that echoed the *Seven Years in Tibet* and *Kundun* threats, China canceled meetings with Mongolian officials to discuss much-needed loans and Chinese development projects after Buddhist leaders there invited the Dalai Lama for a visit. Mongolia was in the middle of an economic crisis, with a budget deficit of more than $1 billion, and in desperate need of the financial relief now jeopardized by a political misstep. Less than a month later, Mongolian leaders said the Dalai Lama was no longer welcome in their country. Hua Chunying, the spokeswoman for the Chinese Ministry of Foreign Affairs, issued a statement: "We hope that Mongolia will truly learn lessons from this incident." Construction has since begun on the railway that was to be on the agenda of that initial meeting between Chinese and Mongolian officials, with plans to connect coal mines in southern Mongolia to buyers in China.

After a high-profile case like that, what other country dependent on Chinese funding is going to publicly disagree with China's politics? Much like Hollywood studios watching Sony and Disney and ingesting the lesson, other countries see what happens when China's politics are crossed. Indeed, the years of Xi's rise would repeatedly show that Hollywood had been the first offender—and therefore the first student—in dealing with an angry China.

XI'S BOLDEST BET FOR ESTABLISHING a contrast with the global power of the West is the Belt and Road Initiative, a collection of Chinese loans and infrastructure investments aimed at redrawing global trade maps. Announced in September 2013, with a name and motive inspired

by the ancient Silk Road trading routes that made the Middle Kingdom
the center of global commerce, the Belt and Road Initiative connects China
to more than sixty-five countries and populations totaling 4.4 billion people, mostly in the form of infrastructure built by Chinese firms or Chinese
loans emanating from Beijing. The initiative includes trains in Egypt, a
nuclear power station in Sudan, a port in Greece, a railway in Azerbaijan,
and a highway in Kazakhstan. These are just a fraction of the deals assem-
bling this new Pangaea, a trading route that will replace the textiles and
spices of the original Silk Road with an interconnected commerce system
for the next century. China offers its own history as the model, holding up
the infrastructure it funds as the first step toward economic activity and
poverty alleviation. "We Chinese often say that if you want to get rich,
build roads first," said Le Yucheng, China's vice minister of foreign affairs. Or as Belt and Road scholar Frankopan put it: "All roads used to
lead to Rome. Today, they lead to Beijing."

Xi was not the first leader to propose reviving activity among Silk
Road countries—U.S. officials, including Secretary of State Hillary Clinton, called for it in a 2011 speech advocating freer trade policies. But Xi
showed up with the money to do it. Less than two years after his Kazakhstan speech, a Chinese bank—led by a cabinet minister and under
the auspices of the State Council—set aside $890 billion that would fund
nine hundred Belt and Road projects spanning central Asian countries
and parts of the world typically not considered to be in China's sphere of
influence, including eastern Europe, the Middle East, and Africa, as well
as the Caribbean, South America, and both poles. More than eighty countries are now considered Belt and Road countries, meaning somewhere
within their borders, China is funding a project that will further connect them to the Middle Kingdom. There's a reason policy expert Jonathan Hillman has called it "the Baskin-Robbins of partnerships, offering
flavors for everyone."

On the original Silk Road established more than two thousand years ago, tradesmen exchanged more than goods. Religions and language, disease and tribalism, plants, customs, food, and culture—all were on offer in this "central nervous system" of the world. New goods cover the new trading routes, which carry oil and natural gas, rice and wheat— and silicon used in semiconductors, along with rare-earth elements like yttrium and terbium that power computers and mobile phones. Nautical discoveries by Christopher Columbus and Vasco da Gama in the fifteenth century shifted global trade to western Europe as its nucleus. Collectively, the Belt and Road Initiative is a bid to reorient global trade that could alter world politics in a way not seen since the fall of the Berlin Wall.

The money has come with strings attached, and the most prominent criticism of the Belt and Road Initiative concerns loan agreements that turn the developing nation into a borrower that can't pay back its loan. Ports in Sri Lanka, the Maldives, and other far-flung locations are now under Chinese control after loans teetered their economies. To have its debts forgiven on a project, Tajikistan handed over a gold mine to China. In other countries, it wasn't uncommon for the loans to account for more than 60 percent of the national GDP. An angry editorial in Angola pointed out that its country's debt to China averaged out to $754 per resident, in a country where per-capita annual income was $6,200. In Kyrgyzstan it was $703 on $1,000 per-capita income. Then there are the unfulfilled promises: the ports that aren't busy, the airports where full flights fail to materialize. Critics have called the Belt and Road Initia-tive little more than effective marketing—a bundling of investments and promises so far-flung and disparate in mission that they lack any unifying purpose. Yet even if it is savvy marketing, the sudden ubiquity of China in these countries has filled a vacuum created in many cases by the retrenchment of the U.S. and Europe.

China's swift signing of loan deals in these countries has led to accu-sations that Beijing is acting as a neo-colonialist power, and the allure of Chinese financing is changing political alliances. Loans flooded into the tiny West African nation of São Tomé and Príncipe as well as Panama and El Salvador after each withdrew diplomatic recognition of Taiwan as an independent state, in accordance with Beijing's wishes. Warming ties between China and some eastern European countries have rattled the European Union and contributed to challenges to the U.S.-led Western supremacy on the world stage. Criticism from the U.S. is cast as a hegemonic expression of Western values—or, in echoes of the language used in the *Kundun* controversy, an interference in China's internal affairs that is inappropriate under Chinese norms that consider such issues none of another country's business.

China's leverage over politicians pining for loans, and the subsequent debt traps that can lead to Chinese control of their countries' assets, have received ample coverage as the Belt and Road Initiative has taken root. Receiving considerably less attention is the cultural complement to its political and economic aims. In addition to laying the tracks for a China-oriented global trading system, the Belt and Road Initiative is creating a distribution network for Chinese movies and TV shows that sell the country to its new beneficiaries. In government documentation outlining the priorities of the initiative, film festivals and film productions are cited as crucial to building a "people-to-people bond," alongside other goals like "policy coordination" and "financial integration." At that first speech of Xi's announcing the Belt and Road Initiative in Kazakhstan, the president mentioned Xian Xinghai, an early twentieth-century Chinese composer who worked in the central Asian country, as a sign of the two countries' history together. A Beijing producer heard the story and decided to adapt it into a movie, called *Composer*, that was the first co-production between China and Kazakhstan when it was released in 2019. It would not be the last movie to use cinema to deepen the ties China was forming around the world.

Audiences in China likely noticed it before anyone else. Parts of the world they'd given little thought to were suddenly woven into their movies' narratives. Xi declared the Belt and Road Initiative a priority of the state; not long afterward, movies went into production with plots set along the ancient trade route or featuring characters from Belt and Road countries coming together. In Hollywood, the slightest whiff of a preference at a studio will get screenwriters to dust off a script—Disney wants family dramas, Paramount is on the hunt for video game adaptations. In China, the same thing happens in response to governmental priorities. Cynical producers noted how even a tangential Belt and Road theme could boost interest from investors or TV channels buying distribution rights. In the 2017 action movie *The China Salesman*, a Chinese cell phone executive successfully outmaneuvers European competitors for a contract in North Africa (between fight scenes starring Mike Tyson and Steven Seagal). The movie does not mention the Belt and Road Initiative, but it's about a Chinese benefactor connecting his country to a part of the world where telecommunications equipment and services from companies like Huawei are a ubiquitous feature of China's new economic diplomacy. When it came time to sell distribution rights to this movie, more than thirty countries along the Belt and Road route bought it.

The distribution network forming around the world was merely one asset that China's film industry had by the time Xi's global ambitions came into focus. But people do not choose what movie to see based on bilateral agreements. The movies need some sex appeal, and in China, new movie stars modeled the chicest clothes, filled gossip websites, and offered Beijing glamorous ambassadors of the country's culture. But even if Xi recognized the *Star Trek* heroes that an Iowan boy celebrated on his bedroom wall, he would preside over an authoritarian China where such actors' fandoms challenged party orthodoxy and a power dynamic calcified over decades. And when those in the U.S. began speaking out against the new president-for-life, Americans doing business in the country would soon learn they too would be expected to behave.

FOURTEEN

Agents of the State

The paparazzi could barely contain themselves as they took in the quintet of stars. China's most famous actress, Fan Bing-bing, joined Jessica Chastain, Penélope Cruz, Lupita Nyong'o, and Marion Cotillard on the red carpet of the Cannes Film Festival in May 2018. Fan and her fellow actresses had just been cast in *The 355*, a forthcoming film about a cadre of female spies, its title inspired by the code name given to a woman who spied for George Washington in the Revolutionary War. *The 355* was not screening at Cannes, but its distribution rights were being sold at the film market that accompanies the glitzy premieres.

It was hard to imagine a hotter package. After more than a year of public #MeToo excoriations against powerful men in the entertainment industry, the time felt ripe for a movie about women kicking ass. The global makeup of its cast—American, European, Kenyan, Chinese—boded well for worldwide box-office tallies. A bidding war broke out for the distribution rights. Universal won with a $20 million bid, with Chinese studio Huayi Brothers kicking in the same amount to release the movie in China.

Seeing a Chinese actress alongside Oscar winners, an equal to the Hollywood A-list, was another vindication of Xi Jinping's new China. A decade after its Olympic opening ceremony, the country had sent one of its biggest stars to the world's most glamorous film festival. Fan wore oversized sunglasses and a white-on-white ensemble, pairing a loose-fitting blouse with a feathered skirt. She had gone the "flower vase" route in the *Iron Man 3* scene that Disney had commissioned and then cut. The following year, she tried again in Fox's *X-Men: Days of Future Past* as Blink, a mutant with teleporting abilities. She had one line: "Time's up." It was not an auspicious start, but Fan held fast to her hopes. In 2017, as her country's politicians were projecting a century of Chinese dominance, Fan predicted she would win the lead role in a Hollywood movie within ten years. She underestimated herself. *The 355* was scheduled to start filming later on in 2018.

But then, when the actresses gathered again for filming, Fan was nowhere to be found. Even one week into the shoot, no one on set knew if she'd show up—or if they were even allowed to talk about why she'd disappeared. With cameras rolling, the cast and crew of Fan's new movie did not know if the authorities would allow her to leave the country—or even to leave her home.

In the year between the Cannes red carpet and the start of production on *The 355*, Fan became the most famous chicken used by Chinese authorities to scare the monkeys of its entertainment industry. Her downfall was a dramatic example of Xi's determination to bring his country's booming film industry underfoot. While Xi moved aggressively against foreign adversaries and internal rivals, he swiftly enlisted China's film industry—and its stars in particular—as part of that campaign. The shift in China would inevitably present Hollywood and American industry with some of the harshest lessons yet about what happens when doing business with the country becomes a tacit endorsement of its policies. A new celebrity class formed in China, just as it had in the early days of Hollywood, but its members would have to navigate a political tight-rope far trickier than their American counterparts ever did. For those in the U.S. who wanted to keep doing business in the country, the balance proved just as treacherous.

FAN'S DOWNFALL CAME JUST WEEKS after her Cannes appearance. Shortly before the release of a new movie she'd just completed, called *Cell Phone 2*, a Chinese newscaster uploaded images of two contracts to his Weibo account. Both were contracts related to Fan's work on the movie, but they showed her reporting wildly different salaries. One, re-ported to the government, said she had made $1.5 million on the film. The other showed the actual amount: $7.8 million. Not bad for four days of work either way, but here was stark proof of so-called ying-yang contracts that allowed Chinese stars to report one set of earnings to tax authorities while secretly pocketing a much bigger one. Fan's lavish lifestyle—already a rebuke to certain communist philosophies—appeared to have been made possible by tax evasion, an infraction punishable by death in China.

Cui Yongyuan, the newscaster who posted the tax returns, was said to be upset about the original *Cell Phone* movie, which featured a lecherous character who viewers believed was a thinly veiled portrayal of him. Post-ing the evidence of Fan's duplicitous contracts was his way of exacting revenge. Authorities launched an investigation into Fan's finances a week later. China's film industry, playing out its role as a reflection of the state's opinion at any given moment, banned Fan from appearing on-screen.

Graphic designers erased her face from movie posters. Longtime ob-servers of the industry drew comparisons to the fate of Tang Wei, a Chinese actress who had starred in Ang Lee's *Lust, Caution*, a riveting

2007 drama about a troupe of university actors who plot to assassinate a politician in Japanese-controlled Shanghai. The movie's explicit sex scenes—and the fact that Tang would agree to star in them—led Chinese authorities to pull a promotional campaign she'd signed with Pond's cosmetics in retribution. Fan was much more famous than Tang had been at the time of her reprisal, and the fact that she was on the verge of becoming better known globally was alarming—it proved Xi was unafraid of overseas criticism. That Chinese officials would turn their country's most famous actress into its most famous cautionary tale became the ultimate example of how the ruling party required Chinese stars to be model, patriotic citizens. If they stepped out of line, they could disappear. This was not a country where a celebrity scandal can lend mystique and a mug shot is eventually sold as kitsch, like Frank Sinatra's or Lindsay Lohan's.

In early July, Fan was placed under house arrest and was not seen in public for months. She was secretly held at a vacation resort for "residential surveillance," the kind of arrest that Xi reserved for senior party members suspected of corruption. She was allowed no phone, pen, or paper. She was watched constantly, even while taking showers. She would not resurface until October, nearly three months after she'd disappeared.

Before that moment, Fan, like any big star in China, had adroitly balanced fame with the party allegiance required to retain it. Her father had been forced to sing Communist anthems, and her mother was a dancer until a family history that flirted with capitalist ventures ruined her career onstage.

"The most unfortunate thing is their dreams were suppressed," Fan said. "For me, nothing is impossible, nothing is beyond consideration."

After starting in costume dramas, Fan got lead roles in commercial hits like Renny Harlin's *Skiptrace* and *I Am Not Madame Bovary*, a marital comedy that won her critical respect. Free of the artistic suppression that her parents faced, Fan challenged norms about fame and women in

China, becoming a larger-than-life role model in the process. "I don't need to marry rich. I am rich," she said in 2015. Fans called her "Fan Ye," or Master Fan, a designation normally bestowed only on men. She flaunted her wealth, buying expensive apartments that challenged Chinese traditions of public modesty. Only the best dressed her: Dior, Versace, Armani.

But Fan also knew how to offset the Western designers and braggadocio with roles that let the government know she wouldn't stray too far afield. One of her movies, *Sky Hunter*, was made in partnership with the People's Liberation Army. A rip-off of *Top Gun*, even down to some of its fighter-jet choreography, *Sky Hunter* followed a group of fighter pilots who must stop an imminent missile attack and free Chinese hostages trapped overseas. The movie performed modestly in China and collected a pittance outside it in only a handful of foreign markets. One Hong Kong–based critic called it "little more than a recruitment drive for the Chinese military." (Michael Gralapp played the American president.) Fan's next movie, *Air Strike*, was scheduled for release just as she disappeared. This was similarly a movie for the Chinese military to show its power on-screen, since it told the true story of an American air force officer training Chinese fighter pilots to take on Japanese bombers destroying the city of Chongqing. (Bruce Willis played the air force officer who trains them.)

China's film industry under Xi Jinping wanted the special effects, the box-office grosses, and the global influence of modern-day Hollywood. But it wanted the stars that such a system creates to remain stuck in the 1920s, when Rin Tin Tin was the ideal star—bankable and trained. "The creation of art can fly with the wings of imagination," Xi had said at his Yan'an speech on art in 2014. "But make sure art workers tread on solid earth." China's quest to balance its consumerism and its Communism resides in these "art workers" who pose for Gucci one day and play a Mao-era soldier the next. Before her arrest, Fan's filmography was a model for every Chinese actor, producer, and director trying to succeed in the country's modern entertainment sector: commercial *and* patriotic.

THE TEMPLATE FOR SUCH A career had been forged by the man once known as the pride of Hong Kong: Jackie Chan. To most American fans, he remains the death-defying stuntman of *Rush Hour*. At home, he has navigated fame and politics better than any modern Chinese star.

Chan was born in 1954, a twelve-pound baby whose weight got him his first press notice—"Giant Baby," the local paper reported. As a kid in Hong Kong, he idolized the cowboys of Hollywood and trained in kung fu at a drama academy where class ran from 5:00 a.m. to 11:00 p.m. His master screamed so much at Chan that the young boy slept on a bed covered in the elder's spittle. Since his parents worked at the French consulate, Chan had access to milk and bread, which made him stronger and better nourished than other kids. It was an origin story that rendered him a distinctly Chinese hero, one strengthened not by a radioactive spider or cosmic event but by training, discipline, and a diet available during a time of mass starvation. When he assumed the mantle left by Bruce Lee's death, Chan signaled he would be a different kind of on-screen hero. Bruce Lee specialized in high kicks; Chan kept his legs low. Whereas Lee yelled when fighting, Chan would grimace and make faces to show the audience how much pain he was in. "Bruce Lee is superhuman in the audience's eyes, but I just want to be a regular guy. I want to play ordinary, flawed people who sometimes despair. They aren't heroes; there are things they can't do," he wrote in a 2018 memoir.

Early in his career, Chan was seen as a potential crossover star and cast in *Cannonball Run*, a 1981 ensemble comedy about a cross-country car race. Chan starred alongside Burt Reynolds, Farrah Fawcett, and Sammy Davis Jr., who spoke Japanese to him on set without Chan ever correcting him. When the movie was released in Japan and Hong Kong,

Chan's name appeared bigger on the posters to draw in local audiences, but they didn't like what they saw. Fans in Hong Kong hated that he'd played a Japanese character and that he was the butt of everyone's jokes on-screen. If Hong Kong's biggest star was going to be part of a cultural exchange with America, this would not be it.

Chan would find greater success more than a decade later when American audiences saw his slapstick style of fighting in *Rumble in the Bronx* and *Rush Hour*, a buddy comedy about an African American detective who teams with a Hong Kong detective to solve a case. The movie was a hit and spawned two sequels. Chan was the most famous Chinese actor in the world, though at the time he was still largely associated with Hong Kong.

Yet as China's film industry grew, Hong Kong's biggest directors and stars were steadily absorbed into the mainland, where bigger budgets and productions meant bigger paydays. Throughout the 1990s, about four hundred movies were made in Hong Kong each year, turning the colony into a capital of global cinema known for edgy noir and heartbreaking romance. Since the handover to mainland China, that annual figure has shrunk to only a few dozen. Instead, several of China's biggest blockbusters, such as *The Mermaid* ($527 million) and *Kung Fu Yoga* ($254 million) were directed by Hong Kong filmmakers, a trend similar to the absorption of German filmmakers like F. W. Murnau into Hollywood in the 1920s. Andrew Lau, who directed *Infernal Affairs*, the 2002 Hong Kong crime drama that served as the inspiration for Martin Scorsese's *The Departed*, signed on to make Chinese propaganda movies like *The Founding of an Army*.

Chan went with them, starring in propaganda movies about significant party anniversaries and stories that always doubled as positive morality tales. If there was a state priority, chances are its themes would appear in a Jackie Chan movie. In *Kung Fu Yoga*, Chan plays an archaeologist who partners with an Indian counterpart to search for lost treasure. In real life, India was skeptical of China's Belt and Road Initiative, since it would improve transportation in Kashmir, including through a hotly disputed region that challenged Indian sovereignty, and boost the economy and defense capabilities of India's main rival in the region, Pakistan. China was pushing a colonialist agenda, Indian critics alleged, one that ignored preexisting international norms like transparency and equality. When a Chinese construction firm started work on a road in Tibet that India said crossed into its territory, soldiers from the two nations started a fistfight. Others feared there could be an all-out war.

Such realities are of no concern to the characters of *Kung Fu Yoga*. When the Indian archaeologist lobbies Chan's character, Jack, to join her effort, she says:

```
                    ASHMITA
     We could increase the cooperation in
     archaeological research between China and
     India. It would also be in line with the One
     Belt One Road policy.


                    JACK
     So well said!
```

It was political product placement—a clumsy attempt to stuff state messaging into a commercial film. And it was far from the only such example in Chan's repertoire. In the summer of 2019, I attended a promotional event in Shanghai for another Chan movie that seemed produced to reflect an off-screen political reality. It was a Russia-China coproduction called *The Mystery of the Dragon Seal: Journey to China*. This movie follows a cartographer as he travels across eastern Russia toward China, a journey that introduces him to wizards and other CGI creations and symbolizes the conjoining of the two countries. The former governor of California, Arnold Schwarzenegger, stars opposite Chan.

The director of the film, Oleg Stepchenko, told me he was proud of the bilateral landmark. "The movies have great power and can unite and inspire people," he said. In the years during the film's development, China and Russia proclaimed their relations the best they had ever been, and they partnered on economic projects and military strategies that deepened their alliance. The summer before, Beijing had sent thirty jets and helicopters, along with more than three thousand soldiers, to participate in a Russian war exercise. On the day of the publicity event for *The Mystery of the Dragon Seal*, news agencies in China reported that Vladimir Putin had sent Xi some Russian ice cream as a birthday present.

Neither movie succeeded in its messaging. The pandering in *Kung Fu Yoga* was torn apart by some Indian moviegoers, and the movie's stereotypical depiction of Indian customs alienated them further. *The Mystery of the Dragon Seal* drew reviews that made it clear it was too confusing a movie to serve any kind of geopolitical purpose. Yet producers far and wide were heeding their government's call to endorse the Belt and Road Initiative through entertainment. While attending a trade show in Hong Kong at which distributors sell overseas rights to shows and movies, I was struck by the amount of children's programming introducing young minds to the plan. One such show, called *Panda and Krash*, was announced during one of Xi's visits to Russia. It was an animated version of the friendship forming between the two countries—Panda, from China, and his best friend, Krash, from Russia. Together they formed a kid-friendly cinematic representation of growing cooperation between China and Russia, two countries with a complicated history that nonetheless have discovered the benefits of joining forces to create an alternative to America's unipolarity. "It praises the virtues shared by the people of the two countries, such as kindness, courage, and inclusiveness," the statement announcing the show declared. Panda also starred in a Czech Republic show with similar themes and a beloved Czech character in Krash's place, called *The Little Mole and Panda*, that premiered around the time of Xi's state visit to the country. The concept, one CCTV representative explained to me, could be replicated across countries—imagine a *Panda and Mickey Mouse*, he said.

On-screen alliances with roots in the Belt and Road Initiative also took shape. Pakistan took the two-pronged approach of making dry testimonials—a short film called *Amity Along the Orange Line*, about a subway built as part of the Belt and Road Initiative—and commercial exploits: *Parwaaz Hai Junoon*, an action film about the Pakistani air force that features JF-17 fighter jets manufactured in the two countries and became the first movie from Pakistan to screen in China in decades. In Egypt, a company called Vibration Studios dubbed Chinese dramas into Arabic for broadcast on Egypt's state television. In Italy, *Chang'an Meets Rome* spanned one hundred mini episodes about landmarks on the Silk Road between the two countries. In the Balkans, Huahua Media—an investor behind several Hollywood movies, including *Godzilla: King of the Monsters*—signed a deal to remake two Balkan films, *The Bridge* and *Walter Defends Sarajevo*. The latter, about a Communist resistance fighter who takes on the Nazis, was one of the few foreign films let into China during the Cultural Revolution, and it grew so beloved that a Chinese beer brand took the name *Walter.* Announcing the remakes, Huahua CEO Wang Kefei said the agreement "responds to the call of the state by bearing the important weight of strengthening 'Belt and Road' cultural exchange." (The week before, China had agreed to build a new subway system in Belgrade.) In a Ukrainian-Chinese movie filmed in Henan Province, where the Silk Road started tracing across the continent, a Chinese painter falls in love with a Ukrainian dancer. In another, set in the Czech Republic, a Chinese man travels there to reunite with his soul mate. That movie was directed by Jackie Chan.

CHAN HAS LEARNED FIRSTHAND what happens when stars fall out of line. In the summer of 2014, his son Jaycee Chan—an aspiring actor named after his father's initials—was arrested in Beijing for marijuana possession. He was sentenced to six months in jail but served only one month. For Kai Ko, a friend who was busted along with Jaycee, the

The original "Hollywood" sign, erected in 1923 to advertise a housing development being built in the hills below, came to signify the glitz and pull of America's most famous industry.

In 2016, a Chinese real estate mogul named Wang Jianlin erected his own version of the Hollywood sign above a massive complex of sound stages built in the eastern Chinese city of Qingdao. It translates to "Movie Metropolis of the East"—and its letters stand taller than those of its Los Angeles counterpart.

In the 1990s, Richard Gere's public friendship with the Dalai Lama inspired him to issue statements in support of Tibet—a political stance that would cost him roles in major studio releases years later.

Chen Kaige's 1993 film *Farewell My Concubine* was one of several Chinese movies of the 1980s and 1990s that heralded a breakthrough in the country's cinema. *Concubine* was celebrated in the West, winning the Palme d'Or at the Cannes Film Festival, but was banned in China until political pressure prompted officials to allow it to screen.

America's leading man John Wayne starred as Mongol empire leader Genghis Khan in the 1956 film *The Conqueror*. Its stereotypically Orientalist portrayal characterized much of Hollywood's treatment of Asians in the midtwentieth century.

Nicole Kidman walks the red carpet at the opening ceremony of Wanda Group's Oriental Movie Metropolis in 2013. She joined John Travolta and other Hollywood stars who welcomed the Qingdao, China, facility into the global filmmaking community—and who were paid handsomely for attending.

Jeffrey Katzenberg, the chief executive of DreamWorks Animation, poses with the animal that would anchor his studio's hit franchise, *Kung Fu Panda*—and prompt Chinese officials to question why their nation's filmmakers hadn't conceived of the film first.

Walt Disney Company chief executive Robert Iger snaps selfies with visitors to the Shanghai Disney Resort, a $5.5 billion attraction that opened in 2016 after years of negotiations and concessions from his entertainment company.

After its TV channel was blocked from Chinese airwaves, Disney opted for an unconventional approach to introducing Chinese children to its characters: opening a string of English-language schools that used Disney properties in the curriculum and encouraged kids to fall in love with Mickey Mouse and his friends.

Concessions-stand employees wear Stormtrooper masks before the first public screening of Disney's *Star Wars: The Force Awakens* at a theater in Shanghai, China. The movie would eventually fail at the Chinese box office, sending Disney executives into a yearslong frenzy to win over the market.

Fan Bingbing, China's most famous actress, attends the Cannes Film Festival in 2018 alongside her fellow stars of the action film *The 355*: Marion Cotillard, Jessica Chastain, Penélope Cruz, and Lupita Nyong'o. Fan would disappear into government custody amid allegations of tax evasion soon after the festival.

Director Renny Harlin, once known for major Hollywood blockbusters, saw his career collapse in the U.S. with the flop *Cutthroat Island* but years later found a second act on China's A-list. Here he congratulates two actors who had finished filming on his 2019 Chinese action thriller *Bodies at Rest*.

Posters for the highest-grossing Chinese movie of all time, *Wolf Warrior 2*, lure audiences in Yichang, China. The movie starred Wu Jing as a Chinese soldier who saves African villagers from violent, racist American mercenaries.

A young Xi Jinping, far right, on his first trip to the United States, where he stayed at the split-entry home of Eleanor, Thomas, and Paula Dvorchak (second, third, and fourth from left) in Muscatine, Iowa, in 1985.

Xi Jinping, then vice president of China, and Joe Biden, then vice president of the United States, signal a new era of cooperation between their two countries during Xi's visit to California in 2012.

Nelly Naimutie, a resident of Suswa, Kenya, and the wife of the town's chief, in front of her home, which in late 2018 was outfitted with a satellite dish that carries Chinese movies and TV shows.

Immaculate Wanjiku, seen in yellow, feeds a baby some medicine with help from her children and some neighbors. The family had just taken a break from watching *Crouching Tiger, Hidden Dragon* on their living-room TV in Suswa, Kenya.

retribution was far worse. He had just finished filming *Monster Hunt*, a comedy in which he was one of four lead actors. The movie's director, Raman Hui, was in the final stages of editing the movie when authorities called to tell him the movie could not be released with an immoral star in it. He would have to reshoot the movie with a different actor. Like Fan Bingbing's face getting scrubbed from posters, it was an example of Chinese authorities wanting the cast on-screen to be uncomplicated role models.

This was a bigger undertaking than swapping out the flags in *Red Dawn* or erasing an actress from a poster. "We looked at one [scene] with no actors, just monsters. And my reaction was, OK, this shot is safe. We don't have to change this. Then I started crying. I just burst into tears," Hui said. In all, he had to reshoot 70 percent of the movie so Chinese audiences wouldn't see a star who'd been caught with a joint. *Monster Hunt* would go on to gross $382 million in China, one of the country's all-time biggest hits. Ko's career would never recover.

Executives in Hollywood traded the story of the *Monster Hunt* removal with equal parts amazement and fear. It was a cinematic disappearing. Chinese actors were quick to point out, several years later, that the #MeToo movement had forced Hollywood directors to do the same thing, such as when Christopher Plummer reshot scenes originally completed by Kevin Spacey in *All the Money in the World*, a drama about the Getty kidnapping scheduled for release soon after the original actor was accused of sexual misconduct. Plummer was the first of many such swaps as #MeToo allegations spread.

I got a firsthand look at how China's politics shape Chan's life when I briefly met him in Salt Lake City in early 2019. He was there to promote his environmentalism initiative, and a local museum had mounted an exhibit of art pieces made of recycled components; Chan spoke at a podium under a copper dragon with teeth made out of nails and a tail of frayed wicker branches. Before he arrived, assistants with earpieces scurried around like a head of state was due.

I was scheduled to sit down with Chan at 10:50 a.m. for twenty minutes, at which point he would move on to a general press conference. I'd
assumed we would meet in a boardroom away from the others but was
instead ushered to an art gallery surrounded by surrealist pieces inspired
by Chan. I sat near *Jackie Lisa*, an appropriation of the *Mona Lisa* with a
grinning Jackie Chan face implanted in place of *Mona*'s enigmatic smile.
Chan arrived with a team of fifteen handlers, all wearing puffy jackets with
"JC Stunt Team" embossed on them. He was surrounded by photogra-
phers and multiple cameramen who documented our entire interview. To
be around Jackie Chan is to be part of a roving, constant documentary.

Chan's responses to my questions were relentlessly on message: He
wanted Chinese kids to toughen up like he did. He wanted young men
to avoid nightclubs. He wanted Chinese actors and movies to travel the
world so people can come together and understand one another's culture.
After the conversation, I realized the more telling moment had come in
the seconds before I sat down with Chan, when one of his staff members—
until then a friendly and accommodating coordinator of the chat—pulled
me aside. Chan, she said, was not to be asked about certain topics or
mentioned in any way that related to them. U.S.-China relations, Tibet,
the Dalai Lama—these subjects were radioactive, and he could not be
near any such topics.

"He is our national treasure," she explained.

EIGHTEEN MONTHS AFTER Fan's arrest and disappearance, prodemocracy protests in Hong Kong drew the world's attention to the province
and to Xi's crackdown on dissent and free expression. Young people
taking to the streets adopted a namesake from Western entertainment,
calling themselves the "cursed generation" for having grown up in Hong
Kong when they did, a moniker derived from *Harry Potter*. According to
"Xi Jinping Thought," a political philosophy named for the leader and

encoded in the constitution of the People's Republic, the city would be subject to national reunification. Xi's power had undeniably reached Hong Kong.

It had also reached America, where corporate interests overruled most objections to the government's power grab. As protests intensified, Daryl Morey, general manager of the National Basketball Association's Houston Rockets, tweeted, "Fight for Freedom. Stand with Hong Kong." Though he quickly deleted it, that single tweet immediately jeopardized decades of business-building the NBA had done in China, where players already sold millions in sneakers, jerseys, and bobbleheads, and where a few games were played each year. CCTV stopped airing games, and Tencent, which had just signed a $1.5 billion deal with the NBA, was no longer allowed to carry them on its streaming platform. As many in Hollywood could have warned Morey, a single tweet that opposed Beijing policy would cost the league and its athletes hundreds of millions of dollars.

Now any stance that Xi disagreed with—such as a prodemocracy movement—was off limits for businesses that wanted to keep making money in China. Morey's colleagues in the NBA, a league typically willing to speak out on social issues like racial equality, took a collective vow of silence. LeBron James, its most visible star and advocate for social justice, said Morey was "misinformed." The NBA said it was "regrettable" to see the tweet had offended their "friends and fans in China," and when the league's statement was translated into Mandarin, it went even further in criticizing Morey for saying what he did. "We feel greatly disappointed at Houston Rockets' GM Daryl Morey's inappropriate speech, which is regrettable," the statement read in Mandarin. "Without a doubt, he has deeply offended many Chinese basketball fans."

The involvement of Tencent, which had partnered with Disney's ESPN to air NBA games in China, presented an issue for Disney CEO Robert Iger. Just as *Kundun* had threatened his company's theme park plans, tensions in one division of Disney were threatening the entire portfolio. An executive usually unafraid to weigh in on political matters— and who had even toyed with running for president himself in 2020—Iger shut up when it came to any question about China or the prodemocracy movement challenging its sovereignty. In an interview shortly after the Morey tweet, as captains of all industry were being pressured to comment on China and its treatment of protesters in Hong Kong, Iger talked about taking a public stance against a Georgia law that made it more difficult to get an abortion and Donald Trump's decision to withdraw the U.S. from the Paris climate accords. He stood up for the immigrants who worked for his company and had seen their status threatened by Trump-backed legislation. But when it came to China, Iger said he had a fiduciary duty to stay silent.

"Damned if you do, damned if you don't," Iger said. "We've learned how complicated this is . . . and I think the biggest learning from that is that caution is imperative, meaning to take a position that could harm our company in some form would be a big mistake."

The journalist interviewing Iger, *Wall Street Journal* editor Matt Murray, asked if a change in circumstances could necessitate a public stance. "I don't know," Iger said. He then made it clear that the China line of questioning was over.

The NBA's effort to defuse the situation in a series of statements that both distanced the league from Morey's comment and defended his right to make it sparked outrage in China and on both sides of the U.S. political aisle. Democratic and Republican lawmakers lambasted the league for not standing behind Morey and the opinion he'd tweeted, turning China's quashing of free speech into one of the very few issues that Senator Ted Cruz and Representative Alexandria Ocasio-Cortez agreed on.

"While it is easy to defend freedom of speech when it costs you nothing, equivocating when profits are at stake is a betrayal of fundamental American values," the lawmakers wrote in a letter to NBA commissioner Adam Silver.

. . .

ONE OF THE HONG KONG residents watching Xi's moves with trepidation was Sophia Shek, a local filmmaker who had been an assistant director on *Transformers: Age of Extinction* several years earlier. She was one of Michael Bay's half dozen assistant directors charged with various tasks that included prepping the main cast for the day's work, explaining to star Nicola Peltz how to use a crouch toilet, or escorting Kelsey Grammer to his dressing room. Shek had been born in Scotland to Asian parents and moved to Hong Kong in 1999 to work in entertainment, mostly drawn to the cinema scene that flourished there. *Transformers* was a bit of a shift, but she enjoyed it. Bay's responsibility—essentially a $200 million business with hundreds of employees—was far beyond the scope of her usual productions. And the movie was given all sorts of allowances that would never have been granted to local filmmakers, like the day they shot a scene that involved blowing up the local Hong Kong government office.

The movie was on her mind when I caught up with her in the summer of 2020. Beijing had recently passed a national security law that made dissent illegal in Hong Kong, turning the activism that had defined the city's streets and character in recent months into offenses punishable by up to a lifetime in jail. Dissident groups dissolved and members rid their social media accounts of any evidence of prior support.

I asked about that scene that came toward the end of the *Transformers* movie, the one that Paramount executives had rewritten at the request of authorities in order to secure the Chinese release date that led to those record-setting Chinese grosses. When she'd gone to see the film in 2014, Shek had little idea the scene was in the movie. The plot had been kept top secret even on set, and she saw only the pages of the script for scenes she was working on.

This is what she and viewers around the world saw as they sat in the darkened auditorium: In the final chapter of the film, Hong Kong officials watch in terror as skyscrapers crumble around them. With their city on the brink of total annihilation, they arrive at only one solution.

"We've got to call the central government for help!" one of them proclaims.

Cut to a hotel in Beijing, where the Chinese minister of defense is told that "there's a crisis in Hong Kong."

The defense minister is resolute.

```
            DEFENSE MINISTER
  The central government will protect Hong
  Kong at all costs. We have fighter jets on
  the way.
```

In the *Transformers* universe on-screen, as in the world China wanted to will into existence off-screen, Hong Kong officials know there is only one logical place to go for protection. As she sat in the theater, Shek realized she had been working on "one of the first films that made Hong Kong completely a part of China. . . . It was the whole package." To Shek and her friends, *Transformers* now feels like a sneak preview, a movie in which Mark Wahlberg says, "Sweetie, hand me my alien gun," becoming an unlikely vehicle in an escalating campaign of aggression. Rob Moore and the other Paramount executives who had approved the scene were fired or left the studio years before that motivation came into focus on the streets of Hong Kong. It all felt like another reminder of a maxim passed through Hollywood: American studios think in stock-market quarters. China thinks in centuries.

Today, Shek fears a loss of the strong identity that once defined Hong Kong filmmaking. "It's very difficult to finance any film. Hong Kong is a tiny market. It doesn't even register on the box office. If you can get one movie released across mainland China, you've made it. But if I wanted to make money, I would not be in this industry." When we spoke in the summer of 2020, she told me she worried about a censorship board being installed that would operate like the one in Beijing. "There's an urgency to document as much of Hong Kong as possible," she said. Less than a year later, the Hong Kong government announced it would ban films it believed were undermining national security and called on officials reviewing movies to "safeguard the sovereignty, unification, and territorial integrity of the People's Republic of China." Shek's fears were coming true. *Age of Extinction* means several things to her now.

HOLLYWOOD'S REACTION TO EVENTS IN Hong Kong followed the trajectory of its attention to Tibet, where once-vociferous support grew silent as China's influence over the entertainment industry grew. No one paid the price for that support like Richard Gere.

Though hardly anyone saw *Red Corner*, Gere's career and activism didn't immediately slow down, and for a time he was permitted to blend the two. He was named *People's* Sexiest Man Alive in 1999, the same year he reunited with *Pretty Woman* costar Julia Roberts in the hit romantic comedy *Runaway Bride*. He tap-danced as the lead in *Chicago* in 2002 and continued his specialty as the tortured leading man trying to navigate love and heartache in 2008's *Nights in Rodanthe*. Through it all, he wore his Buddhist prayer beads on the red carpet and hosted the Dalai Lama at events around the world.

His unapologetic and ceaseless criticism of China eventually caught up with him. As studios realized they could not do anything to jeopardize getting their movies onto Chinese screens, Gere became unemployable.

"There are definitely movies that I can't be in because the Chinese will say, 'Not with him,'" he said.

Gere has not made a movie with a major studio in a decade, instead starring in independent movies made at firms with no parent company ties to China and with no financiers worried about threatening their other holdings in the country. Several years ago, he was attached to star in an independently financed movie that was to be directed by a Chinese director who had no plans to show the film in China. Two weeks before shooting began, the director called Gere on a secure line.

"I can't do it," he said. If he made a movie with Gere, the director and his family would never be permitted to leave China again. The director's own career would dry up, he said, as if Gere's situation were contagious.

Contemporaries like Michael Douglas play supporting roles in Marvel Studios movies like *Ant-Man*, and even Mel Gibson finds big-studio work after making homophobic and anti-Semitic remarks. At Warner Bros., an actor like Gere might be considered for the role of Superman's counselor or a politician in Gotham City, roles that have gone to older actors with gravitas, like Gary Oldman. But it comes down to a matter of risk: If swapping in Jeremy Irons doesn't torpedo the movie creatively, then why chance it? For his part, Gere says he prefers making the smaller, character-driven stories. "I'm not interested in playing the wizened Jedi in your tentpole," he said.

Some studio executives have been skeptical of Gere's insistence that his political stance against China has cost him jobs. One told me Gere was difficult to work with and not worth the trouble. Another said he was getting John Travolta's hand-me-downs even at the height of his career. But Gere is actually correct. He has been blacklisted. According to a casting executive at Warner Bros., the studio that had hired him as recently as 2008 in *Nights in Rodanthe*, Gere became radioactive as China's market power grew.

With him, the rule became: "If you could have somebody else, then get somebody else," this person said.

THE OUTCRY IN THE U.S. over the treatment of Hong Kong, and the fact that international calls for information on Fan Bingbing's well-being were met with silence, contributed to a view held in both countries' film industries that Xi was impervious to criticism or pressure. In March 2018, Xi transferred oversight of his nation's movies from the expansive State Administration of Press, Publication, Radio, Film, and Television to the Ministry of Propaganda. The shift put Chinese movies under the control of a Communist Party overseer that would prioritize the messaging of cinema, as opposed to the previous authority, where growing the market was a top concern. Depending on the film's plot, several other government entities that are essentially police agencies—from the Ministry of State Security to the Ministry of Public Security and the Ministry of Justice—might have to issue an approval.

The crackdown many feared was solidified eight months later, when Ang Lee and actress Gong Li presided over the 2018 Golden Horse Awards, the most prestigious evening in Asian cinema, at a ceremony in Taipei. It was a banner year for mainland China, whose movies accounted for more nominations than Hong Kong or Taiwanese ones—a sign that the mainland was developing into a bona fide filmmaking force. Before Beijing-based producers left for the ceremony in Taipei, they were warned by authorities to be on guard. Officials feared Taiwan's government, Beijing's rival for territory with even more sensitivity than Tibet and Hong Kong, might try to sabotage the proceedings as a political statement against Xi.

It felt like a family reunion in the auditorium that night, a gathering of executives who had been in China from the industry's earliest days and the new filmmakers who were building an exciting market. The evening was going well, with text messages exchanged about which after-ceremony parties everyone was attending, when the winner for best documentary was announced. The award went to *Our Youth in Taiwan*, about young people's attitude toward political advocacy.

One of the winners, Fu Yue, took the stage. From their seats, the audience members could see she was shaking and sweaty. She looked nervous, and those watching her stand at the microphone grew anxious, exchanging the current of anxiety that's invisibly transferred in modern-day China between people when a political third rail appears to be in proximity.

"I really hope that one day our country can be treated as a truly independent entity," she said.

To outsiders, it might have looked like any politically tinged acceptance speech—unremarkable in a world where Michael Moore and Brad Pitt go after the sitting president when they accept their Oscars.

In China, where leaders are easily angered by suggestions that Taiwan is not a part of their country, it was a ten-second bomb blast.

Ang Lee's face went gray. Executives and filmmakers sat frozen in their seats. Phones started vibrating in the pockets of attendees. They were text messages sent by the authorities monitoring the ceremony from Beijing—with instantaneous instructions.

Do not show emotion.

Leave the ceremony quietly.

Cancel your after-party.

Get back to China as soon as possible.

After the ceremony, attendees gathered in a suite that was supposed to have hosted a party. It had the air of a wake. Fu's statement would not have surprised many in the audience, but making such a remark on such a stage was professional suicide—and reacting positively would jeopardize anyone's livelihood. The optimism of those early days in China's new film business had been replaced by creeping dread.

The response spoke to a central irony of working in today's Chinese entertainment industry. It is a collection of producers and directors who believe in film's power, in its ability to change lives and perspectives through persuasion or empathy. But it is also an industry that knows such power is limited by the terms of storytelling imposed by the state—and that if anyone violates those rules, it could all go away.

The absorption continued. In the summer of 2019, the Central Commission for Deepening Overall Reform, led by Xi, distributed new guidelines for the Chinese entertainment industry that a state-affiliated news outlet said made it clear the Communist Party considered the entertainment industry to be under its domain.

"Film and TV work cannot merely be approached from a commercial, market-based or entertainment perspective; it must be undertaken with strategic thinking from the national level, from the same battle lines that the country itself is fighting from," one analysis from a state-backed broadcaster explained. The language could have been an updated translation of Mao's speech in 1942. Fan Bingbing's arrest, the Golden Horse shutdown, the Ministry of Propaganda's new powers—it all added up to a message from Xi Jinping's government to the commercial film industry built since the turn of the century: time's up.

FOLLOWING FAN'S ARREST, the government announced that it would rein in stars' salaries, ruling that they could account for only 40 percent of a film's total budget. The film industry was "distorting social values" through "money worship," the authorities declared. Fan was ordered to pay $131 million in back taxes, though reports of how much came out of her own pocket range from $2 million to $70 million. The government said it collected $1.7 billion in total from the film and television industry's unpaid taxes as other stars and studios were audited. Shares in Chinese movie companies fell an average of 18 percent as investors realized that China's government was on to them.

The stars and studios got to work reacquiring the patriotism points they'd lost in the tax scandal. After the pro-Taiwan comment at the Golden Horse Awards, Fan came out in support of her country on social media, saying, "China cannot miss out on any inch." Feng Xiaogang, the *Cell Phone 2* director who was arrested along with her, announced that his next movie would celebrate the seventieth anniversary of the party. Huayi Brothers, another studio implicated in the tax scandal, established an in-house Communist Party committee. The studio would "integrate the party's achievements into film and television." It was an unusually explicit encroachment of the party into an entertainment company, but not entirely unprecedented. At least 288 companies listed on the Shanghai and Shenzhen stock exchanges had "revised corporate charters to allow a deeper management role" for the Communist Party, according to Nikkei research conducted in 2017. Huayi also announced that its movies would stick to certain themes: coming of age, Communist history, traditional Chinese culture, and the Belt and Road Initiative.

Eventually, Fan was allowed back into polite society, giving interviews in which she positioned her experience as an instructive fable for others. She was permitted to leave China, but not in time to make it to the set of *The 355*. When Chastain, Cruz, and her other costars spent the summer of 2019 filming in Paris and Morocco, a body double was used for all of Fan's scenes. Once production had wrapped, Fan flew to Los Angeles, where she filmed her lines in front of a green screen for director Simon Kinberg. It would be kept top secret, but the real Fan Bingbing would appear in the movie thanks to a postproduction team who inserted her footage. All viewers of the finished film would see was a beautiful and talented Chinese actress, looking perfect on-screen.

FIFTEEN

Wolf Warriors

n 2019, Nathaniel Boyd, the air force veteran who had found work starring as American missionaries, businessmen, and bad boyfriends in Chinese films, suddenly found himself out of work. The U.S.-China trade war prompted Chinese producers to stop hiring Americans in their movies—not because of any official edict, but because they just read the situation as risky. That changed the next year, when Boyd was booked for one job after another, but all for the same kind of role. He was in hot demand because all of these new projects took place during the Korean War, or as it is known in China, the War to Resist the U.S. Aggression. Within a year, Boyd had starred in a Korean War TV series, as well as two movies about the conflict. One focused on the battle of Lake Changjin, when Chinese soldiers defeated American troops despite grueling winter weather. The other—directed by Zhang Yimou—detailed the story of a successful Chinese sharpshooter said to have killed 214 American soldiers in thirty-two days. "With historical facts, the film is going to make audiences once again realize that although the U.S. is strong, it is not unbeatable," said Tan Fei, a producer on the film. The National Radio and Television Administration told provincial officials that they should dust off their library titles with American villains and get them back on TV. CCTV began reairing *Battle on Shangganling Mountain*, a film about a Korean War battle in which China's People's Volunteer Army takes on U.S. troops. The movie had been released in 1956, but it received prime-time placement in the summer of 2020, when COVID-19 ripped through the United States and relations between the two countries sank to new lows. Across China, America once again became the on-screen bad guy.

Postproduction editors—like the *Red Dawn* graphics mavens in 2011—were ordered to adjust finished Chinese movies to do anything possible to bolster Chinese nationalism, even as Hollywood movies continued to cut anything that might anger Chinese censors. One postproduction editor working in China was making a dozen changes to footage a week, under orders to make the movie "feel more Chinese" so it would carry a stronger patriotic message. Entire plot locations were reassigned to China. A computer-generated character lost his hair after the director said a bald head made him look more like a Chinese grandfather. It was the equivalent of a director asking that computer-generated cowboy hats be placed atop characters' heads to boost American patriotism. "Safe to say that we're making a ton of changes and are continually adjusting the aesthetic to try and achieve something that cannot at any point be mistaken as 'Western,'" this editor said. He wanted to get a T-shirt made to wear to the footage reviews with the director. All it would need to say was "This isn't Chinese enough."

One young creative executive, who had grown up watching *Transformers* as a kid in 1990s China, told me of visiting relatives in the countryside in the fall of 2020. They had a TV used by the children of neighboring families. The animation they watched was all made in China and mostly about the historical revolutions the country fights over and over again on-screen. He watched the kids watch movies about heroes from the Communist revolution. Another show followed a child soldier fighting the Japanese, before the station aired another show about fighting the Americans. When he was their age, all he'd heard was a narrative about the country opening up to the world, a narrative that had stayed with him as he moved to attend college in the U.S. It was hard to imagine the young generation of Chinese people, reared on the entertainment of contemporary China, feeling anything but antagonism toward America.

"In another fifteen years, when this generation of Chinese grows up and becomes more the mainstream of the population, what will happen because they grew up with a very different narrative?" he asked. Even Lawrence Zhou, the Captain America superfan, wrote me in the late spring of 2021 to say he viewed his cinematic idol a bit differently—as a symbol, not of what the U.S. represented, but of the aspirations it failed to meet. "America is no longer the nation of the 'American Dream,'" he said. The portrayal of the U.S. as a moral and just nation in the Marvel films he loved so dearly was actually showing audiences "what America is missing or has never had," he added.

Chinese movies were giving the country's audiences a new clarity about the world's good guys and bad guys—a message reflected by Beijing more broadly. President Xi's mission to offer "socialism with Chinese characteristics" as an alternative to the U.S.'s liberal democracy took on a new urgency in the last years of the Trump administration, when a global pandemic put in stark relief the superpower showdown defining the twenty-first century. On-screen, Chinese directors mined the myths of the past for new ways to reflect their country's modern-day swagger, fan the flames of rising nationalism, and provide their industry with the franchise blockbusters that would finally allow it to complete the Hollywood playbook. Outright antagonism toward the U.S. and a new wave of human-rights abuses would put companies like Disney in a geopolitical morass not seen since the *Kundun* days, recasting the years of chasing riches into something that now looked like complicity in a state enemy's rise. The decade had started with *Avatar* and Wanda's blank checks. It would end with the movies becoming a proxy for the broader battle for the future of the world order.

. . .

IN THE YEARS SINCE *Wolf Warrior 2*, other pill-in-the-peanut-butter tales of Chinese heroism hit screens. In 2019, China had its first science-fiction blockbuster with *The Wandering Earth*, about a group of Chinese heroes who pivot the planet off its axis to avoid the blast radius of an imminently exploding sun. The combination of sophisticated special effects, Chinese heroism, and genre novelty helped it make $700 million at the box office—the third-highest gross of all time in the country. Hollywood executives called it China's own *Independence Day*, noting that the movie had even opened on the first day of the Chinese New Year (the Will Smith blockbuster had opened around July 4). In this interpretation, America retained its cultural dominance, since China, with its genre experimentation and release-date strategies, was merely replicating a century of entertainment already culled and packaged by Western tastes.

The Wandering Earth put Chinese taikonauts in the captain's chair. The U.S. is hardly anywhere to be found. In fact, the only reference to the U.S. comes early in the movie, during a fast-moving clip reel of newscasters around the world reporting on the impending doom. The U.S., viewers learn in brief footage from an *NBC News* special report, cannot help save the world. The crawl text along the bottom of the screen explains why.

LABOR STRIKE CAUSES CONSTRUCTION DELAY TO FOUR EARTH ENGINES IN NEW YORK AREA

Unions are stopping the U.S. from helping build the propulsion machines needed to get the Earth to safety. American democracy, with its many stakeholders and noisy chorus of agitators, is going to get the planet destroyed if China and its organized team of taikonauts don't step up. It was the schlocky sci-fi version of the contrast Xi was drawing between his country and the U.S.: order versus chaos.

The spread of COVID-19 provided China a chance to try to prove it. The virus originated in China and spread around the world in a way eerily foreshadowed by Max Brooks in his zombie thriller *World War Z*, in which an authoritarian regime in China tries to message-control its way out of a crisis. In Washington, the coronavirus—and its origins in China—exacerbated a standoff that the countries had been building toward for years. "Today, we're finally realizing the degree to which the Chinese Communist Party is truly hostile to the United States and our values," Secretary of State Mike Pompeo said in October 2019. Chinese state-run media responded by calling him a "public enemy of mankind," and made him such a frequent target that everyday Chinese citizens knew his name. (How many Americans in 2019 could summon the name of a single deputy of Xi's?) Nearly four years into his term, President Trump's repeated assaults on China took on a new ugliness in his adoption of the racist term "kung flu" to describe the coronavirus. U.S. public opinion on China fell to its lowest point since the question started being asked by Pew pollsters in 2005. About two thirds of Americans had a negative view of China, an increase of twenty percentage points from when Trump took office.

In the early weeks of the virus outbreak, China kept American scientific officials away from hot spots and obscured information that could have contained it, leading analysts to wonder if the coronavirus would crack the regime. But once the U.S. was struggling with a rising caseload and Chinese businesses were opening back up, China's propaganda arms got to work using the pandemic as a soft-power opportunity that allowed it to eclipse the U.S. as the global leader to call in an emergency. The Xinhua news service contrasted pictures of a deserted Times Square with a packed Chengdu restaurant.

The Belt and Road Initiative had laid the groundwork for parts of the world to be wooed by the campaign. Three million face masks from Shenzhen went to Hungary, arriving in boxes that said "Hajrá Magyarország!" or "Bring It On, Hungary!," the campaign slogan for Prime

Minister Viktor Orbán, a leader who has tested relations with liberal democratic nations elsewhere in the EU as he has turned toward China. "In the West, there is a shortage of basically everything. The help we are able to get is from the East," Orbán said, in comments picked up and circulated by Chinese state TV—alongside baseless theories that the virus had come to the Chinese city of Wuhan via visiting U.S. Army troops. When Chinese-produced vaccines became available, brokers told Paraguay's foreign ministry their country could receive the shots if they cut diplomatic relations with Taiwan. Onetime adversaries, desperate for the shots, made concessions elsewhere—in Brazil, officials did an about-face and allowed China's 5G telecommunications technology into the country after the vaccinations arrived.

"Almost as soon as the crisis started, they had a propaganda battle to win on this," said Andrew Small of the German Marshall Fund, a policy group advocating stronger ties between the U.S. and Europe. The Chinese foreign ministry countered: "Would they rather China watch on with folded arms, and be indifferent at this time?" The campaign to cast China as the world leader was insulating the country from criticism of its own handling of the virus and provided a new front in what I had observed while reporting in Africa: a filling of the global leadership vacuum left by the U.S. And of course, Xi's film industry started on revisionist history films of China's response to the outbreak, a cinematic campaign to go along with the medical supplies.

Nearly one hundred years after being praised for transporting the Western good around the world in the fight against the Axis powers, Hollywood studios were tarred for placating a country that had emerged as the adversary of the new century. Trump administration officials lambasted Hollywood for sowing the seeds of complacency that had led to China's successful appeals to other countries. Vice President Mike Pence, Attorney General William Barr, and Pompeo all cited *Red Dawn* and *World War Z* as hypocritical examples of a Democratic-leaning industry kowtowing to an authoritarian regime, the case studies in censorship getting more attention from leaders in 2020 than they had when the movies came out. The previous two decades of exploration and investment in China, the box-office tallies and catering to censors' demands—all of it had put Hollywood at odds with its own government.

No Hollywood studio found itself as caught up in the tension as Disney. Two decades of working in China had planted land mines that exploded as the geopolitical fight escalated.

In March 2020, the company had shut down several blocks on Hollywood Boulevard in the heart of Los Angeles for the premiere of its live-action retelling of *Mulan*, the story of a young woman who disguises herself as a man to fight an invading army in her father's stead. It is as well known a parable to Chinese children as Snow White is to Americans, a story more than a thousand years old and interpreted over time by poets and playwrights before appearing on-screen in silent versions and a 1960s musical. The Disney *Mulan* of 1998 likely made it more popular in America than any other piece of Chinese mythology. Its Christina Aguilera anthems and animated cast of wise-cracking characters placed the incognito soldier alongside Belle, Ariel, and Sleeping Beauty in the Disney pantheon.

When Disney began remaking those animated films into live-action versions, it was only a matter of time before the studio landed once again on *Mulan*. The animated movie, like *Kung Fu Panda* after it, had looked to China for its culture rather than targeting it as a major market, and any chance of its taking off there had been torpedoed by the *Kundun* drama anyway. But now, in 2018, when *Mulan* 2.0 started production, China was a box-office power that made such a call a no-brainer.

The premiere took over the Hollywood Walk of Fame with a sprawling red carpet and ornamental warrior spears. Liu Yifei, the lead actress bringing the animated character to life after beating out more than one thousand women for the role, posed for the paparazzi in a gold sequined hoop gown. Young girls at the screening cried as the credits rolled, having seen themselves reflected on-screen as fearsome warriors.

The movie was scheduled to debut in theaters eighteen days later. But by the end of that week, the coronavirus had shut down the U.S. theatrical industry, closing every auditorium in the country and taking *Mulan* and numerous other titles off the release calendar indefinitely. More than two decades after the animated *Mulan* was denied its Chinese windfall, the new version was similarly ensnared in matters beyond its control. Disney said it would try to release the movie that summer, hoping the COVID-19 infection rate would be under control by then.

Instead, that premiere on the Walk of Fame was the last thing about *Mulan* and Disney's plans for the year ahead that went as planned. Few could sense it at the time, but lavish, blocks-long premiere parties would, in retrospect, feel like the last gasp of an industry that would soon be forced to acknowledge the hard realities of a dying model. Disney postponed *Mulan* two more times before ultimately deciding to release it in September 2020 on Disney+, the successful streaming operation it had launched to compete with Netflix that was soon the number one priority for the company. For $30, subscribers could watch *Mulan* at home in the U.S. while it premiered in critical markets where theaters were open, like China.

Disney had tried its best to get Chinese moviegoers on board with the new movie, spending months on historical research and setting scenes along the ancient Silk Road that Xi was rebuilding. To appeal to Chinese sensibilities, the filmmakers also returned to the original myth's core lesson of putting family above the self. The animated movie had been told through a more American lens, focusing on Mulan's personal growth rather than the sacrifice she made for the collective community.

But when the movie premiered in China, it became clear that Disney had once again forgotten a lesson few in Hollywood managed to internalize: no one wants to date someone who tries too hard. By 2020, Chinese studios were making movies about Chinese heroes, leaving little need among some moviegoers for a Western version of their story. Would American families flock to a Chinese telling of the story of Davy Crockett? The disinterested response was compounded by the demographics of the *Mulan* team making such an effort. Veteran executive Bill Kong had come on as an executive producer, but he was one of only a few Asians among the movie's producers. Disney had initially planned to hire a female Chinese director, before settling on Niki Caro, a New Zealander.

By 2020, a steady diet of better Chinese movies had left fans of the original emboldened to criticize its remake. Critics nitpicked historical inaccuracies, such as the rounded houses that Disney sets showed—a common architectural style in southern China, not northern China, where Mulan lives. And a general antagonism toward the U.S. led some to give *Mulan* poor ratings online as a surrogate punching bag for America at large. After once looking like the Chinese box-office hope of 2020, *Mulan* made a paltry $41 million.

The film may have been doomed from the start, but things grew much worse. Soon after its online premiere, Isaac Stone Fish of *The Washington Post* noticed some lines in the closing credits of the film. Disney was offering "special thanks" to government agencies for facilitating filming in China, including eight departments in Xinjiang, the western autonomous region where Xi's government had detained more than a million Uighurs, a Muslim minority that lives in the region.

The premiere of *Mulan* coincided with a human-rights crisis for China over its treatment of Uighurs. The Turkic minority, which is primarily Muslim, has long, and sometimes violently, clashed with Beijing's atheist ideology. Xi has struck harder than his predecessors by forcing Uighurs and other Muslims in Xinjiang into reeducation camps, where more than one million detainees have been fed a steady diet of official propaganda. Xi ordered officials to counter the "toxicity of religious extremism" that he said threatened his country—and, notably, was largely based in a region with gas, oil, and coal reserves critical to the Belt and Road Initiative. Communist Party members spoke of the "ideological illness" pervading the region.

U.S. officials and human-rights advocates called it a genocide. Outside the camps, mothers cannot name their sons Muhammad, and party members move in with families to monitor them. At the camps, Uighurs are urged to denounce Islam and sing Communist Party anthems. Women have reported forced sterilizations aimed at ending the ethnic minority in a generation. Hair believed to be from the shaved heads of prisoners was packaged as weaves and wigs and sent to the U.S. for sale. One of the bureaus involved in operating those camps, the Turpan Public Security Bureau, got a shout-out in the *Mulan* credits. Disney was thanking the authorities of a city where at least four camps were believed to be operating. Some scholars noted the cruel irony of Disney crews going to Xinjiang to make a movie about a heroine helping China trample a rebellious faction in the West.

Behind the scenes, Disney publicists defended the decision, pointing out that the footage from Xinjiang accounted for seventy-eight seconds of the movie. The Chinese production company that Disney had partnered with had requested filming permits in the region in 2017, before the U.S. government had issued any advisories to businesses operating in Xinjiang. But the damage was done. Human-rights advocates lambasted Disney for taking its business to the region. Fans called for a boycott. Chinese authorities forbade articles about the movie in state outlets. It was among the most fraught political morasses Disney could have found itself in, at a time when its dependence on the Chinese consumer was higher than ever. At the time *Mulan* premiered, China's movie theaters and its Shanghai theme park were open while American auditoriums and attractions remained closed due to COVID-19. And in the months ahead, the Chinese economy would recover at a faster rate than that of the U.S., making Disney even more dependent on the country.

If it wanted a future in China, Disney had to keep its response to a minimum. Disney executives could not risk angering the Chinese authorities with an apology or statement that would even acknowledge the *existence* of the detention camps. Such a statement would anger Chinese officials who controlled Disney's presence in the country and inflame Chinese fans sticking up for their country as part of the online brigades of pro-party cheerleaders. Disney had the box-office grosses of future movies to consider. It had toy sales to keep in mind. It had a theme park to worry about.

Soon after the outcry subsided, Joe Biden beat Donald Trump in the U.S. presidential election. In the weeks after his victory, Robert Iger, on the verge of leaving the company he'd led since 2005, told officials close to the transition team that he would be willing to serve in a Biden administration. The job he wanted: ambassador to China. Hollywood allies like Jeffrey Katzenberg endorsed the idea, saying the man who had led the Magic Kingdom to the Middle Kingdom was the best candidate to represent America in Beijing. He had already charmed Xi, they noted. This was the degree to which American business had been the first arena for the U.S.-China dynamic defining the next century: the man who brought Mickey Mouse to the country was floated as an ambassador to it. But Iger's interest did not quite square with reality. After the years of the Trump administration's agitations against China, and Americans' waking up to the moral queasiness of U.S. companies doing business there, success in the country had become as much a liability as an asset. In the eyes of some lawmakers and consumers ready to welcome in a Biden administration that was sure to be more attentive to human-rights violations, Disney now faced the political and moral ramifications of having funneled billions of dollars and priceless legitimacy into the country as Uighurs were forced into concentration camps.

WITH EACH GEOPOLITICAL FLARE-UP, some Chinese officials thought a global chest-pounding was warranted, a commensurate response to "kung flu" and similar attacks. After Venezuelan lawmakers referred to COVID-19 as the "China coronavirus," Chinese embassy officials told them they suffered from a "political virus" and that the first step toward curing themselves of it would be to "wear the masks and shut up." As audiences of *Wolf Warrior 2* had learned when the American embassy hadn't answered its phone and China had to come to the rescue, China's governance was presented as effective where democracy had failed. In Germany, Chinese diplomats asked officials to give public statements praising China's response to the outbreak. After Sri Lankan activist Chirantha Amerasinghe tweeted that the Chinese government was "low class," a representative from China replied that same day: "Total death in #China #pandemic is 3344 til today, much smaller than your western 'high class' governments." No fight was too small: the Sri Lankan activist had shared his opinion with about thirty followers. Forty years after Deng Xiaoping declared China must "hide our light and bide our time," the country was fighting back.

Proponents gave this aggressive approach a name: "wolf warrior diplomacy," using Wu Jing's cinematic rallying cry to describe policy on the world stage. "We will push back against any deliberate insult to resolutely defend our national honor and dignity," said state councilor and foreign minister Wang Yi, a wolf warrior diplomat, in May 2020. It sounded a lot like the closing-credits promise of the movie, telling moviegoers: "Please remember, at your back stands a strong motherland." Wolf warrior diplomats often called out American hypocrisy when it came to complaints of human-rights abuses in China, referencing the mass shootings and racism that racked the U.S., an update of the 1960s propaganda posters showing police beating up anti–Vietnam War protesters. As in the movie, they were quick to point out that America could not be counted on as a reliable world leader.

Factions within Beijing cautioned against wolf warrior diplomacy, worried that it stoked the chance of war between the U.S. and China and turned their country into a tall tree that must face the wind. "History proves that when foreign policy gets hijacked by public opinion, it inevitably brings disastrous results," said former diplomat Yuan Nansheng. That likely explains why, despite the blockbuster success of *Wolf Warrior 2*, there has yet to be a *Wolf Warrior 3*. Had China operated like Hollywood, production on a third film would have started before those first-weekend grosses had been tallied. No movie in America makes more than $900 million without spawning a sequel, a spin-off, or several of both. But when Wu Jing submitted a script for a third *Wolf Warrior* to the film bureau, it was rejected outright. He tried two other times to no avail. Even worse for his prospects, the bureau offered no comments that typically indicate a willingness to negotiate plot details and arrive at a screenplay that can be approved. The movie, according to some corners of the government, portrayed China as overly aggressive, not a harmonious participant in global affairs. Chinese leaders wanted a check on their cinematic hawkishness. The vigilante template that had placed Wu Jing in the echelon of similar "lone warriors" of cinema and mythology also chafed some officials who did not want to see movies in which a single individual does the work of China's armed forces.

"There are still camps out there saying we need to be strong, not to be bullied," said Chinese producer Alex Zhang. "But there is division about how to portray being strong."

WHEN I VISITED THE Qingdao Movie Metropolis in early 2020, I went to the set of a movie trying to provide one answer to the question of how to reflect China's strength and national pride. *Fengshen Trilogy*, a retelling of *Investiture of the Gods*, was filming—a sprawling, sixteenth-century story about a dynasty overthrow, originally told in installments to audiences who gathered in teahouses centuries ago. One of China's most well-known myths, it blended historical fact with fantastical folklore and featured princes, monsters, and other characters known to most Chinese young people. It was getting a cinematic treatment unlike any other in the country's history. Three movies were filming at once with a budget of more than $445 million. The set boasted more than two thousand workers—and more than thirty Thoroughbreds, trained by the horse master from *War Horse*. Its director, who goes by the single name Wuershan, said that his ambitions were nothing less than to create a Chinese *Lord of the Rings*. Naturally, Barrie Osborne, a producer on that trilogy, was brought on as a consultant. *Fengshen* had notes of *Game of Thrones*, as well—one scene in the book featured a queen getting her right eye ripped out and a eunuch delivering the news to the princes. Wuershan put it in contemporarily nationalist terms: he wanted to use an ancient myth to give China its own Marvel universe. He had seen how his son had been brainwashed by American entertainment.

"I can't even buy him Chinese toys—on his birthday, he wants Transformers, and there's nothing I can say to stop him," he said. "All I can do is make a film so that when he grows up, he can say, 'Next theme party, I want *Fengshen*.'"

As I watched an old Chinese actor portray an ancient fisherman in a scene filmed in front of a blue screen that would be filled in with images of a bubbling stream, I thought of a Hollywood executive who had described the millennia of Chinese dynasties to me in terms he could understand. "They have five thousand years of base equity," he said. *Fengshen* was just one of numerous movies that was trading on it. It was telling that for its biggest production ever, China was turning to its oldest stories, a cinematic ode not unlike the impulse of college students during the 2008 Olympics to dress in traditional clothing as a nod to their ancestors.

The crew was filming this paean to Chinese history, though, while surrounded by an homage to Hollywood. Black-and-white headshots of Charlie Chaplin and Marilyn Monroe decorated the facade of the Qingdao Movie Metropolis shopping mall, located half a mile from the sound stage and below the hillside where the city's own "Hollywood sign" spells out "Movie Metropolis of the East." Film canisters decorated everything: park benches, the roof of the mall, the outdoor ashtrays where cigarettes can be stubbed out in their indented holes. As I walked by a statue of Marilyn Monroe fighting her dress over the blow of the subway grate in *The Seven-Year Itch*, I realized that many of the actress's best-known movies were released at a time when Mao had banned Western entertainment from the country. There was a Chinese film industry then, but not this romanticized version of midcentury Hollywood, with its clapper boards, film reels, and Walk of Fame. The city hosting China's future entertainers felt nostalgic for a Hollywood it hadn't been able to access.

In *Fengshen*, China's producers see their best shot at replicating the final—and most challenging—aspect of the Hollywood playbook: franchising. With a movie like *Jurassic World*, for instance, Universal receives box-office revenue that expands into toy sales, a Netflix TV show, and a Universal Studios ride. I spent most of my time in Qingdao with Tyler Lu, a marketing executive on the trilogy who was in his early thirties and charged with doing the same on *Fengshen*. Walking through a mall with Lu, I saw the franchise-building of *Fengshen Trilogy* taking shape. He inspected the tags on DreamWorks Animation dolls to check their source factories. Vocabulary-wise, he held his own with any Disney executive paid to push characters and stories into the product pipeline. All entertainment was "content," and all "content" was "intellectual property." Books were "publishing." Stuffed animals were "plush." For *Fengshen*, there were already plans for mobile-phone apps, a costume line, and logos on the jerseys of the Chinese Basketball Association players that celebrated these myths of kings and spirits the way Shrek becomes a McDonald's Happy Meal toy. Inspiration wasn't hard to find: Lu was wearing a Mickey Mouse sweatshirt.

When I asked Lu if the characters of *Fengshen* should be considered China's version of Marvel superheroes, he was emphatic. These were not superheroes as Western audiences might think of them. In the West, superheroes are just born or happen into their circumstance, by childhood trauma or some fantastical event. In China, heroes "need thousands of years to learn and become immortal," he said. Chinese heroes, he said, had to put in the work.

THE NEXT DAY, Lu and I drove an hour from the Movie Metropolis to visit a set used for the *Fengshen* battle scenes: a built-to-scale re-creation of an imperial palace. Shooting there had finished, but the fortress was being preserved so it could become a tourist attraction after the movie premiered—a Chinese countryside destination for fans that would satisfy another requirement of the ideal franchise model, and perhaps cater to those who wanted to feel a deeper connection to their country's past glories at a moment of national power.

As we approached the area, I noticed a construction crew amid the one-story homes and acres of brown fields. They're building a highway exit that will take cars to the palace once it becomes a tourist attraction, Lu told me. I asked what would happen to the farmers whose land was turning into the exit.

"The government will give them money to move," he said. The land surrounding us looked a lot like where he grew up in the 1990s, north of the Korean Peninsula, he added.

"It's a lucky thing for them," he said, motioning to the farmers outside the window. "They will be rich. I wish my hometown would be removed."

Then, out of nowhere, amid the single-story homes, rose a church with two steeples. Behind it was a fully re-created, life-size New York City street scene, with neon lights hanging off four-story facades and fire escapes lining the side, bursting out of the farmland. There were no leafless trees or soggy grass here. The streets were paved. A fake English tavern called the Playwright stood near a restaurant simply named Italian Sausage. A back lot of several city blocks continued behind them: a theater marquee, a speakeasy, a diner. Here, in the middle of a Chinese field an hour's drive from the nearest city block, were several streets of New York City, translated into the kind of filming location found at Warner Bros., where a collection of facades and storefronts can substitute on-screen for any borough. This architect clearly had a sleazy 1970s New York in mind: the complex is called Hot Sexy Plaza, and its businesses include the XXX Spot, a venue called Girls Girls Girls, and a movie palace showing something called *Angels of Sin*. Depending on the camera angle, only one portrayal of America would be possible here.

"Did you build this?" I asked Lu, confused as to why a grungy cityscape was necessary for the retelling of a three-thousand-year-old myth.

"No," he said. "We built *this*."

He gestured directly across the street from Hot Sexy Plaza, where there sat the enormous Chinese palace constructed out of dark-brown lumber. There were tree trunks sharpened into spikes to fend off enemy invaders. Two cauldrons were stationed outside the palace door, and smaller versions had phoenixes carved into their bases, propping them up. There was a moat cleaved into the ground around the front entrance. Fake trees with golden and yellow leaves ringed the exterior for acres, a burst of color in the winter landscape. There were guard towers and pagodas, a long walkway where I could picture the emperor conferencing with his advisers, fields expansive enough for any battle between troops. No movie magic was required for it to feel like we had been transported back to ancient times. The wood was real, the interiors had actual ceilings, the upper level of those guard towers was accessible by built-in staircases. And when some magic was needed, cranes were there to erect giant blue screens strategically located to block any undue modernity from creeping into the shot. When the director needed to film at an angle where an apartment tower under construction is visible in the background—or that ITALIAN SAUSAGE sign got in the way—the screen would go up, and a visual-effects team would paste a new image over the blue, and suddenly everything in the frame would look like the China of the Shang dynasty.

Later, crew workers told me that filming at this location was a nuisance, because the *Fengshen* producers had designated it a tourist attraction *before* the movie started filming, and they wanted the wood to stay pristine and free of imperfections for when the fans showed up years later. The appeal had been reverse-engineered, a controlled-economy attempt to re-create the gravitational pull that the acres of Iowa corn made famous by *Field of Dreams*, or the Stanley Hotel, located in Estes Park, Colorado, where Jack Nicholson descended into madness in *The Shining*, have on fans of the movies who want to see the location in real life. In China, development around the fake imperial palace is already planned, too, and expected to include hotels, apartments, and a three-story mall not far from the moat.

It was a strategy similar to one China was undertaking out of sight of most Americans, in the Belt and Road Initiative, which had already brought infrastructure, aid, and entertainment to countries on every continent. In Chinese real estate, as in those campaigns introducing China to the world, the hope remained: if you build it, they will come.

SIXTEEN

Watching *Crouching Tiger, Hidden Dragon* in Kenya

One sunny afternoon in September 2018, a gray Toyota van bounced along the unpaved back roads of Suswa, Kenya, a village on the edge of Hells Gate National Park, some eighty miles northwest of Nairobi. Nicholas Nkukuu, who for sixteen years had adjudicated land disputes, paternity dramas, and other village matters as the Kenyan president's representative in Suswa—a position known simply as chief—rode in the back seat along with a gift from China: more than a dozen bright-orange satellite dishes, each stamped with Chinese lettering and the logo of the company providing them, a Beijing-based operation called StarTimes. That afternoon, Nkukuu would determine which homes would be receiving these low-cost StarTimes dishes and gaining access to the hundreds of cable channels they carried. Narrowing the list was not hard. Only a small number of homes in Suswa had electricity at all.

The van pulled up to the sixty-acre farm run by twenty-two-year-old Brian Letayian and his family, on the side of a slight hill accessible via a dirt road that until recently had been impassable every time it rained. Letayian was harvesting maize when Nkukuu arrived with a Chinese man who also got out of the van. StarTimes was distributing dishes to families in Suswa, they explained—six months free, and then a low monthly payment for the channels they provided. Letayian led them into the one-bedroom cabin he'd built for himself, a bachelor pad decorated with posters of American McMansions that featured inspirational sayings like "Today's preparation determines tomorrow's achievements." A dangling electrical cord, worn so thin in some places that its wiring was exposed, hung between the trees from his mother's house to his own. The electricity it carried was popular among Letayian's buddies, who stopped by to charge their phones for a fee of 20 shillings.

It took less than thirty minutes to set up the dish and start receiving its broadcast signals, the Tic Tac–orange circle popping through the verdant green leaves that shade his home much of the day. Suddenly Letayian had so many more channels than he'd had before. He stopped his usual after-work activity—hanging out with his friends to stave off boredom at home—and headed back to watch TV each night. On the third day, he landed on a new kind of program, available only on Star-Times: Chinese kung fu.

Many of the homes in Suswa with televisions used satellite dishes operated by African pay-TV companies, but they were expensive and had fewer channels than the ones being provided by this new company, which offered not only Kenyan news and entertainment but also several channels of Chinese programming. For Nkukuu, the satellite dishes were yet another modern intrusion into his hometown. When he was a kid in the 1970s, evenings were shared trading stories of near-miss lion encounters or singing songs as a group, not looking at smartphones. Girls wore dresses to their ankles when their father was around, not the slitted skirts his own daughter favored. But he wasn't above getting a dish himself, installing it that first day atop his home, a bright-blue shack attached to a converted storage container.

The modern touches were especially apparent in Suswa, home to the Maasai, a Kenyan tribe that had farmed in the region since the eighteenth century. In Suswa today, older residents still wear kaleidoscopic Maasai shawls and jewelry that stretches their earlobes down their necks, but the younger members straddle both worlds. Letayian is a Maasai, and like other Maasai men, he was circumcised in an initiation ceremony at age eighteen—but unlike his father before him, he was taken to a hospital for his procedure. The shawls and coverings come out for weddings and other celebrations; most days he favors a sleeveless Adidas jersey and knockoff Crocs.

Suswa was also accustomed to foreign charity. The number of schools in the area had increased considerably since Nkukuu was a kid, mostly due to an influx of Christian missionaries who arrived in the 1970s. At first the community was skeptical of any outside influence. Parents, fearing the schools would take their children forever, sent only the unruly or challenged kids they considered the most expendable. The churches built by missionaries were eventually embraced, even if they irritated Nkukuu by telling him his rain sacrifices weren't as effective as simply praying to God. American aid in the form of medical supplies and scholarship programs was also now a part of everyday life, entrenched enough to seem invisible at this point.

But in recent years, foreign aid had come from an unlikely source— China—and in a new, tangible form: infrastructure, in what felt like every corner of Africa. China had been in Suswa for more than a year by the time the Toyota van arrived, constructing a massive train station for a stop on the Standard Gauge Railway, a $4 billion Belt and Road Initiative project that connects coastal Mombasa to inner Kenya, with plans to expand to other landlocked economies across Africa. Why exactly the train would stop in Suswa confused some Kenyans, who called it the "train to nowhere," and even some Suswans, who asked, "Why Suswa?" when they heard it was coming. For skeptics, it was another case of a country agreeing to a Chinese loan it would likely never pay. The cost of the railway and accompanying expressway helped raise Kenya's debt from 40 percent of its GDP to more than 60 percent.

Today the station appears in the flat Suswa landscape like a mirage, located about two kilometers off the main drag of shops and commuter van stops. It has a tiered red roof that calls to mind the silhouette of Chinese palaces, and the front of the station is dominated by the kind of wide steps found at the U.S. Capitol, directly across from fields where dozens of goats munch on the grass. The elevated railway heading east toward Nairobi has occasional underpasses big enough to allow migrating elephants to slip through.

Great Britain built a railway across the country when it controlled Kenya from 1920 to 1963, but that one has since been abandoned. Its tracks still cut across the landscape from Nairobi to inner Kenya and serve as a bench for young men congregating in the early evening. The goal of this Chinese-built railway was to open inner Kenya up to the world again, turning what had been a cramped four-hour van ride to Nairobi into a comfortable two-hour trip. Suswan bracelet makers made plans to sell their jewelry in the city. Nkukuu's wife wanted to take the train to the coast and swim in the ocean.

Africa's history of colonial push and pull has given the continent a reputation in business circles as the long untapped market. The Belt and Road Initiative is the most formal, structured means by which China is trying to impose its philosophy on the world—with varying degrees of success. These were the investments and geopolitical priorities that took *Wolf Warrior 2* to Africa, and that would lay the groundwork for the lobbying campaign in the wake of the coronavirus that positioned China, and not America, as the global superpower. Mao first won people over in the Chinese countryside. Remote villages such as Suswa became the global analogue.

But to local critics of the Chinese investment, this railway embodied all that was wrong with China's designs in Africa. The railway construction had cut through Nairobi National Park. Ten elephants died during the construction, and several lions escaped. The loans to build the project were doled out by Chinese banks in the same kind of "debt-trap" deal that had allowed China to wrest control of bridges, ports, and holdings in Kenya and across Africa. Locally, the construction had consumed Nkukuu's docket of disputes. Unemployed Suswans asked why the Chinese weren't hiring locals. A runoff of water generated by the construction destroyed some homes. Construction dust floated through the air and dried out beans and grass, forcing the Chinese firms to pay farmers thousands of shillings in compensation. By the time the StarTimes satellites showed up, China had some winning over to do.

HOLLYWOOD MOVIES REMAIN beloved in Kenya, but an American retreat from the continent has left a vacuum that China is eager to fill. A boost in domestic energy production made America less dependent on African oil. Officials in Washington continued to back U.S. efforts to provide electricity and aid to parts of the continent—but China, said one assistant secretary of state, is often "the only person standing there" when investors knock on the door. When it came to entertainment, the new Will Smith movie played in theaters when I visited in early 2020, but most residents I spoke to were happy to mix their Western entertainment options with Chinese ones in ways Americans have resisted. I went to Kenya to see how China's movies—and therefore its messaging— were received by communities accustomed to decades of outside superpowers trying to exert influence over their opinions. What I found was a populace and a government that, like Hollywood, had barely thought about China several years ago—and now saw it everywhere they looked.

No less than Xi Jinping himself announced the arrival of the Star-Times satellite dishes in Kenya in late 2015. Xi surprised the world when he said China was pledging a massive $60 billion in aid to Africa, more than a tenfold increase from the $5 billion in annual aid China had been giving in 2006. Xi's promises included the usual economic and political

handouts: free-trade agreements, cancellation of debt, and cooperation between counterterrorism forces. Then Xi announced an unusual element of
this "win-win cooperation": satellite TV reception to ten thousand African
villages. China's Ministry of Commerce authorized StarTimes to work in
foreign TV industries, the only private Chinese company granted such a
clearance—an arrangement that gave StarTimes access to significant growth
markets but accentuated its ties to the state. As with that fake fortress
constructed outside Qingdao, China hoped that it could underwrite the
infrastructure and appeal would follow.

When new StarTimes viewers turned on their TVs, Chinese entertainment wasn't the only option, but it quickly became a local favorite.
A twenty-four-hour kung fu network played new releases and Jackie
Chan classics. Elaborate Chinese costume dramas about ancient dynasties competed with Spanish telenovelas. CGTN, a state-owned news operation that had to register as a foreign agent in the U.S. and will never
produce a broadcast critical of Xi, airs alongside Kenyan news. There
were Chinese game shows and Chinese animation produced for kids, all
of it dubbed into English or Swahili for easy viewing. A Kenyan company produced glass-half-full documentaries about friendships between
Chinese and African citizens. In early 2021, a show premiered about Sino-
African relations that would include details on the economic ties between the country and the continent, as well as features outlining what
Africa might learn from China (one episode would highlight the planting of coffee beans to reduce poverty). Its title: *Look to the East.*

The satellite dishes traveling with Nkukuu in the Toyota came courtesy of Beijing, which allotted nearly $8 million in additional funding
to expand the 10,000 Villages Project across Kenya in 2018. More than
sixteen thousand households and 2,400 communal spaces, like schools and
hospitals, would get a dish. But while everyone in Suswa knows that the
Chinese built the railway, fewer know that they built the satellites, too.

At the home of John and Lily Rutto, located in Ainamoi, in the southwest corner of Kenya, and surrounded by thousands of acres of tea-leaf fields, the StarTimes dish was a major improvement over their usual television. When their five children were growing up, the Ruttos had a twelve-inch black-and-white television that screened a single channel, a state-run station showing progovernment news and a few imports like *The Bold and the Beautiful* and professional wrestling. The TV ran off a car battery, and recharging it required an hour-long trip to a store that kept it for a week. They eventually bought a color set with more channels, but it was controlled by an antenna on the roof that required sending one of the kids outside to move it around while everyone shouted about where to stick it. This was how the Ruttos, a retired telecom worker and teacher, watched television until 2018, when StarTimes affixed an orange dish to their roof and more than four hundred channels from around the world were immediately beamed into their home.

Chinese culture pervaded their surrounding community. Nearby, a movie hall, operated by Leonard Biegon, most weekends fills nine rows of stadium seating built out of sanded plywood. Two giant televisions play Chinese action movies like *Wolf Warrior* and CCTV variety shows. On the Saturday morning I visited, about a dozen Kenyan guys had paid 10 cents each to watch Jet Li dispatch half of Japan in *Fist of Legend*. By early afternoon, the room was filled to capacity.

When he opened the cinema in 2002, Biegon was an eighth-grade dropout with one fourteen-inch television. Since then he's outlasted two rival movie houses, has graduated from one small TV to two big screens, and makes enough money to support two wives and four kids—thanks in large part to his customers' appetite for Chinese entertainment. He buys pirated DVDs of Chinese movies from hawkers on the road or at the library, copying the lettering off the poster so his marquee reads in English and Mandarin. The only other programming known to draw such a crowd is English soccer.

Caleb Lang'at, a twenty-two-year-old from town, told me he comes every weekend to watch movies about Chinese heroes, studying their martial arts skills for self-defense tips and picking up a few cues about approaching women.

"What I love about the Chinese people, they are so creative. They make something and it becomes real," he told me.

At the hospital in Ainamoi, not far from the Ruttos' home, a StarTimes-provided television hangs from a strand of coiled barbed wire at the end of a hallway. Patients watch it while recovering, and so do staff members during downtime, the hospital's director of facilities, Milton Kemboi, told me. Growing up, he'd heard whispers of America, a place he thought of as heaven.

"I wanted to visit America. But now my perception is changing slowly. I just realize there is nothing special," he said. After hearing about the TV donation, he and some friends researched China online. As a doctor, he was particularly drawn to the country's aggressive policy making around family planning. "We could learn from them," he said.

He motions to a manual blood pressure machine on the shelf—donated by a Chinese nonprofit, he said. Every three months, a Chinese health worker visits to teach workshops on best practices, like how to organize the tuberculosis records, and neatly hang posters detailing malaria epidemic zones. If he traveled to China today, "I could learn more and come back and help my society. How they managed to get where they are," he said. A year after our visit, a new gift from China would arrive in Kenya: COVID-19 vaccinations, part of a public-health outreach campaign Beijing officials called the "Health Silk Road" that also delivered shots to more than a dozen countries, including Turkey, Morocco, and Egypt.

In towns where the 10,000 Villages Project hands out satellite dishes, StarTimes advertises itself by painting a mural that features the Kenyan and Chinese flags side by side. In Ainamoi the mural is on a storefront at the town's main intersection, steps from the movie theater showing

Chinese films. The actual store is a wholesale outfitter, selling items like toilet paper, straws, pineapple juice, and Coca-Cola—nothing related to TV or satellites. But StarTimes wanted prime placement, so the company offered a free paint job in exchange for the free advertising. The owner's wife, Roseline Chepkwony, doesn't have a TV herself. Hers broke down, and she never replaced it because she wanted her kids to focus on school.

Chepkwony's free advertising is just one soft-power component of a larger Chinese campaign across Kenya. In Nairobi today, Chinese-owned water trucks drive on Chinese-built roads in and out of Chinese-run construction sites. Hundreds of Kenyans pay $320 in rent for a three-bedroom in apartment complexes called the Great Wall, located in the Nairobi suburbs just off Beijing Road. New slaughterhouses ship donkey parts to China, where locals believe they carry medicinal value. Cheaper Chinese tennis shoes have lowered the price of all sneakers, and a Chinese-run hotel prints receipts in Chinese.

The projects, and in particular the new railway, are promoted as a way for Africa to flatten access to parts of the world still cut off from the global economy, and a chance for Africans to travel to new markets and build up their countries through the movement of people and goods. The pragmatic form of aid draws a contrast with America's long-standing approach, which is based on a belief that an empowered and enlightened individual can promote a functioning system that in turn drives economic progress. In touting its outreach to Africa, the U.S. states its mission as follows: "To achieve the great promise of Kenya's Constitution, we will partner with Kenya to strengthen democratic institutions, address ethnic divisions, fight corruption, and help ensure freedom of the media and space for civil society." China, on the other hand, is giving Kenyans what they need to do their jobs today, not some abstract notion about what might come tomorrow. Kenya is a country not far from the shadow of colonialism, and one eager to move beyond the part of the world described as "developing." When I asked Kenyans to describe what China is like, one adjective came up again and again: *developed*. China is building roads they drive on, a railway that can take them to places that were recently too far away. As one observer of China's infrastructure frenzy in Africa put it: "The Western theory of development proposes to tinker with the superstructure, while China proposes to remake the base."

Or as Kenyan official Ezekiel Mutua told me: "People don't eat freedom."

ON THE DAY AFTER THAT Toyota van delivered StarTimes dishes to the villages around Suswa, a Chinese photographer came to the village to take pictures of the new subscribers for *China Daily*, a government-published, English-language newspaper distributed worldwide. In China, some citizens are skeptical of their government's costly outreach to Africa, and StarTimes needed to promote the program to people back home. The photographer gathered folks like Jeremy Saitoti, a brother-in-law of the chief, who had just received a dish. On the day I met Saitoti, he was wearing a white knit baseball cap with a black bomber jacket over a gray T-shirt and salmon-colored jeans. The photographer asked Saitoti and his neighbors to retrieve their Maasai wardrobes.

Saitoti put on a blue-and-yellow plaid Maasai *shuka*, a shawl-like covering that hangs around the neck or off one shoulder. His mother wore one wrapped around her neck in a violet, orange, and yellow geometric pattern. They were joined by eight others, all in crowns and beaded necklaces, many holding Maasai walking sticks above their heads. Now the group looked like a stereotypical *National Geographic* spread of happy Africans, not far removed from the caricatures of *Wolf Warrior 2*. The only inconsistency was what they held in their other hands: a StarTimes dish, a flat-screen television box, a StarTimes decoder.

The *China Daily* photographer had Saitoti and his fellow Maasai place the StarTimes dish on the ground. With a video camera recording them, he had them dance around the dish in a circle, singing a tribal song of gratitude reserved for babies, freshly circumcised men, and newly married couples.

Enechipai enoolong'
Enechipai aake

"It is a happy day for this village / It is a happy day for these people," they sang as they danced around the dish. Then the photographer had Saitoti and his family go inside their living room and turn the TV to the kung fu channel. He staged photographs of them sitting and watching. He asked them to smile.

"I watch a lot of kung fu," says Grace Waithera as soon as I tell her I'm in Kenya to learn about StarTimes.

She lives in apartment number 3 in a strip of single-story rooms, located down a dirt path about a kilometer off Suswa's main drag. Several different families live in these rooms, but the metal cerulean doors stay open, and neighbors float in and out. On a Sunday afternoon, most are still in their church clothes. Waithera, a tailor by trade, is wearing a perfectly fitted black blouse and fire-engine-red skirt.

Waithera subscribed to StarTimes several years ago and quickly became its biggest fan. Until the television broke down recently, she kept to a schedule of shows that ran more than twelve hours a day: Nigerian movies and Swahili shows in the morning, Chinese game shows and kung fu in the afternoon, Kenyan news and Bollywood soaps in the evening. She discovered kung fu after channel surfing for a Bollywood station, before realizing she didn't pay enough to get it. She landed instead on kung fu, which came with basic channel packages. Her daughter stopped washing dishes—soon she stopped washing dishes, too.

"I can spend the entire Sunday watching it," she said.

Since the TV was broken, she's been spending more time in apartment number 8, a living area and bedroom shared by the children of Immaculate Wanjiku that's become a gathering spot for kids in the neighborhood. There are two couches and a chaise lounge facing the television, beyond a front door that's also always open but kept private by a rose-pink bedsheet barely moving in the still air. The voice of a Chinese soprano, singing the theme song of a costume drama about to start, floats through apartment number 8 when Waithera and I step inside.

It's the unofficial playroom of the apartment block. Immaculate, who moved to Suswa in her twenties to study herbal medicine, stays down the hall with her husband. Immaculate largely raised their nine children herself when her husband disappeared for a dozen years, and Charity, a nineteen-year-old, is the oldest still living at home. Charity has long hair dyed maroon and a stud in her right nostril that the Maasai elders do not understand.

Before the TVs arrived, women used to sit outside and talk to one another, Immaculate said. ("About what?" I asked. "Other people," her twentysomething daughter Ann said.) Now they're inside watching TV, but that's not such a bad development, she added. They can follow current events; nearly everyone I speak to considers Kenyan news broadcasts a must-watch. This week, there's growing concern about a locust infestation in the north that's threatening food supplies.

The service grew more essential when the coronavirus spread across Africa in March 2020 and StarTimes became an integral source of information, particularly for remote villages like Suswa. The company launched a new TV show in Kenya with daily updates on the pandemic and how to stop its spread. It aired on seven channels and on the StarTimes mobile app, translated into multiple languages. When Kenyan schoolchildren were still home from school weeks later, StarTimes partnered with a national education institute to broadcast lessons they could watch at home. In the summer of 2021, StarTimes announced another outreach effort, this one a video competition. Viewers were invited to send in short films detailing how Chinese investments had transformed the lives of everyday Africans. The theme of this year's contest was infrastructure, and the Standard Gauge Railway was one suggested subject.

INSIDE THE APARTMENT, the kids from the neighborhood discuss their favorite Chinese hero: the Monkey King, the country's most famous mythical children's figure. They watch him in *Journey to the West* every night at 7:40, and nine-year-old Lucky, a plump boy wearing a knockoff Gucci shirt and jeans, has started imitating his favorite character. The Monkey King is a mischievous prankster, so Lucky hides under the bed or behind the couch so he can jump out and scare everyone.

Waithera says the Monkey King is a good role model. "He comes up with ideas and helps the king," she says.

I ask Lucky who his other heroes are. "Jet Li!" he says. When Dwayne Johnson is on television later, I ask Lucky who it is. "Um, the Rock!" he says. He gives me a power ranking—Monkey King is tops, followed by Dwayne Johnson, then Jet Li.

Lucky's preferences speak to the crowded competitive field Chinese programming is entering here. No matter how cool Jet Li may be, he still can't outrank the Rock, who in turn can't match the five-hundred-year-old Monkey King. Even as Donald Trump turned some Kenyans away from America, most of those I met still embraced American culture, so long as it blended with their new Chinese options. As in most parts of the developing world, the Hollywood they knew was on somewhat of a delay—onetime superstars like Arnold Schwarzenegger still ruled alongside Dwayne Johnson. The Hollywood effort to penetrate the Kenyan market has been piecemeal, though DreamWorks Animation and Warner Bros. launched StarTimes channels that show *Trolls* and Denzel Washington movies on the same TV that Lucky watched. Netflix has invested in the continent, too, seeing it as an untapped frontier in the streaming wars, but its internet-based model has run into issues brought on by slow internet connection speeds and piracy.

Grace and Immaculate, the two moms in the room, agree that Chinese shows like *Journey to the West* are the better family option. "There are some Hollywood ones you won't want to watch with your kids, the ones on late at night," says Waithera.

A high school graduate with few job prospects in the area, Charity spends a lot of her day channel surfing. She loves kung fu movies, even if they have scared her off living in China. Living in the U.S. is preferable, she says, since in China, "you'll be beaten even by children." She worked briefly planting grass at the railway during construction and asked her colleagues about their school system and how hard they study.

The Chinese are "the only ones who can do the building," she says of the railway. "Most of the people here are not educated like them." Grace is an even bigger StarTimes fan, but she's more jaundiced about the Chinese presence in town. "We don't have jobs. There are some Kenyans who can do those jobs."

"They have the skills," Charity says, referring to the Chinese workers. "Their work is perfect." Look at how they cook, she adds, referencing a Chinese cooking show they all watch on StarTimes. They have a methodical style and follow a recipe step by step.

Then the television goes out. It's the midafternoon, and at first it feels like a blackout. But it's because the TV bill needs to be paid. It happens every one or two days, when Charity or her mother must text a code that sends 100 Kenyan shillings—or about $1—to StarTimes for two more days of service. Of course, it often goes out at the worst possible moment.

"I'm crying, hitting the TV," Charity jokes.

Later that night, the TV is back on, after Charity's 100 shillings have gone through. After a Chinese game show airs, a documentary on the origins of kung fu starts. It is exactly the kind of programming that Chinese officials want people like Charity to watch. Men on camels cross the Mongolian desert and a narrator intones: "Chinese martial arts has a long history. . . ." An elderly Chinese man completes calligraphy brush-strokes on-screen. A talking-head kung fu master describes how the fighting style helped fight off bandits, and how it symbolizes the richness of Chinese culture. Charity has seen this show before.

"It's boring," she says, and changes the channel to a Spanish telenovela.

"Don't twist the truth, Barbara!" a young Spanish woman yells at an older *abuela*.

After the telenovela ends, Charity flips back to the kung fu channel, which, she is irritated to see, is still on the boring documentary. She keeps it on, though, because *Crouching Tiger, Hidden Dragon* is starting soon. After Michelle Yeoh and Zhang Ziyi appear on-screen, Immaculate asks her to turn up the volume so she can hear it in the kitchen. A sharp whiff of cooked goat meat hits the living room, and dinner is ready just as the movie is getting good. The family closes their eyes as Immaculate leads the room in a Swahili prayer. On-screen, Zhang Ziyi rides through the desert as everyone eats their soup. There is a fight in the sand. The TV freezes. Charity stands up and presses a button on the decoder. Zhang Ziyi rides again.

The next night, we watch a 1980s kung fu movie, a dubbed escapade about three Chinese women who team up to take down a drug trafficking ring in the U.S. Ryan, a young boy in the room, asks Charity's younger sister to draw a gun on his arm so he can flail it up and down, making spitting noises with his mouth to mimic the shooting of the Chinese soldiers on-screen.

At the end of the movie, the Chinese women take down the ring and are exalted by the American authorities.

"Without the assistance of those three Chinese soldiers . . . it would have been difficult, if not impossible, to crack this case, like stuffing twenty pounds of manure into a ten-pound barrel," the police chief says in a representatively odd translation.

I ask Charity what she thought of the movie.

"The Chinese who were on the mission, they were fighting the drug traffickers," she says. "The American police were not willing to help them. But they fought and won."

THE CHINESE CAMPAIGN FOR African opinion is just the latest example of a superpower trying to win over the continent. In the 1940s, while Nigeria was still under colonial rule, loudspeakers were installed outside libraries, post offices, and other gathering spots so residents could hear English radio broadcasts. Few understood the English being used on the station, but dozens still gathered to listen, the radio "addressing contemporary native subjects as future colonial citizens," as scholar Brian Larkin has put it. The English, hoping to boost crowd numbers, started incorporating music from the local Hausa community, along with recordings of overseas Hausa troops sending well wishes back home, a blending of local and foreign programming similar to the StarTimes channel lineup. It was a British effort to connect rural Nigerian communities, some of which were entertaining the idea of separation, with the larger project of the British Empire.

The loudspeakers were hugely popular, and soon Nigerians were requesting more speakers and more localized programming. The British built a cheaper radio set exclusively for the African market. England's Public Relations Department used the broadcasts to counteract the parochial practices of conservative Islam and promote the investments they were making in the region. The radio programming became a place for boring but safe endorsements of British contributions—their own versions of *Look to the East*. A British engineer came on to talk about "Water Supply and Electricity Provision." A British traffic superintendent filled in listeners on "How Trains Are Moved on the Railways." A British health officer lectured "On Infectious Diseases and Their Prevention."

Like their British predecessors, Chinese producers have exercised strict control over the messaging leaving their borders. Chinese soap operas are a prime example. These programs have been popular, since they often explore themes that will resonate in an evolving Kenya: tensions between the older and younger generations, or the clash of rural and urban communities in a country where development is happening at a dizzying rate.

But Chinese officials have made sure the nation exports only programming that shows their country in the best possible light, according to Dani Madrid-Morales, a professor at the University of Houston who has studied StarTimes. Madrid-Morales analyzed the most popular soap operas in China and found they often had an edge—or as much of an edge as Beijing would allow. There might be allusions to gay characters or story lines involving divorce. Chinese audiences gravitate to these stories, but these aren't the ones that Beijing approves to send overseas. The soap operas available on StarTimes mostly show a China of sparkling new cities, where the young and old live together in harmony and prosperity.

Of the one hundred most popular soap operas in China, none were exported by the government. Instead, the exported programs were soaps that trade appeal for conformism. These main-melody soaps include *Urban Emotion*, which "presents an array of family plots in which the morally righteous protagonists fight against the ills (nepotism, bribery, individualism) of a profit-driven society." Or there's *Naked Wedding*, about a young couple who cause a scandal when they decide to elope but who ultimately learn "the importance of conforming to the norm and social orthodoxy." This kind of entertainment in China follows an inverse dynamic: the more popular a show is in China, the likelier it is to portray a version of the country its leaders don't want foreigners to see.

Here again was China's Achilles' heel, evidenced by the soap opera cleansing and Charity's reaction to the boring documentary. Its leaders wanted to make movies that would charm the world as Hollywood had, failing to understand that it was often the unflattering cinematic portraits of America that had won over audiences. It was more than just *Top Gun* and *Dirty Dancing* that convinced global moviegoers that America was in charge, an idyll of democracy, heartthrobs, and cool clothes. It was also the movies that challenged the state, revealed the country at its most imperfect, shined a light on the mistakes of its past, whether in politics, war, or the community. Movies like *Iron Man 3* and *Transformers* regularly cast the government authorities as bad guys who orchestrated conspiracies that the heroes must take down. These portrayals could convince viewers that American politics are corrupt, but the fact that such a movie could be made with these antagonists served a higher persuasive purpose. If a country is criticizing itself or portraying its leaders in a negative light, it signals an authenticity, a willingness to trust the audience. U.S. officials might prefer a different villain in some Hollywood movies with a cynical view of the American government, but they should understand that it is these very portrayals that might do the most soft-power work for them. Dissent proves openness.

By controlling which programs are exported to StarTimes, China makes sure that Africa watches Chinese entertainment that doubles as Chinese commercials. To a person, StarTimes viewers in Kenya told me China was a place with incredible engineering and construction skills, the kind they'd like to see applied to their country. The only China they saw was in an economic boom that never ended. Harmony and morality always prevailed.

In some cases, Chinese firms have made the programming easier to view by paying to dub the movies into local languages beyond Swahili, like African French, African Portuguese, and African English, which are often spoken by too few people to be considered economically worthwhile for Hollywood. But many of the residents I spoke to are more willing to watch dubbed entertainment than subtitled, and Chinese firms will eat the cost if it shortens the bridge to appeal. A young finance manager at one dubbing firm, Gladys Mwita, told me she worried it was a neocolonial campaign. "You see the way we were colonized by the British. Now we relate more to China, we get to know them, we try to behave like they behave. The kids who are growing up now, in twenty years . . ." She mentioned a niece who gets into debates with friends about preferring Lady Gaga to

Cardi B but who also wants to find a pair of shoes like the ones she sees on Chinese soaps. It made her think her niece's generation will grow up equally aligned with the U.S. and with China. In this family, the future of the global world order—one of smaller countries needing to ally themselves with America or China—came writ small.

Mwita was among those Kenyans I met who drew the strongest parallels between the Chinese and the colonialists, but she admitted she was not the perfect messenger. She signed up for StarTimes herself. It was just too cheap to pass up.

IF THE MONKEY KING CONTINUES to prevail over Dwayne Johnson in the estimation of Kenyan boys like Lucky, it may have as much to do with the mythical creature's natural draw as with the support of politicians like Ezekiel Mutua, the head of Kenya's Film Classification Board. Only months after taking the job in 2015, Mutua appointed himself the "moral policeman" of his country. He has a pencil-thin mustache and a sermonizing delivery that turns his fifteenth-floor office in Nairobi into a street preacher's platform. A large oil painting of him hangs above his desk, not far from a giant monitor displaying the surveillance footage from closed-circuit cameras placed throughout the board's offices. A personal photographer took no fewer than one hundred photos during my ninety-minute interview with him. This is a man who knows the power of an image.

"If you want to change a nation, change it through stories," he told me.

Or by banning them. Mutua has removed dozens of movies, shows, music videos, and commercials from Kenyan screens since taking office. He's implemented a system that requires approval of scripts before a Kenyan movie can begin production that draws inspiration from China's process. As the official in charge of what stories come into his country, Mutua has dozens of counterparts across Africa and other continents weighing whether to mix their usual diet of Western entertainment with these new Chinese options.

Mutua was less concerned with whether movies were entertaining and more with what they represented. What opinions, outlook, priorities were they transporting to Kenyans? "Western ideas go with the Western good," Woodrow Wilson had said, and for Mutua, that was the problem.

"We don't want to keep imbibing Western culture, homosexual films, violent films, as a way of life," he said.

China is a different story. "I never have to worry about bad content, obscenity, whatever. They have taken care of that, naturally."

The Chinese ideas coming in with the movies have convinced Mutua that China offers not just safer entertainment but an alternative to the form of governance America has been trying to export for decades. On the week I visited, that brand was tarnished.

"I mean, look at the way you are treating this guy on TV," Mutua said, gesturing to footage of an impeached President Trump on CNN. "In the name of democracy, then nobody respects anyone. A child can say anything to their father, any guy in the street can insult the president and get away with it 'in the name of freedom.' You get to a point where we can't manage that kind of system. The system that is manageable is that, 'I may not be one hundred percent right, but I'm the one in the office.'"

Hollywood, the industry that is supposed to sell American democracy better than any government ever could, has only worsened things for people like Mutua. Disney's *Black Panther*, which imagined a thriving African country ruled by a superhero king, is the only recent Hollywood release he can think of that doesn't fall into the typical storytelling traps of portraying the continent as a lawless land of disease and despots. When nonfiction stories of black people in the U.S. reach Kenya on the news, they are often about men and women fighting for equality in a nation said to be the freest on earth.

In 2019 the Kenyan high court upheld a colonial-era ban on gay sex, punishable by up to fourteen years in prison, and nothing animates Mutua like ridding Kenya of movies with gay themes or characters. By his logic, Kenya will thrive only if it can grow its population and promote nuclear, heterosexual families. "Strong families contribute to strong communities contribute to strong nations. That, China has done very well," he said. Even as he wants Kenyans to build their own Kenya, he is willing to encourage yet another superpower to come to his country and dictate what his people see and think. "As long as it has the positive social values," he said.

Mutua banned children's animated shows *Hey Arnold!* and *Loud House*, since they were "laced with retrogressive and bizarre messages" that could turn kids gay. He called for the arrest of Kenyan singers who'd been featured in the video of Macklemore's same-sex anthem "Same Love." In 2018 he ruled that the Kenyan film *Rafiki*, about a romance between two Kenyan women, would never show in Kenyan theaters. Like *Farewell My Concubine* more than two decades earlier, the movie had been celebrated at the Cannes Film Festival, but it would not screen in its home country after Mutua claimed it carried a "clear intent to promote lesbianism in Kenya." He warned that anyone found with a copy of the movie could be arrested, giving interviews far and wide to create his own "kill the chicken" moment.

On the afternoon we met, Mutua was feeling proud. He has just come from a meeting to review the hundreds of films submitted to the board over the last seven months. When he took the job, it seemed they had problematic scripts every day, and Mutua banned fifteen commercials in his first two weeks alone. But since he banned *Rafiki*, no other script with gay themes or characters has even been submitted for review, he boasted. At this meeting where his team reviewed some one thousand projects, not a single production was flagged. The filmmakers were doing his work for him.

"There's great compliance," he said.

As Mutua told me about his efficacy, I thought of Will, a twenty-

two-year-old Kenyan I'd met on my first day in the country at the Karen
Blixen Museum, the farm once owned by the Danish author that has
become one of Nairobi's top tourist attractions thanks to the 1985 drama-
tization of her life, *Out of Africa.* We met at a place sustained by the im-
mortalizing effect of cinema, but Will grew up in a country where only
certain images could be shown. When he was younger, he told me, he had
a crush on a boy at school who he thought was gay like him. When he
shared his feelings, the boy told everyone. The principal called an assembly to warn students there was a homosexual among them, telling the
boys to stop wearing baggy trousers to avoid arousing him. Will noncha-
lantly told me of the several times he tried to kill himself, including the
time his sister insisted she join. ("If you're going to kill yourself, I'm going
to kill myself too.") They put poison in their porridge but still woke up
the next day. Now he lives in Nairobi, where he's studying foreign languages, and he's out to himself, some family members, and a few friends.

He relies on piracy websites to access films like *Call Me by Your
Name,* which he's watched five times. He asked me if I worried about my
safety at work, and I reflexively answered that being a journalist can be
dangerous, depending on what you cover and where you report. He'd
meant: When you go to the office, do you worry that you'll be attacked
if your colleagues find out that you're gay? Eventually he wants to run
his own business, because then no one can fire him for his sexuality.
When we said goodbye, he hurriedly stuck his hand out. A hug would
have set off alarms.

The images on-screen condition young people like Will to value their
lives in a certain way. Mutua controls what Kenyans like Will can see,
and he thinks Chinese movies censored by Chinese officials are the more
acceptable option for Will and his family. It is a mission that extends
beyond the movie theater.

"They aren't making movies just to have fun. It is something that
they're doing to change ideology," he said. "That helps me to say, 'Huh,
I can also do it in Kenya.'"

Sequel

O n October 17, 2020, Zhang Jing, a thirty-year-old manufacturing employee in Qingdao, participated in a historic event: she bought a ticket to a movie. Zhang sat
three rows from the back in one of six auditoriums at a
nearby cinema, located inside a mall in the northeast city of Weifang,
for a 12:50 p.m. screening of the animated film *Jiang Ziya*. The ticket
cost 32 yuan, or about $4.80. Since going to the cinema of her own voli-
tion for the first time at age nineteen—all of the movies she attended
growing up were propaganda features organized by her school—Zhang
had gone to about five films a year.

Though they did not know it at the time, she and the others in her
auditorium spent 32 yuan that contributed to a decades-long inevitability for their country. That weekend, Chinese ticket sales for the year
reached $1.998 billion, surpassing the $1.937 billion sold in North America. China had the number one box office in the world.

There was, of course, a significant asterisk on the accomplishment.

Even though analysts had projected that the Chinese box office would surpass North America's within a few years, the trend had been accelerated by the COVID-19 outbreak. At the time of China's ascendance to number one, Chinese theaters were open, while most American theaters had been closed for months. The reranking was nonetheless a seismic shift in global entertainment, the first time the U.S. had been unseated since its rise in the early twentieth century, and one that remained in place as the year ended. The practices and strategies Hollywood had honed over the past twenty-five years of business with China would only further bake themselves into the American entertainment business now.

Few expected North America ever to catch up once its theaters reopened. This assumption was confirmed four months after Zhang's outing, when the Lunar New Year release *Detective Chinatown 3* opened to a record-setting $397 million, the largest opening gross in world history, besting *Avengers: Endgame* by $40 million and allowing another American record to fall. For the entertainment industry, the COVID-19 outbreak appeared to have given China an opening to overtake its main film-market competitor—an echo of the American cinema industry's ascendance during World War I, when bombs shut down European production and moviegoing.

The movie Zhang went to see, *Jiang Ziya*, spoke to the moment. An animated retelling of a character from *Investiture of the Gods*, the classic collection of Chinese myths that was inspiring *Fengshen Trilogy*, it told the story of a military adviser who defies the orders of the heavenly realm to assist mortals, a decision that goes against his fate and fellow man. The movie featured every form of classic conflict: man versus man, when Jiang Ziya must battle his foes; man versus nature, when he must trek across the tundra; man versus self, when he must overcome his urge to stick to his destiny and avoid causing trouble. But a larger conflict pervaded this movie about a hero fighting his birthright, one many young Chinese people might relate to: man versus myth, when Jiang Ziya decides to defy the expectations set for him by custom and culture. It seemed like a theme that would resonate for moviegoers like Zhang, who have grown up in a culture where much can feel preordained even as they see drastic change around them. Chinese audiences have seen their country go from a dark part of the globe to an emerging superpower built on surveillance and control. Young moviegoers were turning to the screen for help figuring out where they fit into it all.

For Zhang, *Jiang Ziya* also offered a matinee refreshingly spent with a distinctly Chinese hero, one who is unafraid to use strategy and deception to win. She's annoyed by the tendency in Marvel movies to depict heroes like Thor as unimpeachable, when she thought it was his power-hungry and conniving brother, Loki, who should be in charge. In explaining this to me, she quoted Sun Tzu: "All warfare is based on deception."

She went back to the cinema the next weekend to see *The Sacrifice*, a Wu Jing film about the Korean War. She watched the story of Chinese soldiers who try to repair a bridge that is repeatedly destroyed by American forces. Years of propaganda movies as a kid had helped Zhang realize that *The Sacrifice* was in theaters because "movies are a tool for the promotion of ideology," and the government wanted to fan the flames of tensions between the United States and China, she said. But *The Sacrifice* could help other Chinese moviegoers who, unlike her, haven't yet learned to be a bit skeptical of Western entertainment.

"Chinese children used to fully accept American culture," she said. "Now China is waking up, so Chinese people think with their own mind."

COVID-19 WAS A ONETIME, CATACLYSMIC event, but it also pushed both entertainment industries more quickly in the direction they were already headed—away from each other. For starters, with Hollywood delaying most of its major 2020 and 2021 releases from their theatrical debuts, Chinese audiences' growing preference for Chinese films became even more apparent. Chinese streaming services had once proven a lucrative outlet for Hollywood studios, which could license an entire annual slate for more than $80 million. But around 2018, viewer interest in such films fell in favor of Chinese TV dramas. The few postpandemic Western movies that were released in China, such as *Wonder Woman 1984* and *F9*, attracted a fraction of the theatrical audiences that were expected. Studio balance sheets continued to plan for nine-figure windfalls out of China, but Chinese audiences were not providing them. The previous several years had dug a hole into the accounting ledgers that became impossible to fill.

While China was cementing its status as the biggest theatrical market, Hollywood was focused on going smaller—and getting people to tune in at home. Executives in Los Angeles directed efforts to the competitive arena of streaming, hoping to draw business away from Netflix. Every major studio but one launched a streaming service between late 2019 and the end of 2020, and their movies became never-ending collections of "content" that filled each platform's library, convinced users to subscribe, and ultimately boosted the share price of the parent company. Netflix, which had started as a DVD-by-mail company, had a considerable head start and released more original movies per year than all of the Hollywood studios combined. The few number of movies still treated to the wide theatrical release now had to convince filmgoers they were better than anything they could find streaming on the couch. The one hundred years of Hollywood dominance, marked by big-screen palaces and stars exalted as gods, felt as though it was being replaced by a shrunken model that treated movies as interchangeable feedstock for streaming services.

Netflix had expanded to dozens of countries around the world; by early 2021, only about a third of its subscribers were in the U.S. The list of countries where Netflix did not operate was short and included Syria, North Korea—and China. The company had tried for years to break into the Chinese market, especially as streaming shows and movies became increasingly popular in the country. Netflix founder Reed Hastings met with authorities to try to convince them to let his company compete alongside streaming services run by Chinese firms like Alibaba. But China wanted its homegrown industry to flourish without foreign competition.

Netflix could get into China only by licensing its most popular shows to Chinese platforms, which turned *House of Cards*—not exactly the most flattering depiction of American politics—into the top-performing American show in the country. Anything more ambitious was unlikely to happen.

Since it sees no future in the market, Netflix has been one of the few entertainment companies operating with little concern about alienating the country's leadership. It regularly signs deals to stream Chinese blockbusters like *The Wandering Earth*, targeting the considerable Chinese diaspora around the world. But its failure in China has also led to the company's green-lighting documentaries about topics otherwise off limits, such as the protests in Hong Kong calling for independence, or even movies like Steven Soderbergh's *The Laundromat*, which featured a subplot on corruption in Xi Jinping's family. Netflix's failure in China has given it a freedom few others in Hollywood enjoy, even as it censors movies and shows for countries where it does operate, such as Saudi Arabia.

As Disney gained traction with its flagship streaming service, Disney+, during the pandemic, share prices climbed as investors valued the company as they would a tech firm, where present-day losses are forgiven in exchange for the promise of continued growth and future profit. Major releases on the Disney slate started premiering on Disney+, skipping the theatrical release. A future of movies streamed at home was very bad news for one of China's most high-profile forays into American entertainment: AMC Theatres. Wanda's investment in the company had initially looked like a moneymaker after AMC went public. But Chairman Wang Jianlin's aspirations to be the biggest movie theater operator in the world stretched AMC past its limit, setting it up for a complete financial meltdown when the pandemic hit. Wanda had pushed AMC to acquire smaller circuits like Carmike Cinemas, deals that gave it bragging rights when it grew to become the number one theater chain in the world. But that distinction also saddled its balance sheet with sticky-floored ghost auditoriums in lousy markets. That became clear when the pandemic closed all theaters and AMC had just barely enough cash to survive. All of its employees were furloughed, including its CEO. While China's box office soared past the U.S. that October, AMC looked like it would end 2020 in bankruptcy proceedings. But then a Reddit community of online traders, many of them nostalgic for the moviegoing of their youth, drove AMC shares to record highs, soaring 470 percent in the early months of 2021. Wanda steadily sold its stake in the chain while the market manipulation allowed it to cash in on the craze, escaping the investment with unexpected riches thanks to a fluke in the American economic system. Besides, Wanda still had theaters in the bigger market, China.

A streaming-first Hollywood not only signals a possible end to the traditional American theatrical experience, but also places more power in the hands of the companies that will likely supplant Paramount and Sony as the most recognized names in entertainment. As tech giants like Apple have moved into film and TV production to support their own at-home services, they have not brought with them a liberalization in storytelling but instead contributed to a risk-averse landscape where certain topics pertaining to China cannot be broached.

"The two things we will never do are hard-core nudity and China," Eddy Cue, Apple's senior vice president in charge of its entertainment strategy, has told creative partners in Hollywood. In China, the company has a maze of supply chains, factories that make the iPhone, and a customer base of Apple users it cannot risk losing by dabbling in themes that might offend or alienate a Chinese audience. To compete with companies as dominant as Netflix, Apple, and Disney, smaller studios will merge and bulk up, further enveloping Hollywood in a morass of complexly connected conglomerates that put multiple holdings at risk if they anger China, which not only is the biggest box office in the world but will soon be the biggest economy in the world.

CHINA'S ECONOMIC RECOVERY FROM COVID-19 made more than just Hollywood reliant on the country's consumers. In early 2021, one company after another reported earnings where China was among the few, if only, bright spots on the balance sheet. iPhone sales in China rose 57 percent for Apple. Louis Vuitton set a global sales record at its Shanghai flagship store, selling $22 million worth of merchandise in a month when most of the U.S. was under lockdown orders. Tesla more than doubled its revenue in China. Same-store sales at Starbucks recovered faster in China than they had in the U.S. Nike reported sales flat in North America but up more than 20 percent in China. Ericsson, the telecom firm, beat Wall Street expectations thanks to 5G contracts in China. It did not matter if you sold cars or coffee. If you wanted your company to survive COVID-19, you would need China.

But as was the case in Hollywood, the increased reliance was merely an exclamation point on a years-long codependency with the country. Books similar to this one could be written about numerous sectors— from fashion to cars to telecom—and the opportunities identified and concessions made by executives who want to woo Chinese shoppers and authorities. China's political priorities have similarly conquered other parts of corporate America as they have the film industry. The evidence is found on the websites of major airlines like Delta and American, which remove references to Taiwan that designate it as its own country. An employee at Marriott was fired in 2018 for liking a social media post that supported Tibet. He lived in Omaha. At Shutterstock, a New York–based image provider, anyone with a mainland Chinese internet address would find nothing if they searched for "dictator" or other Beijing-banned terms. In early 2018, Daimler got in hot water for an Instagram post showing a Dalai Lama quote ("Look at situations from all angles, and you will become more open") above a Mercedes-Benz coupe. The post was deleted— even though Instagram cannot be accessed through China's controlled internet—and the car company apologized. "Although we deleted the post as soon as possible, it has hurt the feelings of people in this country," the automaker said. Just over two years later, in the wake of COVID-19, Daimler chief executive Ola Källenius would report record revenue for the

Mercedes brand in China, calling the sales figures in the market "almost too good to be true."

What had happened to Hollywood—a customer base proves too lucrative to ignore, and its leaders bend companies to their will—was merely one example of a U.S. industry seeing its business plans rewritten by the sheer scope of Chinese consumer demand. And in many cases, China's strategy of partnering with firms and then disposing of them was replicated as well. In the years before the coronavirus outbreak, each time Chinese relations with the U.S. flared, anxious distribution executives would confide in me a fear that the Chinese film bureau might stop accepting American movies as retaliation, depriving them of box-office grosses they'd grown to rely on. They comforted themselves with the knowledge that such a boycott would generate more headlines than the usual tariff, since it dealt with a sexy and symbolic industry—and told themselves that Chinese leaders had been reluctant to make moves that broadcast such friction to their own people. They also knew that stopping the import of American movies would just end up punishing Chinese theater owners, since the Hollywood films, as they had done in *The Fugitive* days, made them so much money. Both arguments hold less credence than they once did. China's leaders are less sheepish about retaliating against America, especially if it might rally their people. And Chinese theaters do not need American movies to keep their theaters open anymore, now that Chinese movies rake in so much money. China allowed Hollywood movies into the country to revitalize its theaters. It took less than two decades for the tables to turn.

TO MANY MOVIEGOERS AT THE time of COVID-19, the most prominent Chinese filmmaker working was Chloé Zhao, a thirty-nine-year-old daughter of a Chinese steel magnate. Educated in the West, her meditations on the American frontier and struggling classes in films like *The Rider* and *Nomadland* won her high praise—and a job directing a Marvel

Studios superhero epic. When Zhao became the front-runner to win a Best Director Oscar at the 2021 Academy Awards for *Nomadland*, about a sixtysomething from Empire, Nevada, who must live in a van following the 2008 financial crisis, it appeared the little gold statue that China's executives and leaders had so desired was within reach—and in the same year as its box-office ascendance, no less. But when an eight-year-old interview with *Filmmaker* magazine surfaced in which Zhao said China was a place with "lies everywhere" and that she considered her country to be the United States, a filmmaker whom state media had called "The Pride of China!" was blacklisted. References to *Nomadland*, which Chinese fans had cited as proof that America offered no safety net for its most vulnerable residents, were scrubbed from Chinese movie websites. Zhao's comments made her a new target for the rising movement of ultranationalist Chinese citizens, online mobs who policed the comments and actions of those in the West. Many of them had grown up watching pro-China movies during the *Wolf Warrior* era of Chinese filmmaking, and they took the fight online.

If Zhao had assumed she would be moving to a freer industry when she left China to make movies in the U.S., she was rudely reminded that America's entertainment business was already playing by Beijing's rules. The studio behind *Nomadland*, the Disney-owned Searchlight, successfully lobbied *Filmmaker* to remove Zhao's comment from the online version of the interview. But the damage was done. When Zhao won the Oscar for Best Director, it was heralded as a breakthrough in the U.S., since she was the first woman of color to receive the honor. In China, it was as if the Oscars had not been held, and Zhao's career were frozen in time. The day after the ceremony, searches for Zhao on the country's major sites yielded only old news. The country's propaganda ministry ordered state media journalists to ignore the story, and celebratory messages posted by everyday Chinese citizens were found and deleted. The Oscar had loomed large in the collective imagination of China's entertainment pursuits, and now it was finally in hand. But in the eyes of

Chinese leaders, national pride and sovereignty would always trump glitz or approval on the world stage.

To China's leaders, the Oscars incident justified a more intense crackdown on their country's filmmakers. Popular commercial directors whose careers had risen with the box-office were expected to declare publicly they were "of the system" and would make movies that backed the state. The names of Hong Kong–based producers were ordered off movie credits. The Ministry of Propaganda, now years into controlling the country's entertainment industry, functioned like a studio in Hollywood's original system, overseeing a collection of actors, directors, and craftsmen it could plug into any pro-Party movie it wanted. A list of approved plots and themes was maintained by party officials. Winning over audiences in foreign countries took a back seat to rallying the faithful at home.

China's leaders had already signaled where the country's entertainment industry was heading in a plan outlined in 2019 by authorities at the National Film Bureau and the Central Propaganda Department. By 2035, authorities said, China should be a "strong" film power, one that produces movies that stir patriotic feeling in viewers, written and directed by teams with a "clear ideological bottom line." A strong film power was distinct from what China had, which was a big film power, capable of large grosses but little influence. It harkened to a description Chinese intellectual Jiang Shigong made of his country. The story of China under Mao, he said, was one of "standing up." Under Deng Xiaoping, it was a story of "becoming rich." Under Xi Jinping, the story is one of "becoming strong."

Xi had enlisted his country's entertainment industry, reimposing the Maoist expectation that art would serve the state. China's film business can look a lot like America's from a distance, with its studios, national theatrical footprint, and glamorous movie stars. Like many technology transfers, this one would take the tools of the West while maintaining its Chinese essence—and in this case, its Communist Party mandates. Above all, China's on-screen reality would reflect its off-screen moment in history, the officials at the National Film Bureau declared. "A country's level of film development reflects its total national strength," officials said. No one believes this more firmly than Hollywood, where a different bottom line first intertwined studios with the country more than twenty years ago.

As tensions flared between the two countries, sources and friends in the China-Hollywood ecosystem operated with even greater trepidation. "We need to speak in code," one executive cautioned at the start of a phone call from Beijing. Any remark that accidentally veered into a sensitive topic caused the conversation to fall silent, a self-censorship record scratch. For years, China's entertainment industry followed a pattern of opening and then contraction, but in a two-steps-forward, one-step-backward march of progress. Now, under Xi, it was all moving in the wrong direction. Any plans Hollywood had for a conquest of those screens have turned in on themselves.

Can that conquest be reversed? Almost as soon as he became president, Joe Biden began repairing relations around the world that had been frayed by Donald Trump's presidency. Even in his administration's early days, Biden sought alliances that might build a bulwark against the Chinese influence of his former film-quota negotiations partner, Xi. He called it a Summit of Democracies. Together these countries would work on deepening investment and technological ties that reduced dependence on China, especially in sectors, like artificial intelligence, that China sought to dominate. A renewed focus on democratic values would turn back the autocratic trends deep in China and festering elsewhere.

But he may have been too late. Countries across the European Union and democratic nations already had established investment ties to China. Around the world, including in Kenya, Biden officials pursued trade agreements and alliances that would try to counter the China sales pitch. But whereas China's entertainment industry was considered an arm of Beijing's campaign, Hollywood was focused on streaming subscribers and still making sure it did not alienate its most important foreign market. It was a different reality than the one seen in the previous century, when people in every corner of the world absorbed a romantic vision of America from the movies and other forms of soft power. China's challenge to the American model revealed the degree to which the U.S. had taken such influence and easy affection for granted.

Whether China's entertainment industry ultimately prevails in its greater ambition of selling its country and its values to the world will be determined in this next century. That quest will also serve as a global referendum on which system will most inform the way leaders govern, states surveil, consumers spend, and citizens converse. Hollywood, once America's most persuasive evangelist, remains beholden to another country.

We are about to watch the final act in a classic tale. China started this century as the savvy ingenue, eager to learn. Countless Hollywood movies have taught us what happens next.

The ingenue grasps for the leading role.

ACKNOWLEDGMENTS

This book was edited by Emily Cunningham at Penguin Press. When we first met in late 2018 to discuss working together, I could hardly believe my good fortune—how clearly Emily articulated what this book should aim to accomplish, and the precision, nuance, and sense of possibility she brought to the reporting process and eventual manuscript. I thank her first because she illuminated every page you just read. There is a reason she is known in my house as "the LeBron of editors."

My agents, David Kuhn and Nate Muscato at Aevitas Creative Management, were a similarly perfect fit and the most fun duo I could have at my back. They were immediate supporters of the idea, knew where it should land, and made it happen. (I am grateful to be Maer Roshan's friend for many reasons, only one of which is the introduction he made between David and me.)

Reporting this book over several years has been a blast and taken me to very different parts of the world. I would often show up to a stranger's door unannounced, eager to ask about their hosting of Chinese bureaucrats in 1980s Iowa or about the Chinese satellite dish mounted on their roof in

Suswa, Kenya. I thank the dozens of people I met in every location across three continents for the universal spirit of generosity they provided in telling me their story and answering my questions. It was a regular reminder of the privilege this job carries. I am especially grateful to those who spoke with me despite fear of personal or professional harm. It was a regular reminder of the privilege I have living in a country where publishing such a book is possible.

This book, like any piece of nonfiction, depends on the work of others. I am grateful for the research and reporting on China and Hollywood that have come before mine. In particular, I want to acknowledge the insightful work of Aynne Kokas (*Hollywood Made in China*) and Wendy Su (*China's Encounter with Global Hollywood*), two scholars of China-Hollywood relations whose own books illuminate this issue brilliantly, as well as the scholarship of Sir David Puttnam, Stanley Rosen, and Jeffrey Wasserstrom, all of whom became friends and helpful resources throughout this process.

Similar thanks are owed to the journalists whose daily coverage provides the building blocks for this book, stretching back to those first reporters allowed into China thirty years after the 1949 revolution, especially Fox Butterfield. I've never been so grateful for the attention my fellow journalists bring to writing these first drafts of history. I want to thank especially Rebecca Davis and Patrick Frater at *Variety* and Patrick Brzeski and Tatiana Siegel at *The Hollywood Reporter* for doing a remarkable and thorough job at the difficult task of chronicling the shifting dynamics in today's Chinese film industry. The team at *China Film Insider* provides a critical resource as well.

Numerous translators, research assistants, and company employees helped the reporting of this book. In China, I worked with Ann Cao, a wonderful journalist who approached the assignments ("Can we find someone who went to the movies on October 17?") with aplomb and care. In Kenya, I worked with Carlos Mureithi, who spent more than a week helping with reporting and serving as a guide to his home country. He was a sharp and smart partner who made much of that reporting possible. Thank you also to Dominic Kirui for joining us for part of the trip and for the empathy and observation he lent the visit. Amanda Tust provided scrupulous fact-checking. Jasmine Blevins came in with enthusiastic help on the photos. My friend Jim Oberman helped track down people as only he can.

I have worked for eight years at *The Wall Street Journal*, the entire time in its dynamic Los Angeles bureau. The *Journal*'s specific approach to journalism, one that looks to business reporting to illuminate larger truths about the way we live now, informs this entire book and the approach I took to each chapter. I would not have written this book without the *Journal* more generally. It grew out of reporting I did there when my editor, former Los Angeles bureau chief Ethan Smith, gave me freedom to explore the theme. His successor, Liz Rappaport, reminds me we have the coolest job on the planet. Our boss, Jamie Heller, defines dedication to the craft of figuring out what is happening and telling the world about it. I am also grateful for the leadership and standard-setting of the *Journal*'s newsroom leaders, many of whom edited those first China-Hollywood stories: Jason Anders, Tammy Audi, Lisa Bannon, Jonathan Cheng, John Corrigan, Carrie Dolan, Sam Enriquez, Charles Hutzler, Lisa Kalis, Yael Kohen, Kim Last, Sofia McFarland, Matt Murray, Karen Pensiero, Matthew Rose, and Nikki Waller.

Covering Hollywood for the *Journal* is an all-time job, one I get to share with colleagues who have become friends. Those I have collaborated with on the show-business and China beats have been particularly special: Laurie Burkitt, Barbara Chai, Joe Flint, Ben Fritz, Ellen Gamerman, Wayne Ma, and R. T. Watson. A special shout-out to the *WSJ* book-writing club for the constant note-swapping and advice-giving: Eliot Brown, Liz Hoffman, Cameron McWhirter, Tripp Mickle, Katherine Sayre, and especially my writing-day texting buddy, Rob Copeland.

My friend and colleague Josh Mitchell gave me the best book advice I received when he told me to write long emails detailing my days spent reporting overseas, and then to send them to friends each morning. I thank him for the advice and the friends who served as those readers. They and others offered conversation and inspiration that made this book better: Brent Baughman, A. Scott Berg, Alexandra Berzon, Shane Boris, Chris Burick, Amy Chozick, Margeaux Cronce, Evin Ashley Erdoğdu, Will Frank, Brian Goldsmith, Claire Goldsmith, Bekah Grim, Jordan Heimer, Sarah

Idzik, Miriam Jordan, Terry Ann Knopf, Kenny Kyle, Marty LaSalle, Lauren Lexton, Crispin Leyser, Jules Leyser, Stephanie Lowden, Nour Malas, Emily Mohn-Slate, Joe Morgenstern, Wesley Morris, Erica E. Philips, Rachel Beth Polan, Josh Raffel, Sara Randazzo, Dr. Douglas Sadownick, Allison Sanders, Sam Sanders, Lauren Schuker Blum, Leo Seigal, Tomasz Skowronski, my Sunday morning creativity group (Tina Hsu, Joey Kuhn, and Justin Simien), Constance Vale, and Jeanne Whalen.

Several friends helped shape this book by reading early versions of it: Maxwell Anderson, the friend every author should have and the world's best two-person book club member; Daniel Wilner, whose brilliant comments scribbled in the margins brought the final version a new clarity; Sasha Issenberg, answerer of every book-writing question I could ask; and James T. Areddy, who set a land-speed record when he returned the manuscript with detailed notes in twenty-four hours. Sewell Chan and Isaac Chotiner weighed in with helpful insight and enthusiasm as well.

This book is dedicated to my mother, a former high school teacher who demonstrated how a job can be a calling, and my father, who told me that any job worth doing is worth doing right. Special thanks also to my older sister, Gretchen Vogle, and my younger sister, Kirsten Schwartzel, for their continuous support and for being the original targets of my reportorial tendency to interrogate. In the time working on this book, I have had the pleasure of growing closer to the Arnovitz-Plasker and Arnovitz-Kozarsky families, as well, and I thank them for their warm welcome. Diane Ravis made much of this possible when she moved in across the street from my family in 1995 and became my best friend.

My final thanks are reserved for my partner, Kevin Arnovitz, who has built a home and a life with me and our golden retriever, Howard. Kevin championed this book, and his intellect fills it. He is my first reader, my best reader, my travel agent, my love.

NOTES

This book is the result of hundreds of interviews, long and short, conducted over five years of reporting on China's evolving relationship with Hollywood. In the course of reporting this book, I had conversations with studio executives, filmmakers, moviegoers, and residents in China, the U.S., and countries around the world. Many of those people, for fear of professional or political retribution, asked to remain anonymous, and I've changed the names of some sources to protect them. In some cases, I have relied on notes from interviews I did on China and Hollywood for *The Wall Street Journal*. In a small number of instances, interviews were conducted by Ann Cao, a reporting assistant I hired when COVID-19 prevented me from traveling to China.

EPIGRAPHS

vii "Every film that goes": Richard Maltby, "The Americanisation of the World," in *Hollywood Abroad: Audiences and Cultural Exchange*, ed. Richard Maltby and Melvyn Stokes (London: Bloomsbury, 2004), 1.

vii "During its 5,000-year history": Xi Jinping, *The Governance of China* (Beijing: Foreign Languages Press, 2014), 179.

INTRODUCTION

xi Inside the UCLA classroom: Michael Cieply, "China's Media Moguls Tutored by Masters of Hollywood," *New York Times*, September 14, 2008.

xvi turned Maverick's love interest: David L. Robb, *Operation Hollywood: How the Pentagon Shapes and Censors the Movies* (Amherst, NY: Prometheus Books, 2004), 94.

xvii **Chinese investors on the movie:** Author interviews with executives familiar with the matter, June 2020.

CHAPTER I

3 **it was clear the country:** Author interview with Peter Murphy, February 15, 2019.

4 **about 80 percent of its revenue:** The Walt Disney Company, Form 10-K, September 30, 1993, http://edgar.secdatabase.com/1229/95013194000021/filing-main.htm.

4 **"had a lot of money":** Author interview with Lawrence Murphy, February 2019.

5 **known as "the Enforcer":** Richard Verrier, "Disney 'Enforcer' Stripped of Power," *Los Angeles Times*, March 26, 2005.

6 **received a perplexing phone call:** Author interview with Hope Boonshaft, December 22, 2018.

7 **"Fabulous," thought Annaud:** Author interview with Jean-Jacques Annaud, February 8, 2019.

7 **the December issue of French *Vogue*:** "French Vogue Hands Reins to Mandela," *News & Record* (Greensboro, NC), November 21, 1993.

7 **"horrendous, horrendous human rights":** Friends of Tibet, "Richard Gere's 'Unofficial' Oscar Presentation (March 29, 1993)," filmed March 29, 1993, posted January 28, 2018, YouTube video, 00:01:49, https://www.youtube.com/watch?v=mh8cAlNGQxI.

7 **anointed a *tulku*:** Michael Medved, "Hollywood's China Policy," *Wall Street Journal*, June 24, 1998.

8 **met a tour guide:** Melissa Mathison, "Where Is Gendun Rinchen?," *New York Times*, October 2, 1993.

8 **Mathison was there preparing:** Caroline Lees, "Hollywood Does Double Take on the Dalai Lama," *Sunday Times*, October 15, 1995.

8 **"Part of the tragedy":** Rick Lyman, "In Two Looks at Tibet, No Sign of Shangri-La," *New York Times*, September 7, 1997.

8 **"Harrer is one":** Lees, "Hollywood Does Double Take."

9 **"rally calling for Hawaii":** Jeffrey N. Wasserstrom and Maura Elizabeth Cunningham, *China in the 21st Century: What Everyone Needs to Know* (New York: Oxford University Press, 2018), 130.

9 **"I'm not doing this":** James Andrew Miller, *Powerhouse: The Untold Story of Hollywood's Creative Artists Agency* (New York: Custom House, 2016), 507.

9 **"We are resolutely opposed":** Seth Faison, "Muffling the Roar of 'The Lion King,'" *New York Times*, November 27, 1996.

10 **Annaud visited Tibet:** Author interview with Annaud.

11 **purple-inked thumbprints:** Author interview with *Seven Years in Tibet* casting assistant Lucinda Syson, August 10, 2020.

11 **"*yak de compagnie*":** Author interview with Annaud.

11 **The movie opens:** *Seven Years in Tibet*, directed by Jean-Jacques Annaud (Los Angeles: Sony Pictures, 1997).

13 Scorsese's *Kundun*: *Kundun*, directed by Martin Scorsese (Burbank, CA: Buena Vista Pictures, 1997).

14 Disney ultimately decided: Author interview with Peter Murphy.

15 "The reason the Chinese": Stephen Schaefer, "Cause Celeb; Anti-China Activist Richard Gere Suddenly Finds Hollywood in His 'Corner,'" *Boston Herald*, October 26, 1997.

16 "It was like being": Schaefer, "Cause Celeb."

16 In *Red Corner*, Gere stars: *Red Corner*, directed by Jon Avnet (Los Angeles: Metro-Goldwyn-Mayer, 1997).

16 Jiang dined with: Laura Myers, "Protestors Plan to Follow Chinese President Across the United States," Associated Press, October 8, 1997.

17 The crowd at the White House: Jeannie Williams, "'Red Corner' Fires Up Gere's Political Passion," *USA Today*, October 23, 1997.

17 Spike Lee, Barbra Streisand: "Film Stars Send Letter of Protest to China," Reuters, December 12, 1996.

17 "Who cares what I think?": Myers, "Protestors Plan to Follow."

17 *Red Corner* is: Schaefer, "Cause Celeb."

18 "We're not pursuing": Bruce Orwall, "Tibet or Not Tibet: For MGM and Its Star, That Is the Question," *Wall Street Journal*, November 3, 1997.

18 "When you're talking": Schaefer, "Cause Celeb."

18 "There are bad guys": Robert W. Welkos and Rone Tempest, "Hollywood's New China Syndrome," *Los Angeles Times*, September 1, 1997.

18 "MGM is not joined": Orwall, "Tibet or Not Tibet."

18 "today's Chinese wear": Karl Schoenberger, "China Isn't a Three-Act Script," *Los Angeles Times*, November 24, 1997.

18 forty Chinese dissidents: Schoenberger, "China Isn't a Three-Act Script."

19 To help cast: Author interview with Mike Medavoy, May 18, 2021.

19 "The best I have seen": Welkos and Tempest, "Hollywood's New China Syndrome."

19 "We don't want": "Hong Kong: Territory Is Newest Battlefield on Tibet," Inter Press Service, November 4, 1997.

19 *His Powerful Device*: Hal Lipper, "Will 'Mr. Cat Poop' Clean Up at the Box Office in Hong Kong?," *Wall Street Journal*, April 13, 1998.

19 "The Chinese aren't going": Richard W. Welkos, "China Film Rift Will Not Last, Valenti Believes," *Los Angeles Times*, November 1, 1997.

20 "Those three American companies": Brooks Boliek, "Offended China Cuts Off Three H'wood Studios," *Hollywood Reporter*, November 3, 1997.

20 "All of our business": David Barboza and Brooks Barnes, "How China Won the Keys to Disney's Magic Kingdom," *New York Times*, June 14, 2016.

20 The other releases that day: "Domestic Box Office for Dec. 25, 1997," Box Office Mojo, https://www.boxofficemojo.com/date/1997-12-25/?ref_=bo_rl_rl.

20 *It's not like we're burying* Raging Bull: Author interview with Murphy.

21 "Well," he scoffed: Author interview with Boonshaft.

22 **"Can any of us"**: Author interview with former Sony executive, February 2019.

CHAPTER 2

23 **Ming dynasty emperor**: Terry McCarthy, "Zhu Rongji's Year of Living Danger-ously," *Time*, April 12, 1999.

23 **"irrational high growth"**: McCarthy, "Zhu Rongji's Year."

23 **a Park Avenue family**: Mark I. Pinsky, *The Gospel According to Disney* (Louisville, KY: Westminster John Knox Press, 2004), 124–26.

24 **stopped by children**: Laura M. Holson, "A Quiet Departure for Eisner at Disney," *New York Times*, September 26, 2005.

24 **"We made a stupid mistake"**: Zhu Rongji, *Zhu Rongji on the Record: The Road to Reform: 1998–2003* (Washington, DC: Brookings Institution Press, 2015), 92–97.

25 **an evening at the movies**: David Puttnam, *The Undeclared War: The Struggle for Control of the World's Film Industry* (London: HarperCollins, 1997), 17–18.

26 **"Demand for American films"**: Puttnam, *Undeclared War*, 76–77.

26 **"Western ideas go in"**: Puttnam, *Undeclared War*, 89–90.

26 **"undeclared war"**: Puttnam, *Undeclared War*.

26 **movies about American manufacturing**: Puttnam, *Undeclared War*, 91.

27 **"What we wanted"**: George Creel, *How We Advertised America* (New York: Harper & Brothers, 1920), 281.

27 **"was like picking up"**: Puttnam, *Undeclared War*, 86–87.

28 **invested in new movie theaters**: Puttnam, *Undeclared War*, 125–26.

28 **30 percent and 40 percent of studio revenues**: Puttnam, *Undeclared War*, 140–42.

28 **"as a means of reminding them"**: Puttnam, *Undeclared War*, 95.

29 **banned the martial arts films**: Chris Berry and Mary Farquhar, *China on Screen: Cinema and Nation* (New York: Columbia University Press, 2006), 225.

29 **eyed such cultural intrusion warily**: Puttnam, *Undeclared War*, 150.

29 **"adjunct of our State Department"**: Will H. Hays, *The Memoirs of Will H. Hays* (Garden City, NY: Doubleday, 1955), 333–34.

30 **first recorded movie screening**: Berry and Farquhar, *China on Screen*, 223.

30 **"There is, in fact"**: Mao Zedong, "Talks at the Yenan Forum on Literature and Art," May 2, 1942, translation by the Maoist Documentation Project, https://www.marxists.org/reference/archive/mao/selected-works/volume-3/mswv3_08.htm.

31 **"I very much admire"**: Zhu, *Zhu Rongji on the Record*, 92–97.

32 **"An otherwise harmless"**: Hays, *Memoirs of Will H. Hays*, 531.

32 **a subsidiary of the Defense Department**: Mark Harris, *Five Came Back: A Story of Hollywood and the Second World War* (New York: Penguin Press, 2014), 158.

33 **"I want every mother in America"**: Harris, *Five Came Back*, 158.

33 **"Some carping individuals"**: Harris, *Five Came Back*, 161.

33 **"in the stands of ball games"**: Harris, *Five Came Back*, 134.

34 **"often as grotesque stereotypes"**: Harris, *Five Came Back*, 127.

34 **"has helped to define Europe"**: Edward Said, *Orientalism* (New York: Pantheon Books, 1978), 1–2.

34 **asked a Ouija board**: Phil Baker, "Fu Manchu and China: Was the 'Yellow Peril Incarnate' Really Appallingly Racist?" *Independent*, October 20, 2015.

35 **"new wine in old bottles"**: Berry and Farquhar, *China on Screen*, 59.

35 **The only American movie**: Wendy Su, *China's Encounter with Global Hollywood: Cultural Policy and the Film Industry, 1994–2013* (Lexington: University Press of Kentucky, 2016), 1.

35 **It was among the first recordings**: Harris, *Five Came Back*, 370.

36 **"reflect credit on the good name"**: Puttnam, *Undeclared War*, 212–13.

36 **The movies lifting Europe's mood**: Sandra Schulberg, "Selling Democracy: Films of the Marshall Plan; 1948–1953," presented by the Academy Film Archive of the Academy of Motion Picture Arts and Sciences, 2005–2006.

37 **"American campaign to create"**: Schulberg, "Selling Democracy," 10.

38 **paint a tractor or power lines**: Fox Butterfield, *China: Alive in the Bitter Sea* (New York: Bantam, 1982), 437.

38 **a three-room tour**: Author visit to Shanghai Propaganda Poster Art Centre, June 2019.

39 **expression as a form of treason**: Butterfield, *China*, 365.

39 **charged for the bullet**: Butterfield, *China*, 17–18.

40 **a scientist who happened**: Butterfield, *China*, 351.

40 **MGM banned reference**: Puttnam, *Undeclared War*, 231.

40 **considered selling the back lot**: Puttnam, *Undeclared War*, 263.

41 ***Star Wars* generating**: Domestic box office for *Star Wars: Episode IV: A New Hope*, Box Office Mojo, https://www.boxofficemojo.com/release/rl2759034369/?ref_=bo_fr_table_7.

41 **and the other films**: Domestic box office for *Close Encounters of the Third Kind* and *Saturday Night Fever*, Box Office Mojo, https://www.boxofficemojo.com/title/tt0075860/?ref_=bo_se_r_1 and https://www.boxofficemojo.com/title/tt0076666/?ref_=bo_se_r_1.

41 **the first *Rambo* movie**: Domestic box office for *First Blood*, Box Office Mojo, https://www.boxofficemojo.com/title/tt0083944/?ref_=bo_se_r_1.

41 **like *Dirty Dancing***: Domestic box office for *Dirty Dancing*, Box Office Mojo, https://www.boxofficemojo.com/title/tt0092890/?ref_=bo_se_r_1.

41 **Of the one hundred top-grossing films**: Samuel P. Huntington, *The Clash of Civilizations and the Remaking of the World Order* (New York: Simon & Schuster, 1996), 58.

42 **"a narcotic which the capitalist"**: Jim Mann, "'Superman' Shanghaied in Peking Screen Test," *Los Angeles Times*, January 25, 1986.

42 **"soft power"**: Joseph S. Nye Jr., *Bound to Lead: The Changing Nature of American Power* (London: Basic Books, 1990).

42 **"empire by invitation"**: Joseph S. Nye Jr., *The Future of Power* (New York: PublicAffairs, 2011), 97.

43 **"Somewhere in the Middle East"**: Huntington, *Clash of Civilizations*, 58.

44 **"how China greets"**: Zhu, *Zhu Rongji on the Record*.

CHAPTER 3

45 **denounced his father:** Peter Brunette, "Chen Kaige: From His Act of Betrayal Comes the Stuff of a Career," *New York Times*, December 12, 1999.

45 **one cinematography student:** Author interview with Lora Chen, Beijing Film Academy contemporary of Chen Kaige and Zhang Yimou, June 16, 2020.

46 **encouraged the peasantry:** Patrick E. Tyler, "Deng Xiaoping: A Political Wizard Who Put China on the Capitalist Road," *New York Times*, February 20, 1997.

47 **"bogus bourgeois science":** Fox Butterfield, *China: Alive in the Bitter Sea* (New York: Bantam, 1982), 338.

47 **In 1979, Hollywood movies:** Author interview with Lora Chen.

47 **"main-melody" narratives:** Wendy Su, *China's Encounter with Global Hollywood: Cultural Policy and the Film Industry, 1994–2013* (Lexington: University Press of Kentucky, 2016), 20.

48 **"If we can reach":** Tyler, "Deng Xiaoping."

49 **"We face a lot of pressure":** Patrick E. Tyler, "China's Censors Issue a Warning," *New York Times*, September 4, 1993.

50 **"attitude problems":** Tyler, "China's Censors Issue a Warning."

50 **"Even more disturbing":** Steven Spielberg and Kathleen Kennedy, "China and the Oscars," *New York Times*, March 25, 1991.

51 **who first traveled:** Author interview with Ellen Eliasoph, March 3, 2020.

52 **one of three categories:** Su, *China's Encounter with Global Hollywood*, 21–22.

52 **"Main-melody films":** Su, *China's Encounter with Global Hollywood*.

52 **she sensed that movies:** Author interview with Eliasoph.

53 **broke even or made a profit:** Su, *China's Encounter with Global Hollywood*, 14.

54 **"unexpected money in the street":** David Puttnam, *The Undeclared War: The Struggle for Control of the World's Film Industry* (London: HarperCollins, 1997), 86–87.

55 **to see it five times:** Rone Tempest, "How Do You Say 'Boffo' in Chinese?," *Los Angeles Times*, November 29, 1994.

55 **"an underground agent":** Su, *China's Encounter with Global Hollywood*, 18.

56 **generation of young people:** Author interview with Dan Glickman, August 7, 2020.

56 **Chinese writers reminded readers:** Su, *China's Encounter with Global Hollywood*, 55–60.

57 **Box-office grosses surged:** Su, *China's Encounter with Global Hollywood*, 19.

57 **a quid pro quo system:** Su, *China's Encounter with Global Hollywood*, 22.

58 *yi wo wei zhu:* Su, *China's Encounter with Global Hollywood*, 20.

58 **"Fax machines enable":** Ken Auletta, "The Pirate," *New Yorker*, November 5, 1995.

58 **flipping his portfolio:** John Lippman, Leslie Chang, and Robert Frank, "Rupert Murdoch's Wife Wendi Wields Influence at News Corp.," *Wall Street Journal*, November 1, 2000.

59 **The company bought the rights:** Michael Laris, "Mickey Gets China's Ear," *Washington Post*, February 8, 1999.

59 **"Liberty will be spread":** William J. Clinton, "Remarks at the Paul H. Nitze School of Advanced International Studies," March 13, 2000.

60 *Forrest Gump* playing to sold-out crowds: "'Forrest Gump' Takes China by Storm," United Press International, June 14, 1995.

60 ready access to American movies: Ann Hornaday, "A Director's Trip from Salad Days to a 'Banquet,'" *New York Times*, August 1, 1993.

60 "told the world": Author interview with Ang Lee, August 25, 2020.

61 "I love stirring things up": Patrick Pacheco, "Cultural Provocateur: In 'The Wedding Banquet,' Ang Lee Stirs Up Custom," *Los Angeles Times*, August 4, 1993.

62 "People asked me": Author interview with Lee.

62 What was everyone seeing?: Author interview with Hope Boonshaft, December 22, 2018.

63 "did not have that cultural burden": Author interview with Lee.

CHAPTER 4

65 Ben Zhang loved: Author interview with Ben Zhang, March 2019.

66 composed 20 percent: Wendy Su, *China's Encounter with Global Hollywood: Cultural Policy and the Film Industry, 1994–2013* (Lexington: University Press of Kentucky, 2016), 19.

66 the movie demonized the rich: Emily Parker, "'Titanic' Takes China by Storm Following Jiang's Endorsement," *Wall Street Journal*, April 14, 1998.

67 "learn from capitalism": Erik Eckholm, "Why 'Titanic' Conquered the World," *New York Times*, April 26, 1998.

67 asked a classroom: Author interview with Michael Werner, June 2, 2019.

68 sold for $1.20: Craig S. Smith, "A Tale of Piracy: How the Chinese Stole the Grinch," *New York Times*, December 12, 2000.

69 "China has a lot of potential": Author interview with Barry Meyer, February 18, 2020.

69 "Meg Ryan was just": Author interview with Zhang.

70 lived in rural areas: "Percentage of Population in Urban and Rural Areas: China," World Bank staff estimates based on the United Nations Population Division's World Urbanization Prospects, 2018.

70 only about 45 percent: "More Than 55 Percent of Chinese Now Live in Urban Areas," Associated Press, April 21, 2016.

70 the number of movies: Craig S. Smith, "China's WTO Deal: Pact May Not Live Up to Expectations," *Asian Wall Street Journal*, November 16, 1999.

71 seed a theatrical ecosystem: Author interview with Meyer.

72 Warner Wanda Cinemas: Warner Bros., "Wanda Group and Warner Bros. International Cinemas Jointly Create Warner Wanda Cinemas" (press release), January 17, 2004, https://www.warnerbros.com/news/press-releases/wanda-group-and-warner-bros-international-cinemas-jointly-create-warner-wanda-cinemas.

73 The government hastily pulled: Jim Puzzanghera and Mark Magnier, "Studios Still Bit Actors in China," *Los Angeles Times*, June 18, 2006.

73 the terms had changed: Author interviews with former executives and people familiar with the matter, 2019 and 2020.

75 **"You don't understand"**: Author interview with Dan Glickman, August 7, 2020.

76 **a Sioux City native**: Author interview with Michael Gralapp, August 15, 2020.

77 **"I'm either a guy"**: Author interview with Nathaniel Boyd, April 23, 2019.

78 **"an effort to recast"**: "Popular PRC Film Redraws Taiwan Propaganda," U.S. diplomatic cable, created December 29, 2009, https://wikileaks.org/plusd/cables/09BEIJING3482 _a.html.

79 **China was a "sinkhole"**: Author interview with Richard Gelfond, February 6, 2019.

79 **The two men spoke**: Author interview with Gelfond.

CHAPTER 5

81 **a giant clock**: "Beijing Olympics Countdown Begins," *China Daily*, September 22, 2004.

82 **to learn English**: "Chinese Ban 'Chinglish' for Olympics," Associated Press, April 11, 2007.

82 **weather was tamed**: "Beijing Aims to Control Weather at Olympics," Associated Press, February 28, 2008.

82 **two major concessions**: David Barboza and Brooks Barnes, "How China Won the Keys to Disney's Magic Kingdom," *New York Times*, June 14, 2016.

83 **"the greatest opportunity"**: Barboza and Barnes, "How China Won the Keys."

84 **focus group of young children**: Ben Fritz, *The Big Picture: The Fight for the Future of Movies* (New York: Houghton Mifflin Harcourt, 2018), 63.

85 **totaled $2.5 billion**: Nicole LaPorte, "DVD Sales Way Down; High-Def Slow to Rescue," *The Wrap*, February 15, 2009, https://www.thewrap.com/dvd-sales-way-down-high -def-slow-rescue-1404.

85 **eight million DVDs**: "'Nemo' Breaks Sales Records," Associated Press, November 5, 2003.

85 **"When will China"**: Susan Brownell, "America's and Japan's Olympics Debuts: Lessons for Beijing 2008 (and the Tibet Controversy)," *Asia Pacific Journal* 6, no. 5 (May 3, 2008).

85 **When St. Louis**: Brownell, "America's and Japan's Olympics Debuts."

86 **"All the shitty directors"**: "Ai Weiwei: Designer of the Olympic Stadium," *Guardian*, August 9, 2007.

86 **Ang Lee would also consult**: "Ang Lee Joins Team Creating the Beijing Olympics' Opening Ceremony," *Guardian Unlimited*, October 17, 2006.

87 **but edited it**: "Chinese TV Cuts Ang Lee's Speech," *BBC News*, March 7, 2006.

87 **"the pride of Chinese people"**: "Ang Lee Named China Olympics Consultant," Associated Press, October 19, 2006.

87 **criticizing China's support**: Ronan Farrow and Mia Farrow, "The 'Genocide Olympics,'" *Wall Street Journal*, March 28, 2007.

87 **a week later, he did**: Dave Skretta, "Farrow, Spielberg Assail China on Darfur," Associated Press, February 12, 2008.

87 **"aligned with imperialist"**: Eric Sommer, "Spielberg's Decision Misdirected," *China Daily*, February 20, 2008.

88 **A former television producer**: Author interview with Ric Birch, December 11, 2019.

88 "In 1644 the last": Author interview with Birch.

89 a narrative that combined: Jeffrey N. Wasserstrom and Maura Elizabeth Cunningham, *China in the 21st Century: What Everyone Needs to Know* (New York: Oxford University Press, 2018).

89 The seven-year-old girl: Jim Yardley, "In Grand Olympic Show, Some Sleight of Voice," *New York Times*, August 12, 2008.

89 A majority of respondents: Joseph S. Nye Jr., *The Future of Power* (New York: PublicAffairs, 2011), xii.

90 holiday break with homework: Author interview with Jeffrey Katzenberg and other DreamWorks Animation employees, 2019 and 2020.

91 The filmmaking team immersed themselves: Author interviews with DreamWorks Animation employees, May 2020 and June 2020.

91 color theory: Robert W. Butler, "Directors Relied on Improv and 'Happy Accidents' to Polish 'Kung Fu Panda,'" *Kansas City Star*, June 5, 2008.

92 *How does this monk*: Author interview with Melissa Cobb, June 18, 2020.

92 "The film's protagonist": Simon Rabinovitch, "'Kung Fu Panda' Prompts Soul Searching in China," Reuters, July 5, 2008.

93 "Is it subversive?": Author interview with Katzenberg.

93 "That's why we feel": Author interview with Andre Morgan, August 19, 2019.

93 "I cannot help": Li Chuan, "'Kung Fu Panda' Gives Food for Thought," *China Daily*, July 5, 2008.

94 designated animation as an area: Fei Jiang and Kuo Huang, "Hero Is Back—the Rising of Chinese Audiences: The Demonstration of SHI in Popularizing a Chinese Animation," *Global Media and China* 2, no. 2 (June 2017): 122–37.

94 "Although there is no secret": Jonathan Watts, "Film: Hollywood's Panda Hit Makes China Bare Its Soul," *Guardian*, July 8, 2008.

95 Moviegoers waited in line: Fritz, *Big Picture*, 209.

95 Members of the politburo: Author interview with Richard Gelfond, February 6, 2019.

95 Chinese authorities pulled it: Melinda Liu, "In China, Moviegoers Choose *Avatar* over Confucius," *Newsweek*, February 3, 2010.

96 "tight controls": "NPC Delegate Discusses Migrant Labor, Graduate Employment, NPC Experiences," diplomatic cable, April 1, 2009, https://wikileaks.org/plusd/cables /09BEIJING872_a.html.

96 *Battleship Potemkin* premiered: David Puttnam, *The Undeclared War: The Struggle for Control of the World's Film Industry* (London: HarperCollins, 1997), 105–6.

96 the country had installed: Richard Taylor, "From October to 'October': The Soviet Political System in the 1920s and Its Films," in *Politics and the Media: Film and Television for the Political Scientist and the Historian*, ed. M. J. Clark (Oxford: Pergamon, 2014).

98 knew this better: Author interview with Gerry Lopez, July 31, 2019.

98 *Say what?*: Author interview with Lopez.

98 "By 2020, we should": Clifford Coonan, "Richest Man in China Sees 20 More Years of Growth to Come," *Irish Times*, September 17, 2013.

99 "There is a love of something": Author interview with Lopez.

99 **founded in Kansas City:** Diana B. Henriques, "Stanley Durwood, 78, Inventor of Multiplex," *New York Times*, July 16, 1999.

99 **jumped 61 percent:** Willy Shih, "Dalian Wanda Group: The AMC Entertainment Acquisition" (case study), Harvard Business School, December 10, 2014.

100 **among the biggest acquisitions:** Shih, "Dalian Wanda Group."

100 **They certainly could:** Author interview with Lopez.

101 **"When foreign dynasties":** Henry Kissinger, *On China* (New York: Penguin Books, 2011), 22.

102 **new business cards:** Author interview with Katzenberg.

102 **"I would not see myself":** Author interview with distribution executive, April 2019.

CHAPTER 6

103 **Chinese officials thought the drying clothes:** Aynne Kokas, *Hollywood Made in China* (Oakland: University of California Press, 2017), 77.

104 **thought that such an outbreak:** Max Brooks, "China Barred My Dystopian Novel About How Its System Enables Epidemics," *Washington Post*, February 27, 2020.

104 **removed the plot point:** Lucas Shaw, "Fearing Chinese Censors, Paramount Changes 'World War Z,'" *The Wrap*, March 31, 2013, https://www.thewrap.com/fearing-chinese -censors-paramount-changes-world-war-z-exclusive-83316.

104 **became a metaphor:** Steven Zeitchik, "Will Smith's 'Men in Black 3' Censored in China," *Los Angeles Times*, May 31, 2012.

104 **"the disintegration of a regime":** Charles Edel, "Four Theories of Modern China," *American Interest* 15, no. 3 (November 21, 2019).

105 **portrayed a malevolent force:** "China Censors 'Pirates' for 'Vilifying Chinese'" Reuters, June 14, 2007.

105 **a Chinese security guard:** Clarence Tsui, "Chinese Censors Clamp Down on 'Skyfall,'" *Hollywood Reporter*, January 16, 2013.

105 **A gay love scene:** Clarence Tsui, "Chinese Censors Snip 40 Minutes off 'Cloud Atlas,'" *Hollywood Reporter*, January 22, 2013.

105 **Chris Pratt's bare butt:** Erich Schwartzel, "Hollywood's New Script: You Can't Make Movies Without China," *Wall Street Journal*, April 18, 2017.

105 **had nineteen codicils:** Hong Kong Trade Development Council, "SARFT Reiterates Film Censor Criteria" (business alert), April 1, 2008, http://info.hktdc.com/alert/cba -e0804c-2.htm.

107 **"We decided to play safe":** Shabana Ansari, "Chinese Pressure Forces Tibetan Films' Ouster," *Times of India*, August 18, 2004.

108 **a lobbying process:** These and other details on the censorship process are from interviews with American and Chinese film executives.

110 **distressing to screenwriter Ryan Condal:** Author interview with Ryan Condal, November 10, 2019.

114 **didn't drink or smoke:** David Puttnam, *The Undeclared War: The Struggle for Control of the World's Film Industry* (London: HarperCollins, 1997), 129.

114 **by other constituents:** Will H. Hays, *The Memoirs of Will H. Hays* (Garden City, NY: Doubleday, 1955).

115 **Under the Hays Code:** Hays, *Memoirs of Will H. Hays*, 434.

115 **Rhett Butler's most famous line:** Eric Gardner, "The Czar of Hollywood," *Indianapolis Monthly*, February 2005.

115 **Pope Pius XI thanked Hays:** Hays, *Memoirs of Will H. Hays*, 449.

116 **sixty-seven plays or novels:** Hays, *Memoirs of Will H. Hays*, 432.

116 **"The best way":** Hays, *Memoirs of Will H. Hays*, 456.

116 **forced new warnings:** Mark Harris, *Mike Nichols: A Life* (New York: Penguin Press, 2021), 194.

117 **Brownshirts in the audience yelled:** Thomas Doherty, *Hollywood and Hitler: 1933–1939* (New York: Columbia University Press, 2013), 4.

117 **"Victory is ours!":** Ben Urwand, *The Collaboration: Hollywood's Pact with Hitler* (Cambridge, MA: Belknap Press of Harvard University Press, 2013), 30.

117 **they resubmitted it:** Urwand, *Collaboration*, 33.

118 **introduced Article 15:** Urwand, *Collaboration*, 48.

118 **create Universum-Film AG:** Puttnam, *Undeclared War*, 98–99.

118 **"moral, political, and eugenic":** Doherty, *Hollywood and Hitler*, 25.

118 **Universal delayed production:** Urwand, *Collaboration*, 54.

118 **scrapped a project:** Urwand, *Collaboration*, 51.

119 **Hitler's ambassador to Hollywood:** Doherty, *Hollywood and Hitler*, 175.

119 **moments of German indignity:** Urwand, *Collaboration*, 55.

119 ***Are We Civilized?*:** Doherty, *Hollywood and Hitler*, 315.

119 ***Give Us This Night*:** Urwand, *Collaboration*, 144.

119 ***The General Died at Dawn*:** Urwand, *Collaboration*, 144.

119 **studio chief's notes:** Urwand, *Collaboration*, 189–91.

119 **"no more or less":** Doherty, *Hollywood and Hitler*, 26.

119 **The British didn't like:** Author interview with Thomas Doherty, March 2020.

120 **too much comingling:** Urwand, *Collaboration*, 152–53.

120 **"the highest sense":** Urwand, *Collaboration*, 130.

120 **created a marketplace:** Doherty, *Hollywood and Hitler*, 44.

120 **"While it might serve":** Doherty, *Hollywood and Hitler*, 58.

121 **Gyssling appears to have threatened:** Urwand, *Collaboration*, 68.

121 **"occurred in the first year":** Urwand, *Collaboration*, 75.

121 **"It is only logical":** Urwand, *Collaboration*, 209.

121 **"will make pictures":** Urwand, *Collaboration*.

121 **set up a loan business:** Urwand, *Collaboration*, 146–47.

121 **overplay his hand:** Doherty, *Hollywood and Hitler*, 217–20.

121 **twenty-one cuts:** Urwand, *Collaboration*, 183.

122 **kicked Universal out:** Urwand, *Collaboration*, 184.

122 **several European markets out of distribution:** Urwand, *Collaboration*, 211.

122 **"With all hope":** Urwand, *Collaboration*.

122 **"sold the American way":** Urwand, *Collaboration*, 222–24.

123 **"pillar industry":** Liu Wei, "Culture to Be Pillar Industry," *China Daily*, February 16, 2012.

123 **more than 15 percent per year:** Priscilla Jiao, "Culture a Key Priority in Five-Year Plan," *South China Morning Post*, March 28, 2011.

123 **expand access to the market:** Author interview with Greg Frazier, May 8, 2019.

124 **"Absolutely, Mr. Vice President":** Author interviews with Jeffrey Katzenberg, 2018 and 2019.

CHAPTER 7

128 **one of those teenagers:** Author interview with Jeremy Passmore, August 2019.

130 **47 percent of respondents:** John Pomfret, "A Fearful View of China," *Washington Post*, October 29, 2010.

130 **"I don't want to do Fakeistan":** Author interview with Carl Ellsworth, August 25, 2019.

133 **"Tempers here will probably":** Brad Webber, "Film Rewinds the Cold War," *China Daily*, April 19, 2010.

133 **MGM executives quietly told crew members:** Author interviews with *Red Dawn* production crew members, August 2019.

133 **$3.7 billion loan:** Brooks Barnes, "MGM Replaces Chief Executive," *New York Times*, August 18, 2009.

135 **"oh shit" jobs:** Author interviews with Custom Film Effects employees Adam Gass, Mark Dornfeld, Jamie Baxter, and Mikyoung Hahm, July 2019 and August 2019.

138 **Ellsworth and Passmore added lines:** *Red Dawn*, directed by Dan Bradley (Los Angeles: FilmDistrict, 2012).

139 **"copout":** Mike Wilkinson, "New 'Dawn' Invaders Make Mich. Militia See Red," *Detroit News*, April 7, 2011.

139 **"without a single word":** Mark McDonald, "Remake of 'Red Dawn' Changes Its Political Hue," *New York Times*, November 21, 2012.

CHAPTER 8

143 **"These are our superheroes":** Author correspondence with Michael Bay, May 2021.

143 **were both to be released:** Pamela McClintock, "Box Office Report: 'Amazing Spider-Man' Beats 'Dark Knight Rises' in China," *Hollywood Reporter*, August 28, 2012.

143 **hurriedly paid a local:** Author interview with person familiar with the situation, 2020.

144 **But Moore reasoned:** Author interview with Rob Moore, July 21, 2020.

147 *No one watching*: Author interview with Moore.

148 **"[export] the U.S.'s rebalancing":** Clifford Coonan, "Chinese PLA Officer Tells Troops 'Pacific Rim' Is Hollywood Propaganda," *Hollywood Reporter*, August 27, 2013.

149 **After a car accident:** May Jeong, "The Big Error Was That She Was Caught," *Vanity Fair*, March 26, 2019.

150 **An additional four minutes:** Clarence Tsui, "'Iron Man 3' China-Only Scenes Draw Mixed Response," *Hollywood Reporter*, May 1, 2013.

151 "flower vases": Erich Schwartzel, "Hollywood Under Pressure to Put More Chinese Actors in the Spotlight," *Wall Street Journal*, September 19, 2016.

151 Roughly a third: *Transformers: Age of Extinction*, directed by Michael Bay (Los Angeles: Paramount Pictures, 2014).

152 Greenberg suspected some other: Author interview with Jonah Greenberg, October 20, 2020.

153 "I didn't think": Vivienne Chow and Michael De Waal–Montgomery, "Mark Wahlberg, Li Bingbing Kick Off Transformers World Premiere in Hong Kong," *South China Morning Post*, June 19, 2014.

153 "I am not sure": "Angelina Jolie Hurts the Feelings of the Chinese People," Associated Press, June 10, 2014.

154 taking dim-sum classes: "Brad Pitt Breaks the Ice with China Visit After Tibet Row," Agence France-Presse, June 3, 2014.

154 Executives split up the cast: Author interview with Marc Ganis, July 29, 2020.

154 "The food was fantastic": Karen Chu, "'Transformers 4' Premiere: Michael Bay Talks Air Conditioner Attack, Optimus Prime Guards Red Carpet," *Hollywood Reporter*, June 20, 2014.

154 farmers in Shandong Province: Abid Rahman, "Chinese Villagers Give Up Farming to Build Giant Transformers from Old Car Parts," *Hollywood Reporter*, July 16, 2014.

155 its quarterly earnings: Meg James, "'Transformers,' 'Turtles' Help Drive Viacom's Revenue Up 9% in Quarter," *Los Angeles Times*, November 12, 2014.

CHAPTER 9

157 reason to be bullish: Author interview with Gerry Lopez, October 9, 2019.

157 the refurbished auditoriums: Erich Schwartzel, "Comfiest Seat in the House: Struggling Movie Theaters Go Upscale to Survive," *Wall Street Journal*, April 9, 2018.

159 the scrawny son: Malcolm Moore, "The Rise and Rise of Wang Jianlin, China's Richest Man," *Telegraph*, September 21, 2013.

159 renovating slum housing: Matthew Miller, "Wang Jianlin, China's Property Tycoon, Finds Golden Path to Billions," Reuters, December 22, 2014.

159 had been given early stakes: Michael Forsythe, "Wang Jianlin, a Billionaire at the Intersection of Business and Power in China," *New York Times*, April 28, 2015.

159 the Confucian ideal: Willy Shih, "Dalian Wanda Group: The AMC Entertainment Acquisition" (case study), Harvard Business School, December 10, 2014.

159 an annual company: Author interviews with former and current Wanda employees, December 2019.

160 "So later, I asked": Moore, "Rise and Rise of Wang Jianlin."

160 more than $30 billion: *Forbes*, "Wang Jianlin Reclaims Top Spot on 2015 Forbes China Rich List" (press release), October 26, 2015.

161 one for each front leg: Rob Price, "The Son of China's Richest Man Wang Jianlin Bought 2 Gold Apple Watches for His Dog," *Business Insider*, May 27, 2015.

161 **a head start:** Wayne Ma and Ben Fritz, "China's Tough-Talking Theme-Park Mogul Surrenders to Minnie Mouse," *Wall Street Journal*, July 20, 2017.

162 **controlled $660 million:** Ben Fritz, "Hollywood's New Backer: China," *Wall Street Journal*, July 25, 2015.

162 **self-driving cars:** Author interview with Zhang Zhou, November 10, 2015.

162 **"This is really":** Ben Fritz, *The Big Picture: The Fight for the Future of Movies* (New York: Houghton Mifflin Harcourt, 2018), 218.

162 **approved a sequel:** *Pacific Rim: Uprising*, directed by Steven S. DeKnight (Universal City, CA; Universal Pictures, 2018).

163 **a record $24 million:** Erich Schwartzel, "'Warcraft' Deal Sets Record for Streaming Video in China," *Wall Street Journal*, August 18, 2016.

164 **"We want films":** Amy Qin and Audrey Carlsen, "How China Is Rewriting Its Own Script," *New York Times*, November 18, 2018.

164 **a forty-acre entertainment and retail campus:** Renderings of DreamWorks Animation's Shanghai Dream Center, *Variety*, March 20, 2014.

164 **"Frankly speaking":** Xu Jing, "Meet the Man Behind Screen Hit Animation Monkey King," *China Daily*, July 31, 2015.

164 **factored into major decisions:** Erich Schwartzel and Laurie Burkitt, "'Kung Fu Panda 3' Aims to Kick-Start Chinese Studio," *Wall Street Journal*, January 26, 2016.

165 **grabbed the extra Oscar:** Author interview with Hawk Koch, October 7, 2019.

167 **Wang had his eye:** Author interviews with former Wanda employees, July 31, 2019.

168 **"It is the beginning":** Malcolm Moore, "Welcome to Chollywood," *Telegraph*, September 24, 2013.

168 **"I am hoping":** Moore, "Welcome to Chollywood."

168 **promised the world:** Clifford Coonan, "China's Wanda Unveils $8.2 Billion Movie Fund as Hollywood A-Listers Lend Support," *Hollywood Reporter*, September 21, 2013.

168 **biggest sound stage:** Dinny McMahon, "The Wanda Warning," *The Wire China*, June 28, 2020.

168 **the real moneymakers:** Descriptions based on author visit to Qingdao Movie Metropolis, January 2020.

169 **pouring cheap wine:** Author interview with Lopez.

169 **"foreign propaganda influence":** Erich Schwartzel, "Congressman Calls for Review of Wanda Group's Hollywood Ambitions," *Wall Street Journal*, October 7, 2016.

170 **"dream factory":** Hortense Powdermaker, *Hollywood: The Dream Factory* (Boston: Little, Brown and Company, 1950).

170 **axed a movie:** Author interview with Hope Boonshaft, December 22, 2018.

170 **underreporting American grosses:** Wayne Ma, "Hollywood Finds Chinese Cinemas Fudging Box-Office Figures," *Wall Street Journal*, October 3, 2017.

171 **noticed their ticket stubs:** Lilian Lin and Laurie Burkitt, "China's Movie Executives Cry Foul over Propaganda Film's Box-Office Success," *Wall Street Journal*, September 9, 2015.

171 **Xinke New Materials was going to buy:** Patrick Frater, "Chinese Metals Firm Xinke Buys Voltage Pictures for $345 Million," *Variety*, November 13, 2016.

171 **a deal spearheaded:** Author interview with Rob Moore, July 21, 2020.

171 **about a third of that:** Erich Schwartzel and Wayne Ma, "Dalian Wanda's Dick Clark Deal Hits Hurdle," *Wall Street Journal*, February 21, 2017.

171 **would be barred:** Author interview with Hollywood Foreign Press Association member, 2017.

172 **ordered a twist ending:** Erich Schwartzel, Kane Wu, and Wayne Ma, "Hollywood Is Left Hanging as China Reins In Investments," *Wall Street Journal*, February 24, 2017.

172 **the acquisition was canceled:** Wayne Ma and Kane Wu, "Chinese Metals Manufacturer Scraps Bid for Hollywood Production Company," *Wall Street Journal*, December 22, 2016.

172 **That would be dead:** Anita Busch, "Millennium Films' Deal with China's Recon Now 'Dead,' Says Avi Lerner," *Deadline*, August 31, 2017.

172 **fall 79 percent:** "China Issues Guidelines on Curbing Outbound Investment," Dow Jones Newswires, August 18, 2017.

172 **looking for the cash:** Erich Schwartzel, "Paramount Working to Keep Film-Financing Deal on Track," *Wall Street Journal*, March 16, 2017.

173 **drove Zhang across town:** Author interview with Jonah Greenberg, October 20, 2020.

174 **"How do I look":** Erich Schwartzel, "As 'The Great Wall' Hits Theaters in China, Hollywood Is Watching," *Wall Street Journal*, December 15, 2016.

175 **"white savior" narrative:** Graeme McMillan, "Constance Wu on 'The Great Wall': 'Our Heroes Don't Look Like Matt Damon," *Hollywood Reporter*, July 29, 2016.

175 **personally barred China's:** Lingling Wei and Chao Deng, "Xi's Sign-Off Deals Blow to China Inc.'s Global Spending Spree," *Wall Street Journal*, July 23, 2017.

175 **"When private entrepreneurs":** Wei and Deng, "Xi's Sign-Off Deals."

175 **"the O Project":** Wayne Ma and Erich Schwartzel, "This Billionaire Had an Oscar Dream, but His Hollywood Ending Was Spoiled by China," *Wall Street Journal*, October 4, 2017.

176 **facilities in Qingdao:** Wayne Ma, "Chinese Billionaire Scales Down His Hollywood Dreams," *Wall Street Journal*, July 27, 2017.

176 **faded but still visible:** Author visit to Qingdao.

CHAPTER 10

177 **he spent much of his life:** Author interview with Tang through researcher Ann Cao, September 2020.

178 **ninth-busiest airport:** Katia Hetter, "This Is the World's Busiest Airport," CNN .com, September 16, 2019.

178 **Confetti blasted across:** David Barboza and Brooks Barnes, "How China Won the Keys to Disney's Magic Kingdom," *New York Times*, June 14, 2016.

179 **More than 1,200 tombs:** "Shanghai Disney Park to Be Built on Graveyard: State Media," *Independent*, December 20, 2009.

179 **biggest of any Disney castle:** Author interview with Walt Disney Imagineering president Bob Weis at U.S.-Asia Entertainment Summit, Los Angeles, November 5, 2019.

181 **"acting in much the same way"**: Aynne Kokas, *Hollywood Made in China* (Oakland: University of California Press, 2017), 50–51.

181 **saw two objectives**: Author interviews with former Disney executives, March 2017 and December 2017.

182 **"What is the root cause"**: Fox Butterfield, *China: Alive in the Bitter Sea* (New York: Bantam, 1982), 200.

182 **immersed in the Disney way**: Author interview with Ivan Encinas, June 2019.

185 **called it whitewashing**: Alyssa Sage, "Marvel Responds to 'Doctor Strange' 'Whitewashing' Criticisms over Tilda Swinton Casting," *Variety*, April 27, 2016.

185 **"The Ancient One was a racist"**: "Exclusive! Doctor Strange Writer C. Robert Cargill—Double Toasted Interview," https://www.youtube.com/watch?v=PlKC2NeWaQM.

186 **found *Iron Man* by accident**: Author interview with Lawrence Zhao through Cao.

189 **storm troopers stand in formation**: Nancy Groves, "500 Star Wars Stormtroopers March on Great Wall of China in Epic Disney Event," *Guardian*, October 21, 2015.

190 **they shrank Boyega's image**: Author interviews with former Disney executive, 2019.

190 **Roffman started interviewing fans**: Author interview with Howard Roffman, December 4, 2019.

191 **"I know nothing"**: Dan Jolin, "Rogue One: A Star Wars Story—the Complete History, Part II," *Empire*, December 13, 2016.

192 **"In America, people like you"**: *Ip Man 4: The Finale*, directed by Wilson Yip (Hong Kong: Mandarin Motion Pictures, 2019).

193 **"I suggest that we"**: Barboza and Barnes, "How China Won the Keys."

194 **I visited Shanghai Disneyland**: Author visit to Shanghai Disneyland, June 2019.

194 **eleven million visitors**: Themed Entertainment Association, "Global Attractions Attendance Report," 2019, https://www.aecom.com/wp-content/uploads/2019/05/Theme-Index-2018-4.pdf.

196 **"I think being"**: Author interview with Tang through Cao.

CHAPTER 11

197 **Michael Douglas quit**: Marilyn Beck and Stacy Jenel Smith, "Illnesses Plague Cast and Crew of 'Island' Production," *Los Angeles Daily News*, March 2, 1995.

197 **crew got food poisoning**: Beck and Smith, "Illnesses Plague Cast and Crew."

197 PIRATE MOVIE'S SO BAD: Rod Dreher, "Pirate Movie's So Bad, It Should Cut Its Own Throat," *Sun-Sentinel* (Ft. Lauderdale), December 22, 1995.

197 **The life Harlin had constructed**: Author interview with Renny Harlin, November 2017.

199 **Western crew members noticed**: Author interviews with *The Great Wall* crew members, November and December 2016.

199 **"A man of my stature"**: Author interview with Bruce Feirstein, June 2, 2020; Bruce Feirstein, "The Dawn of the Chinese Blockbuster," *Strategy + Business*, July 23, 2019.

200 **"on no account"**: Mao Zedong, "Talks at the Yenan Forum on Literature and Art," May 2, 1942, translation by Maoist Documentation Project, https://www.marxists.org/reference/archive/mao/selected-works/volume-3/mswv3_08.htm.

200 she learned a dialectic: Author interview with Ellen Eliasoph, March 3, 2020.

201 He arrived on the set: This and other details taken from author's time with Harlin in Huairou in November 2017.

201 "Renny has prestigious": Author interview with Peggy Pu, November 2017.

203 "China boasts a long": Ryan Nakashima, "China Woos Hollywood Studios with Film Fund," Associated Press, March 7, 2012.

203 a fracking company: Jim Fuquay, "FTS Announces China Joint Venture with Sinopec," *Fort Worth Star-Telegram*, June 10, 2014.

203 flagship 787 Dreamliner: David Barboza, Christopher Drew, and Steve Lohr, "G.E. to Share Jet Technology with China in New Joint Venture," *New York Times*, January 17, 2011.

203 share with a local Chinese firm: Keith Bradsher, "G.M.'s Electric Car Push Could Put China in the Driver's Seat," *New York Times*, January 29, 2021.

204 "Can I tell": Erich Schwartzel, "China Wants to Beat the U.S. in Movies. So It Turned to the Guy Who Made 'Die Hard 2,'" *Wall Street Journal*, December 28, 2017.

205 Ming left his job: Author interview with Ming Peng, November 2017.

205 "It's not easy": Author interview with Yang Zi, November 2017.

206 "You know, James": Author interview with James Schamus, August 17, 2020.

207 "This is an action-adventure film": Steven Smith, "Born in Finland but Banned There," *Los Angeles Times*, February 10, 1986.

208 "Tall Director and Actress": "Tall Director and Actress to Become Tall Newlyweds," *Orlando Sentinel*, July 10, 1993.

208 "He got hit": Schwartzel, "China Wants to Beat the U.S."

209 "I'm sorry": Author interview with Jean-Jacques Annaud, February 8, 2019.

211 "Due to the lack": James Tager, "Made in Hollywood, Censored by Beijing," *PEN America*, August 5, 2020.

212 "What would we think": Jonathan Landreth, "Time Heals an Old Wound," *Los Angeles Times*, June 16, 2012.

212 The movie had followed: *Bodies at Rest*, directed by Renny Harlin (Beijing: Wanda Media, 2019).

214 "The number of 'fate' stories": Author interview with Feirstein; Feirstein, "Dawn of the Chinese Blockbuster."

CHAPTER 12

217 Mel Gibson movie *The Patriot*: Author interview with a Sony Pictures executive, 2020.

218 "worth a whole regiment": Ben Urwand, *The Collaboration: Hollywood's Pact with Hitler* (Cambridge, MA: Belknap Press of Harvard University Press, 2013), 226.

219 became an immediate phenomenon: Patrick Frater, "China Box Office: 'Wolf Warriors [*sic*] 2' Tops Global Rankings with $127 Million Debut," *Variety*, July 30, 2017.

221 "There's our hero!": *Wolf Warrior 2*, directed by Wu Jing (Beijing: Beijing Culture, 2017).

222 "It feels good": Chris Buckley, "In China, an Action Hero Beats Box Office Records (and Arrogant Westerners)," *New York Times*, August 16, 2017.

223 **"after more than one hundred"**: François Bougon, *Inside the Mind of Xi Jinping* (London: Hurst, 2018), 25.

223 **"never forget national humiliation"**: Jonathan Kaufman, "Are Hong Kong Protests a Preview of China's Uncertain Future?," *Boston Globe*, September 6, 2019.

223 **"perfect mold"**: Joan Didion, *Slouching Towards Bethlehem* (New York: Farrar, Straus and Giroux, 1968), 31.

223 **"Why do only foreign nations"**: Anthony Kuhn, "Chinese Blockbuster 'Wolf Warrior 2' Mixes Jingoism with Hollywood Heroism," *All Things Considered*, August 10, 2017.

223 **born in Beijing**: "An Actor Prepares: From China's Rambo to Sci-fi Blockbuster," *People's Daily*, February 25, 2019.

223 **a second mortgage**: Rebecca Sun, "Meet the Director Behind China's Highest-Grossing Film of All Time," *Hollywood Reporter*, December 8, 2017.

224 **When it was founded**: Rebecca Davis, "Beijing Culture Blasts Off in China by Backing Hits like 'The Wandering Earth,'" *Variety*, May 9, 2019.

224 **As thanks to Beijing Culture**: Author interviews with executives familiar with the matter, 2020.

224 **"Though we should learn"**: "An Actor Prepares."

225 **"Just imagine what that"**: "Wu Jing, Reeves Could Join 'Hobbs & Shaw' Sequel," China.org, August 8, 2019.

226 **Gralapp started to notice**: Author interview with Michael Gralapp, August 15, 2020.

228 **"hero's journey" template**: Joseph Campbell, *The Hero with a Thousand Faces* (Princeton, NJ: Princeton University Press, 1949).

228 **"private, unrecognized, rudimentary"**: Campbell, *Hero with a Thousand Faces*, 4.

229 **China's wealthiest man**: Russell Flannery, "Alibaba's Jack Ma Overtakes Wang Jianlin as China's Richest Man," *Forbes*, May 14, 2017.

230 **Wei grew up**: Author interview with Wei Zhang, August 26, 2020.

231 **offered a better shot**: Brook Larmer, "Home at Last," *Newsweek*, July 30, 2000.

233 **"Some of the things"**: Chris Lee, "Why *Crazy Rich Asians* Flopped in China," *Vulture*, December 4, 2018.

235 **Amblin raked in**: Erich Schwartzel and Ben Fritz, "Why 'A Dog's Purpose' Soared in China While 'Lego Batman' Flopped," *Wall Street Journal*, June 19, 2017.

236 **"How do we come up"**: Author attendance at Chinese Film Industry Summit at 22nd Shanghai International Film Festival, June 16, 2019.

237 **The shooting scripts**: Author visit to Shanghai International Film Festival, 2019.

CHAPTER 13

241 **Not content to live**: Author interview with Paula Dvorchak, June 27, 2019.

242 **total button revenue**: National Pearl Button Museum, located in Muscatine, Iowa, https://muscatinehistory.org.

243 **an exchange program**: Kyle Munson, "Italian Convinced Xi of Iowa's Greatness," *Des Moines Register*, December 9, 2016.

243 "Come to America": Author interview with Sarah Lande, December 1, 2019.

243 joined the Communist Party from jail: Evan Osnos, "Born Red," *New Yorker*, March 30, 2015.

244 read by night: Jeremy Page, "How the U.S. Misread China's Xi: Hoping for a Globalist, It Got an Autocrat," *Wall Street Journal*, December 23, 2020.

244 "you had to act": "Cultural Revolution Demons Haunt Chinese Billionaire Huang Nubo," Agence France-Presse, May 16, 2016.

244 an Iowa boy in the 1980s: Author interview with Paula Dvorchak; author interview with Gary Dvorchak, June 2, 2019.

245 "It was *American Graffiti*": Author interview with Bill Maeglin, June 1, 2019.

245 The Long John Silver's: Kirk Johnson, "For the Vice President of China, Tea Time in Iowa," *New York Times*, February 15, 2012.

246 interior design has been maintained: Author visit to Muscatine, November 2019.

246 When another Muscatine guest: Author interview with Lande.

247 "The cave-houses": François Bougon, *Inside the Mind of Xi Jinping* (London: Hurst, 2018), 61.

247 "Winnie the Pooh": Tatiana Siegel, "Disney's 'Christopher Robin' Won't Get China Release amid Pooh Crackdown (Exclusive)," *Hollywood Reporter*, August 3, 2018.

248 "In one part of the world": Peter Frankopan, *The New Silk Roads: The Present and Future of the World* (London: Bloomsbury, 2018), 42.

248 nearly 80 percent: Liu Jia and Du Simeng, "The Research Report on Chinese Film Industry," China Film Association, Film Art Center of China Federation of Literacy and Art Circles, 2018, https://www.mpa-apac.org/wp-content/uploads/2018/10/2018-Research -Report-on-Chinese-Film-Industry.pdf.

249 leaving a screening: Author interview with Jonah Greenberg, October 17, 2020.

250 He had been summoned: "Galloping Horse CEO's Death Linked to China Corruption Probe (Report)," *Hollywood Reporter*, January 31, 2014.

250 "We must make patriotism": "Xi Jinping's Talks at the Beijing Forum on Literature and Art," China Copyright and Media, posted October 16, 2014, https:// chinacopyrightandmedia.wordpress.com/2014/10/16/xi-jinpings-talks-at-the-beijing -forum-on-literature-and-art.

251 approved TV shows and movies: Phoebe Zhang and Oasis Li, "No Period Dramas or Pop Idols: Chinese Censors Say Patriotic Shows Must Mark 70th Anniversary of People's Republic," *South China Morning Post*, August 1, 2019.

251 "alleviate the problem": iQIYI Inc., "iQIYI CSR Initiative Uses Film to Enrich Life in Poverty Stricken Areas" (press release), October 11, 2018.

251 taken off streaming sites: Zhang and Li, "No Period Dramas or Pop Idols."

252 was summoned from the set: Author interview with person familiar with the situation, 2020.

252 "We will seek friendship": "Full Text: 2017 Donald Trump Inauguration Speech Transcript," *Politico*, January 20, 2017, https://www.politico.com/story/2017/01/full-text -donald-trump-inauguration-speech-transcript-233907.

252 **"Many people feel":** "Full Text: Xi Jinping's Keynote Speech at the World Economic Forum," Xinhua, April 6, 2017, http://www.china.org.cn/node_7247529/content_40569136.htm.

253 **an inevitable clash:** Graham Allison, *Destined for War: Can America and China Escape Thucydides's Trap?* (New York: Houghton Mifflin Harcourt, 2017).

253 **Steelworkers and teamsters:** Charles Hutzler and Naomi Koppel, "China, U.S. Sign Breakthrough Trade Deal," Associated Press, November 15, 1999.

253 **Trump performed best:** Andrea Cerrato, Francesco Ruggieri, and Federico Maria Ferrara, "Trump Won in Counties That Lost Jobs to China and Mexico," *Washington Post*, December 2, 2016.

254 **"erode norms, such as":** Daniel R. Coats, "Worldwide Threat Assessment of the U.S. Intelligence Community," Senate Select Committee on Intelligence, January 29, 2019, https://www.dni.gov/files/ODNI/documents/2019-ATA-SFR---SSCI.pdf.

254 **canceled meetings with Mongolian officials:** "China Cancels Mongolia Talks Indefinitely After Dalai Lama's Visit," *Bloomberg*, November 26, 2016.

254 **"We hope that Mongolia":** "Mongolia Pledges to Halt Visits by the Dalai Lama," *Bloomberg*, December 22, 2016.

254 **Construction has since begun:** David Stanway, "Mongolia Plans Coal Rail Link to China by 2021: Official," Reuters, November 8, 2018.

255 **"We Chinese often say":** Jamil Anderlini, "Interview: 'We Say, If You Want to Get Rich, Build Roads First,'" *Financial Times*, September 25, 2018.

255 **"All roads used to":** Frankopan, *New Silk Roads*, 117.

255 **in a 2011 speech:** Frankopan, *New Silk Roads*, 91.

255 **"the Baskin-Robbins of partnerships":** Jonathan Hillman, "Opinion: A Chinese World Order," *Washington Post*, July 23, 2018.

256 **"central nervous system":** Frankopan, *New Silk Roads*.

256 **handed over a gold mine:** Eiji Furukawa, "Belt and Road Debt Trap Spreads to Central Asia," *Nikkei Asia*, August 29, 2018.

256 **angry editorial in Angola:** Frankopan, *New Silk Roads*, 126.

257 **"people-to-people bond":** Erich Schwartzel, "China Recreates the Silk Road to Challenge Hollywood," *Wall Street Journal*, December 27, 2017.

258 **more than thirty countries:** Schwartzel, "China Recreates the Silk Road."

CHAPTER 14

260 **With cameras rolling:** Author interviews with people familiar with the situation, summer 2020.

261 **Both were contracts:** May Jeong, "The Big Error Was That She Was Caught," *Vanity Fair*, March 26, 2019.

262 **pull a promotional campaign:** Karen Chu, "'Lust, Caution' Actress Banned in China," *Hollywood Reporter*, March 9, 2008.

262 "residential surveillance": Nectar Gan, Xie Yu, and Jun Mai, "Chinese Actress Fan Bingbing Tells Fans She Is 'Ashamed, Guilty' as She Gets US$129 Million Tax Bill," *South China Morning Post*, October 3, 2018.

262 "The most unfortunate thing": Hannah Beech, "How China Is Remaking the Global Film Industry," *Time*, January 26, 2017.

263 "I don't need to marry": Jeong, "Big Error Was That She Was Caught."

263 "little more than": James Marsh, "Film Review: Sky Hunter—Real-Life Couple Li Chen, Fan Bingbing in Chinese Military Propaganda," *South China Morning Post*, October 17, 2017.

263 "The creation of art": "Xi Jinping's Talks at the Beijing Forum on Literature and Art," *China Copyright and Media*, posted October 16, 2014, https://chinacopyrightandmedia .wordpress.com/2014/10/16/xi-jinpings-talks-at-the-beijing-forum-on-literature-and-art.

264 "Giant Baby": Jackie Chan with Zhu Mo, *Never Grow Up* (New York: Gallery Books, 2018), 2.

264 access to milk and bread: Chan with Zhu, *Never Grow Up*, 28.

264 "Bruce Lee is superhuman": Chan with Zhu, *Never Grow Up*, 79.

265 that annual figure has shrunk: Celine Ge, "It's Fade Out for Hong Kong's Film Industry as China Moves into the Spotlight," *South China Morning Post*, July 28, 2017.

265 In real life: Peter Frankopan, *The New Silk Roads: The Present and Future of the World* (London: Bloomsbury, 2018), 127–34.

266 Such realities are of no: *Kung Fu Yoga*, directed by Stanley Tong (Beijing: Shinework Media, 2017).

266 "The movies have great power": Author interview with Oleg Stepchenko, June 16, 2019.

267 Beijing had sent thirty jets: Colin Dwyer, "Russia Prepares 300,000 Troops for Its Largest War Games in Nearly 4 Decades," *National Public Radio*, August 29, 2018.

267 Russian ice cream: "Russia's Putin Gives China's Xi Ice Cream on His 66th Birthday," Reuters, June 15, 2019.

267 The pandering in *Kung Fu Yoga*: Suparna Dutt D'Cunha, "Why Indian-Chinese Venture 'Kung Fu Yoga' Failed to Impress Bollywood," *Forbes*, February 6, 2017.

267 "It praises the virtues": CCTV 2018–2019 Chinese TV Program, acquired by reporter at Hong Kong International Film Festival in 2019.

267 a beloved Czech character: "Panda to Join Little Mole in New Cartoon Series," *China Daily*, March 28, 2016.

268 became the first movie: "Pakistan's Parwaaz Hai Junoon Premiers [*sic*] in China," *News International* (Pakistan), November 12, 2020.

268 dubbed Chinese dramas: Mahmoud Fouly, "Dubbing Chinese Drama Helps Introduce Chinese Culture to Arab World," *China Daily*, February 18, 2019.

268 one hundred mini episodes: "4K Micro-documentary 'Chang'an Meets Rome' to Debut in China Thursday," *CGTN*, January 30, 2020.

268 "responds to the call": Rebecca Davis, "China to Remake Classic Balkan Films as Part of Diplomatic Charm Offensive," *Variety*, May 9, 2019.

268 a new subway system: Snezana Bjelotomic, "Chinese Company to Build Belgrade Subway," SerbianMonitor.com, April 24, 2019.

269 "We looked at one": Julie Makinen, "'Monster Hunt,' a Monster Hit in China, Was a Scary Journey for Director Raman Hui," *Los Angeles Times*, July 31, 2015.

270 Chan's responses to my questions: Author interview with Jackie Chan, January 24, 2019.

270 "cursed generation": Emanuele Berry and Ira Glass, "Umbrellas Down," *This American Life*, July 10, 2020.

271 "Fight for Freedom": Scott Neuman, "Houston Rockets GM Apologizes for Tweet Supporting Hong Kong Protesters," NPR, October 7, 2019.

271 decades of business-building: James T. Areddy and Ben Cohen, "The NBA's New Normal in China," *Wall Street Journal*, October 25, 2019.

271 "misinformed": William Mauldin and Ben Cohen, "Pence Slams NBA, Nike over China Stance," *Wall Street Journal*, October 24, 2019.

271 "We feel greatly disappointed": Jeff Zillgitt, "NBA Statements on Hong Kong Tweet Different in English and Chinese," *USA Today*, October 7, 2019.

272 "Damned if you do": Robert Iger, interview with Matt Murray, *WSJ Tech Live*, October 22, 2019.

272 lambasted the league: Sylvan Lane, "Ocasio-Cortez, Ted Cruz Join Colleagues Blasting NBA for 'Outrageous' Response to China," *The Hill*, October 9, 2019.

273 that included prepping: Author interview with Sophia Shek, July 10, 2020.

275 "safeguard the sovereignty": The Government of the Hong Kong Special Administrative Region, "Amendments to Guidelines for Censors Under Film Censorship Ordinance" (press release), June 11, 2021, https://www.info.gov.hk/gia/general/202106/11/P2021061100239.htm.

275 "There are definitely movies": Tatiana Siegel, "Richard Gere's Studio Exile: Why His Hollywood Career Took an Indie Turn," *Hollywood Reporter*, April 18, 2017.

276 "If you could": Author interview with former Warner Bros. executive, August 4, 2020.

276 Xi transferred oversight: Chris Buckley, "China Gives Communist Party More Control over Policy and Media," *New York Times*, March 21, 2018.

277 "I really hope that one day": Ko Yu-hao, Chung Chih-kai, and Sherry Hsiao, "Winner's Golden Horse Speech Leads to Protests, Support," *Taipei Times*, November 19, 2018.

278 Phones started vibrating: Author interviews with several attendees, 2020.

278 "Film and TV work": Rebecca Davis, "China's Top Brass Says Stricter Film, TV Censorship 'Will Be the Norm,'" *Variety*, June 6, 2019.

279 "distorting social values": Jeong, "Big Error Was That She Was Caught."

279 "China cannot miss out": Jeong, "Big Error Was That She Was Caught."

279 "integrate the party's achievements": Marrian Zhou, "China Movie Studio Embraces Communist Party as Industry Turns Red," *Nikkei Asian Review*, July 14, 2019.

280 stick to certain themes: Marrian Zhou, "Embattled Chinese Studio Hops on Belt and Road Bandwagon," *Nikkei Asian Review*, August 7, 2019.

280 in front of a green screen: Author interview with person familiar with the situation, 2020.

CHAPTER 15

281 **the air force veteran:** Author correspondence with Nathaniel Boyd.

281 **a successful Chinese sharpshooter:** Huang Lanlan, "Zhang Yimou to Direct 'Sharpshooter' Film Commemorating 70th Anniversary of Korean War," *Global Times*, October 9, 2020.

281 **"With historical facts":** Lanlan, "Zhang Yimou to Direct 'Sharpshooter' Film."

282 **dust off their library titles:** Sophia Yang, "China to Film Anti-American Movies to Mark 70th Anniversary of Korean War," *Taiwan News*, August 4, 2020.

282 **began reairing:** Iris Zhao and Alan Weedon, "Chinese Television Suddenly Switches Scheduling to Anti-American Films amid US-China Trade War," *ABC* (Australian Broadcasting Corporation), May 20, 2019.

282 **"Safe to say":** Author interview with China-based postproduction worker, 2019.

283 **"In another fifteen years":** Author interview with China-based professional, September 14, 2020.

284 LABOR STRIKE CAUSES: *The Wandering Earth*, directed by Frant Gwo (Beijing: Beijing Culture, 2019).

285 **"Today, we're finally realizing":** Michael R. Pompeo, "The China Challenge," remarks delivered at the Hudson Institute's Herman Kahn Award Gala, New York, October 30, 2019, https://sv.usembassy.gov/secretary-pompeo-the-china-challenge.

285 **"public enemy of mankind":** Michael R. Gordon and William Mauldin, "Pompeo, Top Chinese Envoy Meet amid Heightened Tensions," *Wall Street Journal*, June 18, 2020.

285 **two thirds of Americans:** Laura Silver, Kat Devlin, and Christine Huang, "Unfavorable Views of China Reach Historic Highs in Many Countries," Pew Research Center, October 6, 2020, https://www.pewresearch.org/global/2020/10/06/unfavorable-views-of -china-reach-historic-highs-in-many-countries.

285 **wooed by the campaign:** Philip Wen and Drew Hinshaw, "China Asserts Claim to Global Leadership, Mask by Mask," *Wall Street Journal*, April 1, 2020.

286 **Paraguay's foreign ministry:** Emma Graham-Harrison, "China Denies Offer of 'Vaccine Diplomacy' Deal to Paraguay," *Guardian*, March 24, 2021. (Chinese officials denied the charge.)

286 **5G telecommunications technology:** Ernesto Londoño and Letícia Casado, "Brazil Needs Vaccines. China Is Benefiting," *New York Times*, March 15, 2021.

286 **"Almost as soon":** Wen and Hinshaw, "China Asserts Claim to Global Leadership."

286 **revisionist history films:** Ji Yuqiao, "Epidemic-Themed Film and Television Works on the Rise in China," *Global Times*, July 27, 2020.

286 **Vice President Mike Pence:** Vice President Mike Pence, "Remarks on the Administration's Policy Towards China," remarks delivered at the Hudson Institute, Washington, DC, October 4, 2018, https://www.hudson.org/events/1610-vice-president-mike -pence-s-remarks-on-the-administration-s-policy-towards-china102018.

286 **Attorney General William Barr:** Attorney General William P. Barr, "Remarks on China Policy at the Gerald R. Ford Presidential Museum," Grand Rapids, MI, July 16, 2020,

https://www.justice.gov/opa/speech/attorney-general-william-p-barr-delivers-remarks
-china-policy-gerald-r-ford-presidential.

288 **myth's core lesson:** R. T. Watson, "How Disney Enlisted 'Mulan,' a $200 Million
Folktale, to Court China," *Wall Street Journal*, September 2, 2020.

289 **nitpicked historical inaccuracies:** Rebecca Davis, "China Loves New 'Mulan'
Trailer, Except Its Historical Inaccuracies," *Variety*, July 11, 2019.

289 **"special thanks":** Isaac Stone Fish, "Why Disney's New 'Mulan' Is a Scandal," *Washington Post*, September 7, 2020.

289 **"toxicity of religious extremism":** Austin Ramzy and Chris Buckley, "'Absolutely No
Mercy': Leaked Files Expose How China Organized Mass Detention of Muslims," *New
York Times*, November 16, 2019.

290 **"ideological illness":** Sigal Samuel, "China Is Treating Islam like a Mental Illness,"
Atlantic, August 28, 2018.

290 **cannot name their sons:** Javier C. Hernández, "China Bans 'Muhammad' and 'Jihad'
as Baby Names in Heavily Muslim Region," *New York Times*, April 25, 2017.

290 **sing Communist Party anthems:** Gerry Shih, "China's Mass Indoctrination Camps
Evoke Cultural Revolution," Associated Press, May 17, 2018.

290 **reported forced sterilizations:** "China Cuts Uighur Births with IUDs, Abortion,
Sterilization," Associated Press, June 28, 2020.

290 **packaged as weaves and wigs:** Allison Gordon, "13-Ton Shipment of Human Hair,
Likely from Chinese Prisoners, Seized," *CNN*, July 2, 2020.

290 **in state outlets:** "Exclusive: China Bars Media Coverage of Disney's 'Mulan' After
Xinjiang Backlash—Sources," Reuters, September 10, 2020.

290 **most fraught political morasses:** Chun Han Wong and R. T. Watson, "Disney's
'Mulan' Faces Controversy over Filming in China's Xinjiang," *Wall Street Journal*, September 8, 2020.

291 **ambassador to China:** Erich Schwartzel, Ken Thomas, and Emily Glazer, "Disney's
Chairman Robert Iger Is Game for a New Job: U.S. Ambassador to China," *Wall Street
Journal*, December 17, 2020.

292 **"wear the masks":** Chun Han Wong and Chao Deng, "China's 'Wolf Warrior' Diplomats Are Ready to Fight," *Wall Street Journal*, May 19, 2020.

292 **In Germany, Chinese diplomats:** Luke Baker and Robin Emmott, "As China Pushes
Back on Virus, Europe Wakes to 'Wolf Warrior' Diplomacy," Reuters, May 14, 2020.

292 **"low class":** Chirantha Amerasinghe (@chirantha7777), "The low class authoritarian
Chinese government that was a curse to the Chinese people, became a curse to the world.
thats the reality @ChinaEmbSL must understand. #Stand #Against #The #LowClass
#Chinese #Government #lka," Twitter, April 9, 2020, https://twitter.com/chirantha7777
/status/1248158680174006274.

292 **"Total death in #China":** Chinese Embassy in Sri Lanka (@ChinaEmbSL), "You are
right that the 'low class' Chinese government are serving 1.4billion Chinese people, even
the grass root or the 'lowest class' included. Total death in #China #pandemic is 3344
till today, much smaller than your western 'high class' governments. Who are cursed?,"
Twitter, April 9, 2020, https://twitter.com/ChinaEmbSL/status/1248168334899712002.

292 "We will push back": "China's 'Wolf Warrior' Diplomacy Gamble," *Economist*, May 28, 2020.

293 "History proves that": Wong and Deng, "China's 'Wolf Warrior' Diplomats."

293 offered no comments: Author interview with person familiar with the situation, June 29, 2020.

293 "There are still camps": Author interview with Alex Zhang, July 9, 2020.

294 more than thirty Thoroughbreds: Author interview with *Fengshen Trilogy* horse trainer Bill Lawrence, December 2019.

294 her right eye: *Tales of the Teahouse Retold: Investiture of the Gods*, trans. Katherine Liang Chew (Lincoln, NE: Writers Club Press, 2002).

294 "I can't even buy him": Rebecca Davis, "Director Wuershan Wants to Make China's 'Lord of the Rings' with 'Fengshen Trilogy,'" *Variety*, August 14, 2019.

294 Black-and-white headshots: Author visit to Qingdao Movie Metropolis, January 2020.

295 the franchise-building: Author interview with Tyler Lu, January 6, 2020.

296 a tourist attraction: Author interviews with *Fengshen Trilogy* crew members, January 7, 2020.

CHAPTER 16

299 a gift from China: Author interview with Nicholas Nkukuu, January 20, 2020.

300 was harvesting maize: Author interview with Brian Letayian, January 20, 2020.

302 helped raise Kenya's debt: Allan Olingo, "IMF Raises Kenya's Debt Risk to Medium but Remains Cautious," *East African*, October 31, 2018.

303 "the only person standing there": Elliot Smith, "The US-China Trade Rivalry Is Underway in Africa, and Washington Is Playing Catch-Up," *CNBC*, October 9, 2019.

303 massive $60 billion: Norimitsu Onishi, "China Pledges $60 Billion to Aid Africa's Development," *New York Times*, December 4, 2015.

304 "win-win cooperation": Xi Jinping, "Open a New Era of China-Africa Win-Win Cooperation and Common Development," remarks at the Forum on China-Africa Cooperation, Johannesburg, December 4, 2015.

304 granted such a clearance: Jenni Marsh, "How China Is Slowly Expanding Its Power in Africa, One TV Set at a Time," *CNN Business*, July 24, 2019.

304 $8 million in additional funding: Marsh, "How China Is Slowly Expanding Its Power."

305 eventually bought a color set: Author interviews with John, Lily, and Amos Rutto, January 18, 2020.

305 fills nine rows: Author interview with Leonard Biegon, January 18, 2020.

306 "What I love": Author interview with Caleb Lang'at, January 18, 2020.

306 "I wanted to visit America": Author interview with Milton Kemboi, January 18, 2020.

307 Hers broke down: Author interviews with Roseline Chepkwony and Mercy Chemutai Chepkwony, January 18, 2020.

307 "To achieve the great promise": U.S. Department of State et al., "U.S. Government Investments in Kisii County" (brochure), https://www.usaid.gov/sites/default/files/documents/1860/Kisii_Brochure.pdf.

308 **"The Western theory":** Tom Baxter, "Dreams and Infrastructure—Common Destiny, the First Belt and Road Movie," *Panda Paw Dragon Claw*, November 13, 2019.

308 **"People don't eat freedom":** Author interview with Ezekiel Mutua, January 21, 2020.

308 **dance around the dish:** Author interview with Jeremy Saitoti, January 20, 2020.

309 **"I watch a lot":** Author interview with Grace Waithera, January 18, 2020.

310 **Before the TVs arrived:** Author interviews with Immaculate Wanjiku and Ann Sanaipei, January 18, 2020.

310 **updates on the pandemic:** "China's StarTimes Launches New TV Program in Kenya to Help Fight COVID-19 Pandemic," Xinhua, March 25, 2020.

310 **When Kenyan schoolchildren:** Molly Wasonga, "StarTimes Launches a Homeschooling Program for Students," *CIO East Africa*, April 6, 2020.

310 **In the summer of 2021:** "China's StarTimes Announces Short Video Contest to Showcase BRI Projects in Africa," Xinhua, July 13, 2021.

311 **"Jet Li!":** Author interview with Lucky Njoroge, January 18, 2020.

312 **"the only ones":** Author interview with Charity Kishooyian, January 18, 2020.

314 **"addressing contemporary native subjects":** Brian Larkin, *Signal and Noise: Media, Infrastructure, and Urban Culture in Nigeria* (Durham, NC, and London: Duke University Press, 2008), 53.

314 **boost crowd numbers:** Larkin, *Signal and Noise*, 48–49.

314 **boring but safe endorsements:** Larkin, *Signal and Noise*, 59.

315 **most popular soap operas:** Author interview with Dani Madrid-Morales, November 11, 2019.

315 **"presents an array":** Dani Madrid-Morales, "Soft Power in the Living Room: A Survey of Television Drama on CCTV's Foreign-Language Channels," in *Screening China's Soft Power*, ed. Paola Voci and Luo Hui (London: Routledge, 2017), 45.

315 **"the importance of conforming":** Madrid-Morales, "Soft Power in the Living Room."

316 **paying to dub:** Author interviews with audiovisual and dubbing firm Hiventy employees Gladys Mwita, Philip Obwogi, and Juliette Vivier, January 20, 2020.

317 **"If you want":** Author interview with Ezekiel Mutua, January 21, 2020.

319 **"laced with retrogressive":** Jennifer Anyango, "Film Board Bans Six TV Programs 'for Promoting Homosexuality,'" *Standard* (Kenya), June 15, 2017.

319 **called for the arrest:** Eyder Peralta, "Kenya's Censorship King: Head of Film Board Accused of Overstepping," *All Things Considered*, February 22, 2017.

319 **"clear intent to promote":** Tom Odula, "Kenya Bans 1st Cannes-Bound Feature Film over 'Lesbianism,'" Associated Press, April 27, 2018.

EPILOGUE

321 **sat three rows:** Author interview with Zhang Jing, October 24, 2020.

321 **reached $1.998 billion:** Patrick Brzeski, "It's Official: China Overtakes North America as World's Biggest Box Office in 2020," *Hollywood Reporter*, October 18, 2020.

325 **top-performing American show:** Shefali S. Kulkarni, "China Can't Get Enough of 'House of Cards' and That Scares Washington," *The World*, March 4, 2015.

325 **sees no future:** Kevin Stankiewicz, "Netflix's Reed Hastings: 'We Have Not Been Spending Any Time' Trying to Get into China," *CNBC*, September 9, 2020.

325 **theater chain in the world:** Erich Schwartzel, "AMC's Deal for Carmike Cinemas Boosts Chinese Control of U.S. Theaters," *Wall Street Journal*, March 4, 2016.

325 **enough cash to:** Alexander Gladstone and Erich Schwartzel, "AMC Entertainment Lenders Hire Lawyers for Restructuring Talks," *Wall Street Journal*, April 1, 2020.

326 **drove AMC shares:** Jacky Wong, "AMC and Wanda's Unlikely Happy Ending," *Wall Street Journal*, May 24, 2021.

326 **"The two things":** Ben Smith, "Apple TV Was Making a Show About Gawker. Then Tim Cook Found Out," *New York Times*, December 13, 2020.

327 **iPhone sales in China:** Tim Higgins, "Apple's iPhone 12 Helped Deliver a Record $111.4 Billion Quarter," *Wall Street Journal*, January 27, 2021.

327 **Shanghai flagship store:** Tianwei Zhang, "Louis Vuitton's Biggest Shanghai Store Sees Record-High $22M in August Sales: Sources," *Women's Wear Daily*, August 24, 2020.

327 **Tesla more than doubled:** Evelyn Cheng, "Tesla's China Sales More Than Doubled in 2020," *CNBC*, February 8, 2021.

327 **recovered faster in China:** Heather Haddon, "Starbucks Sales Slide but Show Signs of Recovery in China," *Wall Street Journal*, January 26, 2021.

327 **Nike reported sales:** Khadeeja Safdar, "Nike Powers Through Pandemic with Digital Push," *Wall Street Journal*, December 18, 2020.

327 **thanks to 5G contracts:** Callum Keown, "Ericsson Stock Jumps as 5G Success in China Boosts Earnings. There's More to Come," *Barron's*, October 21, 2020.

327 **employee at Marriott:** Brendan Dorsey, "Marriott Employee Fired After Liking Tweet That Offended Chinese Government," *Points Guy*, March 5, 2018.

327 **searched for "dictator":** Sam Biddle, "Shutterstock Employees Fight Company's New Chinese Search Blacklist," *The Intercept*, November 6, 2019.

327 **"Although we deleted":** Sui-Lee Wee, "Mercedes-Benz Quotes the Dalai Lama. China Notices. Apology Follows," *New York Times*, February 6, 2018.

328 **"almost too good":** Joe Miller, "Daimler Chief Hails 'V-Shaped' Recovery in China Car Sales," *Financial Times*, December 2, 2020.

329 **became the front-runner:** Amy Qin and Amy Chang Chien, "In China, a Backlash Against the Chinese-Born Director of 'Nomadland,'" *New York Times*, March 25, 2021.

329 **successfully lobbied** *Filmmaker***:** Patrick Brzeski and Tatiana Siegel, "From Deal Frenzy to Decoupling: Is the China-Hollywood Romance Officially Over?," *Hollywood Reporter*, May 21, 2021.

329 **as if the Oscars had not been held:** Liza Lin, "China Censors 'Nomadland' Director Chloé Zhao's Oscar Win," *Wall Street Journal*, April 26, 2021.

330 **a more intense crackdown:** Interviews with China-based executives, May 2021.

330 **"strong" film power:** Rebecca Davis, "China Aims to Become 'Strong Film Power' like U.S. by 2035, Calls for More Patriotic Films," *Variety*, March 3, 2019.

330 **"standing up":** Peter Frankopan, *The New Silk Roads: The Present and Future of the World* (London: Bloomsbury, 2018), 147–48.

331 **Summit of Democracies:** Bob Davis and Lingling Wei, "Biden Plans to Build a Grand Alliance to Counter China. It Won't Be Easy," *Wall Street Journal*, January 6, 2021.

BIBLIOGRAPHY

Berry, Chris, and Mary Farquhar. *China on Screen: Cinema and Nation.* New York: Columbia University Press, 2006.

Bougon, François. *Inside the Mind of Xi Jinping.* London: Hurst, 2018.

Butterfield, Fox. *China: Alive in the Bitter Sea.* New York: Bantam, 1982.

Campbell, Joseph. *The Hero with a Thousand Faces.* Princeton, NJ: Princeton University Press, 1949.

Chan, Jackie, with Zhu Mo. *Never Grow Up.* New York: Gallery Books, 2018.

Creel, George. *How We Advertised America.* New York and London: Harper & Brothers, 1920.

Doherty, Thomas. *Hollywood and Hitler: 1933–1939.* New York: Columbia University Press, 2013.

Frankopan, Peter. *The New Silk Roads: The Present and Future of the World.* London: Bloomsbury, 2018.

Greene, Naomi. *From Fu Manchu to Kung Fu Panda: Images of China in American Film.* Honolulu: University of Hawai'i Press, 2014.

Harris, Mark. *Five Came Back: A Story of Hollywood and the Second World War.* New York: Penguin Press, 2014.

Kissinger, Henry. *On China.* New York: Penguin Books, 2011.

Kokas, Aynne. *Hollywood Made in China.* Oakland: University of California Press, 2017.

Maçães, Bruno. *Belt and Road: A Chinese World Order.* London: C. Hurst, 2018.

Nye, Joseph S., Jr. *Bound to Lead: The Changing Nature of American Power.* London: Basic Books, 1990.

——. *The Future of Power.* New York: PublicAffairs, 2011.

Osnos, Evan. *Age of Ambition: Chasing Fortune, Truth, and Faith in the New China.* New York: Farrar, Straus and Giroux, 2014.

Puttnam, David. *The Undeclared War: The Struggle for Control of the World's Film Industry.* London: HarperCollins, 1997.

Su, Wendy. *China's Encounter with Global Hollywood: Cultural Policy and the Film Industry, 1994–2013.* Lexington: University Press of Kentucky, 2016.

Urwand, Ben. *The Collaboration: Hollywood's Pact with Hitler.* Cambridge, MA: Belknap Press of Harvard University Press, 2013.

Wasserstrom, Jeffrey N., and Maura Elizabeth Cunningham. *China in the 21st Century: What Everyone Needs to Know.* New York: Oxford University Press, 2018.

Xi Jinping. *The Governance of China.* Beijing: Foreign Languages Press, 2014.

IMAGE CREDITS

INDEX